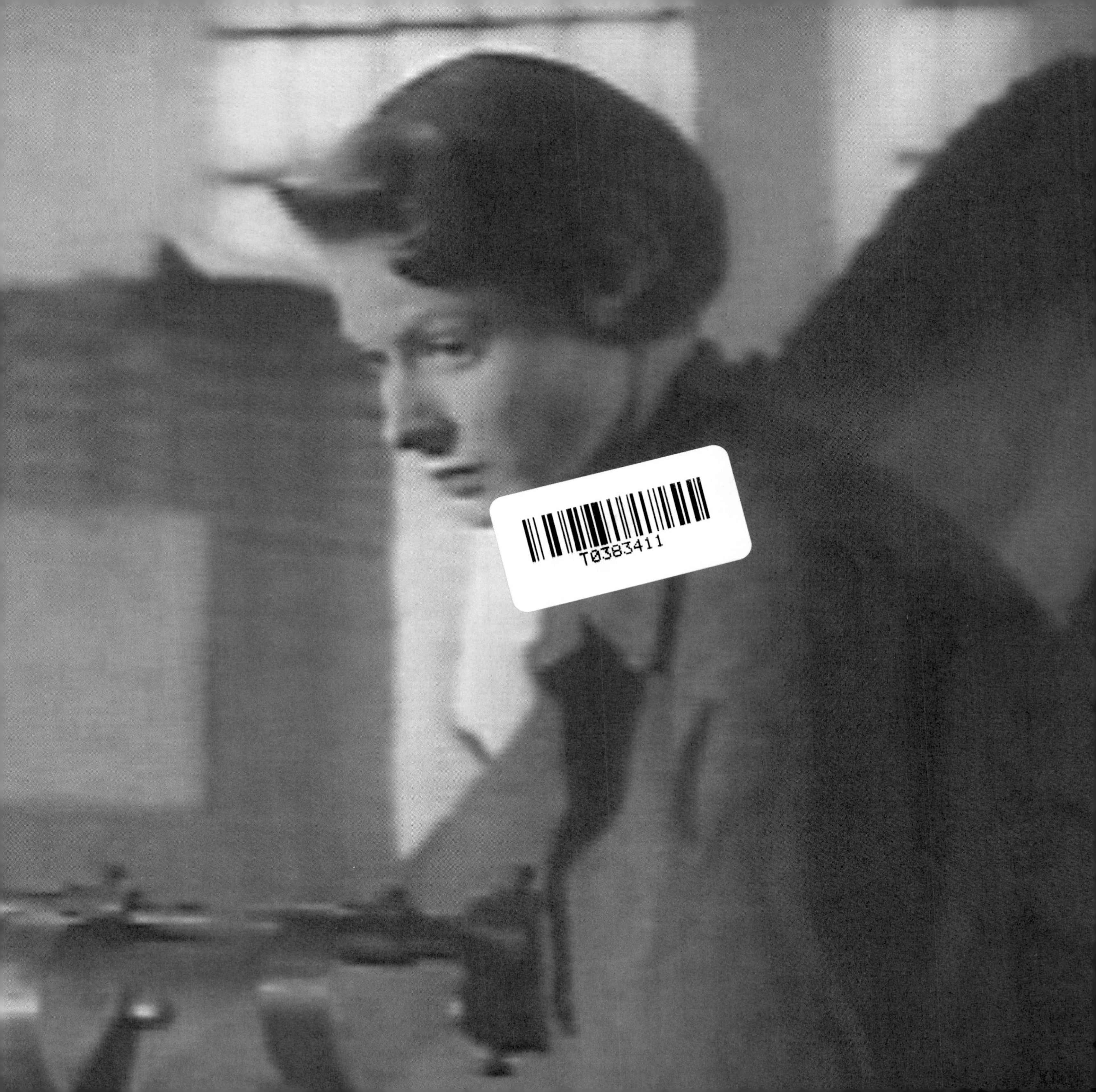

CGIL100

# MADE IN ITALY

TEXTS

UMBERTO GALIMBERTI
ENRICO GHEZZI
CURZIO MALTESE
SAID QASSEM

PHOTOGRAPHS

MASSIMO BERRUTI
GIANCARLO CERAUDO
EMILIANO MANCUSO
RICCARDO SCIBETTA
MARIO SPADA

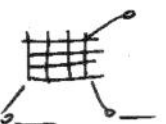

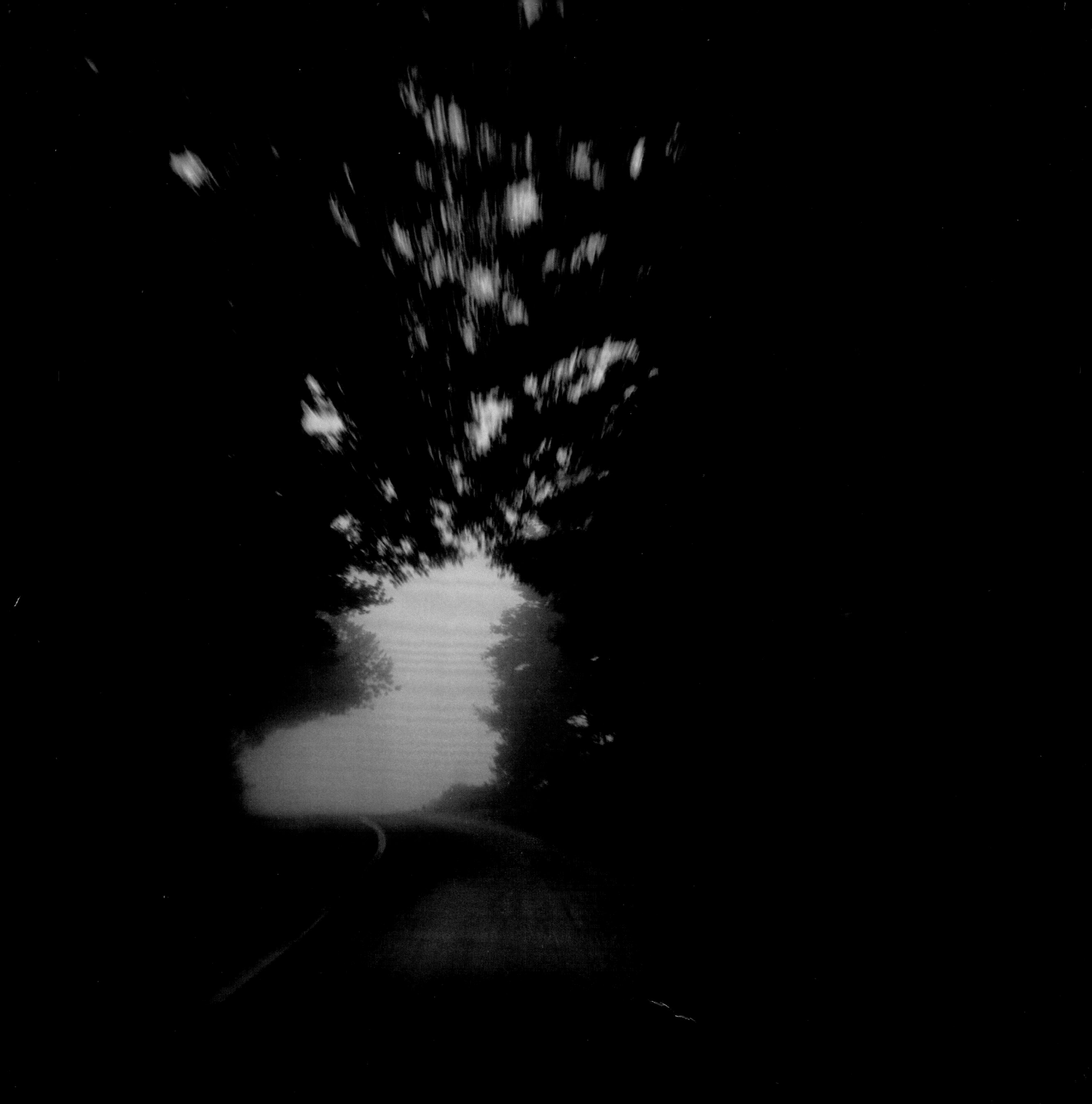

# CONTENTS

08 FUTURE POSTPONED
Enrico Ghezzi

22 THE ITALIAN DECLINE
Curzio Maltese

60 THE ENEMY STATE
Umberto Galimberti

96 THE GLOBAL REBELLION
Umberto Galimberti

108 WHAT LAND IS THIS?
Said Qassem

134 THE INDIVIDUAL AS A COMMODITY
Umberto Galimberti

178 LOVE AND THE POPE
Umberto Galimberti

206 CENSORSHIP
Umberto Galimberti

## PHOTOGRAPHS

MB Massimo Berruti
GC Giancarlo Ceraudo
EM Emiliano Mancuso
RS Riccardo Scibetta
MS Mario Spada

The Salerno-Reggio Calabria highway, November 2004 (GC)

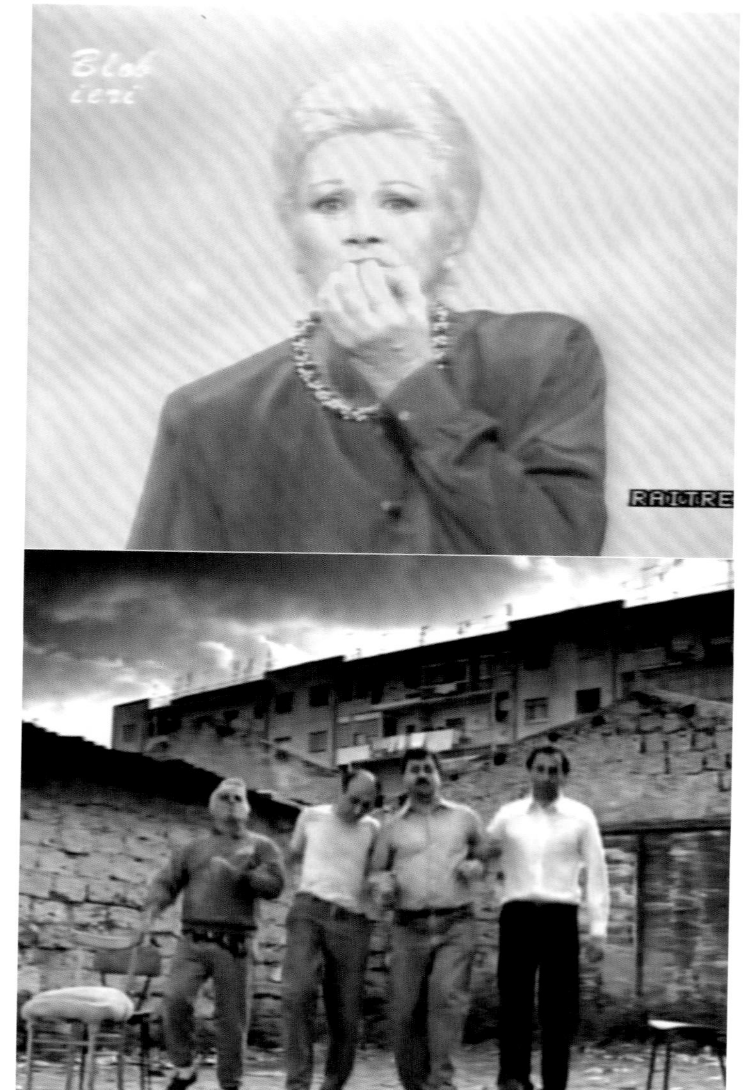


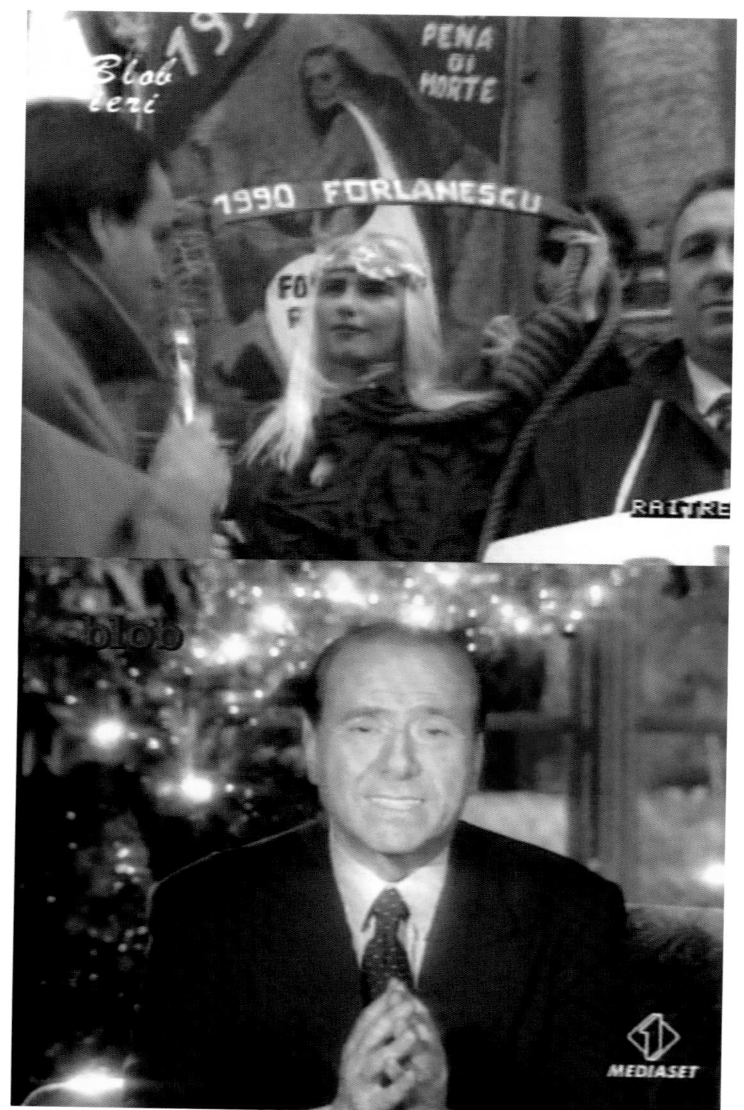


Takes from the Italian T.V. satirical review *Blob*, directed for the last 17 years by Enrico Ghezzi

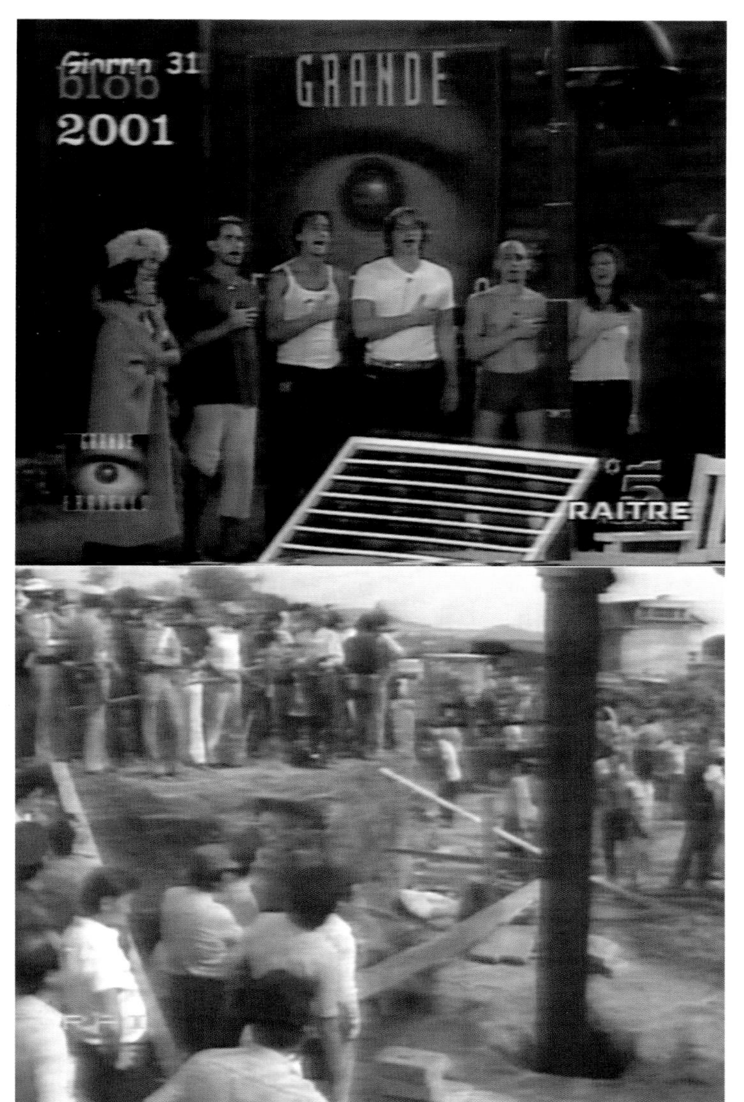
Giorno 31
blob
2001
GRANDE
RAITRE

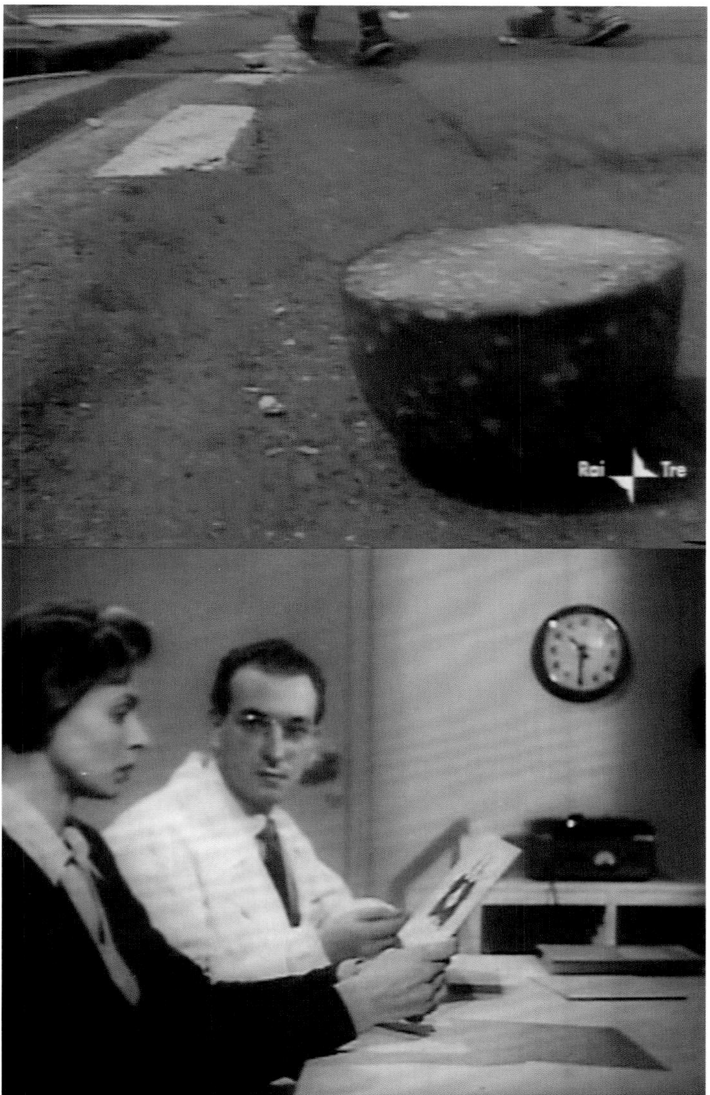
Rai Tre

# FUTURE POSTPONED

## The game of the factory, the factory game: neither exit nor entrance

Enrico Ghezzi

Everything started to become (too) clear when it fell through the Lumière brothers' automatic eye and happened in their automatic light, some hundred and ten years ago.

Because of an inevitability so bright as to blind us, the first images produced by and for that machine (the cinematograph), the first instances of the fake motions of cinema, are those often savoured and repeated ones of the Workers Leaving the Factory. These precise and ambiguous images (ambiguous because, paradoxically, for reasons of banal convenience with regard to sets and human resources, it is the gates and workers of the Lumière factory itself that are being filmed), of what form of 'life' are they a trace and report? Of what are they a calm and terrible premonition as well as already a documentation? What 'state' do these images place in superimposition on the one by Pelizza da Volpedo, without being stopped by the monumental 'click' of that painted image or by the eye in the 'one, two, three, star!'-game, even though they are in fact already called a halt to in the invisible fixedness of the frames?

One asks oneself to what non-work the people being filmed advance, heading as they are for an off-screen in which we spectators are waiting, being at (non-)work ourselves, that is to say: all of us are already recruted for the work that is, and that makes us a 'performance'. (But I wouldn't want to be too general or Debord-ian, going overboard, so to say, into the diffuse and titanically catastrophic water of the performance).

It seems to me that Italy is a country, a place, a geographic expression, and a social agglomerate that is tragically at the vanguard, an image clearer than any other of the 'pins and needles' state of stalemate and (I would say) of 'postponed future' that human society is living world-wide. Its own backwardness, aggravated by misgovernment that is obvious from the unnoticeable take-off of the millenium, supports how evident this view is (and it will be remembered that, also in light of the twin antiglobalist riots – between Naples and the G8 in Genoa – that sought to undermine the very technical illusions themselves of the same 'governability', for Italy the millennium started in the months previous to 9-11).

I have been asked, perhaps by chance and unmerited, for ten 'images' for this photo book of the greatest and most glorious of Italian unions. They, then, approached the author (or in fact: non-author, or re-author, if anything) of the most anarchical and at the same time most tritely institutional television programme in the world, a programme that is absolutely 'innovative' exactly and only for the precision with which it is influenced by the obsessive repetition and repetitiveness that allow the 'image(of the)world' to consist and subsist.

I postponed the choice to the utmost, up to only a moment before that small technical, economical, and editorial disaster of having to redo the cover in order to remove my name or leave it there 'by mistake'. Or perhaps it wouldn't even be (or have been) mistaken. In fact, hesitation cropped and crops up all the time. All the usual images, captured in seventeen years of Blob seemed and seem right, exact, and inevitable: Italian or American ones, exotic or aereal ones, flagrant ones with bodies and blood and sweat and tears, digital artificial synthetic ones, European advertising animated static ones. Therefore the Rossellini of Europa '51: Irene/Ingrid Bergman, the lady and diva who turns herself into a worker alla Simone Weil, and in the end decides to let herself be called 'crazy' and unable to live, locked away in a madhouse. Obstinate in refusing to give an exact meaning to the (test) image of Rohrschach. When you look at what are said to be its images, and especially when you look at its images of work, pretty much the whole country becomes a Rohrschach test, in which the images ruthlessly and dangerously expound their 'indifference', showing rather the 'workings of images', the automatic play-work that the image itself is.

Called upon (chosen to choose) because of my work on and with images, I cannot but answer like this, unsure in descrying light or dark (i.e. chiaroscuro) in the destiny that the image is, and in the work and the game that moves and condensates within it.

There is no country in the world so perversely polymorph, so secretely, profoundly, and, in the end, visibly formed by history. It is preserved in its changes, being more like the 'Theatre of Marcellus' (which is too shapeless to be iconic) than the 'Colosseum'. And it is literally incapable to preserve its status of 'Beautiful Country' (the whole state budget would not suffice even to renovate or protect all the baroque churches that are crumbling in Sicily alone), it is an immens and (fortunately?) difficult to run historico-artistical theme park.

It is not a marginal phenomenon, this 'Venice-isation' (or 'Chianti-isation'; for with the sublime casual irresponsibility of the authors and artists of cinema, and thus with that commendable automatic 'obtuseness' of cinema, this is the brilliantly clear subject of Bernardo Bertolucci's Stealing Beauty, a film anything but decorative and mooshy). Or the phenomenon is marginal to the extreme, in experiencing or being influenced by the margin itself, in which seeing yourself live is to live, the performance is a non-stop job without margines, the image becomes the most material form of existing.

The "Reality shows" which were prefigured within the programming of this television, were a unique moment worldwide for what was RAI Tre of Angelo Gugliemi between the end of the Eighties and early Nineties. A "great game" whose elements were continuously re-anagrammed (this included Chi l'ha visto, Blob, Un giorno in Pretura and Samarcanda, from Telefono Giallo to il Postino) they were born of the country itself, convened in its whole to work at the same game, to play at the same job; a rash move both surely crazy and extreme, if we think about Un Giorno in Pretura, a true transparency of language crashing and masked, a ritual that is the daily class fight. It was a program fifteen years ahead of its time, surely a TV that is still not there, bridled by now in Italy like in Europe and in the world is still shape, not just past, but more clear – albeit distorted, degraded manipulated, accurately and badly regulated and dramatized –

Finally and less honestly attempting to take advantage of the power of television, moralizing cultural merits and titles without becoming conscious how much near and dedicated to the same "job" of depreciated, uncultivated vulgarity, like dancers that cannot dance. The atrocious cynicism of a country, which only expects unforeseeable problems with an immigration catastrophe (including the " Berlusconi catastrophe ") has up to now prevented it from waking itself up, contentedly sleeping in an extended ministerial museum, allowing a wild way, a rebellion, to show up the materiality of its appearance, an empty authority and multi-shape of the show.

For example - no doubt an intense specific truth implemented the collapse of the Soviet regimen, bringing about the phenomenon of the Albanian attack to the coasts of that country with shimmering television, revealing the illusion of the plan for structural political reforms, Perestroika, and the unconscious shattering force that would have had excited the circulation of the Coca-Cola image and a little of "western television". As far as Berlusconi: instead of continuing with the usual legislative emptiness and rules that permitted tacit agreement of everybody in the wild race to the West for the indisputable but bootleg private television frontier, the misunderstanding of false danger of a '1984 Orwell' regime by the owner of TV nets had Media King also allow us to try to throw away the chance to understand how necessary connections are the evidence of blossoming cinetelevision, producing material "immaterial" but with value and the obscurity of the dark riches of all the Mafias

that are the true world-wide financial motor. While complaining rightly of the " research escape " and of freedom of thought, we try not to be blind inside the laboratory where we more or less unconsciously explore, sometimes both guinea-pigs and crazy scientists.
This old and 'crepuscolare' country, full of history, beauty and culture, put under protection if protection could indeed exist, swollen with original memory and of mixed and interlaced memories, therefore untiring to concentrate and give shape to the already formed, to sketch with the shades of the global anonymity, to reduce the birth-rates in a sort of obligation, to which we can recognize already deposits the virus of the extreme contemporaneity, that of the postponed future (the most evident shape today is that of eternal instantaneous "dismissal" that is the Internet) its deferred future, continuously expanded in a telephonic mobile outbreak and distribution of electronically communicated messages.

Needing of nothing but just the saying, in a carefully distracted dumbfound, empty community. Nearly an ancestral political culture of fuzzy improvisation, both cynical and scoundrel and getting closer to advanced technology, to more scientific daring hypotheses. The issue is not to resist to this, but to resist in this (with all the backwardness and contradictions, I think that this is the contemporary and historical sense and merit of the workers union: assuming also or just blindly the role of who resists).

Choosing and resisting in the same heart, this is where it job and work and exisitence seems to dissolve itself – and therefore in some way- the difference between thing and image dissolves, hard job, hard work of uncertain yield and of perhaps painful enjoyment - Illuminist. Therefore we can discover that this rear country more equipped in order to understand the fire and flames of the Parisian banlieu, the signs of inner division, separation in the social individual subject more than race, religion, census or culture.

The director of the ephemeral way, the spectacular fireworks of machines given to flames, in order to see itself again, face the mirror, ("endured" extended and then swallowed suddenly by the archives), spectator of itself.

The bel paese and the dolce vita, in same boldness of knowing or defining themselves, enjoying until they are exhausting feeling how hard it is to live knowing (if not giving up and yielding to the national virtue of the hypocrisy, this is the historical acknowledgment of the image autonomy) that it is a re-living.

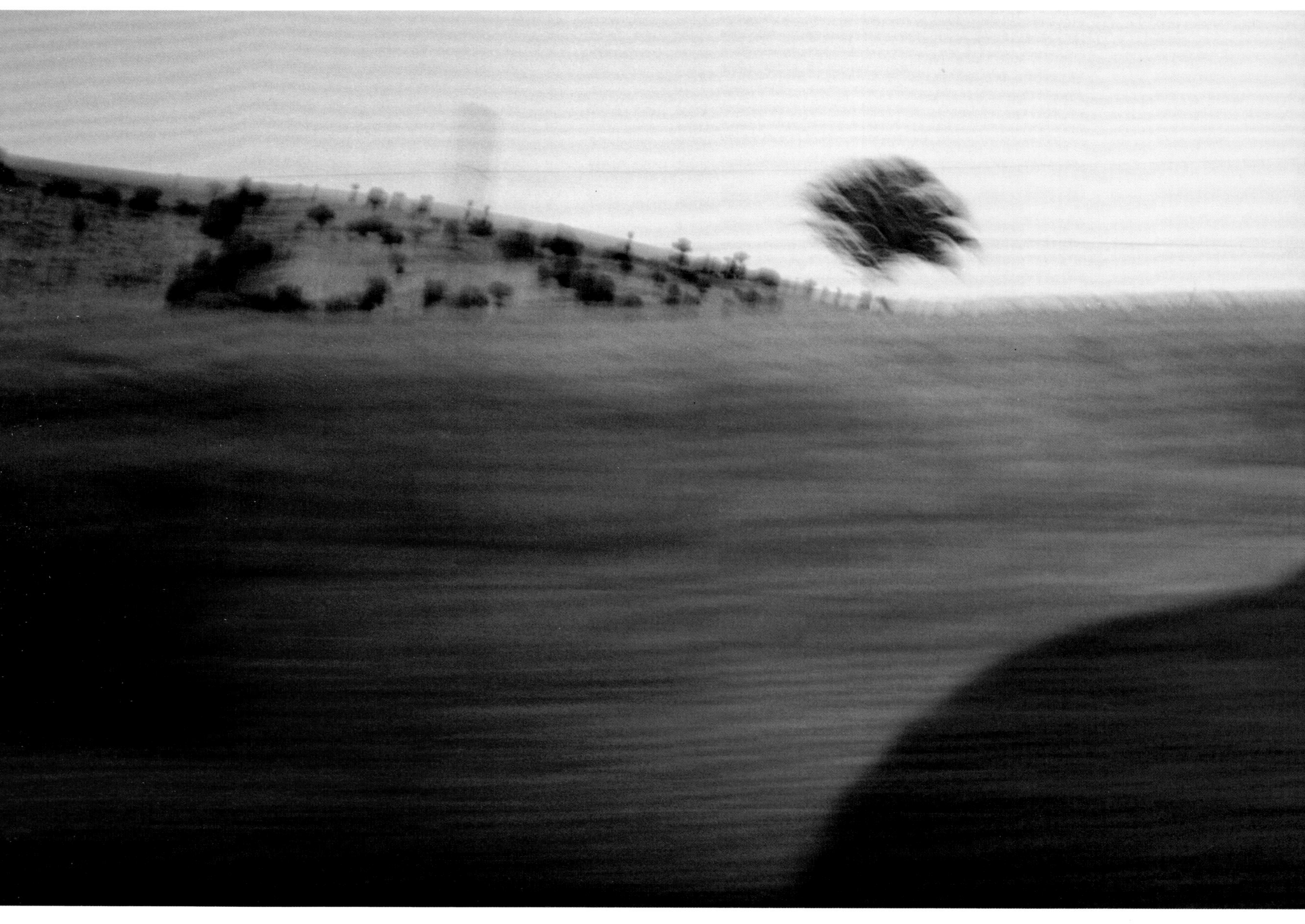

Barbagia, Sardinia, August 2005 (MB)

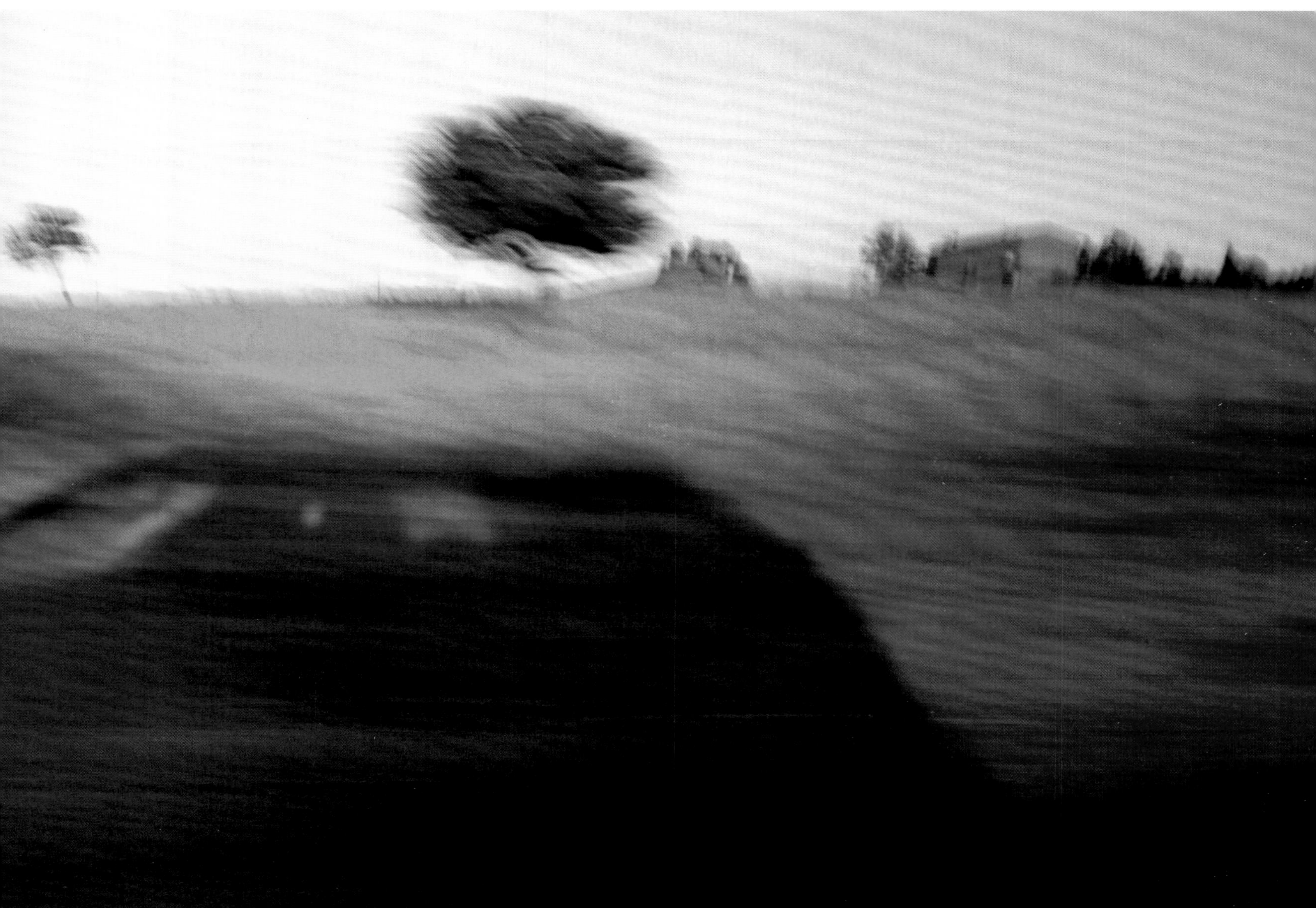

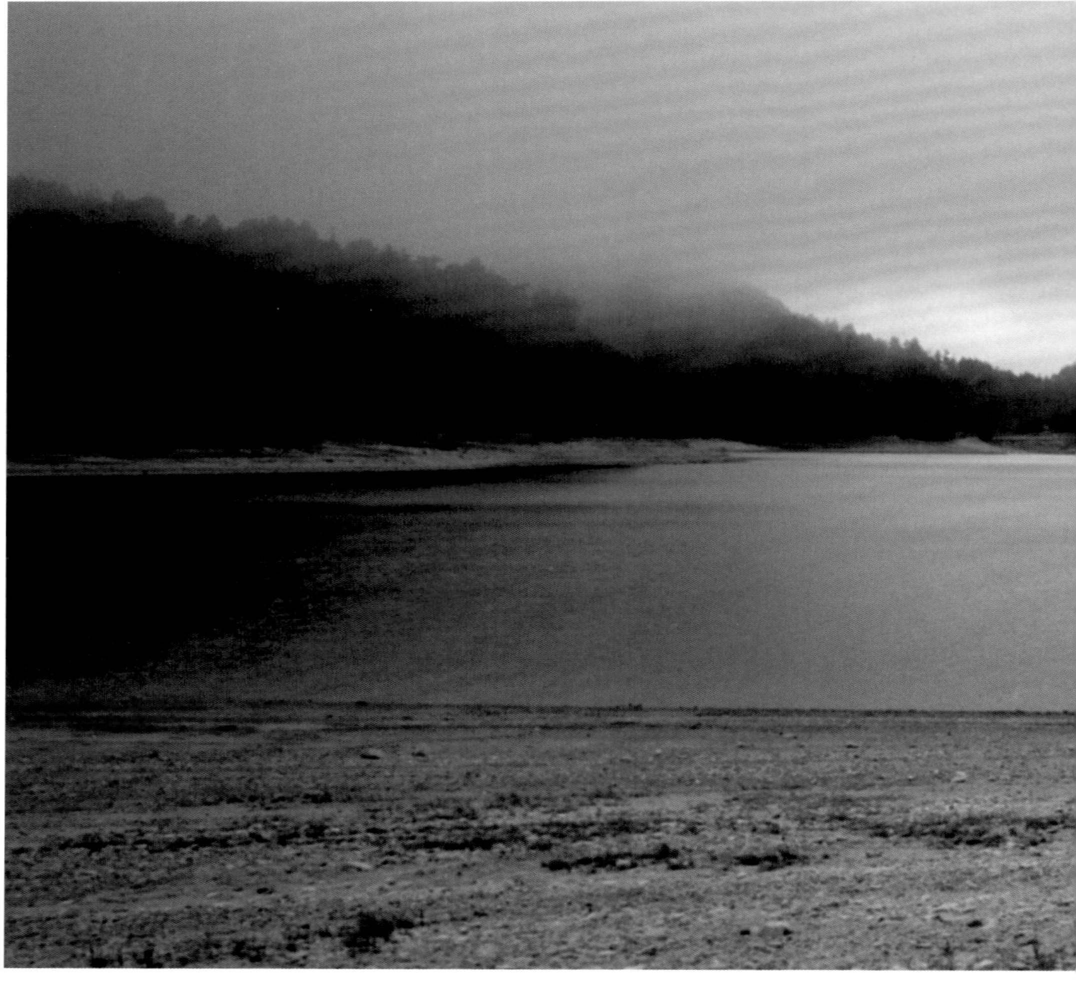

Sila, Lake Ampollino, Calabria, December 2004 (GC)

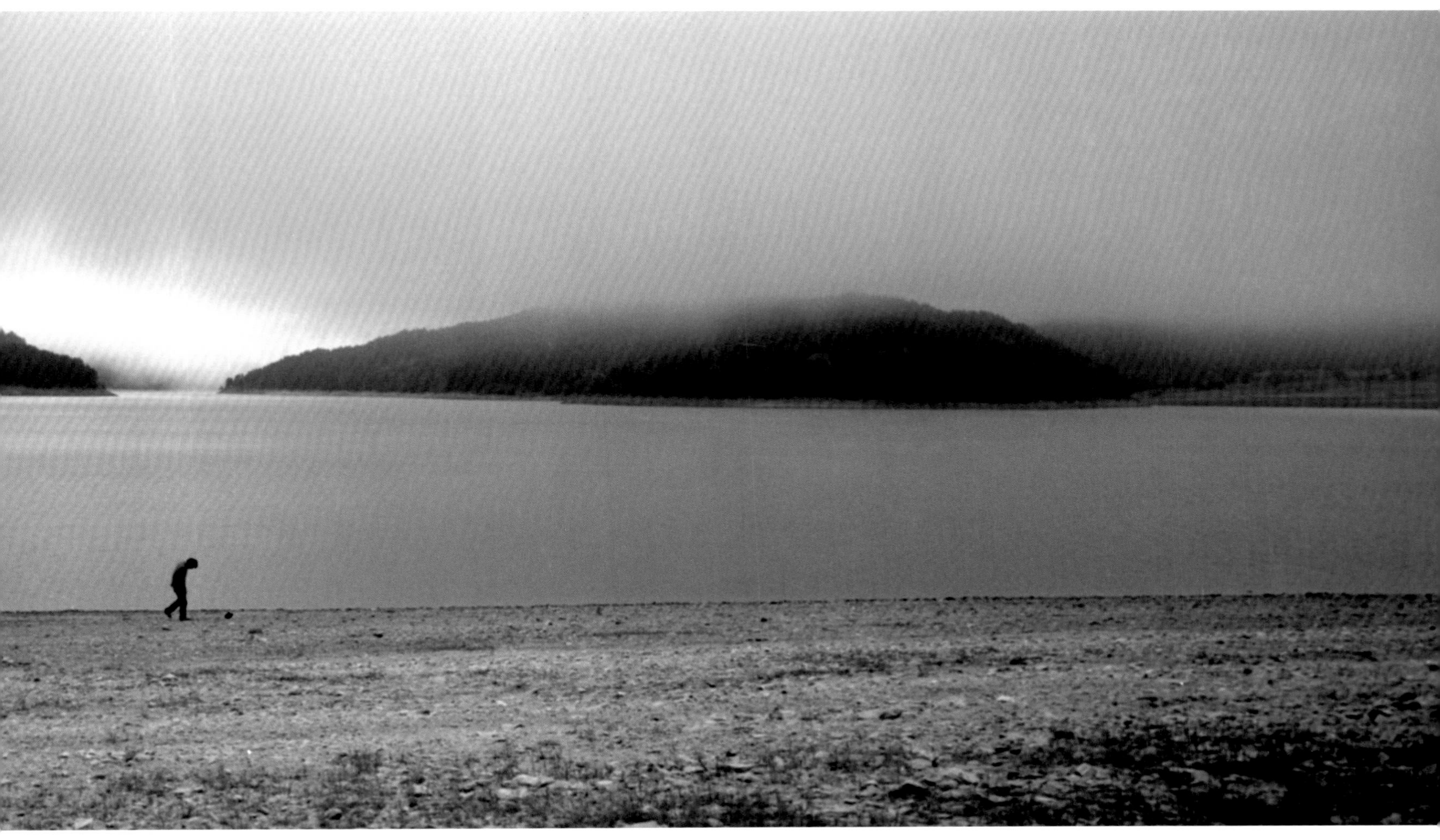

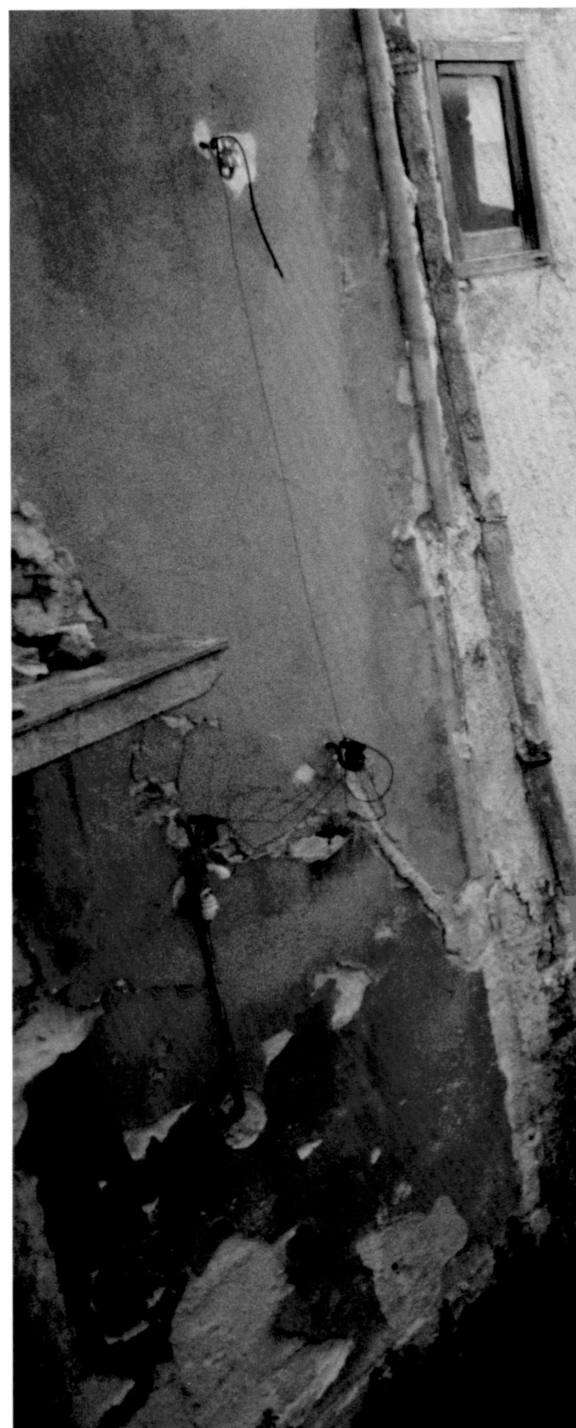

Gibellina, Sicily, June 2004 (RS)

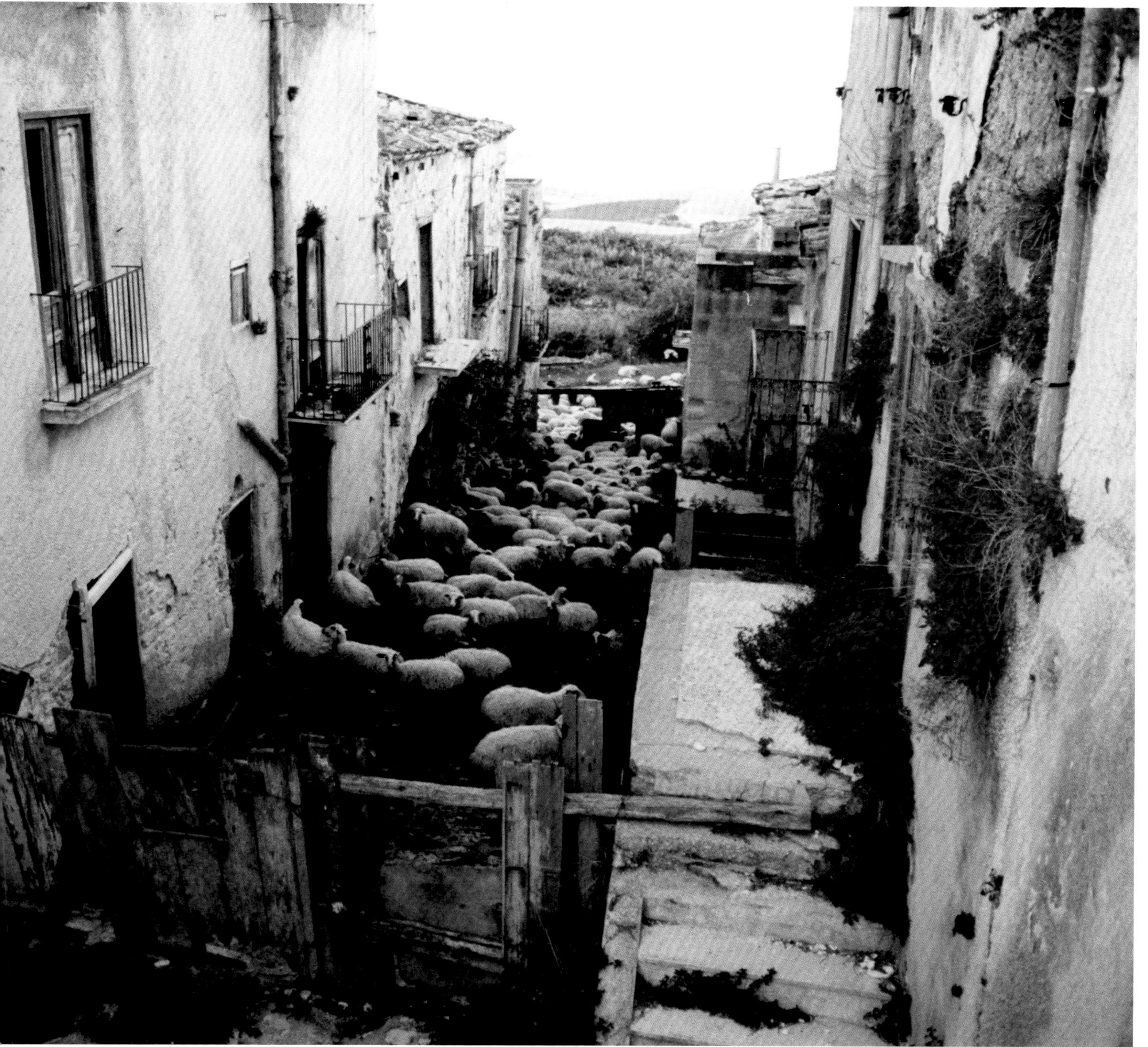

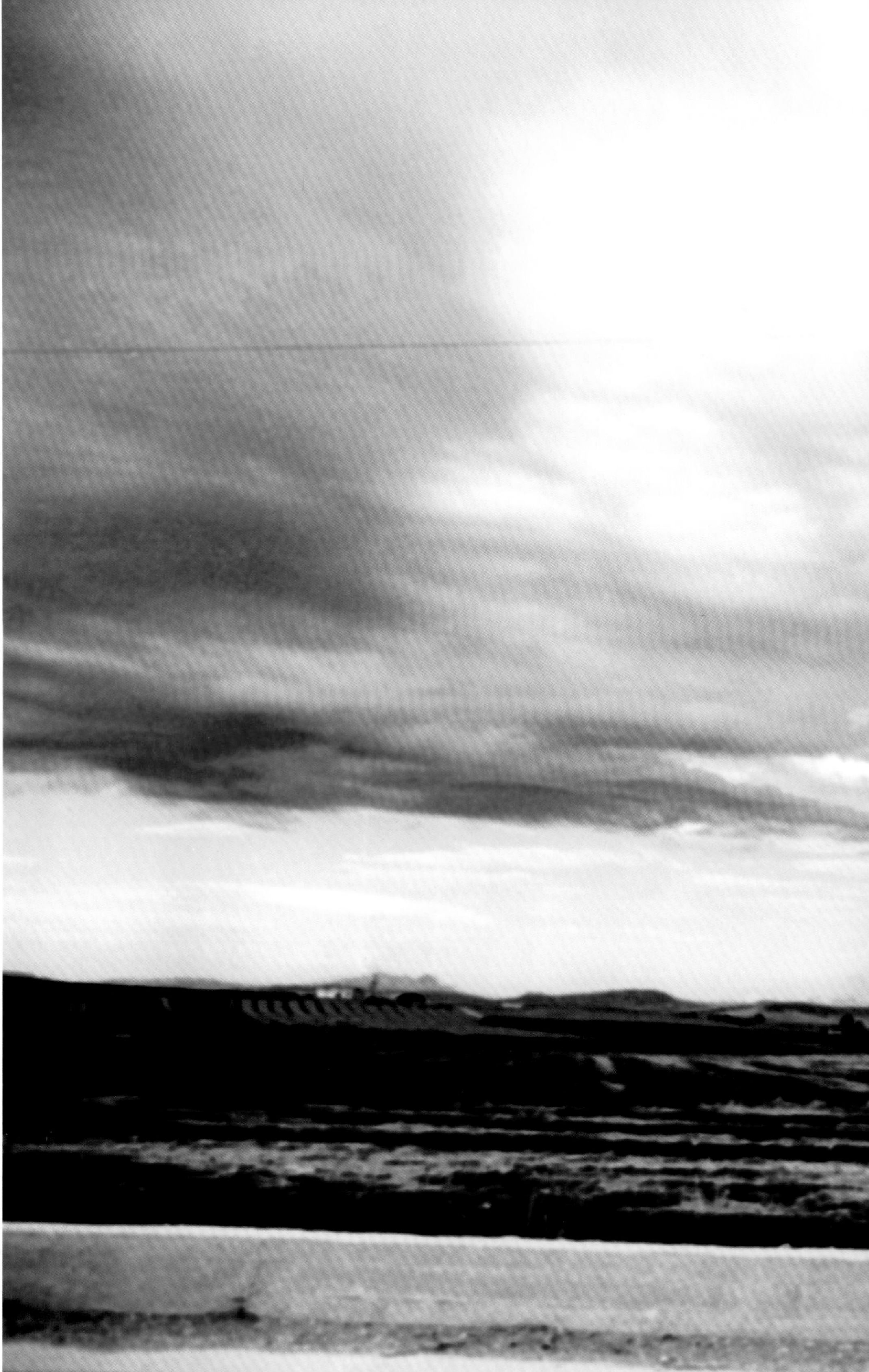

Gibellina, Sicily, June 2004 (RS)

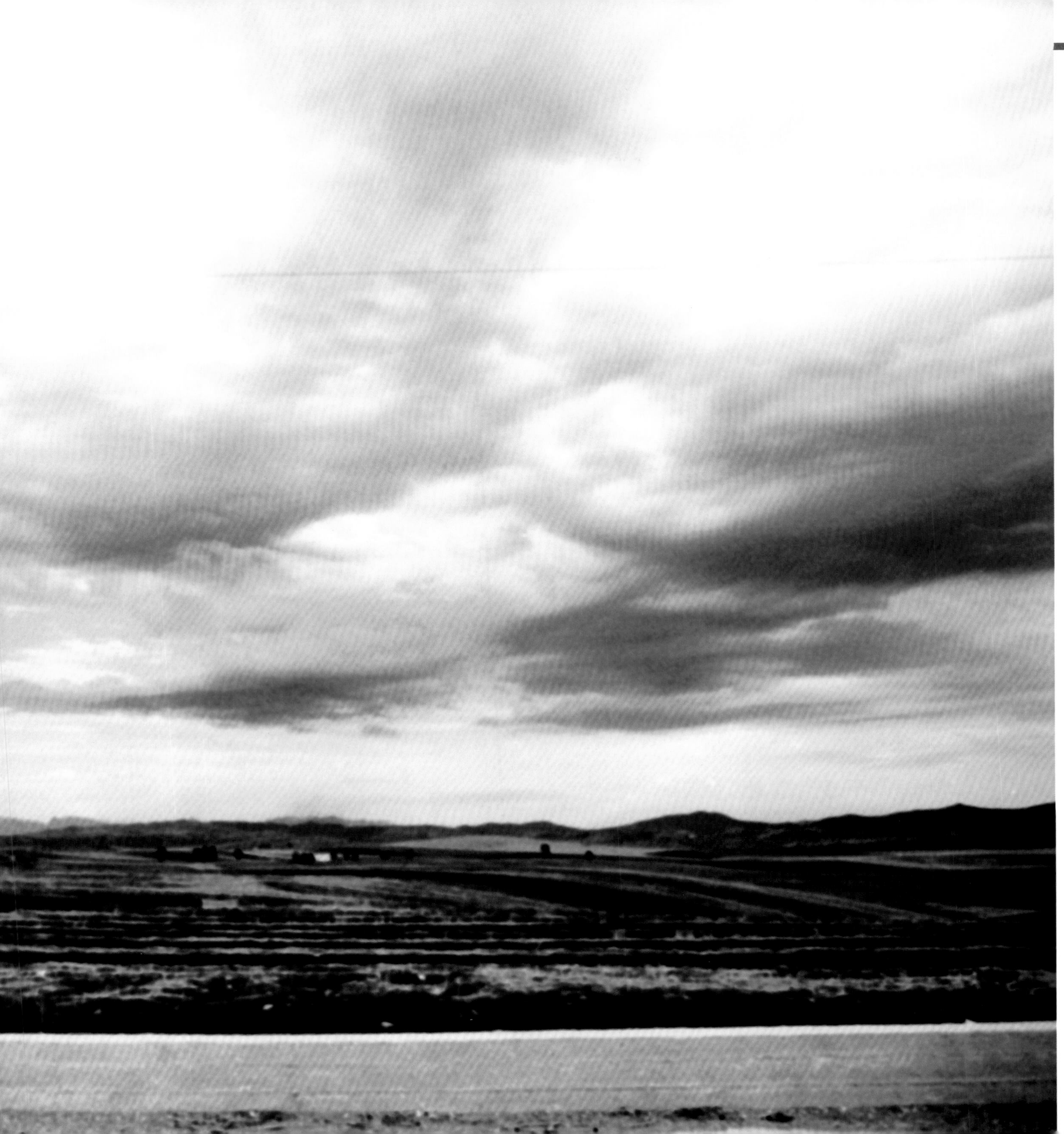

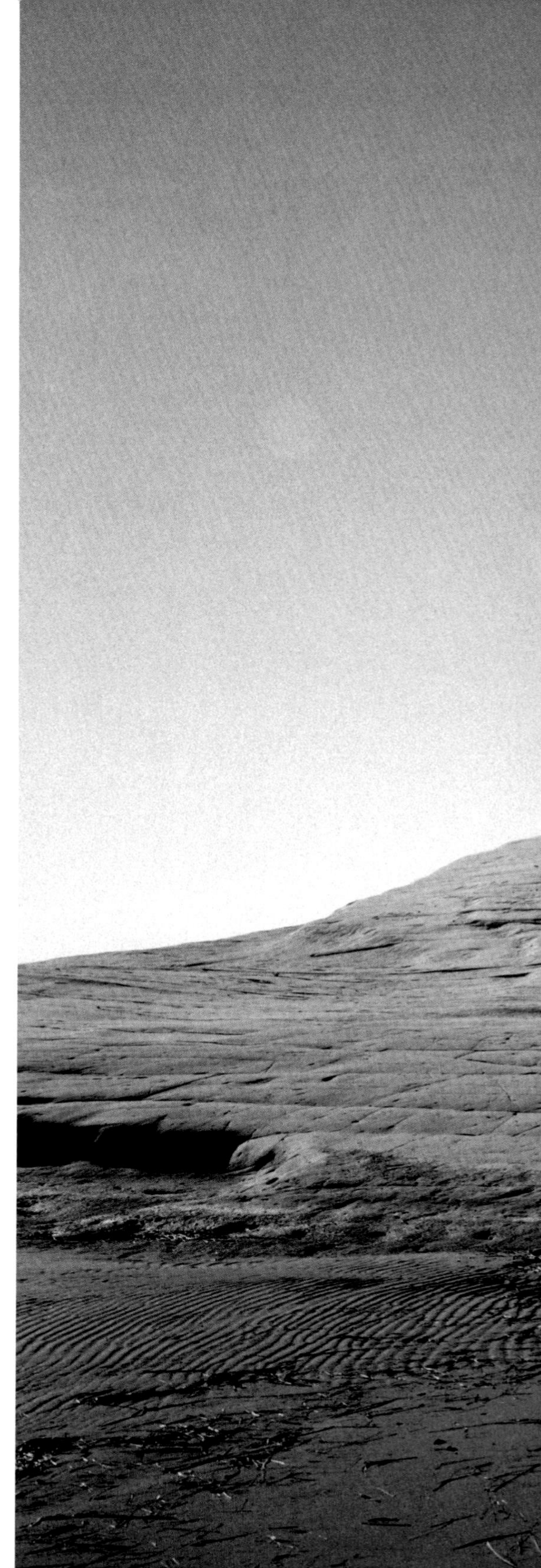

The Bay of Turks, Agrigento, Sicily, December 2005 (EM)

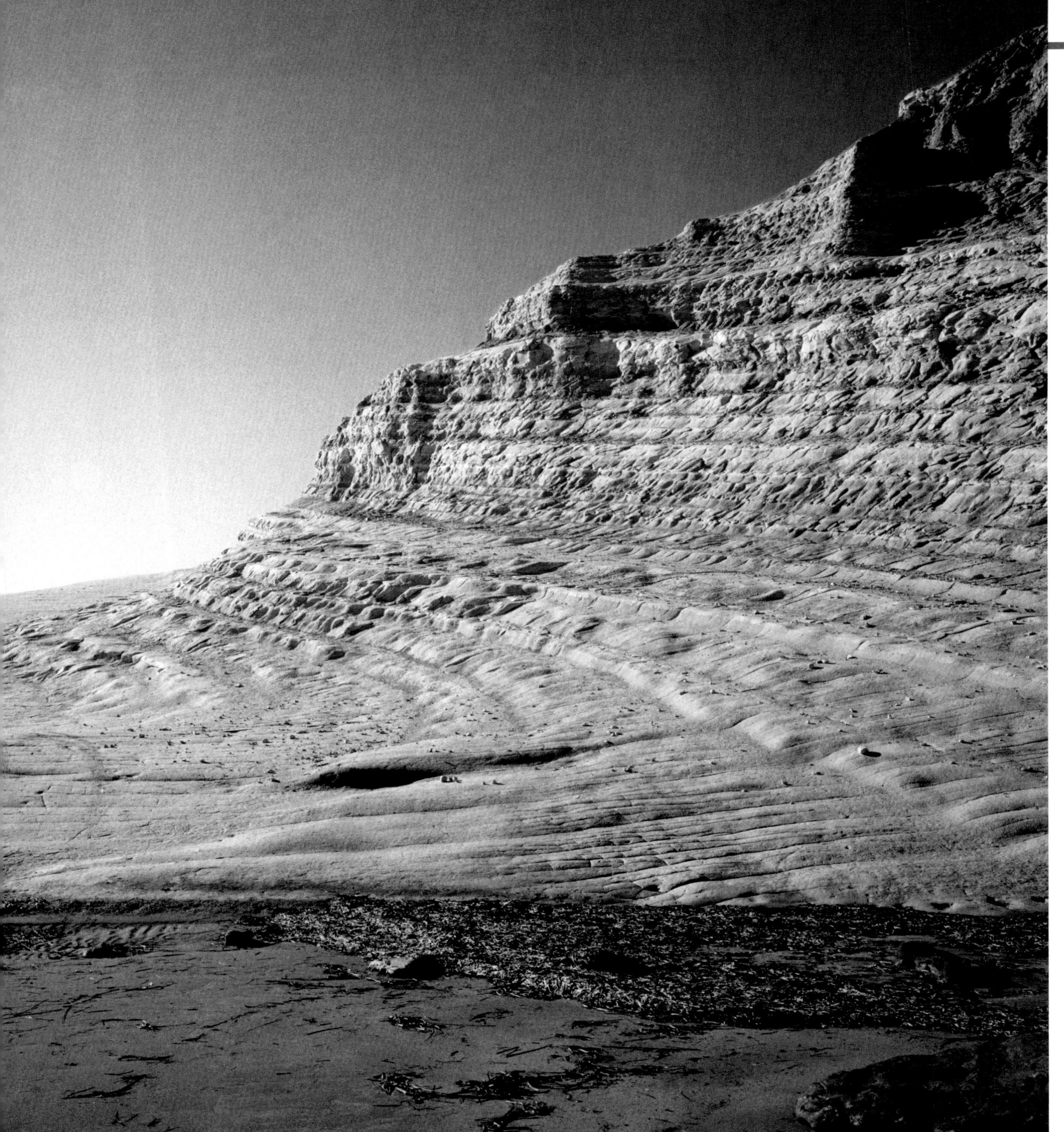

# THE ITALIAN DECLINE

## Curzio Maltese

The debate surrounding the cultural and economic decay of Italy, and its marginalisation by new global markets, has been at the centre of many recent economic inquiries. Perhaps the most infamous, yet authoritative and brilliant, was that printed by the UK magazine *The Economist*, "Addio Dolce Vita", in 2005. The article was received with irritation and annoyance not only by the Berlusconi government but also by Italian institutions beyond the Berlusconi sphere. *The Economist* inquiry was deemed to have been the product of an arrogance with which, over the centuries, the English have patronised 'picturesque' Italy. The accusations are misinformed. In fact the only misrepresentation of the Italian condition in the magazine's survey was the title, which we will come to later. Consequently our colleagues of *The Economist* have not written anything different from what the authors of this book propose through their images, which is simply to photograph a truth and a reality apparent to all.

The decline in Italian production and exports lies at the heart of the issue, and provides the most alarming evidence of the decay. In just ten years, from '96 until today, 'Made in Italy' has collapsed from 4. 6% of the world-wide market to a share of barely 3%. The economic model of the Italian North East has failed to replace the capitalism of the great Italian dynasties.

While chasing the dream of challenging globalization through hard-working industrial units of small and medium enterprises, the few monolithic industries have broken down; wrecked by scandal, as in the case of Parmalat and Cirio, or by an inability to renew themselves and understand the new logic of the market, as with Fiat and Alitalia. Small is beautiful, indeed, but as *The Economist* states, bigger is better. Now the illusion is clearly over.

The pictures here describe a country that has wasted in just a few decades a wealth of talents. Industrial plastic was invented by an Italian, the Nobel Prize winner Natta, yet the chemical industry has failed. Once ahead of its time in civil aeronautics, Italy is now the only major European nation excluded, due to myopic politics, from the European Airbus project; further, Italy is facing a catastrophic crisis with its national airline. Olivetti of Ivrea patented the first desktop computer, yet Italy has no current computer production, let alone part of any other advanced technology production. Fiat, Lancia and Alpha Romeo have for decades supplied models imitated the world over, yet Italy today faces the disappearance of its entire automobile industry. The list of these lost enterprises could continue for a long time yet, and include the mechanical, design, fashion and food industries.

But the Italian decline is not only apparent in its financial accounts. Indeed, in some way, the crisis is the consequence of a slow but unstoppable process begun elsewhere. Signs were detectable at an earlier stage of a civil, cultural, moral, social and demographic decline. It is here that the title of The Economist's piece is erroneous. It is a blithe turn of phrase, evoking the pleasures of life, the taste of Italian beauty. Fellini's film tells of the opposite in the first and perfect representation of a society that, in the throes of its wealth, harboured the disease that would bring it to recession.

The reportage featured in these pages is an attempt to read the anthropological change of the Italians through images, details, faces, scenes of decadence, taking in the rich and affluent cultural side-shows, the deprived wastelands of the Italian city suburbs, even the television studios where power rituals are celebrated. The stages of this journey through Italy are divided mainly into categories: illegal construction, the so-called abusivismos; industry, employment, youth, the elderly and the home; and the South. They are important topics, with profound historical lessons, but they are virtually excluded from the current national debate.

The abusivismos have been one of the great topics in Italian journalism. Who does not remember the famous inquiry of *L'Espresso*, "Corrupted Capital, Infected Nation"? It cannot be said that the situation has improved. To the old disasters new must be added, a result of the building regulations amnesty managed by Berlusconi-Tremonti. The evidence left by these landscaped disasters brings to mind the sarcasm of Ennio Flaiano: "Of all the foreign occupations of Italy, the worst has been the Italians".
In fact our cities are the most damaged of all Europe, cities with huge treasures of beauty that somehow manage to be ugly; unliveable in, polluted, dirty, and incapable of expressing such 'urban' qualities as welcome, vitality, the art of conviviality. The issue of the old and the young is another rarely addressed. While Italy is a country that is getting older it demonstrates no particular love for its young, removing them to the margins of public life in an everlastingly uncertain and unhappy kind of adolescence.
The South, meanwhile, lives in a world denied any media attention, a sort of parallel country rarely investigated for good or bad.

But nowhere is Italy's decline more evident than in employment. In this respect it seems as if a form of censorship is at work. Employment is a stranger to the press, other than reports of the odd disruptive protest causing a street block, or a delegation of workers at the festival of Sanremo, or the interruption of the Giro d'Italia. Reflection and comment on employment and industry has been excised and replaced by a panoply of slogans. One year wild liberalism was in fashion. In another it was privatization that would resolve all problems. Article 18 was attacked, along with workers rights, and finally the short term contract was hailed. It was believed that to address any historical process it was enough to find extemporaneous solutions, una tantum. The solutions failed, one after the other.

Those who sought to unravel the truths of the economy found few listening and were branded as either reactionaries or dangerous reformists, regardless of the legitimacy of their claims. In any case, Italy could not compete with China, India, Vietnam or Indonesia in terms of their employment rates. Meanwhile the short term contract has not helped to conquer new markets but to depress internal consumption. A decade has been lost discussing nothing as any realistic means of inspiring Italian industry, research and the skills of its workers have been abandoned.

The workers unions, the CGIL in particular, have played an unwelcome and thankless role in warning of the dangers of de-industrialization, of privatization without an integrated industrial agenda - as in the case of Telecom - and revealing the Holy Grail of flexibility as no more than the expedient of a short-sighted entrepreneurial class. But their warnings have been lost in a blizzard of show policies that promised instant miracles.

Maybe the period of illusion is coming to an end. Italy is tired of promises and looks to the future with a wary eye but also, for the first time for many years, with a healthy realism. It is an important step but perhaps not enough. In order to escape the decline it is necessary to invert the clichés that have dominated the debate for the past decade, to radically change the point of view with regard to opportunities that were previously perceived as threats or obstacles - globalization, immigration, foreign investments, inward investment in the independent system, workers skills, protecting the landscape, fighting the Mafia.

In order to do this it is necessary to tear down the papier-mâché wall of images and curtains constructed by Berlusconism, and to voyage around an Italy unseen on TV for the past few years, to travel the roads and public squares of our hundred cities, to cross the industrial districts of the North to see how much they are changed, to return to the Camorra and 'Ndrangheta districts while also discovering the new high-technology industrial areas in Catania and Puglia. It would then be apparent that the difference between the country represented in the media and the one experienced in daily life by millions of citizens is far greater than imagined. This is the disease at the heart of the crisis: the false perception of oneself. This book offers many reasons to rediscover our country. Buon viaggio.

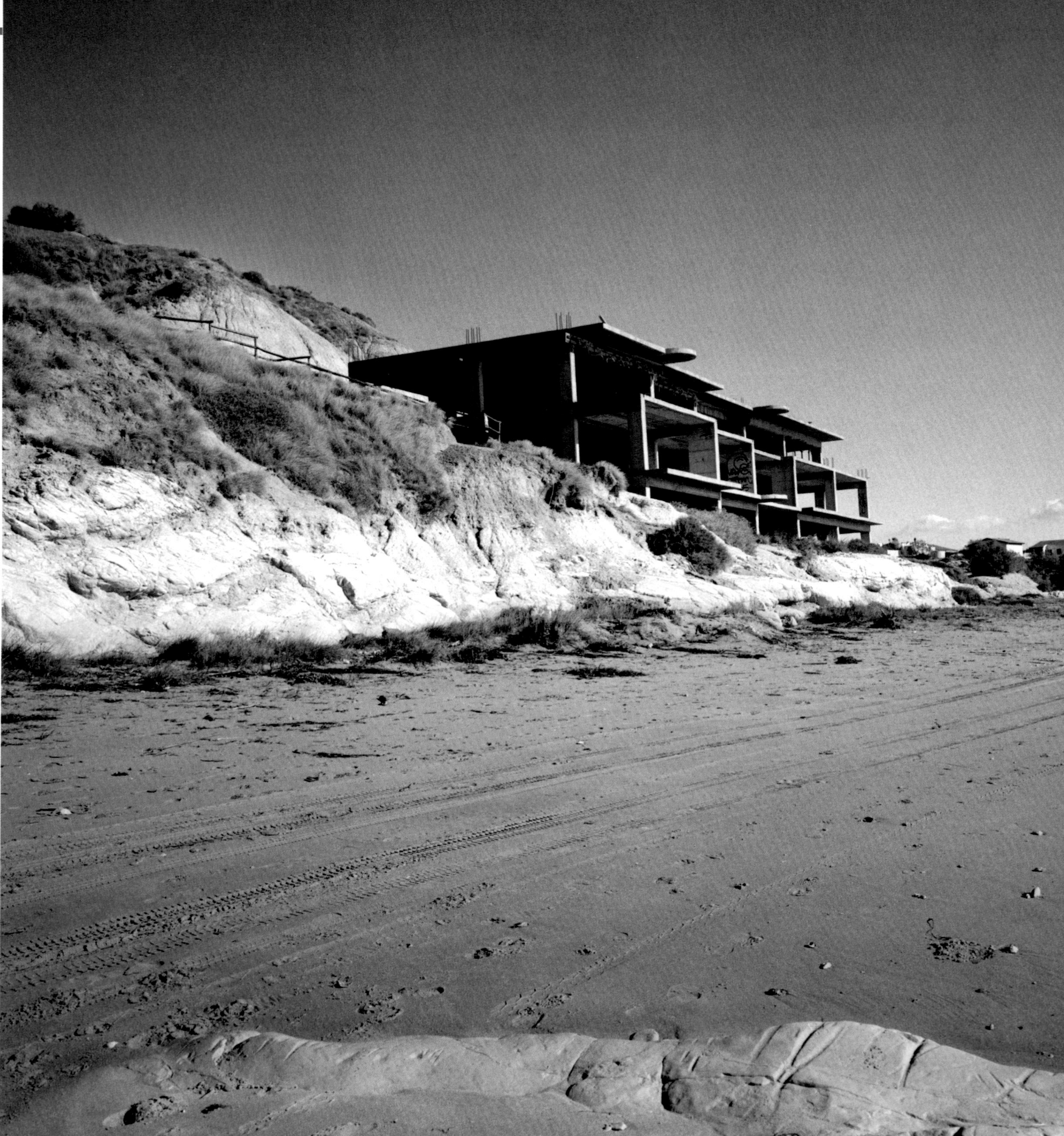

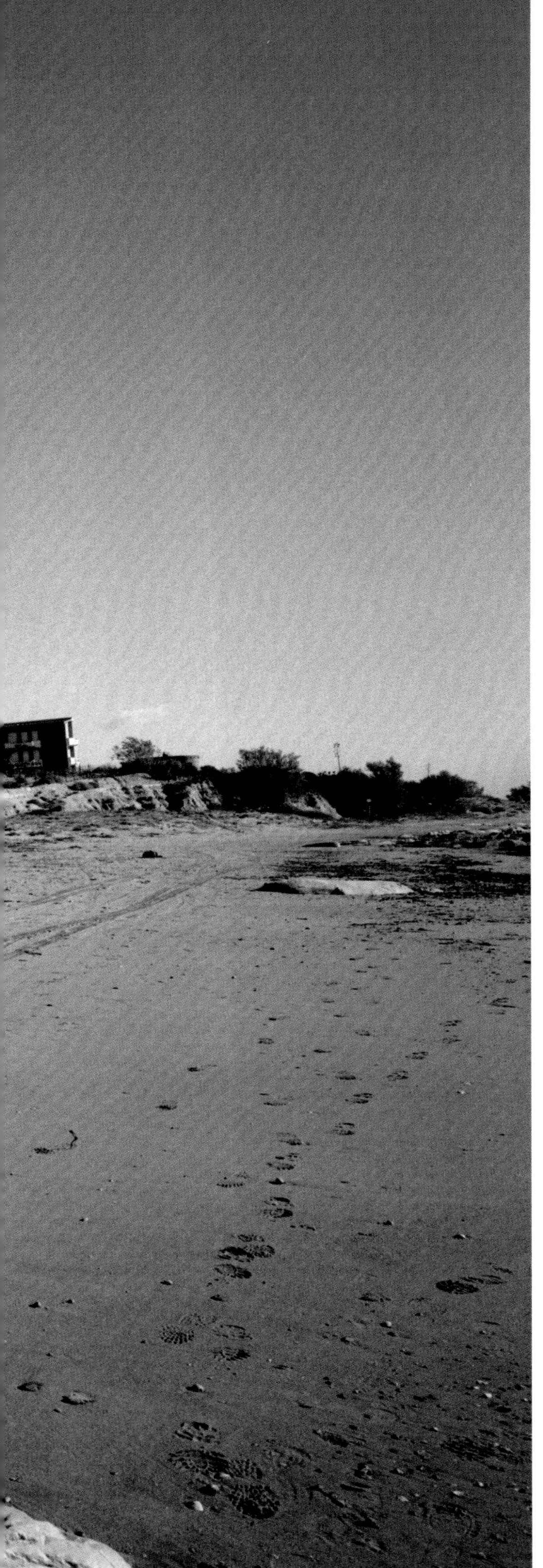

Cammarata, Agrigento, December 2005 (EM)

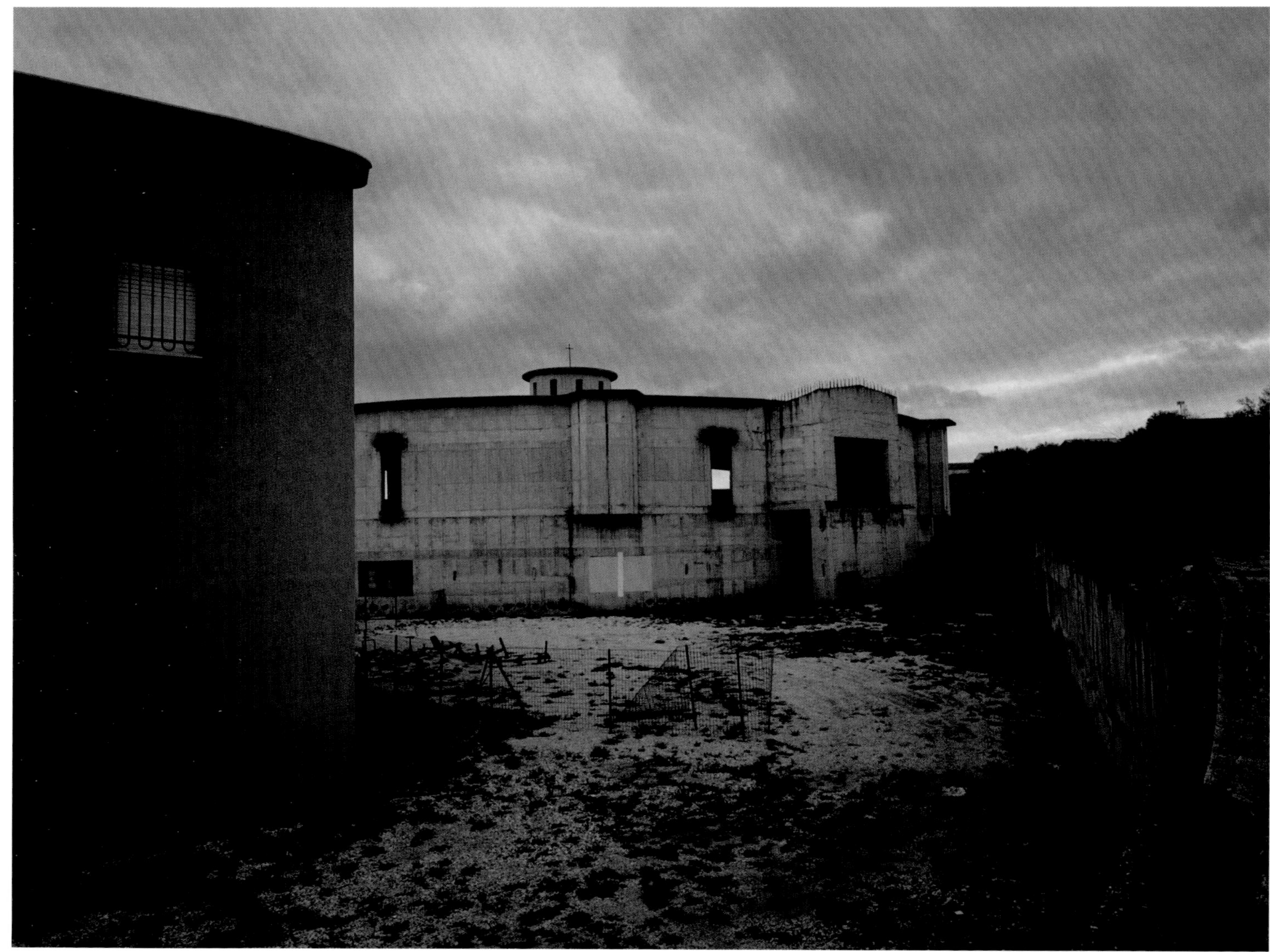

Unauthorised church building (abandoned for 20 years), San Giovanni Gemini, Agrigento, December 2005 (EM)

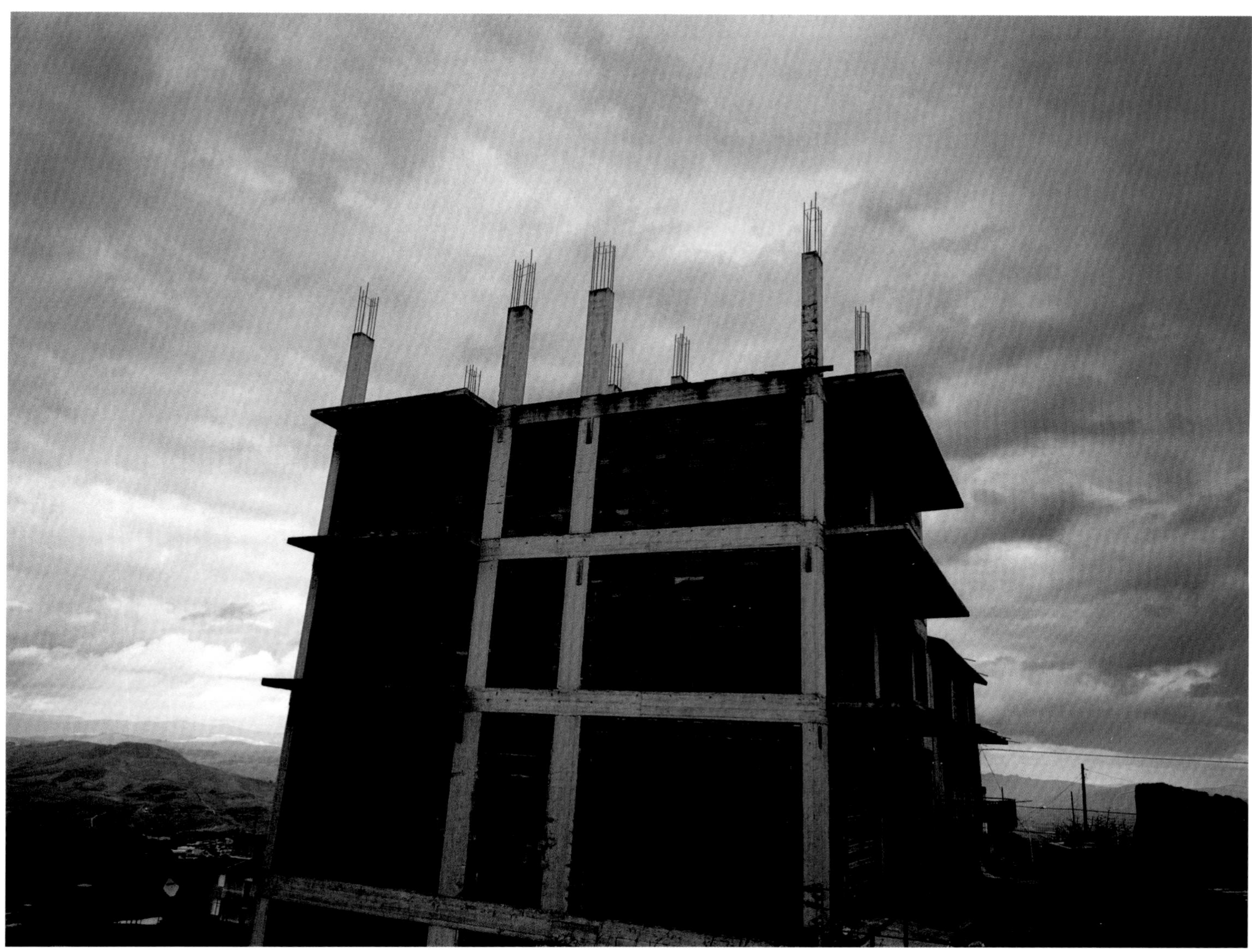

San Giovanni Gemini, Agrigento, December 2005 (EM)

In 1985, 1994 and 2003 three bills
were passed to condone illegal constructions,
which consequently raised money for the Italian treasury.

Each bill caused an increase in illegal constructions in the
immediate years before and after the bill passes.
The market reaction before each bill was termed
*Announcement Effect*, and after *Pulling Effect*.

Ostia, september 2003 (GC)

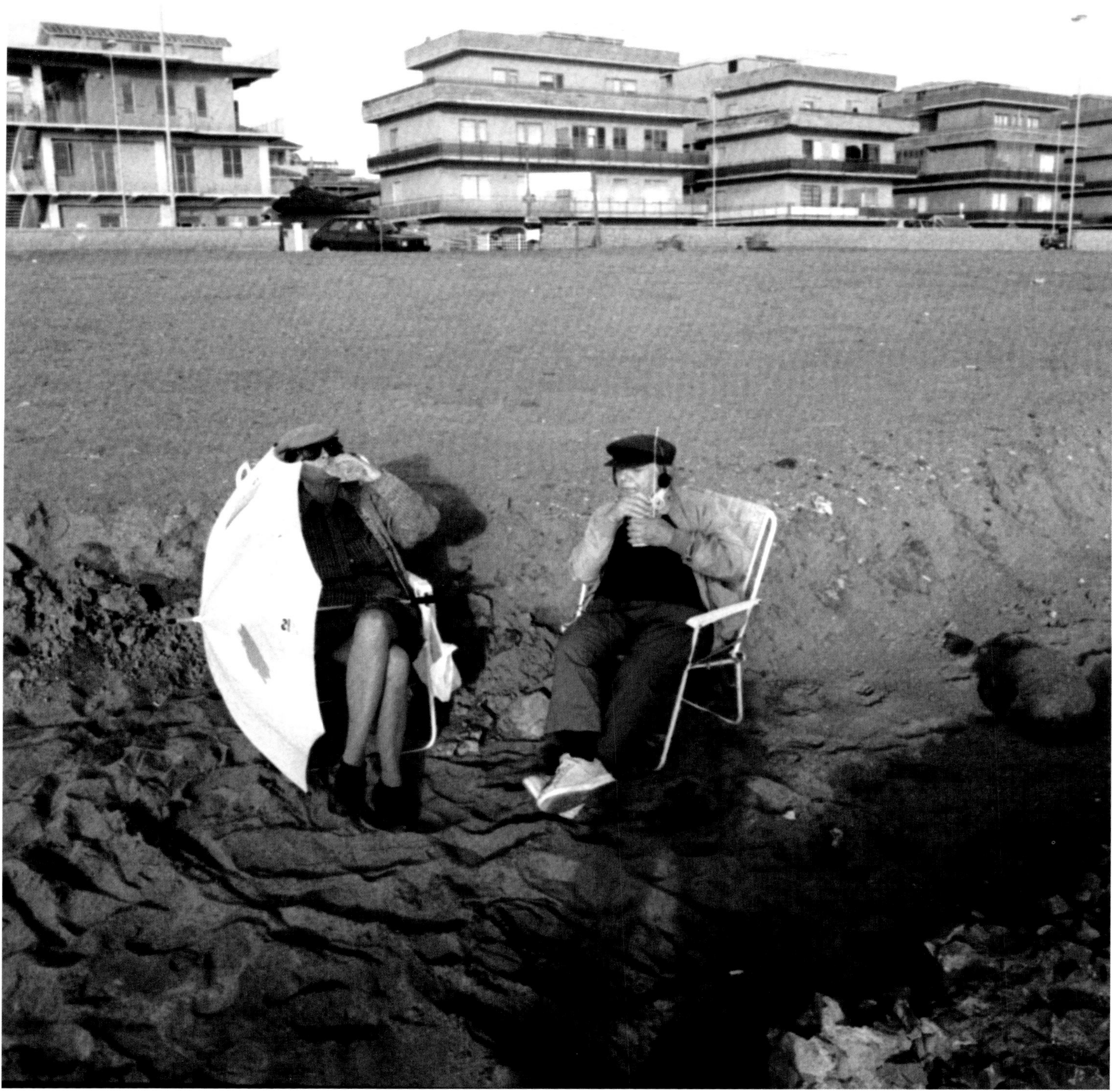

*Right* Augusta, Siracusa, The Paradiso beach, september 2004, (EM)
*Next page* San Paolo quarters, Bari, July 2004 (EM)

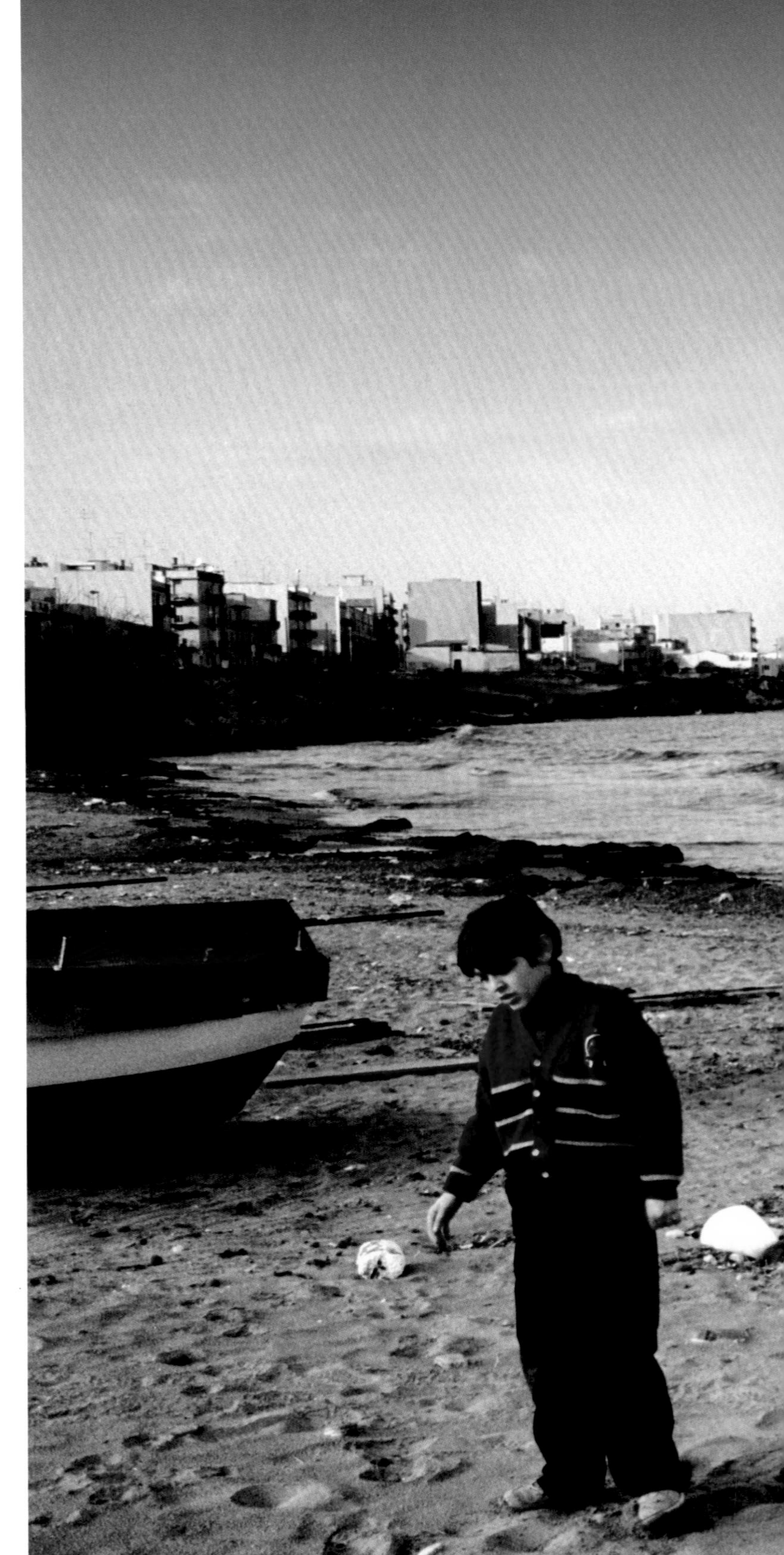

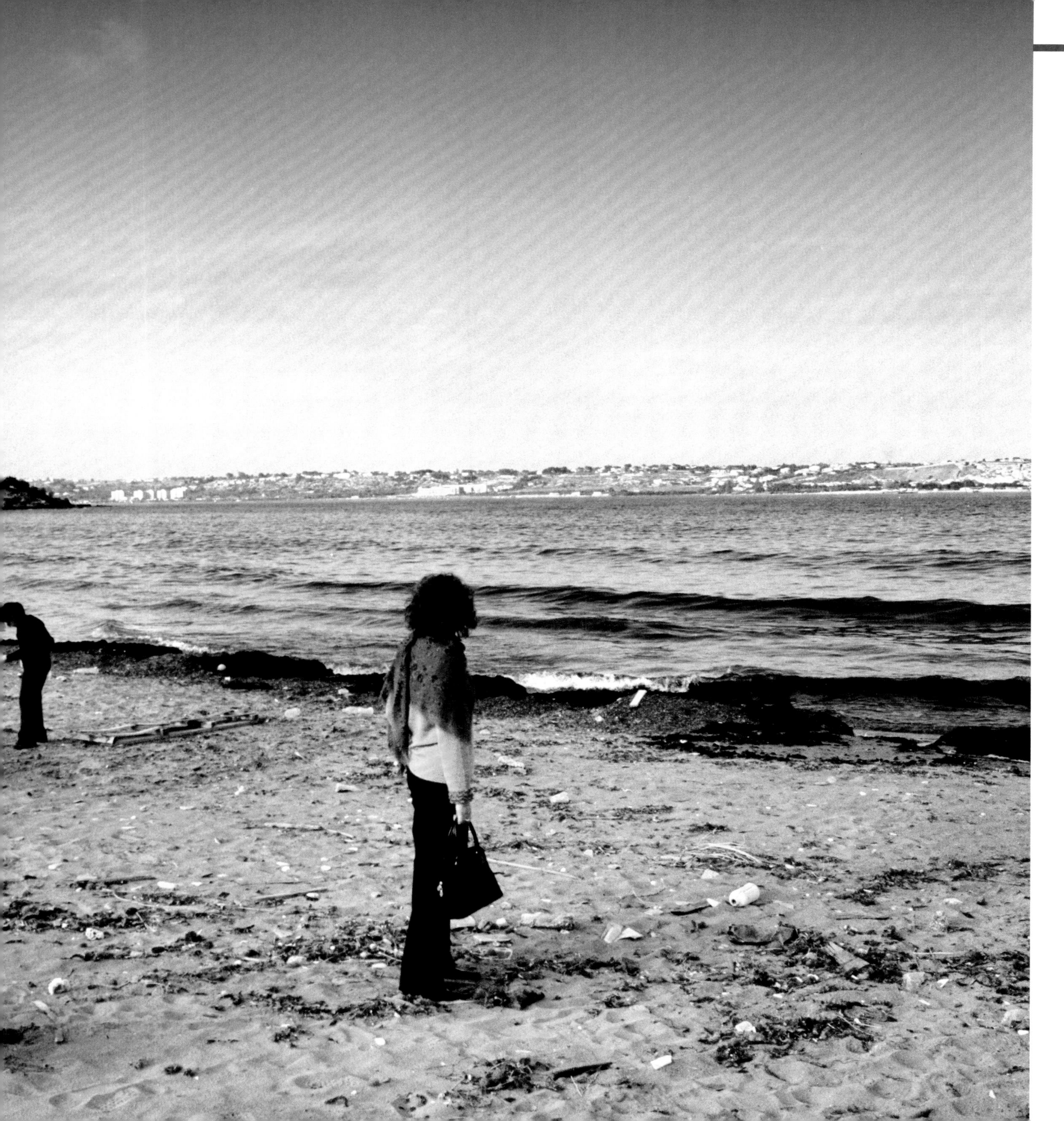

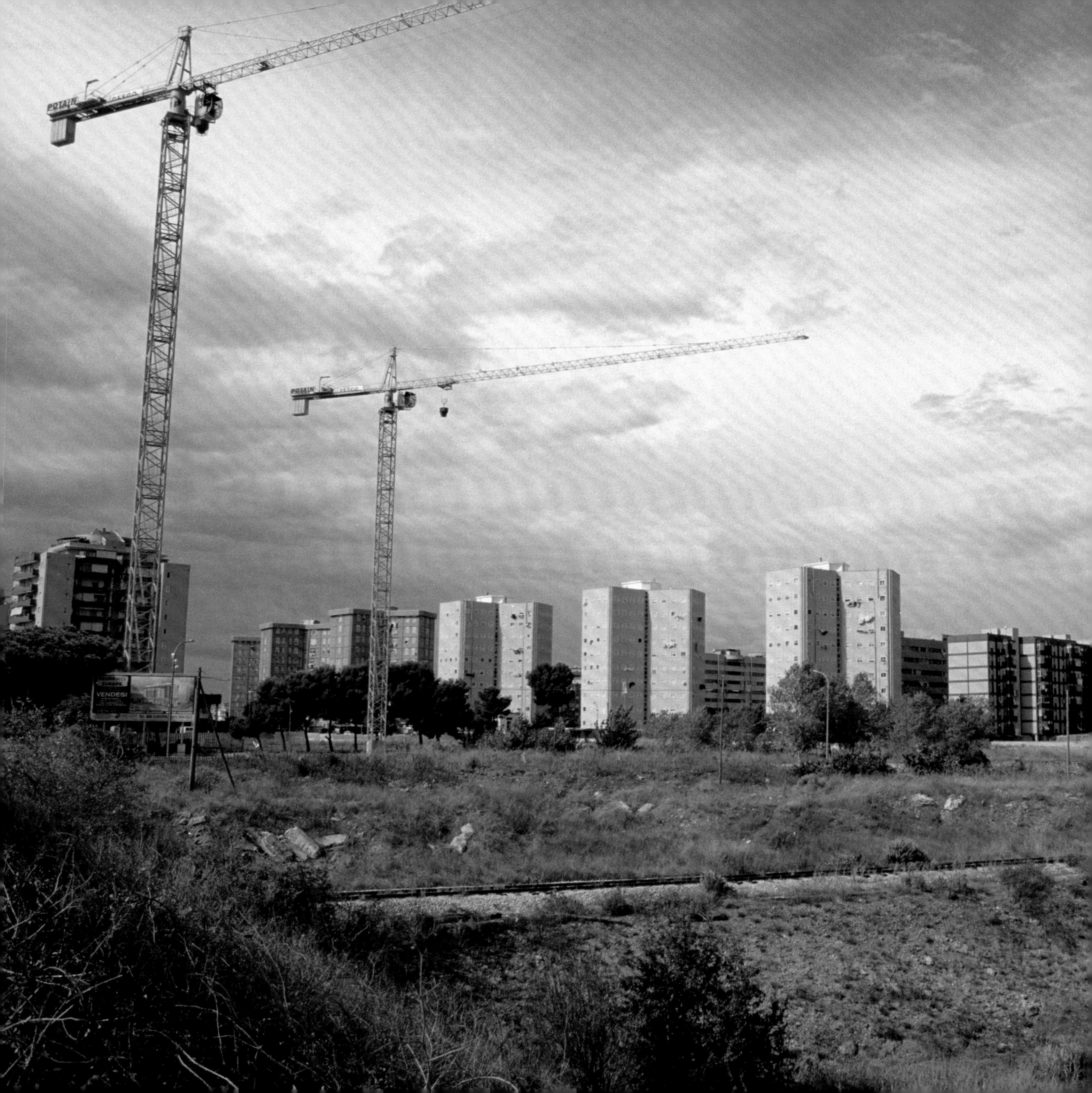
POTAIN
VENDESI

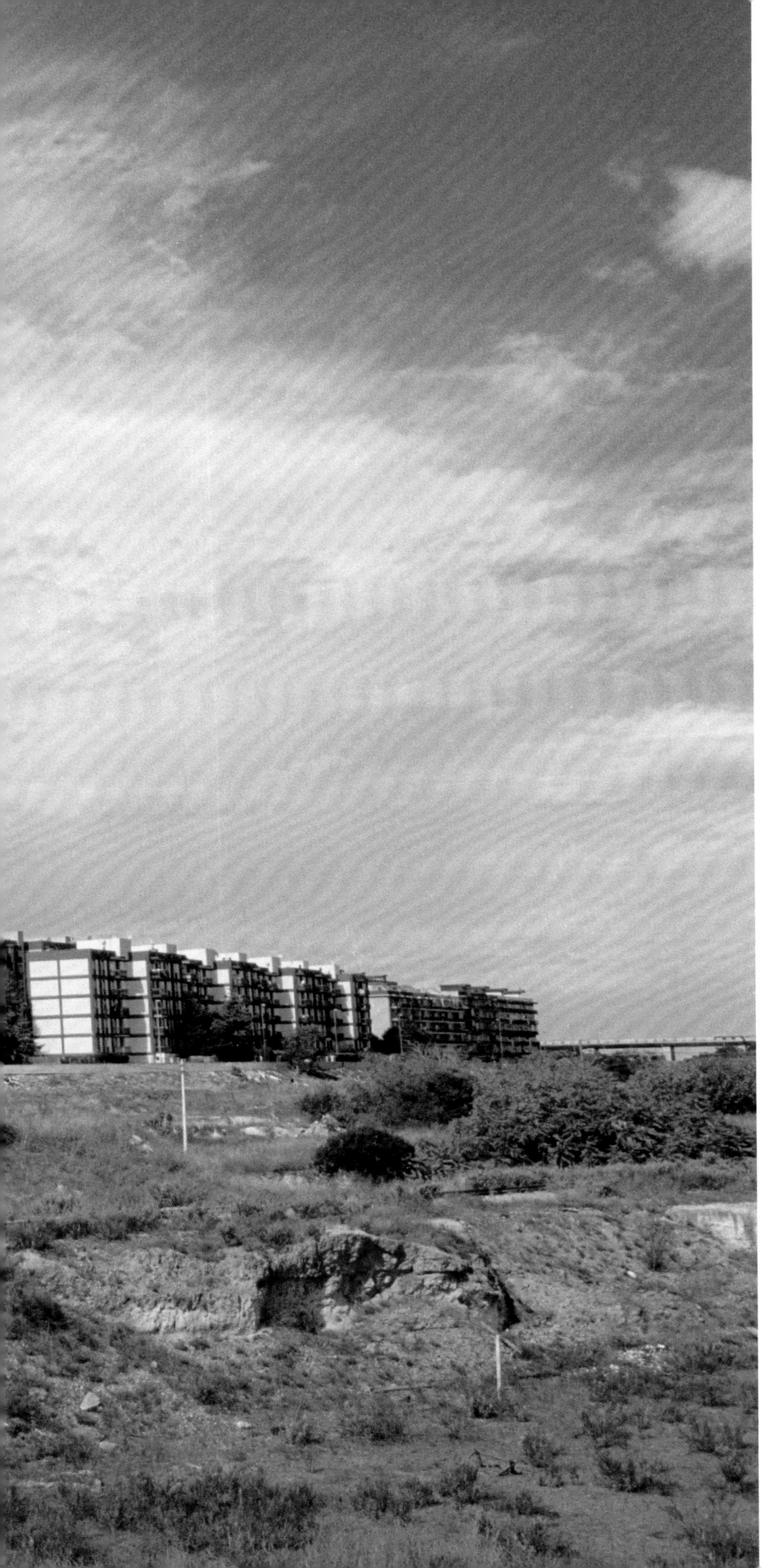

225,000 flats were built in the immediate years before and after the 1985 bill was passed. In 1994 142,000 units were built.

San Paolo quarters, Bari, July 2004 (EM)

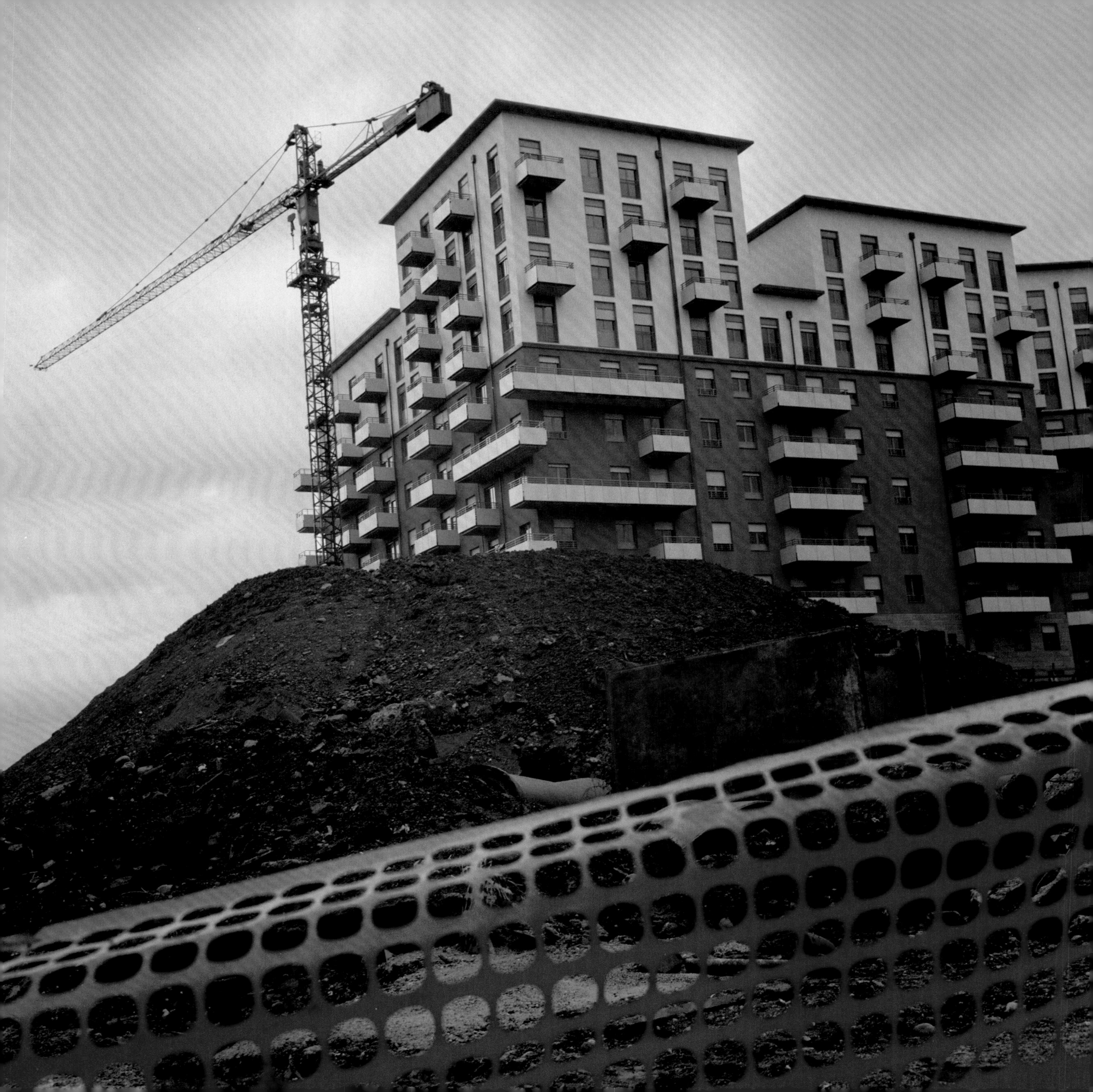

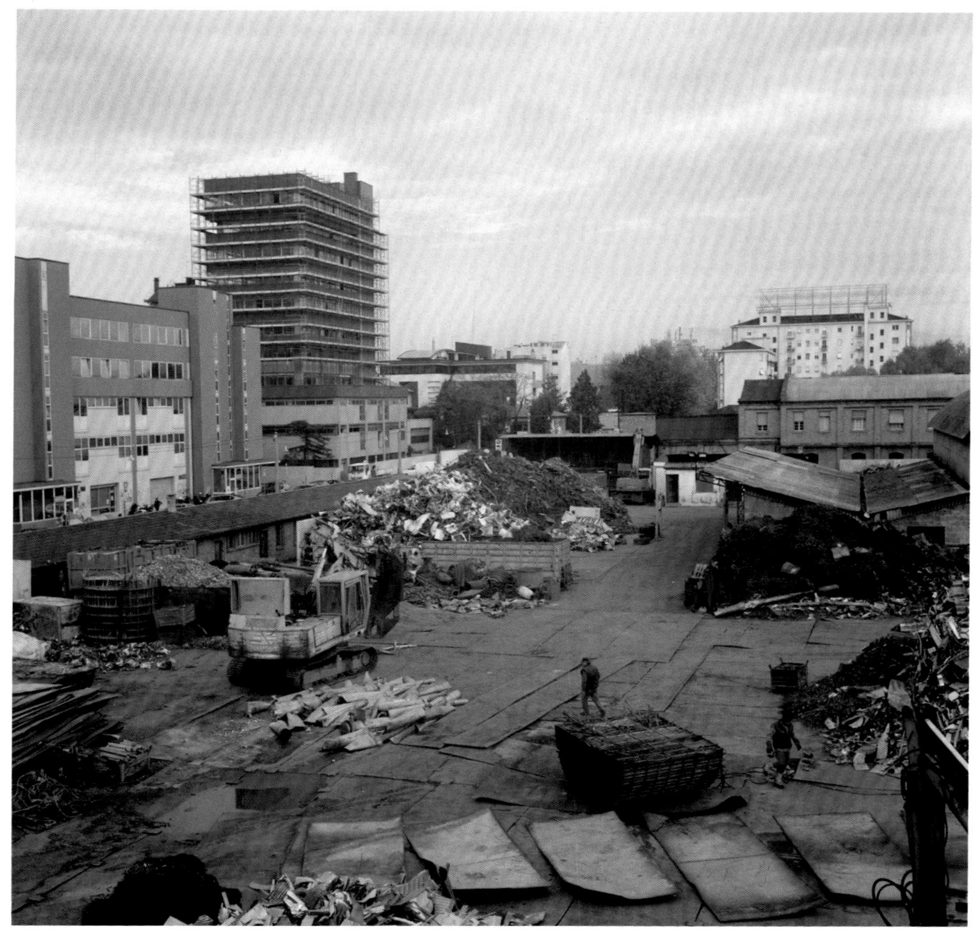

*Above* Porto Marghera, Venezia, December 2004 (MB)
*Left* Quartiere Spina Tre, Torino, October 2005 (MB)

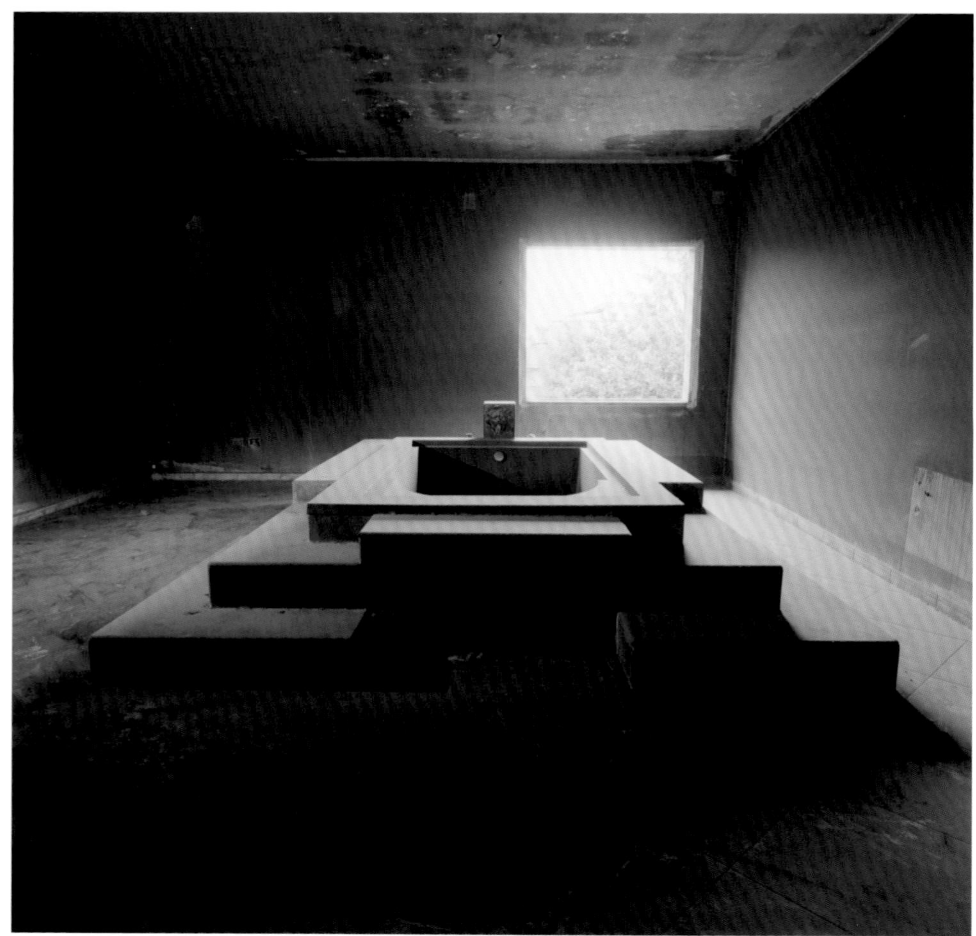

*Above, right and next page* Ville della Camorra (clan dei Casalesi), Caserta, June 2005 (MS)

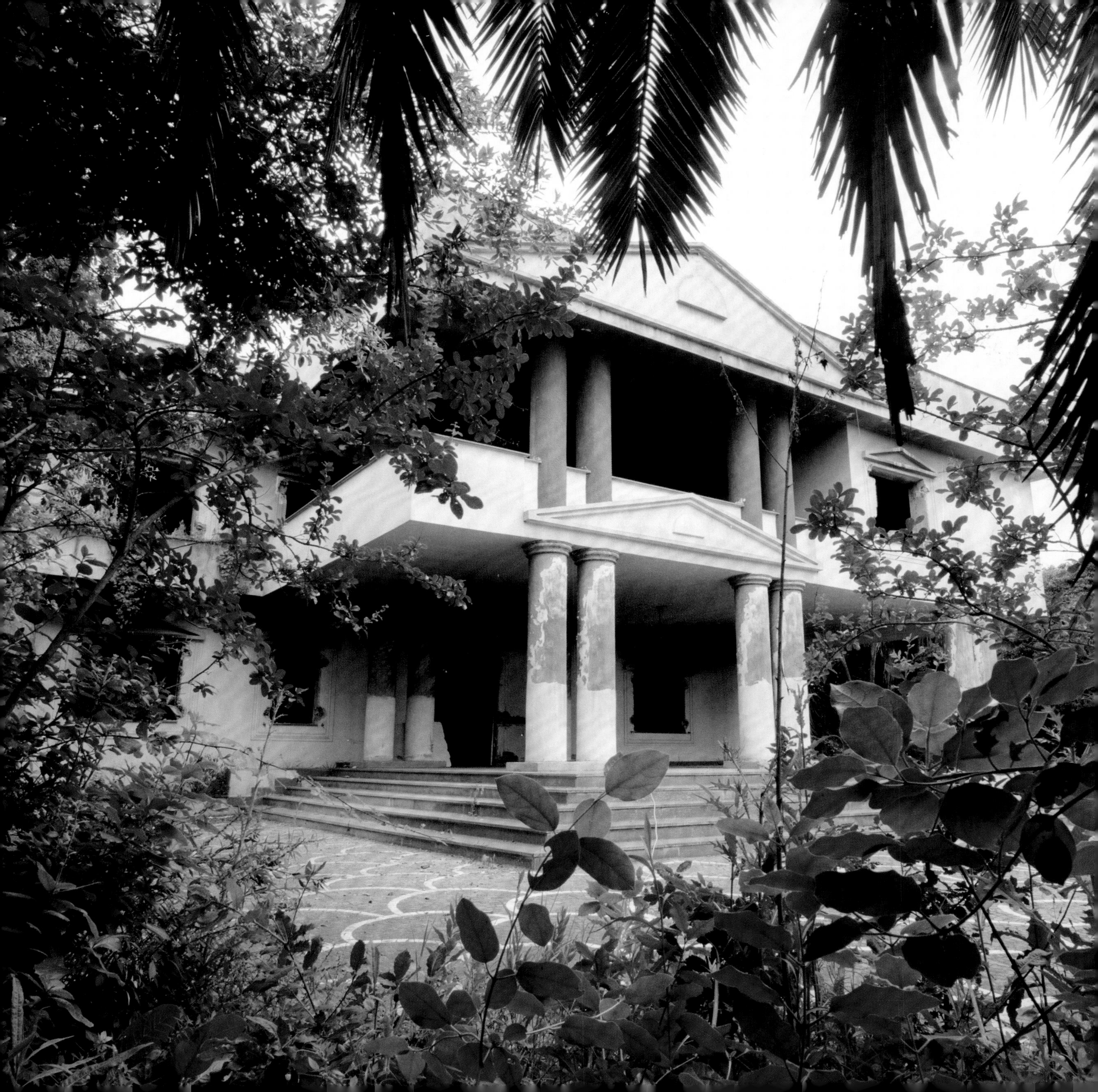

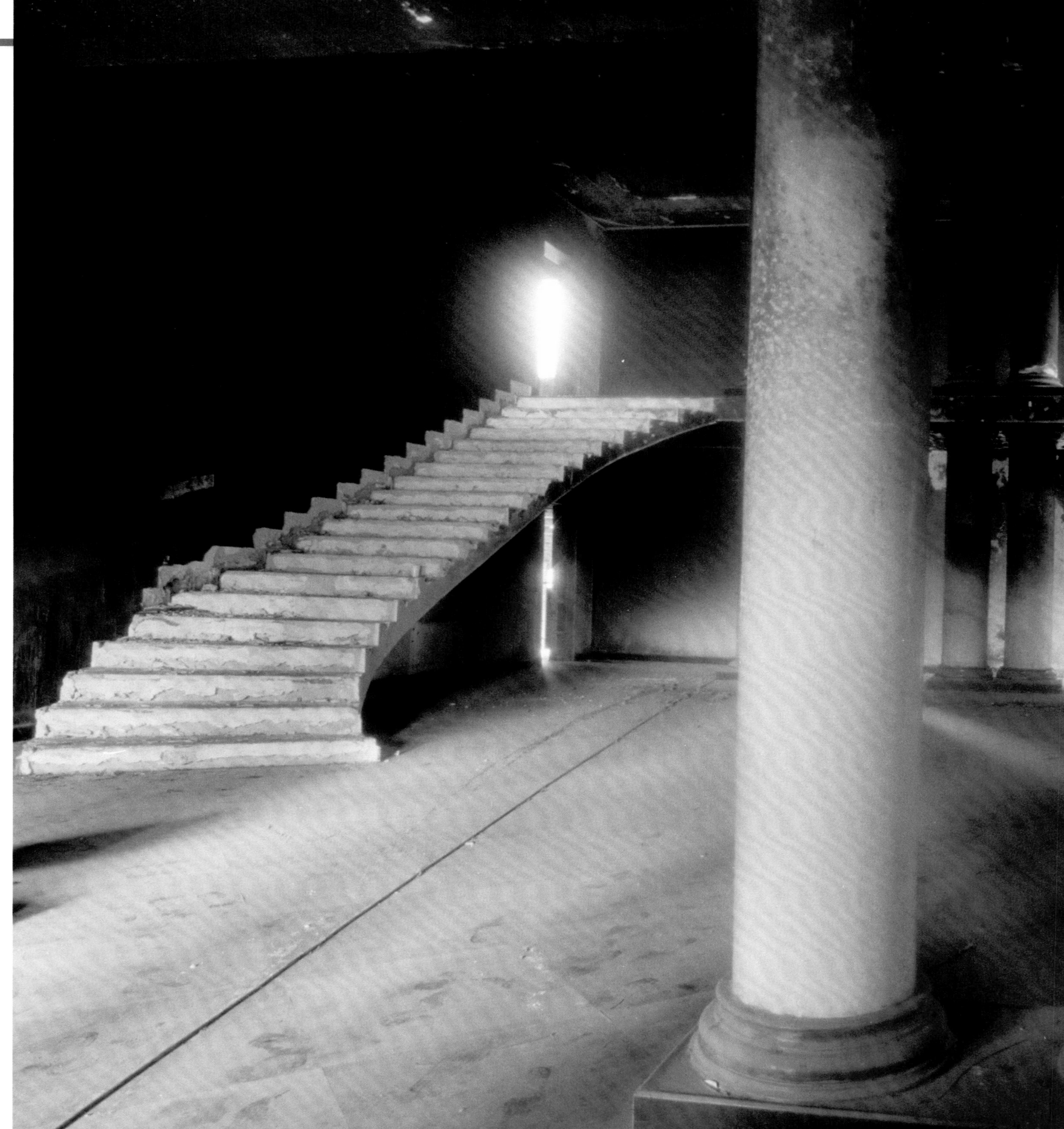

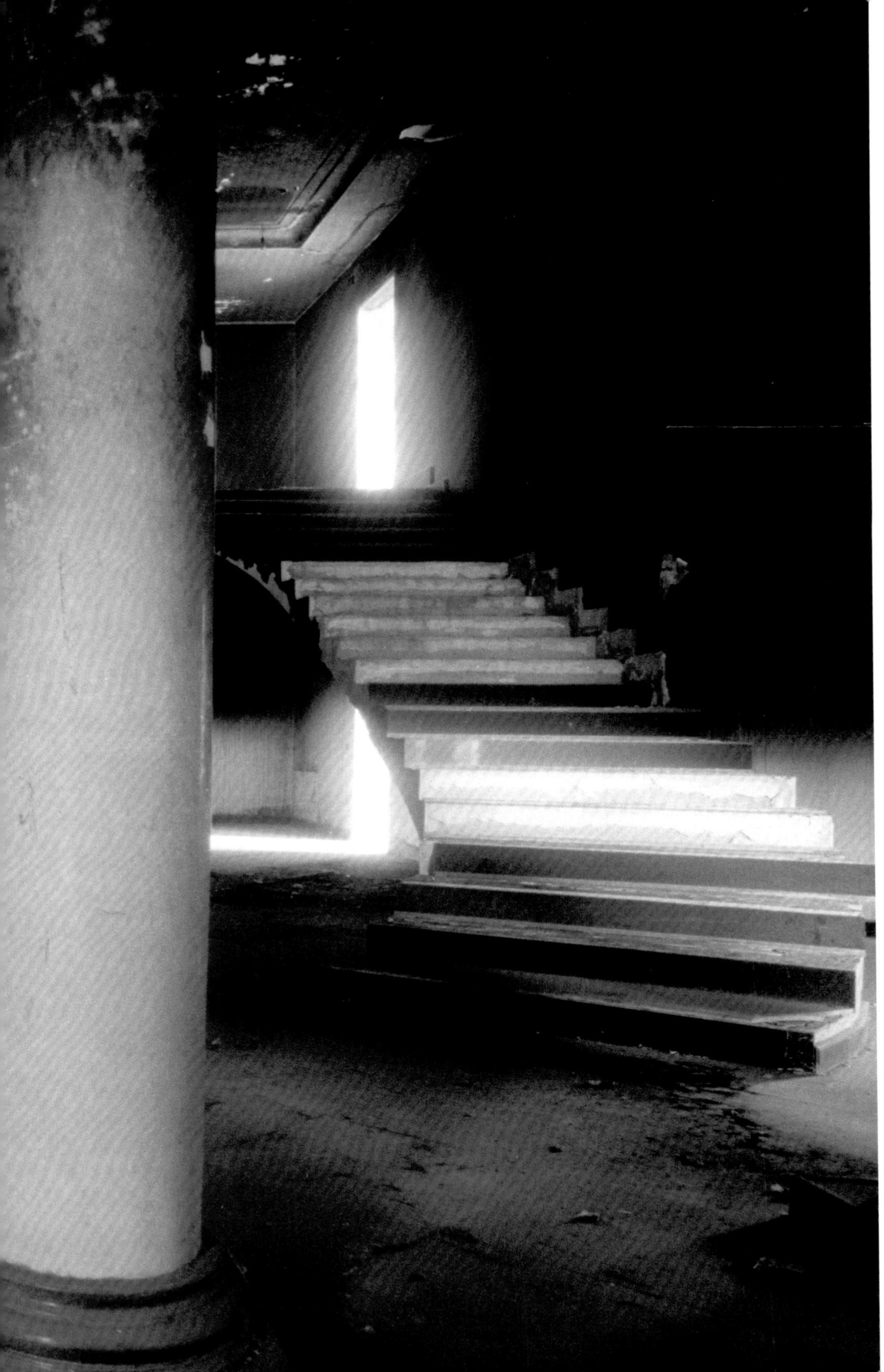

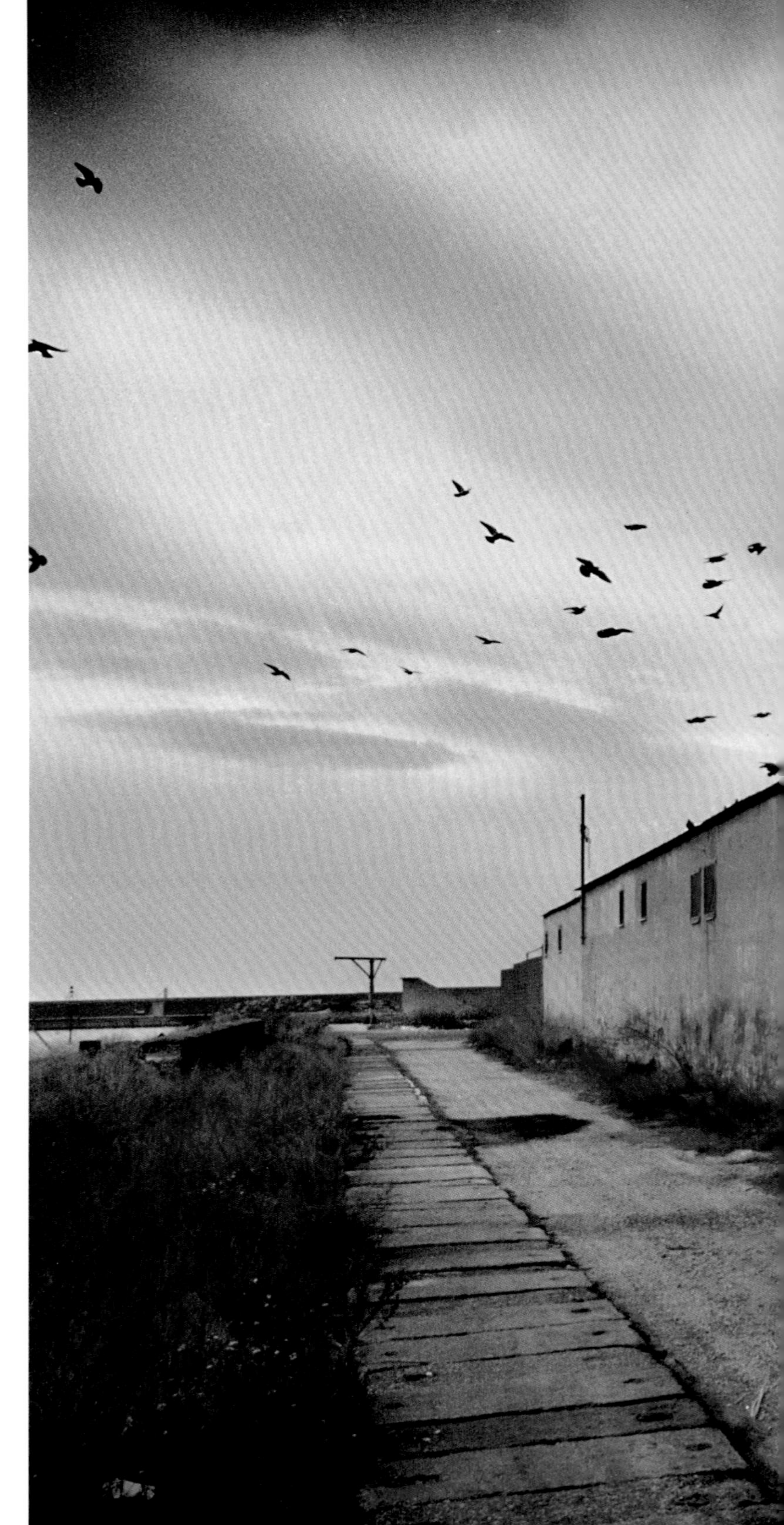

Torre Annunziata docks, March 2003 (EM)

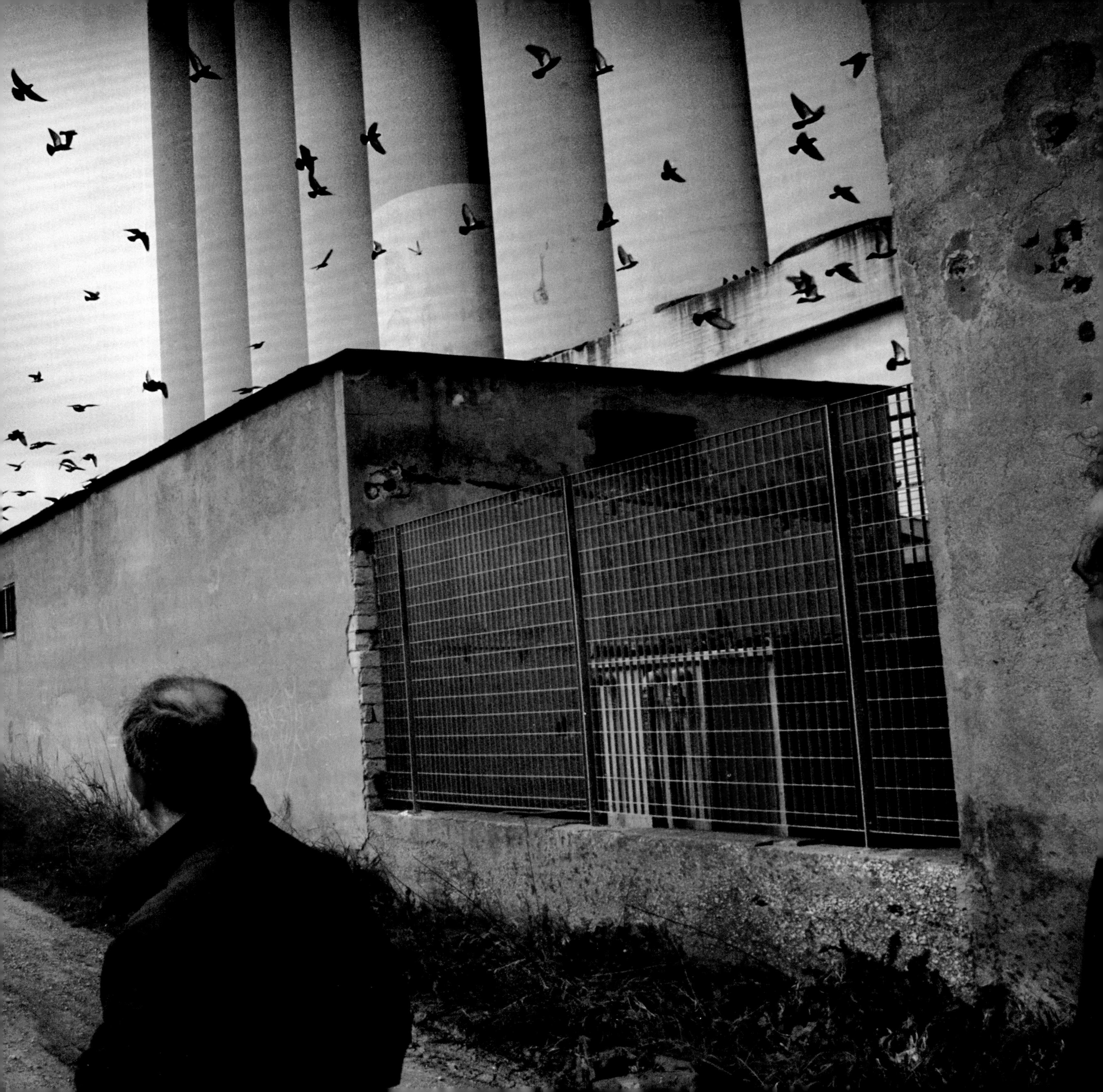

32,000 new illegal constructions were built in 2004,
an increase of approximately 10% over 2003.
A further 10% increase was forecast for 2005.

Genoa – Olbia ferry , July 2005 (MB)

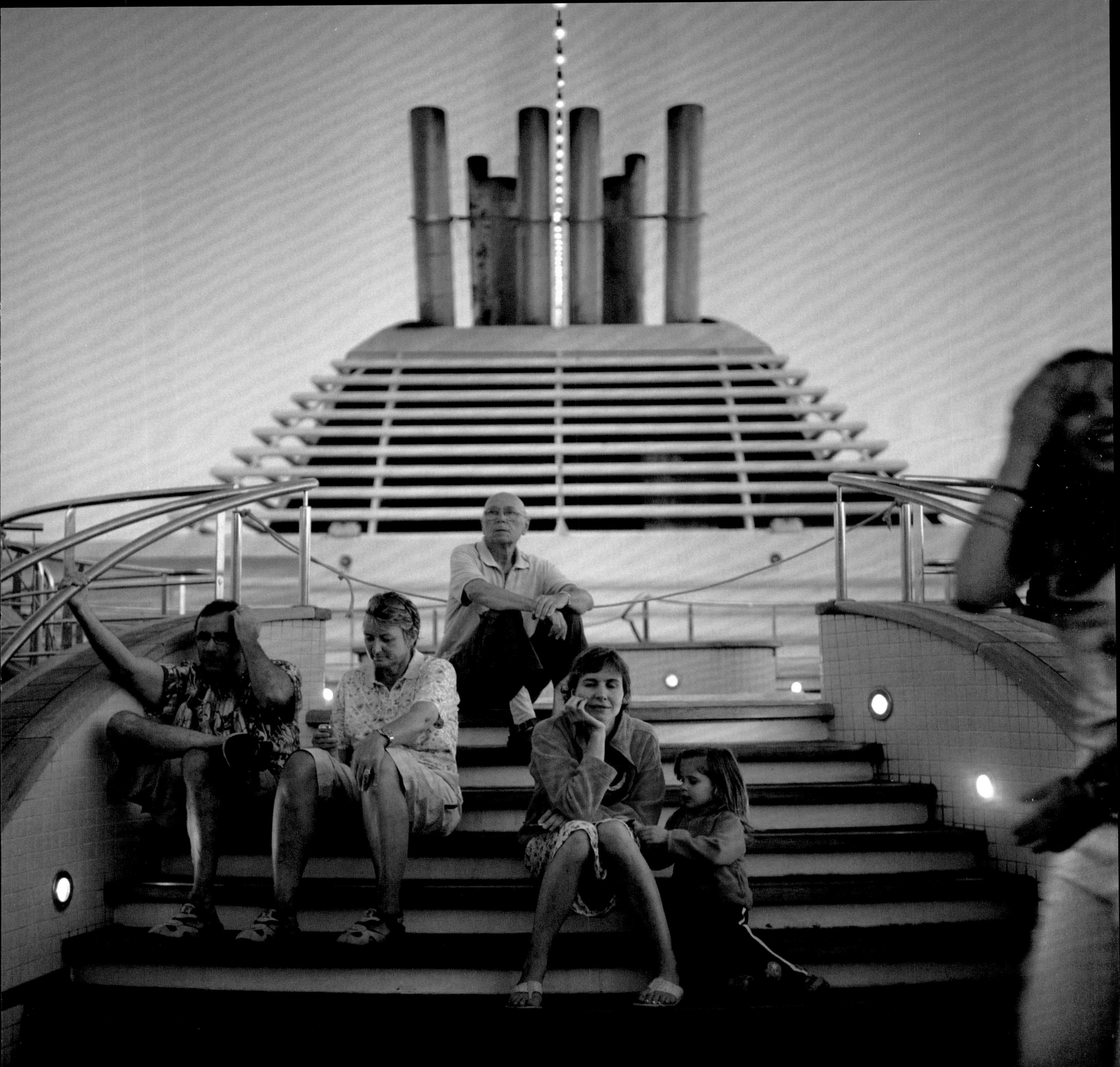

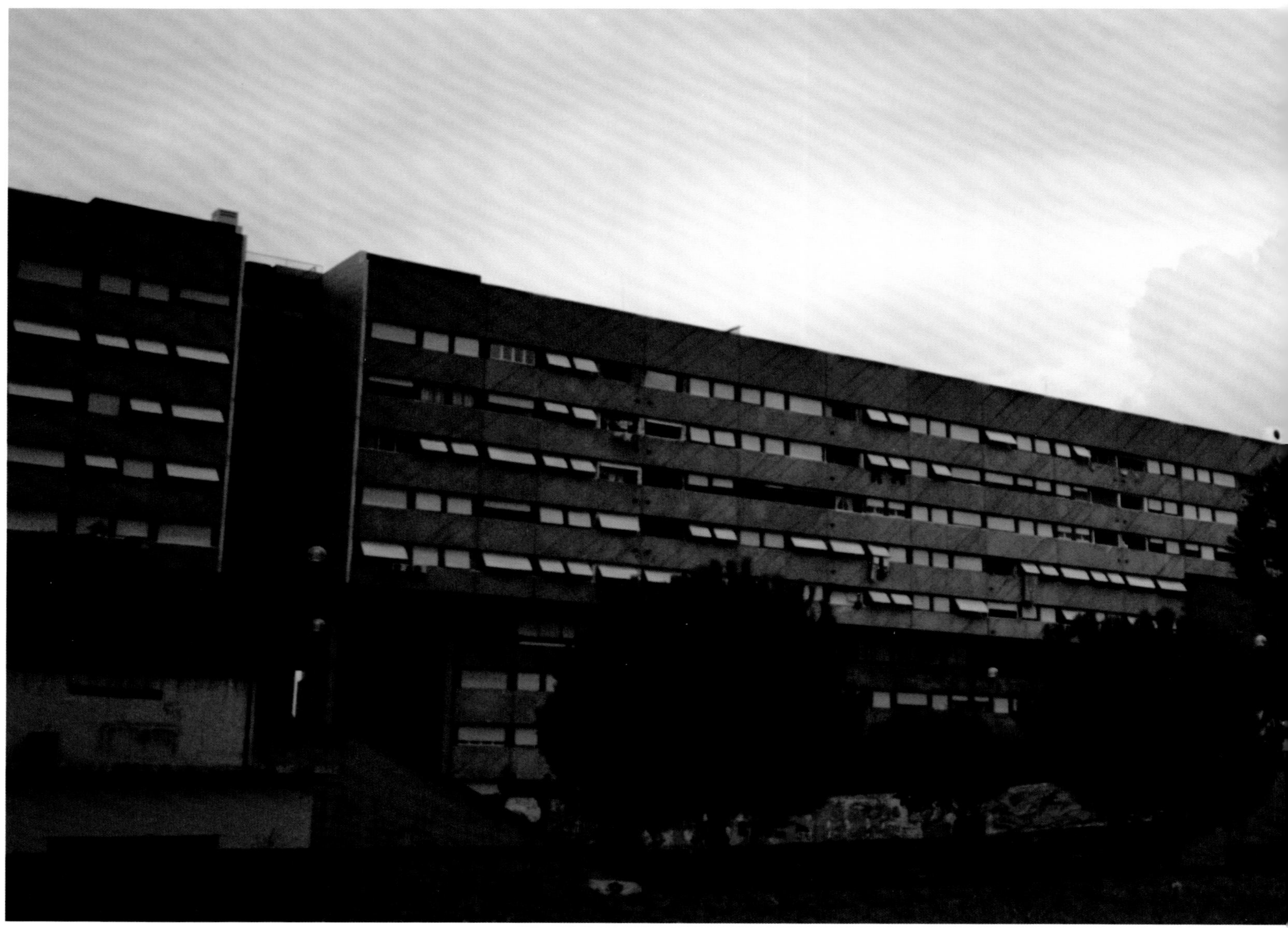

Corviale, Roma, September 2004 (MB)

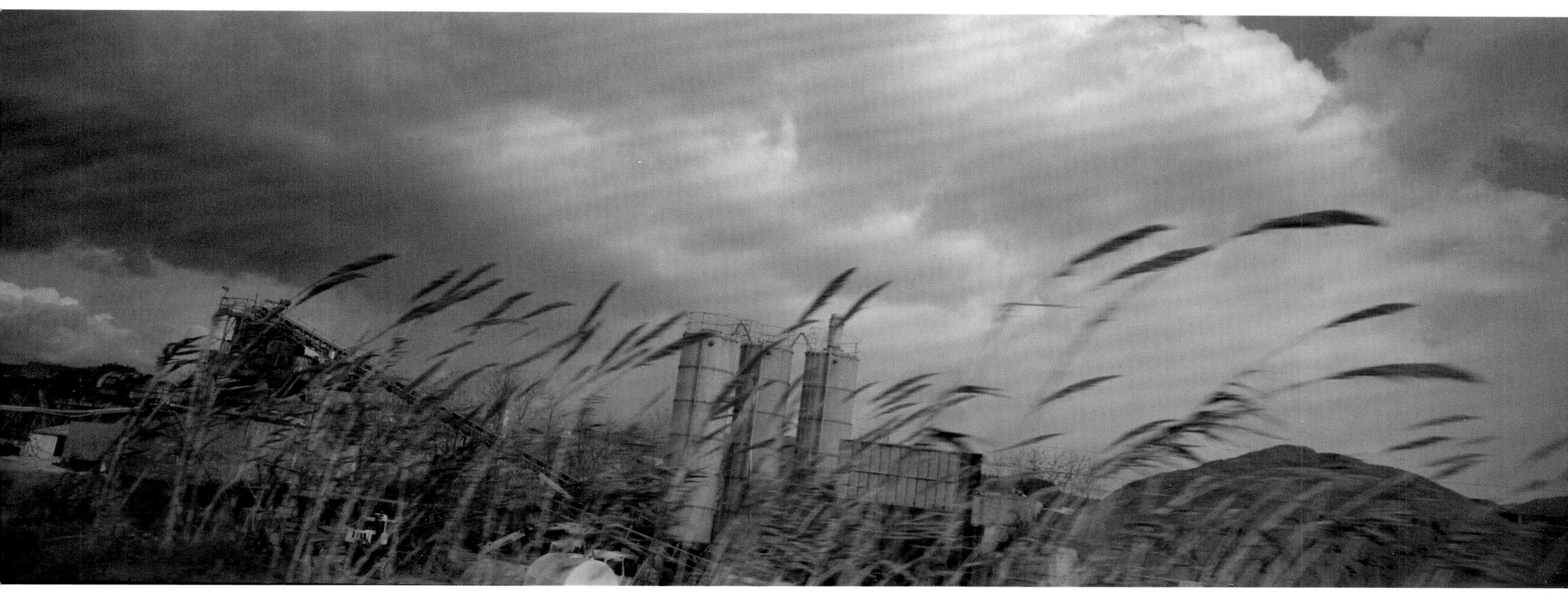

Salerno-Reggio Calabria highway, November 2004 (GC)

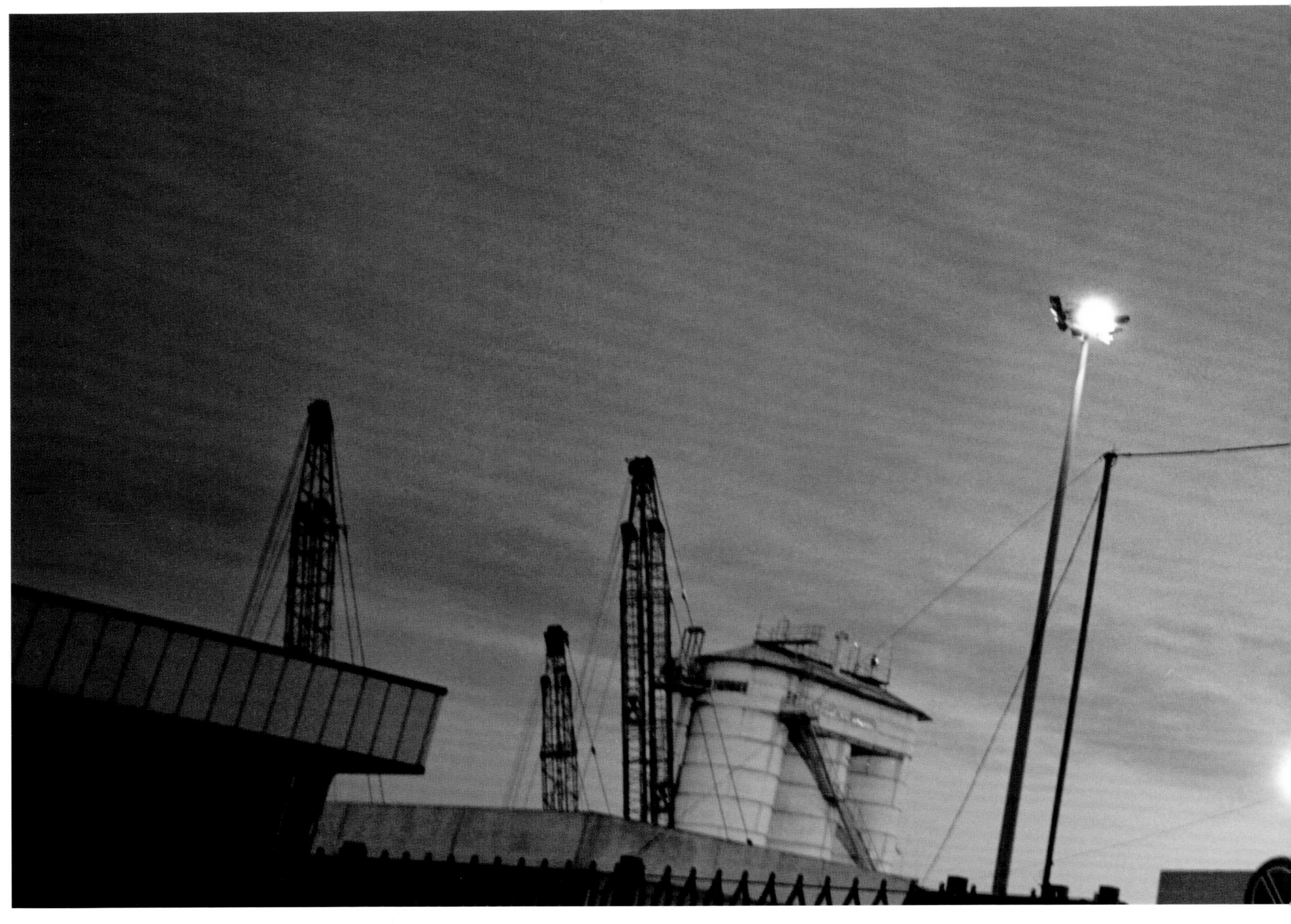

*Above* The port of Pescara, October 2003 (GC) (© by kind permission of Darc, photograph in permanent collection of Maxxi, Rome)
*Next page* Porto Marghera, Venezia, December 2004 (MB)

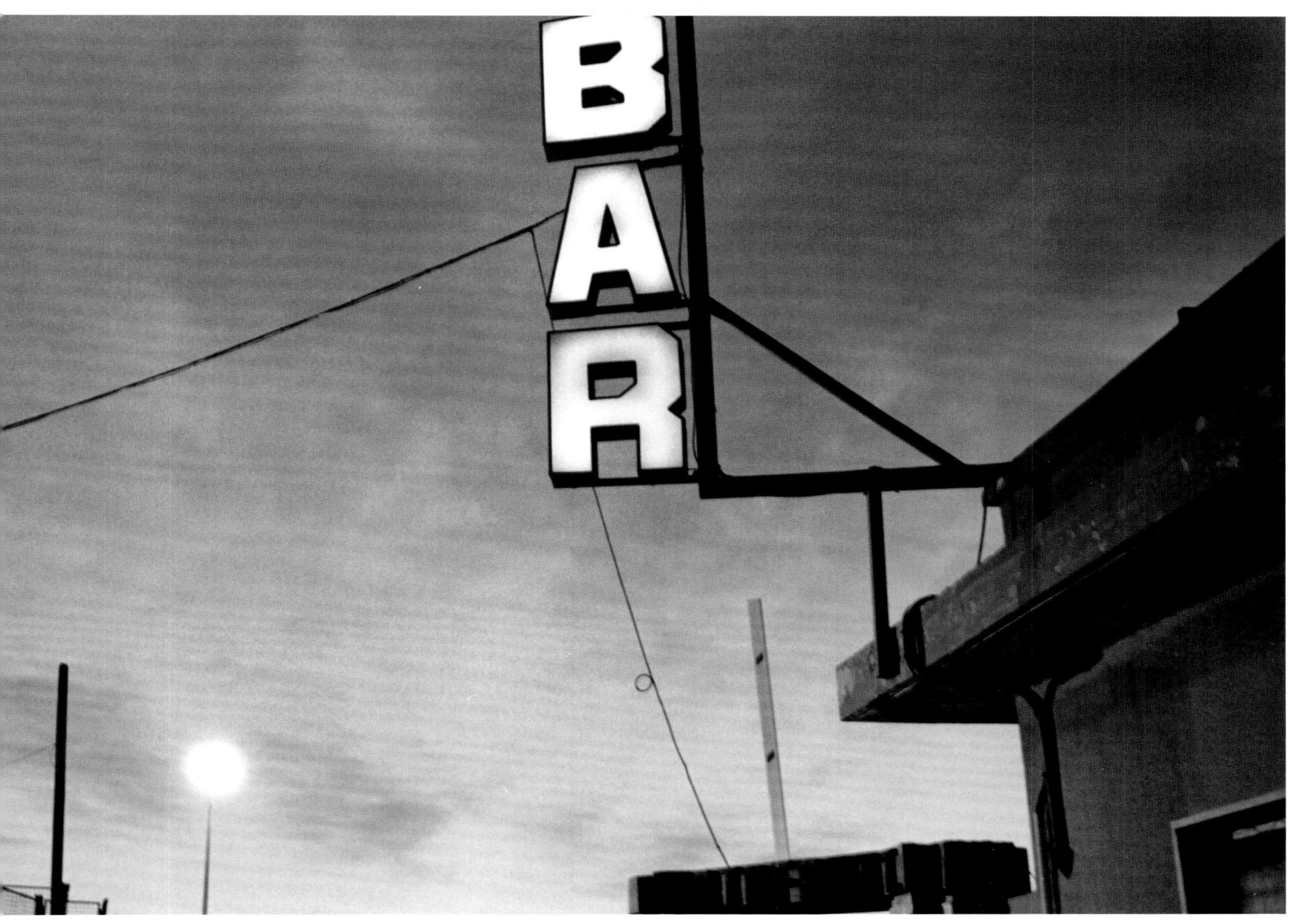
BAR

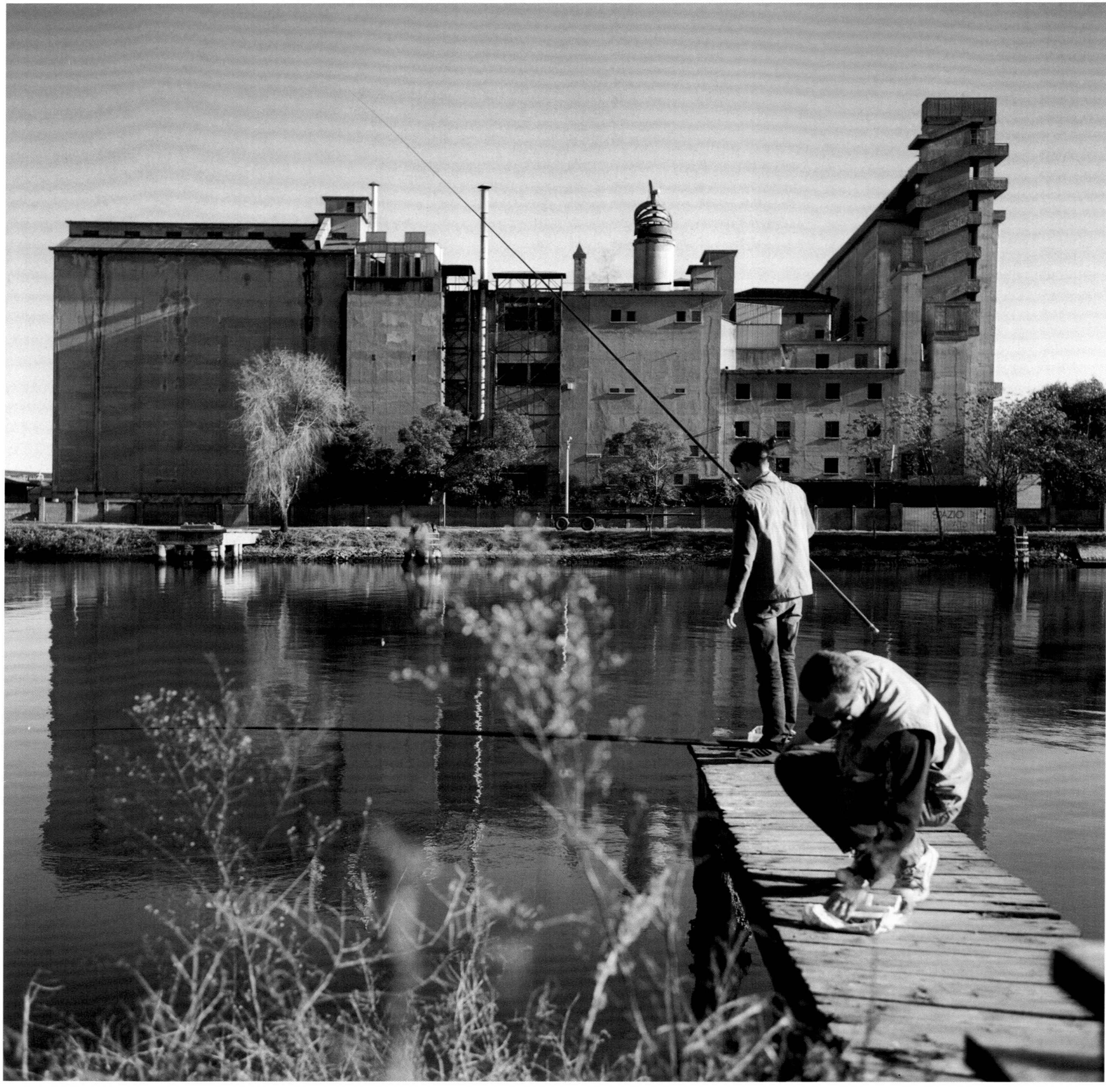
SPAZIO

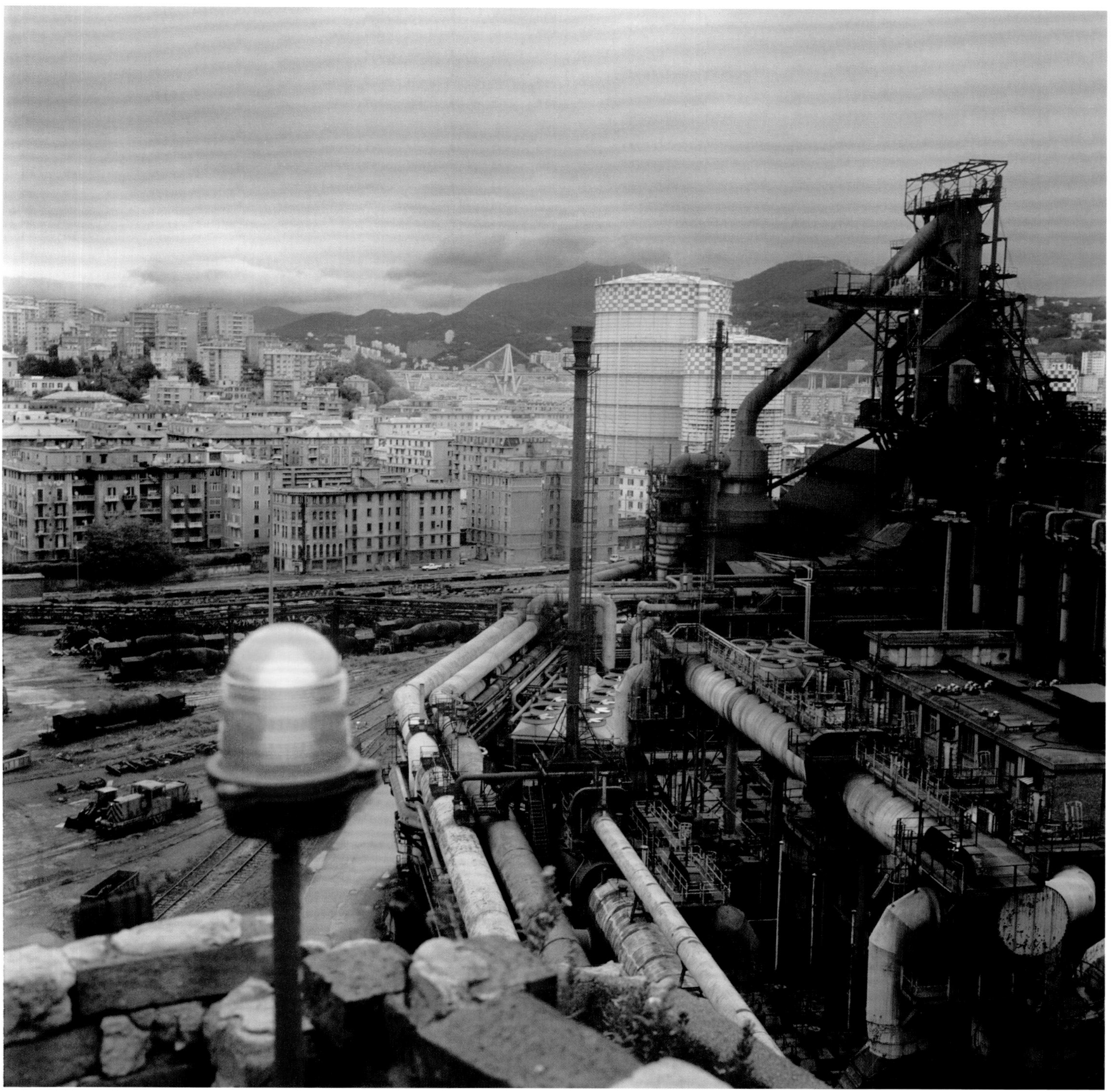

In 2004 the number of breaches reported to the police increased by 3.6% on the previous year; seizures increased by 17.7% to 1,675.

*Previous page* Cornigliano steel foundry, Genova, February 2005 (MB)
*Right* The Gulf of Termini Imerese , Sicily, October 2002 (EM)

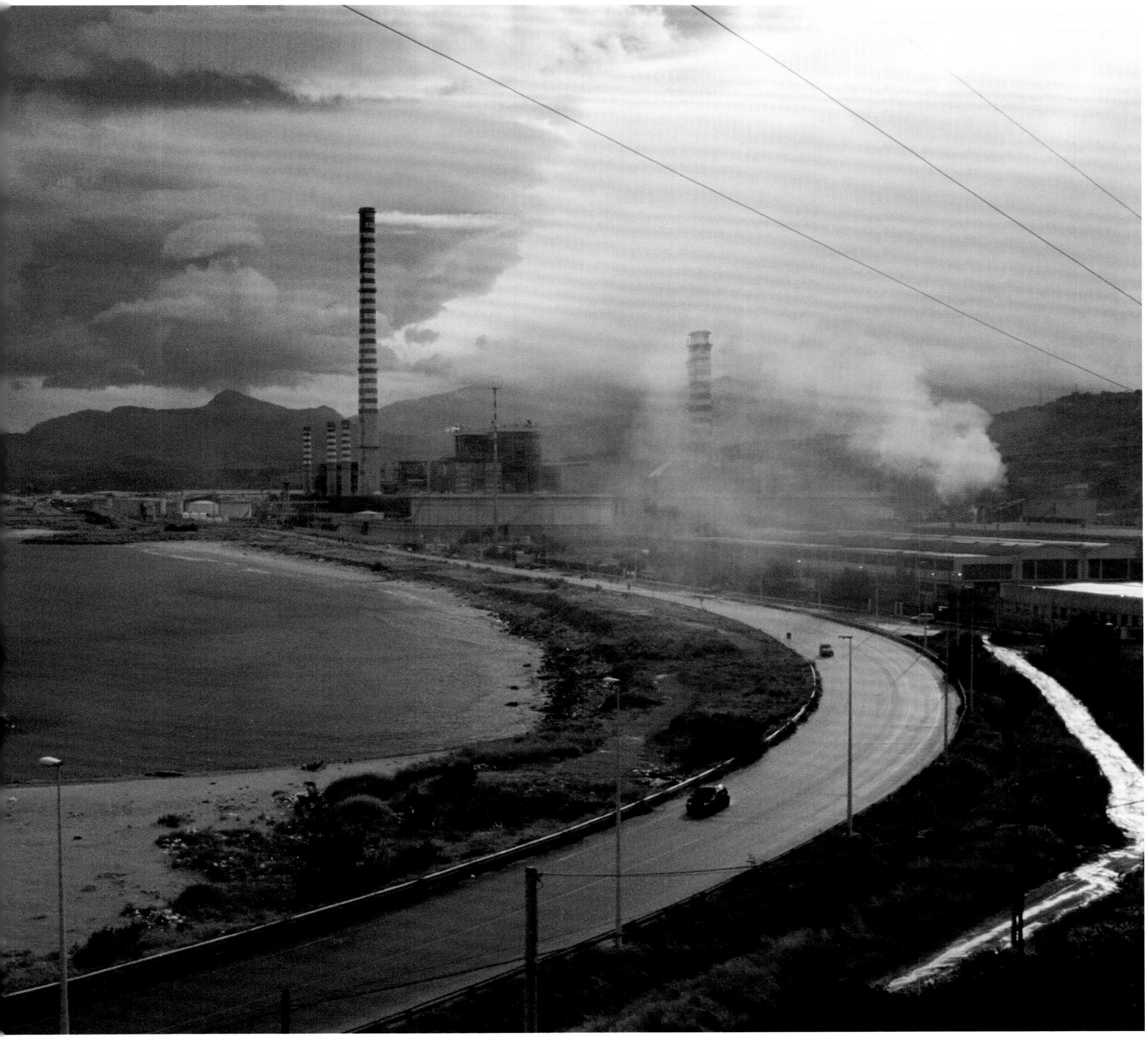

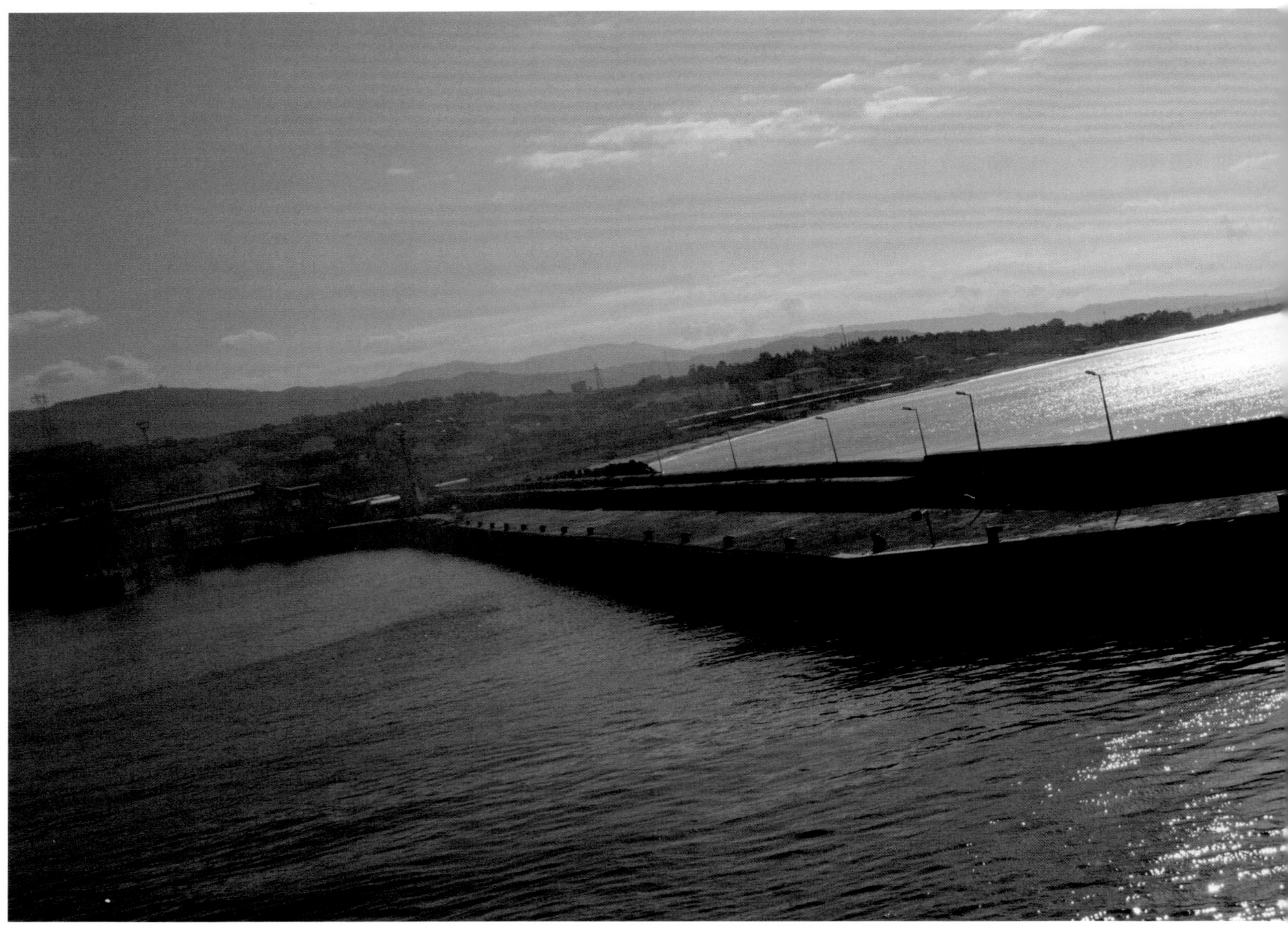

*Above* Messina Straits, November 2004 (GC)
*Next page* Fano, June 2003 (GC) (© by kind permission of Darc, photograph in permanent collection of Maxxi, Rome)

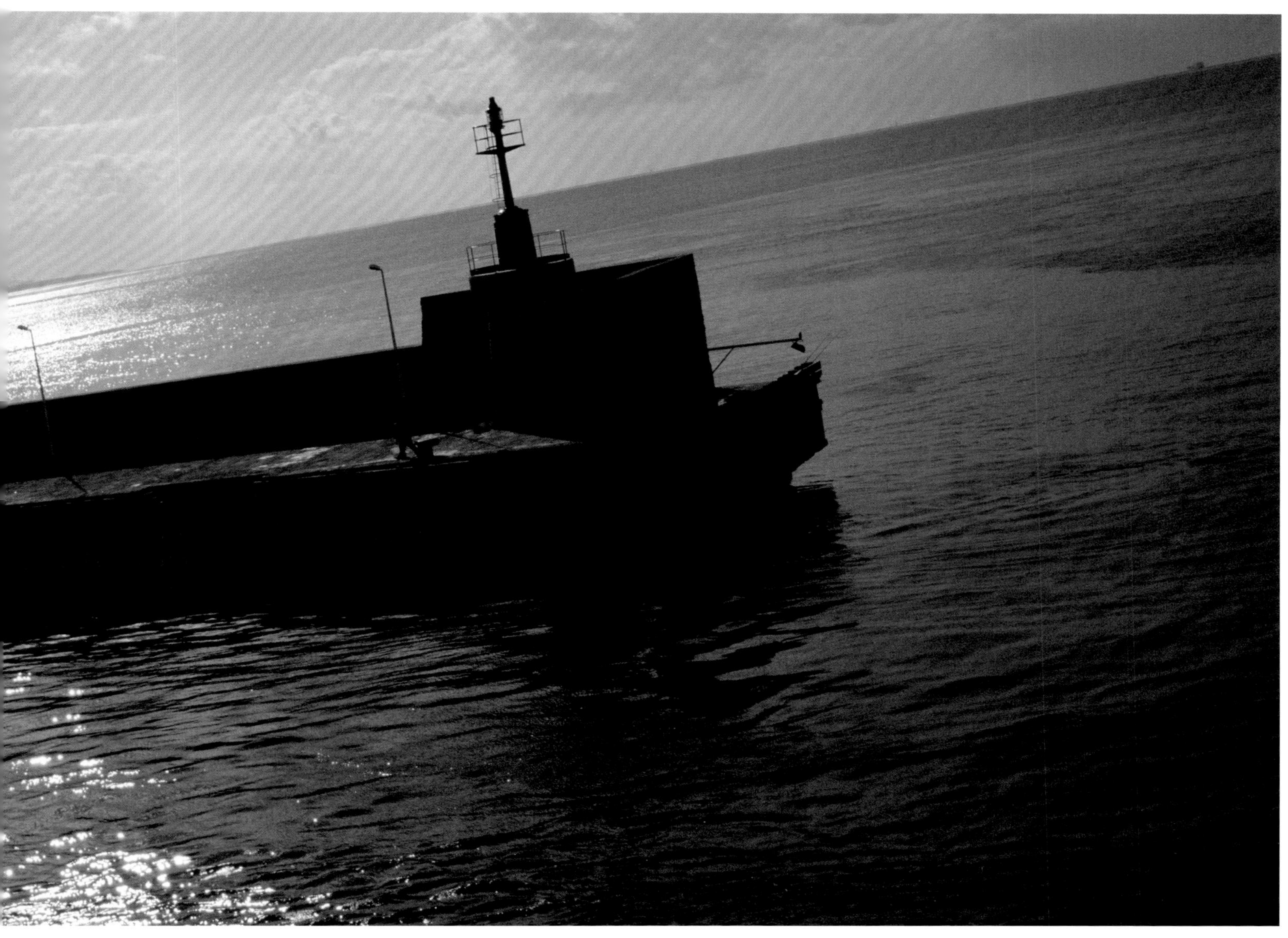

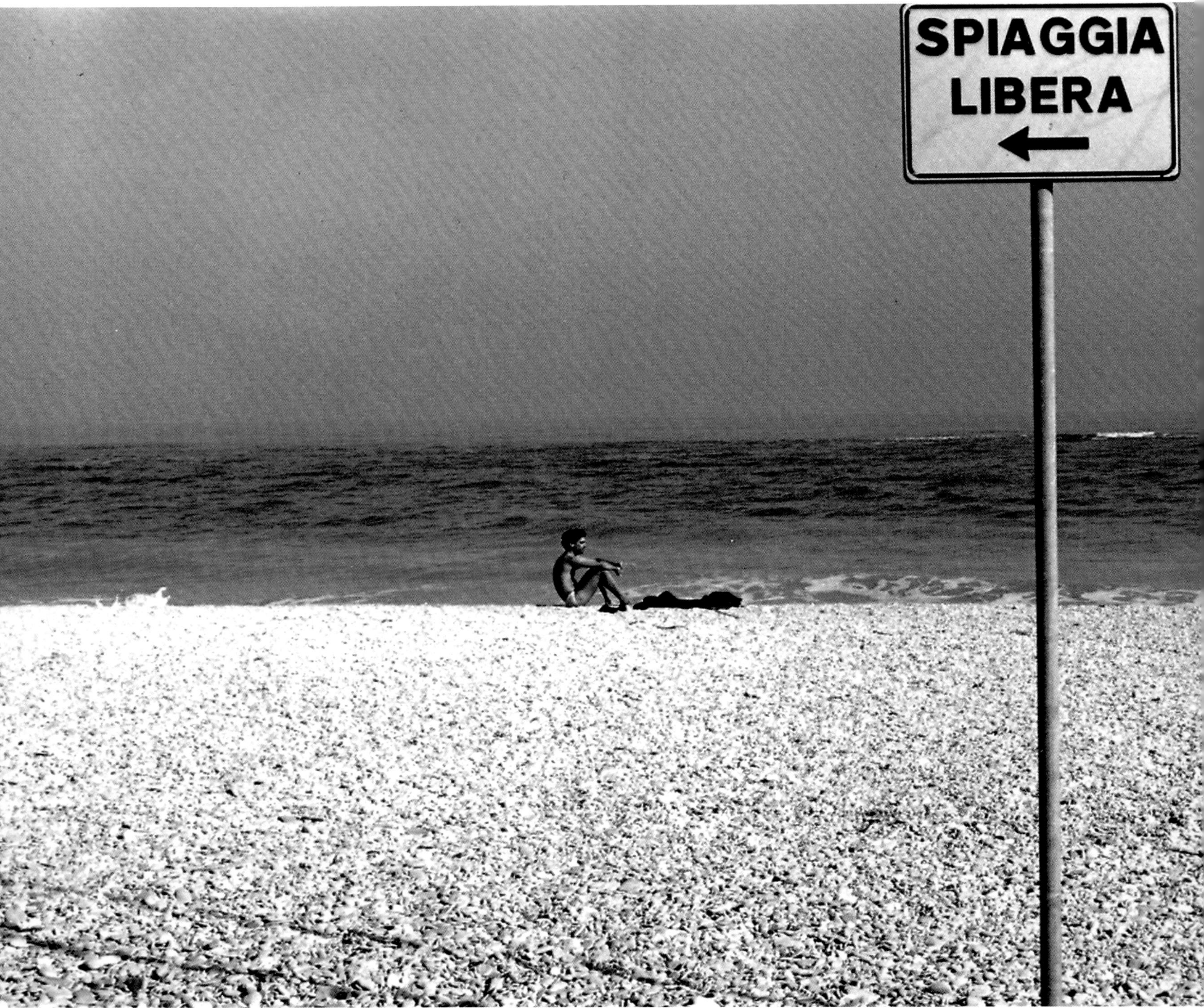
SPIAGGIA
LIBERA

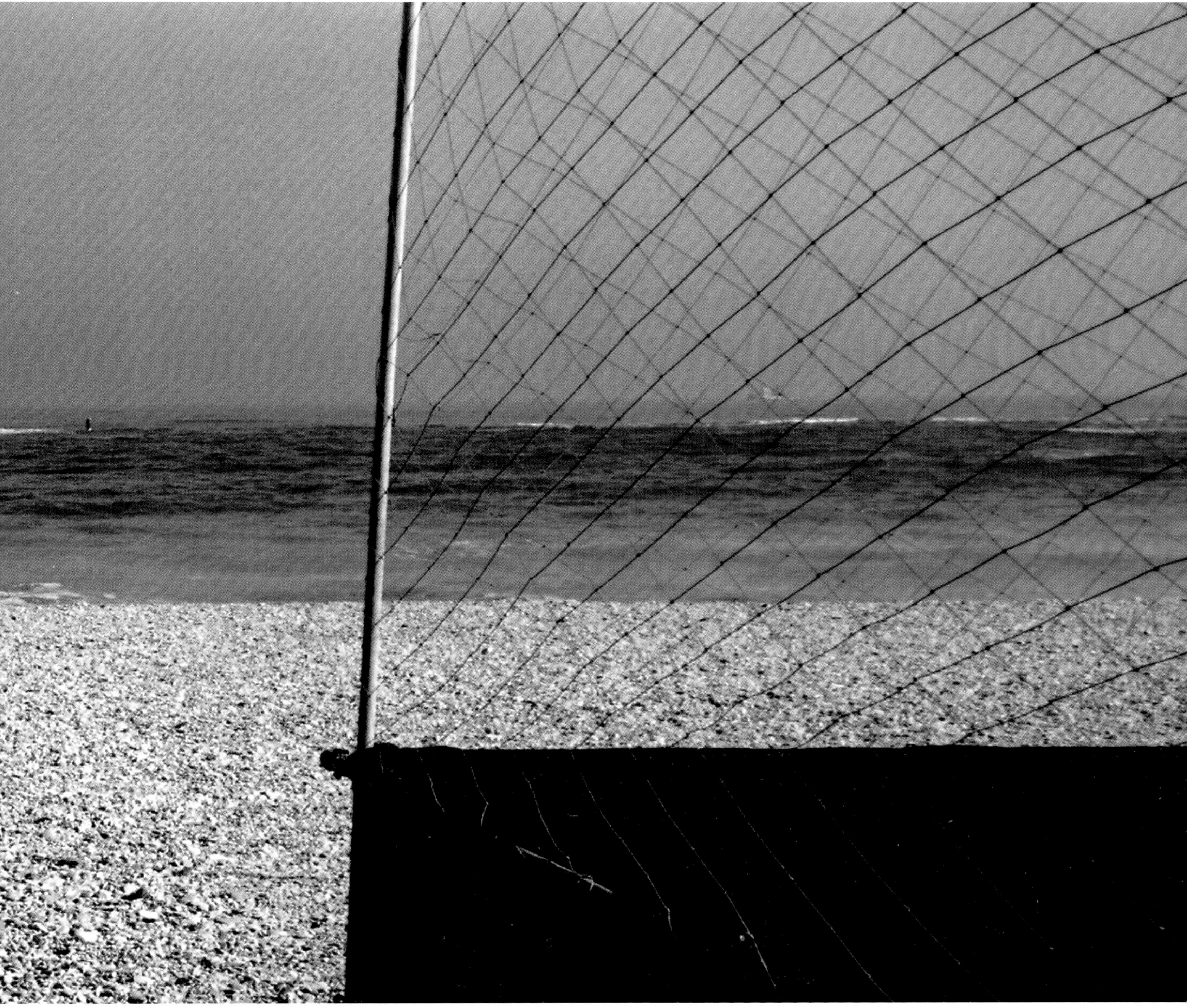

# THE ENEMY STATE

## Umberto Galimberti

The revelations of the Italian Central Bank's aberrations, and sundry other ambiguous operations by financial institutions in Italy, raise important questions. Why, for example, is there no realisable concept of the integrity of the State and its institutions? Why is there no comprehensive civic sense of ethics?

There appear to be three fundamental considerations that provide answers. The first is that the Italian experience of statehood is no more than 150 years old, while those of France, the United Kingdom and Scandinavian countries is some hundreds of years older.

For several centuries Italy was ruled by foreign powers. The state, per se, was a foreign organisation which had no representation of the Italian people and the population, not unnaturally, was hostile to that "enemy state". The consequence was that the people, exasperated by the state, developed individual aims and ambitions that had no room for the concept of *res publica*.

Secondly, it should be remembered that Italy is a Christian, Catholic country, where the realities of the world are subject to supernatural definitions as dictated by Augustinian philosophies. The roots of these ideas are to be found in the belief that the Christian has a life after death. The Christian, so he believes, inhabits this world but will inevitably be removed from it to a new life. Necessarily such a belief demands a division between the Christian's morals and his politics, since his ultimate destination is not the society in which he lives, or the betterment of it, but a metaphysical world.

The philosopher Jean-Jacques Rosseau understood this paradigm when he wrote that the ardent Christian is unlikely to be a good citizen. He believed that a Christian's commitment to the society in which he lives is no more than a pragmatic understanding of his earthly existence, and that he has no tenets dedicated to that society, since he will be moving on. Rousseau asked himself: Why is Paradise so essential to a Christian?

The Christian Catholic's understanding of society is that it is a conduit to the salvation of his soul, wherein he may demonstrate his goodness, rather than an activity directed towards the benefit of the many. It is the reason why morals and politics fail to live in harmony in a Christian Catholic society.

The third consideration is that Italian society is governed by ethical principles of behaviour that are, frankly, primitive.

They concentrate on the physical violation of the individual, including murder and rape, and theft. Italian prisons are awash with felons convicted of such banal crimes.

The more complex financial crimes, that earn huge profits for their perpetrators, operate at a less visible level in society, since they have yet to enter the collective consciousness. If and when they are recognized by the legal system the exemplary sentences required to recognise society's repugnance and moral indignation are very hard to find.

The combination of these three prevailing factors - the perception of the state as hostile, the Catholic ethic that separates ambition from moral politics, and the inability to recognise immorality for what it is, make Italy what it is today. This is exactly where the culture of our country resides.

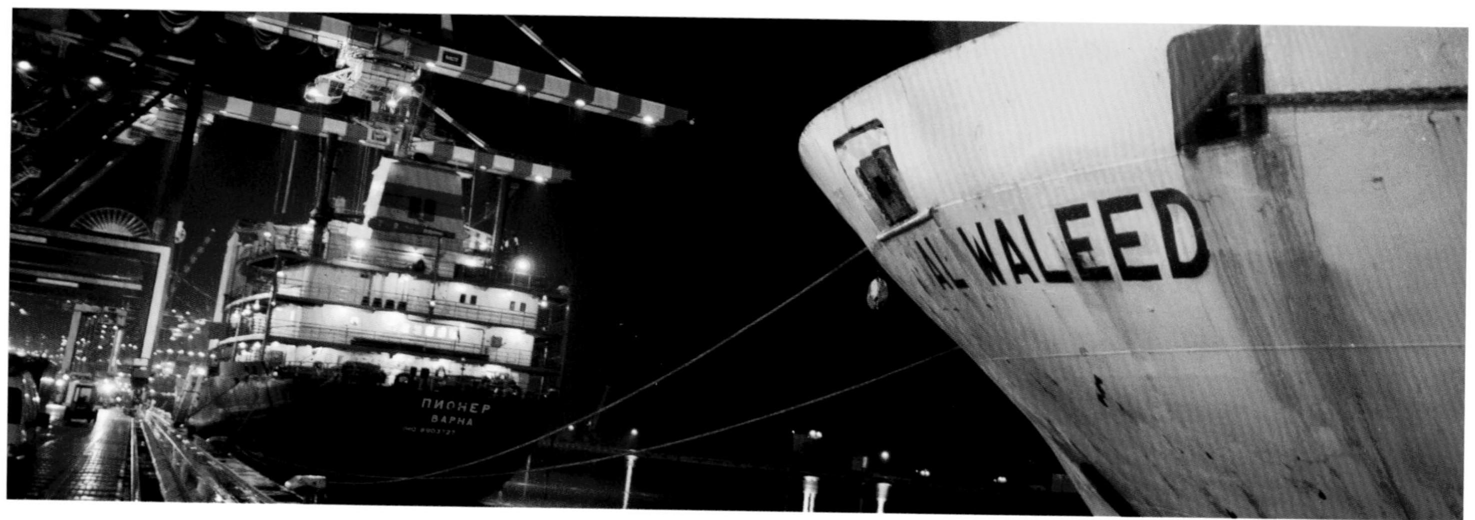


In 2005 the Italian GNP fell by between 0.1 and 0.2 % (ISTAT).

*Above and right* Port of Gioia Tauro, Reggio Calabria, January 2005 (GC)

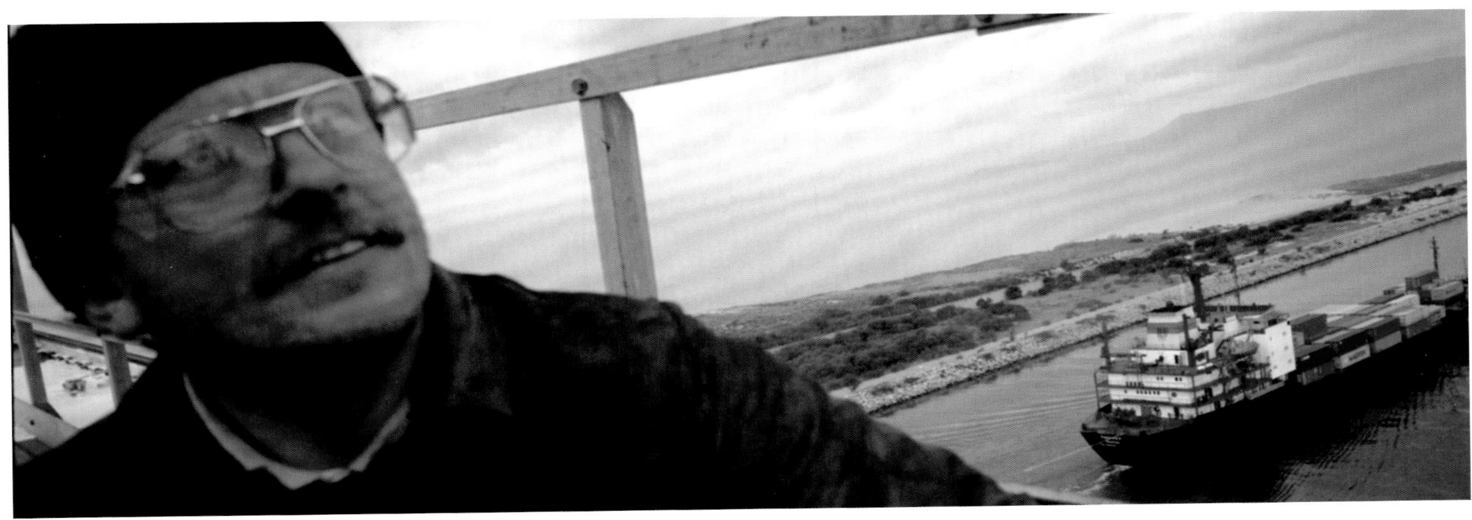

Between 1994-2004 expenditure on Research and Development in Italy was approximately 1% of GNP (ISTAT).

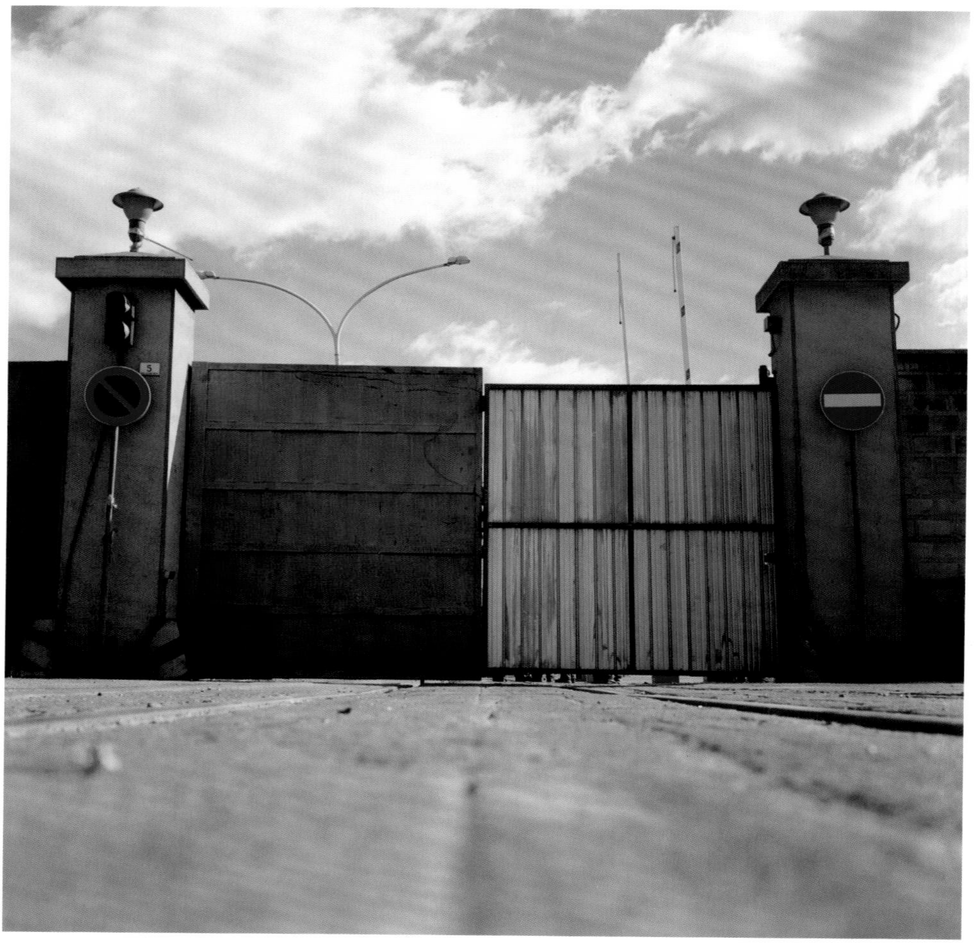


*Above and right* Strike against the proposed closure of the Thyssen Krupp steelworks, Umbria, September 2004 (MB)

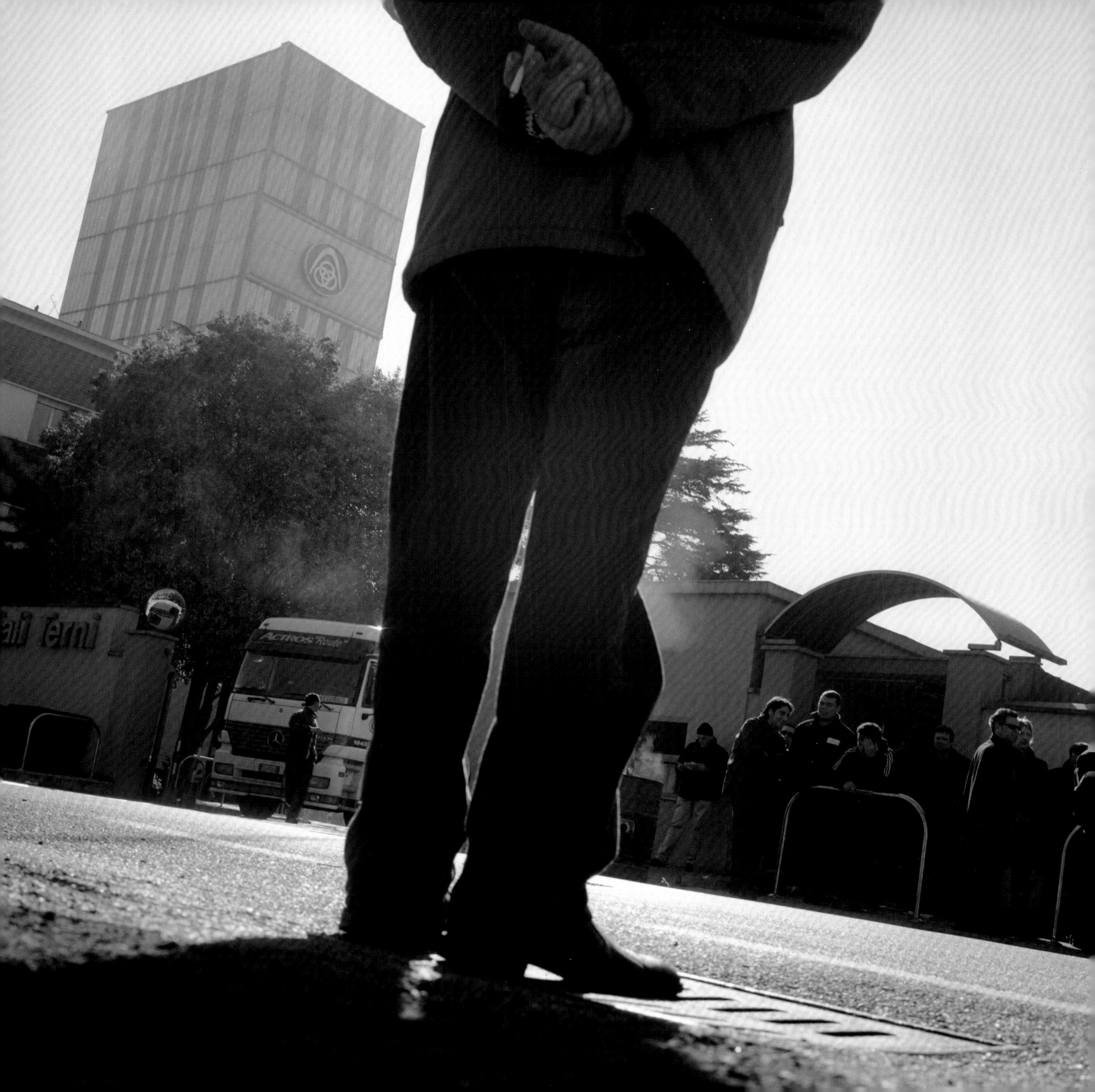
Terni
Actros "Route"

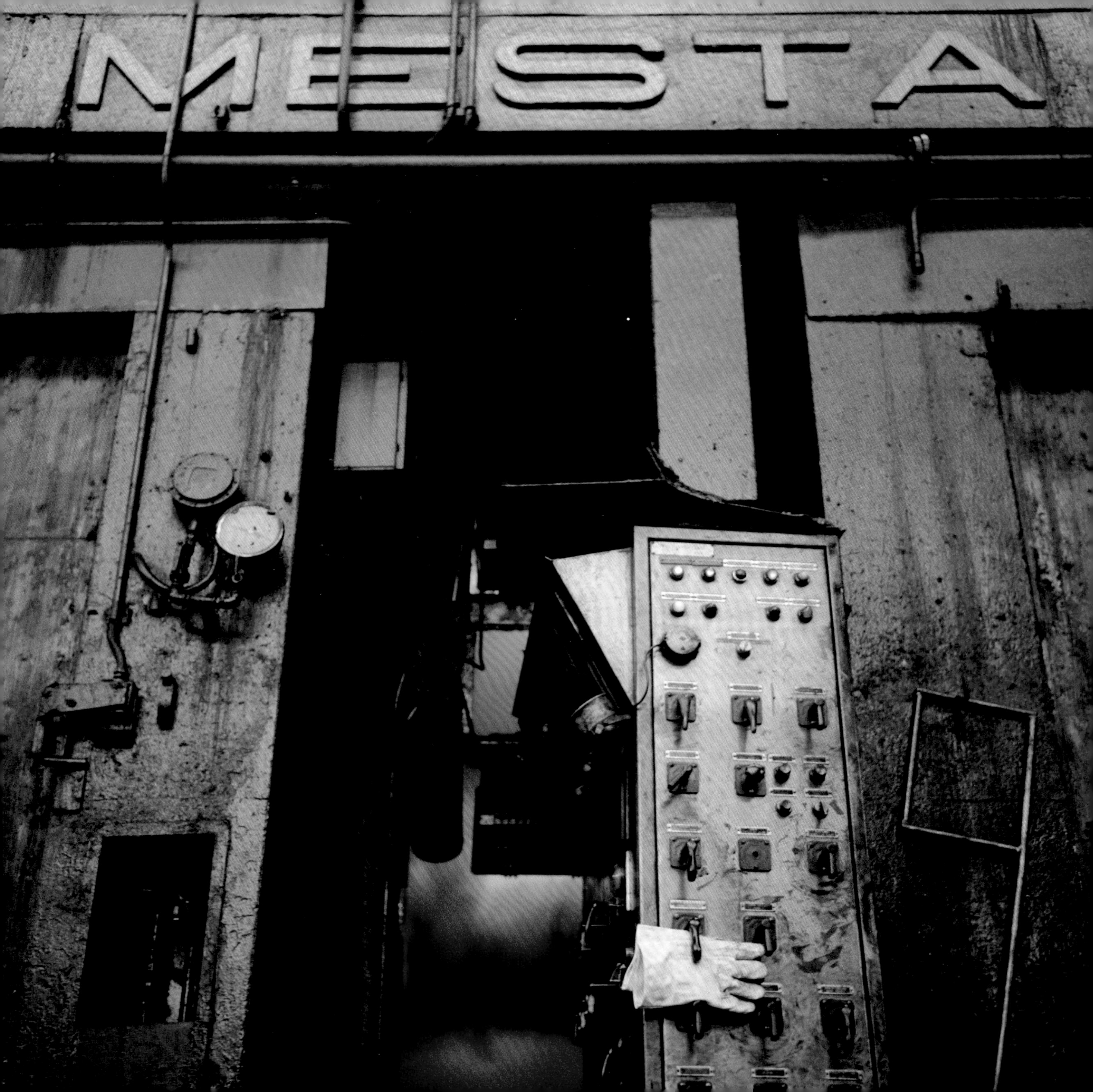
MESTA

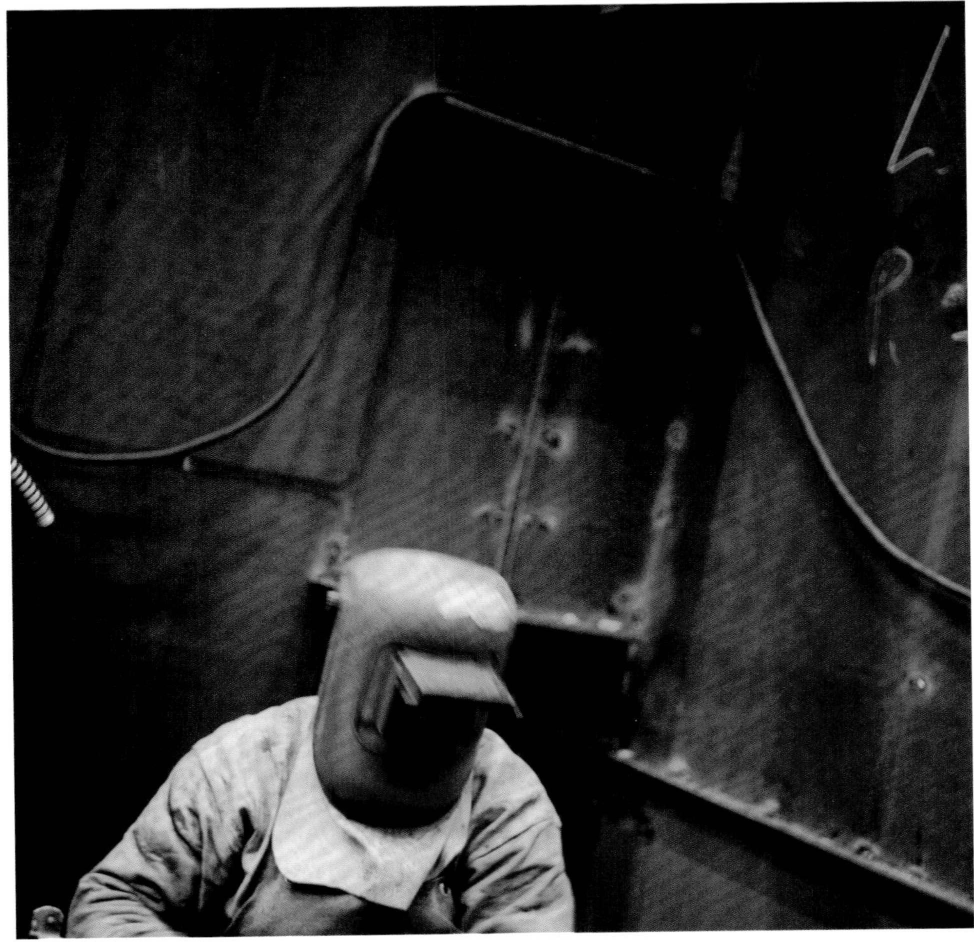

*Above* Porto Marghera, Venezia, December 2004 (MB)
*Left* Cornigliano Steelworks, Genova, October 2005 (MB )

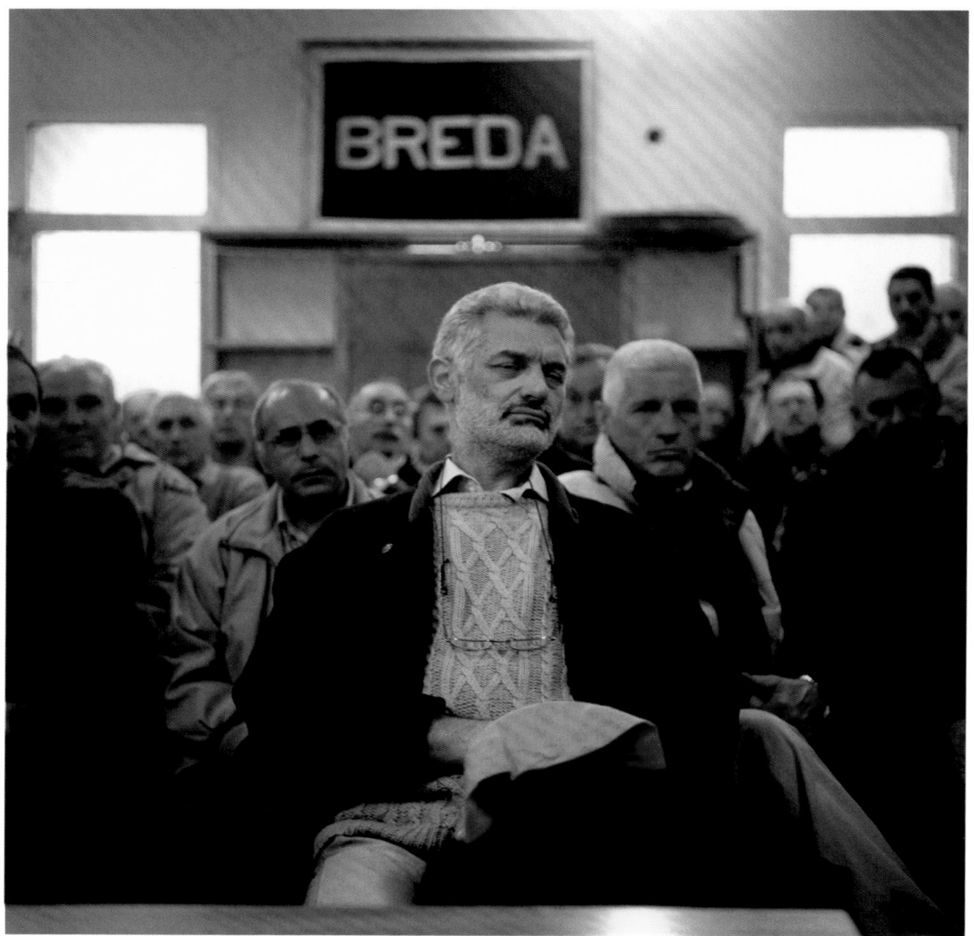


*Above* Reunion of workers made redundant after illness caused by pollution from the chemical plant at Porto Marghera, Venezia, December 2004 (MB)
*Right* Industrial complex, Porto Marghera, Venezia, December 2004 (MB)

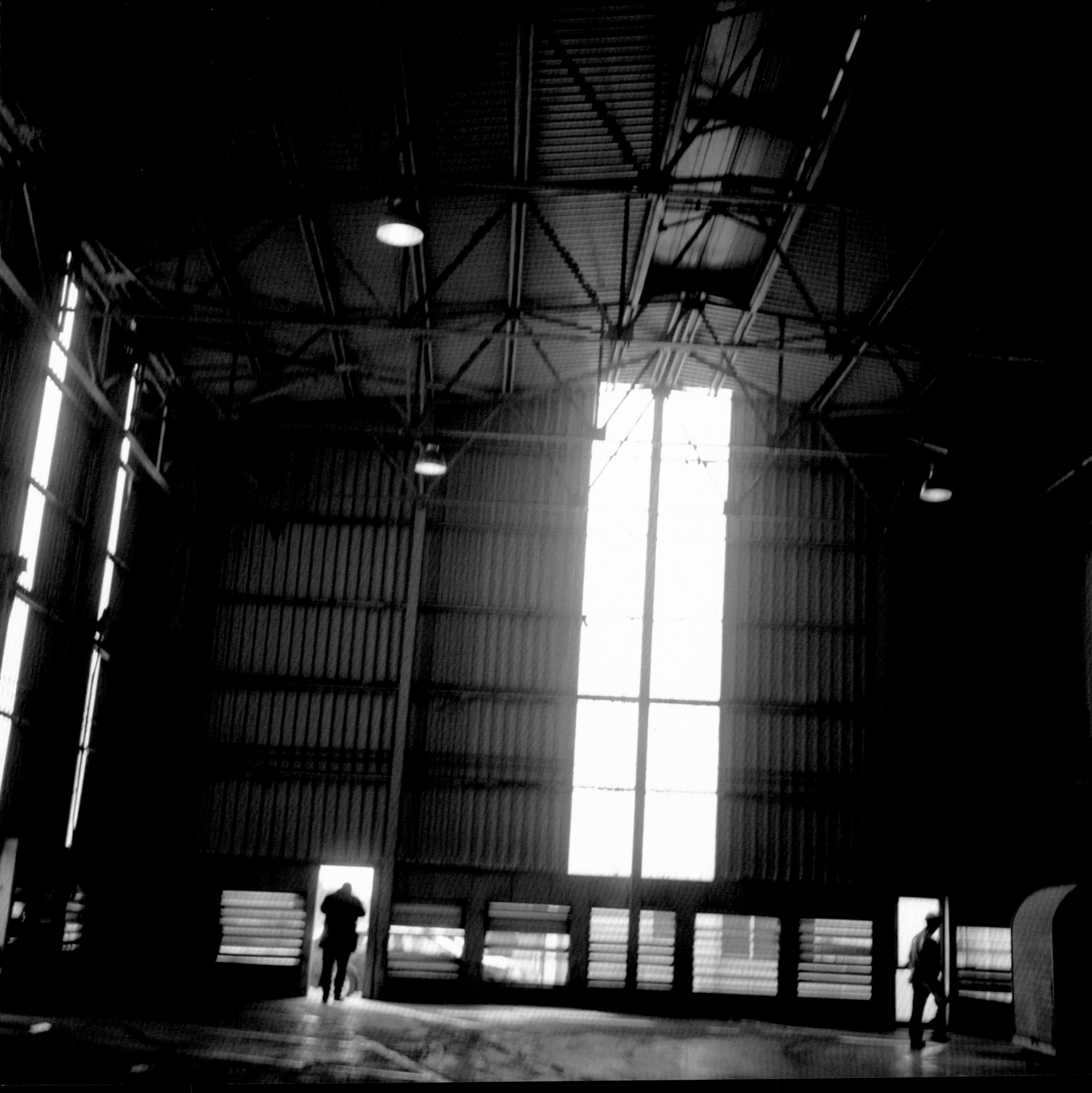

Between 2001 - 2005 inflation in Italy rose by 23.7% , representing a loss in purchasing power of 20.4% for white collar employees, of 14.1% for blue collar, of 12.1% for managers and of 8.3% for directors (Eurispes).

Call center in Torino, Ottobre 2005 (MB)

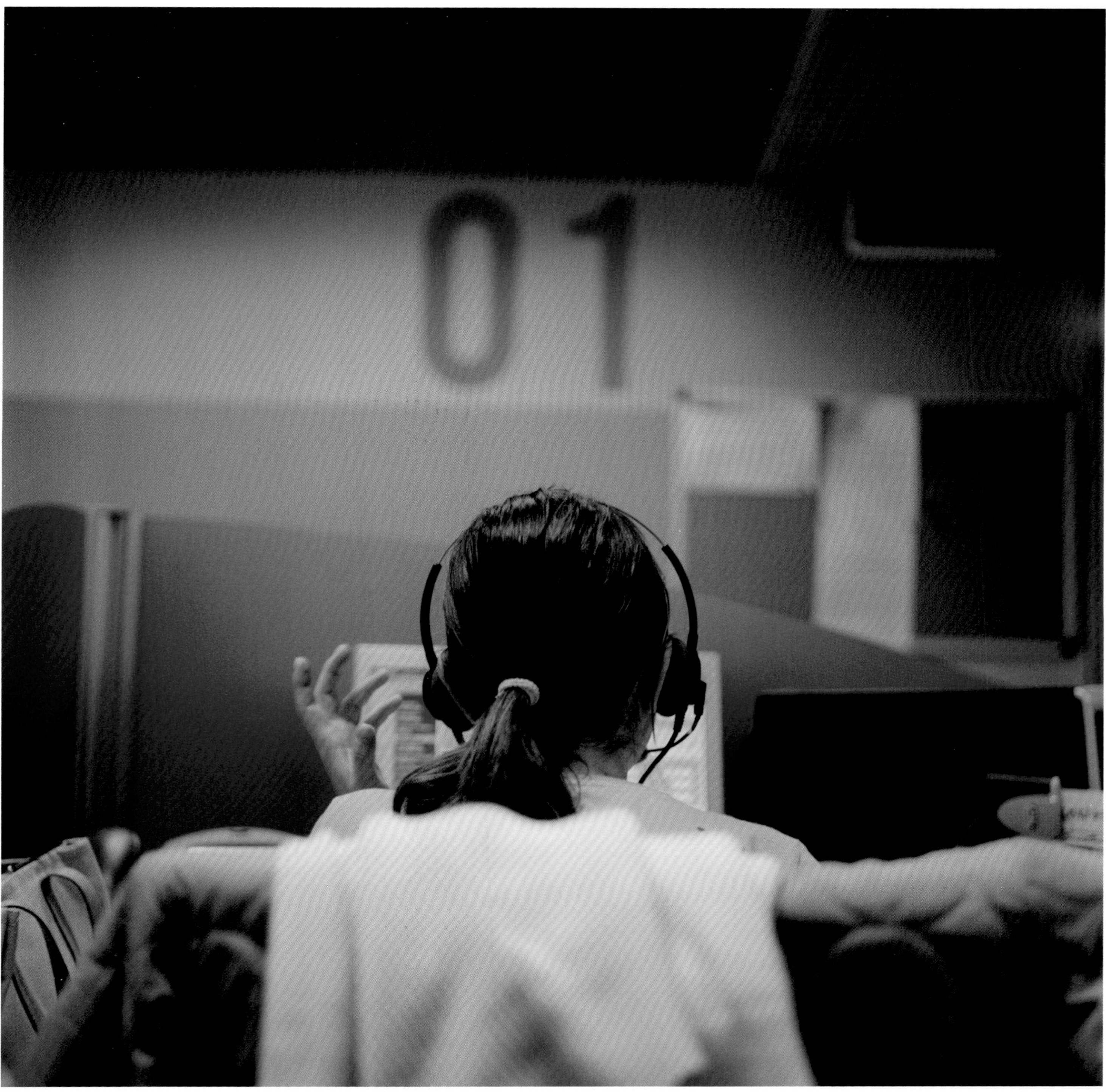
01

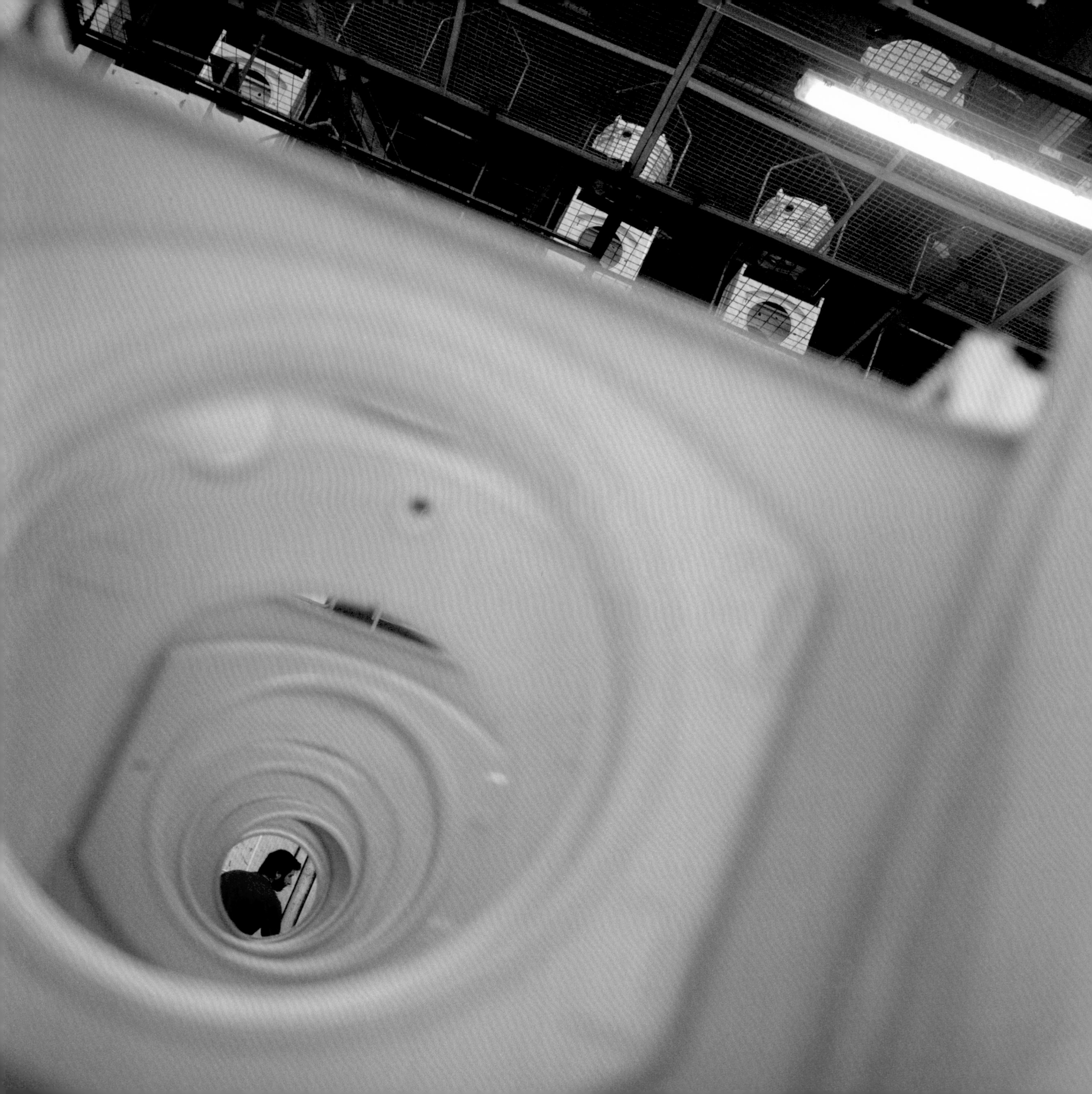

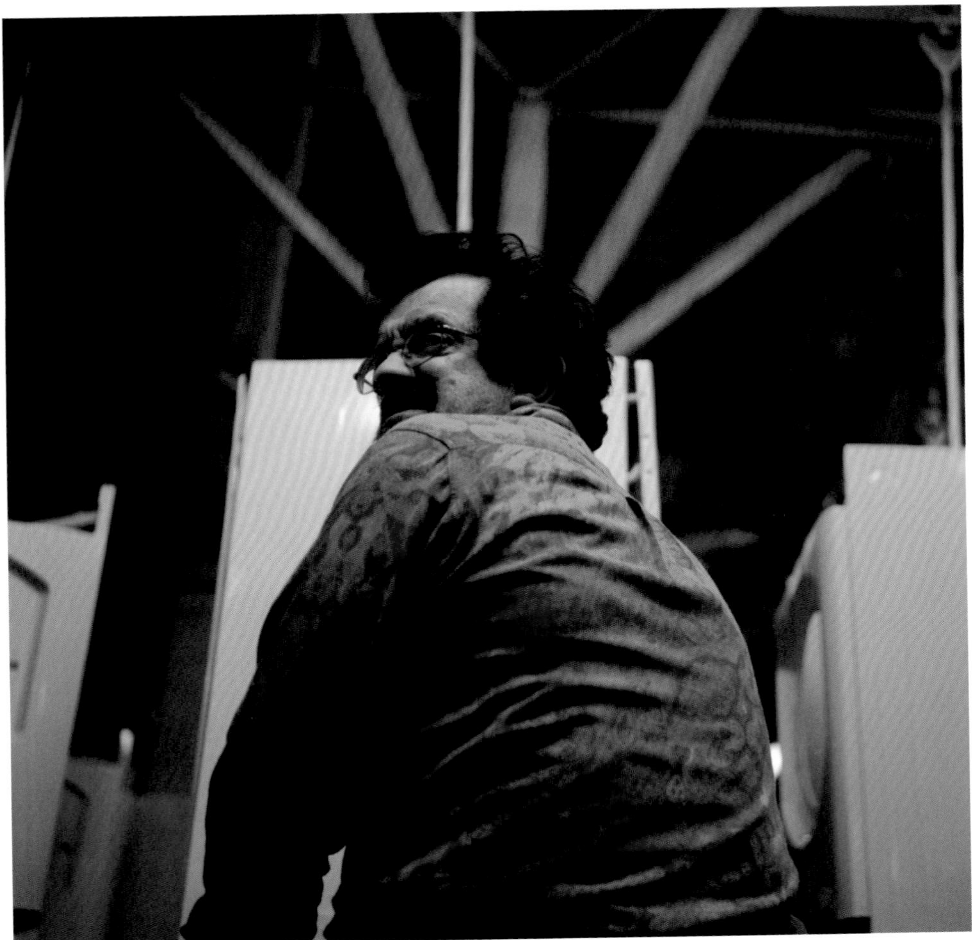

*Above and left* Merloni plant, Albacina, Marche, May 2005 (MB)

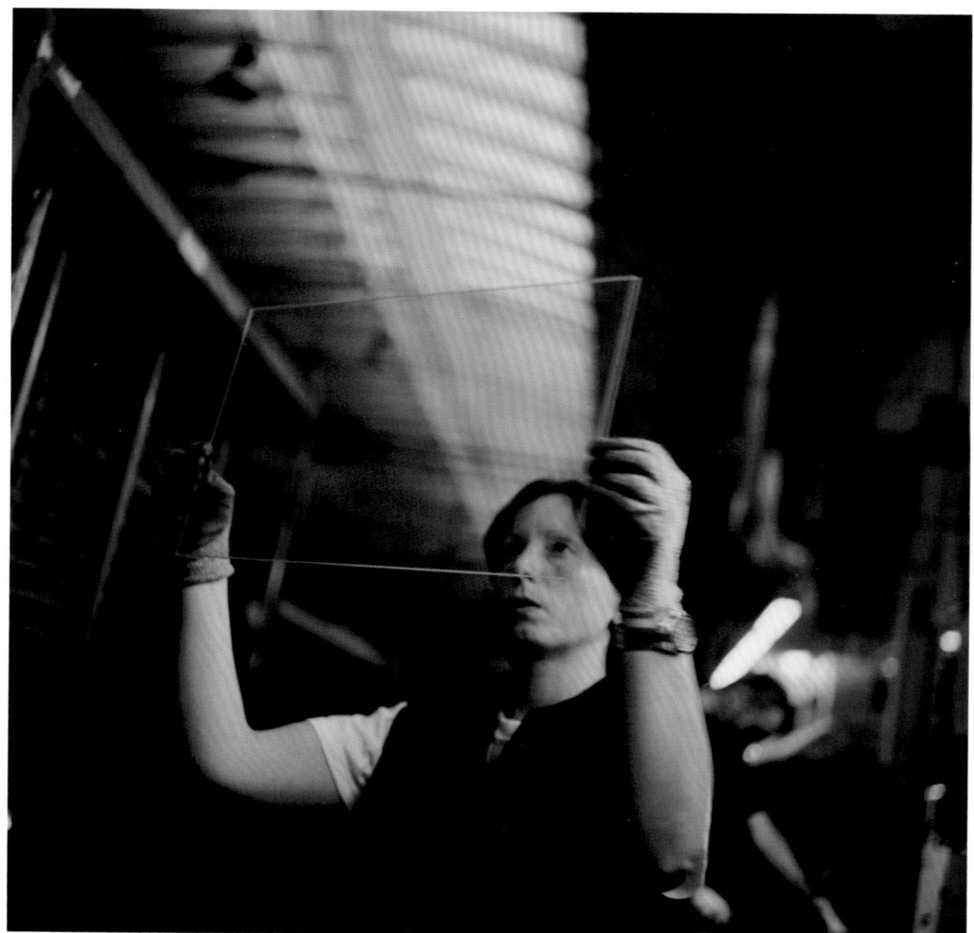

*Above and right* Merloni plant, Albacina,Marche, May 2005 (MB)

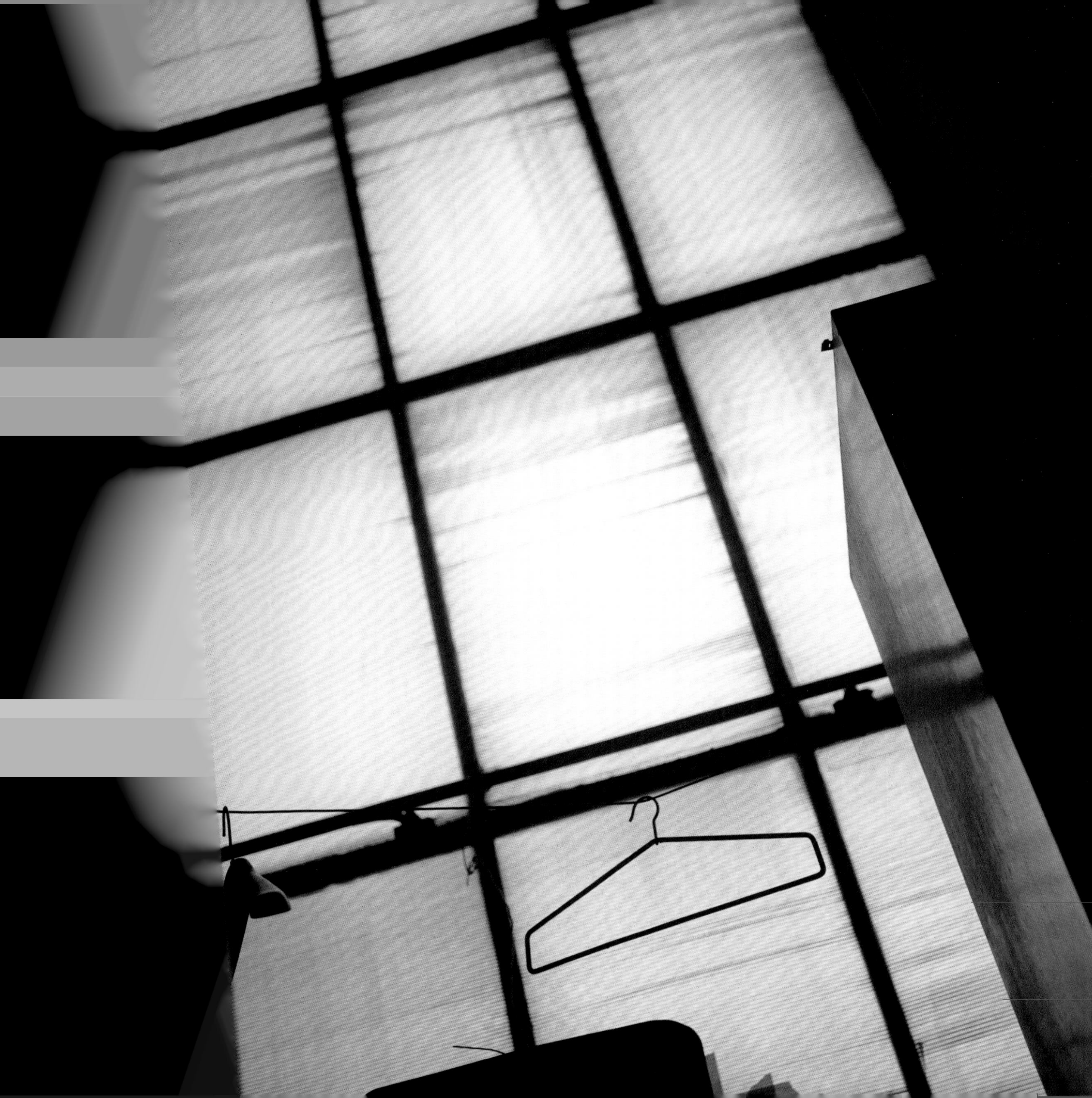

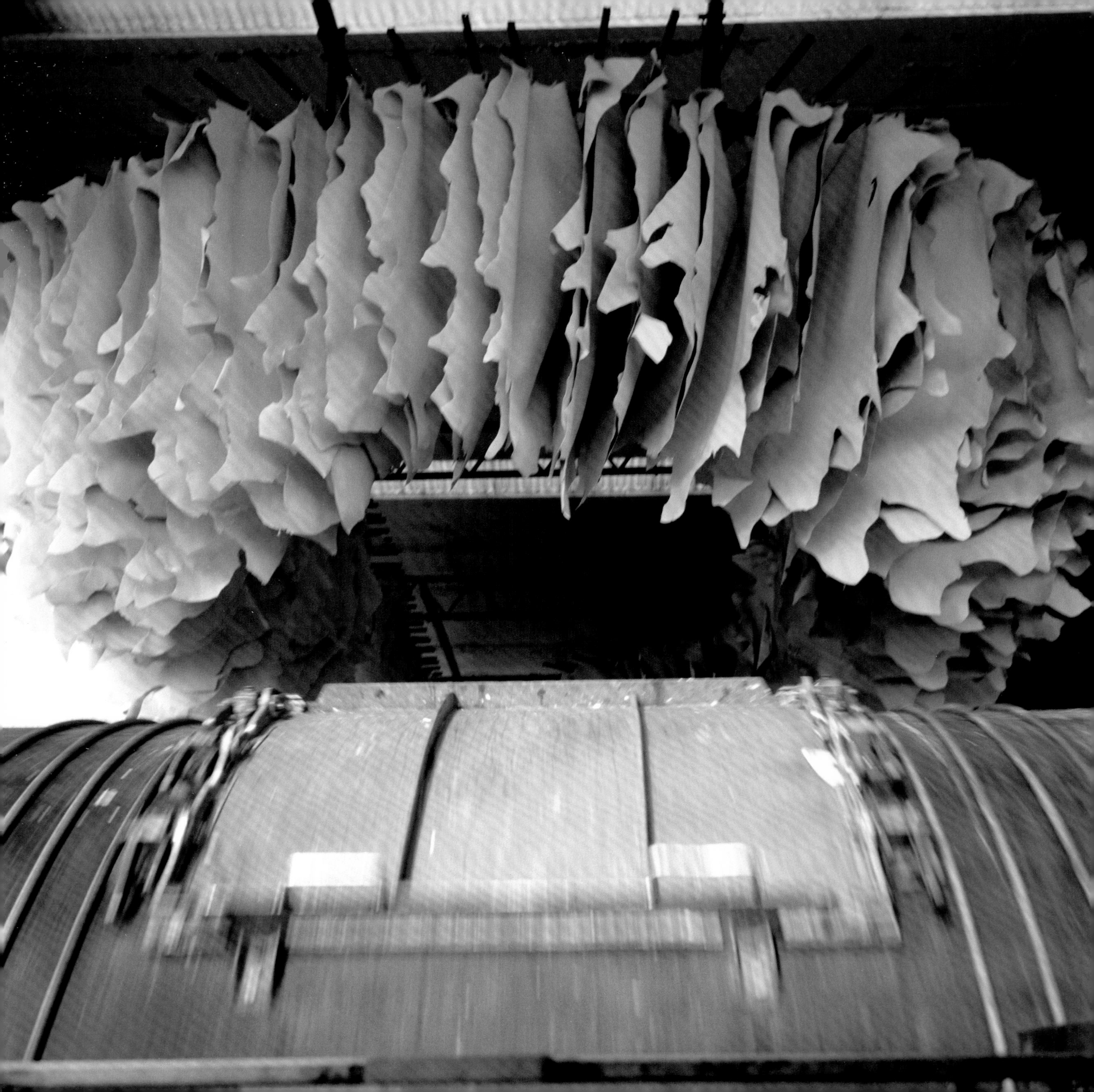

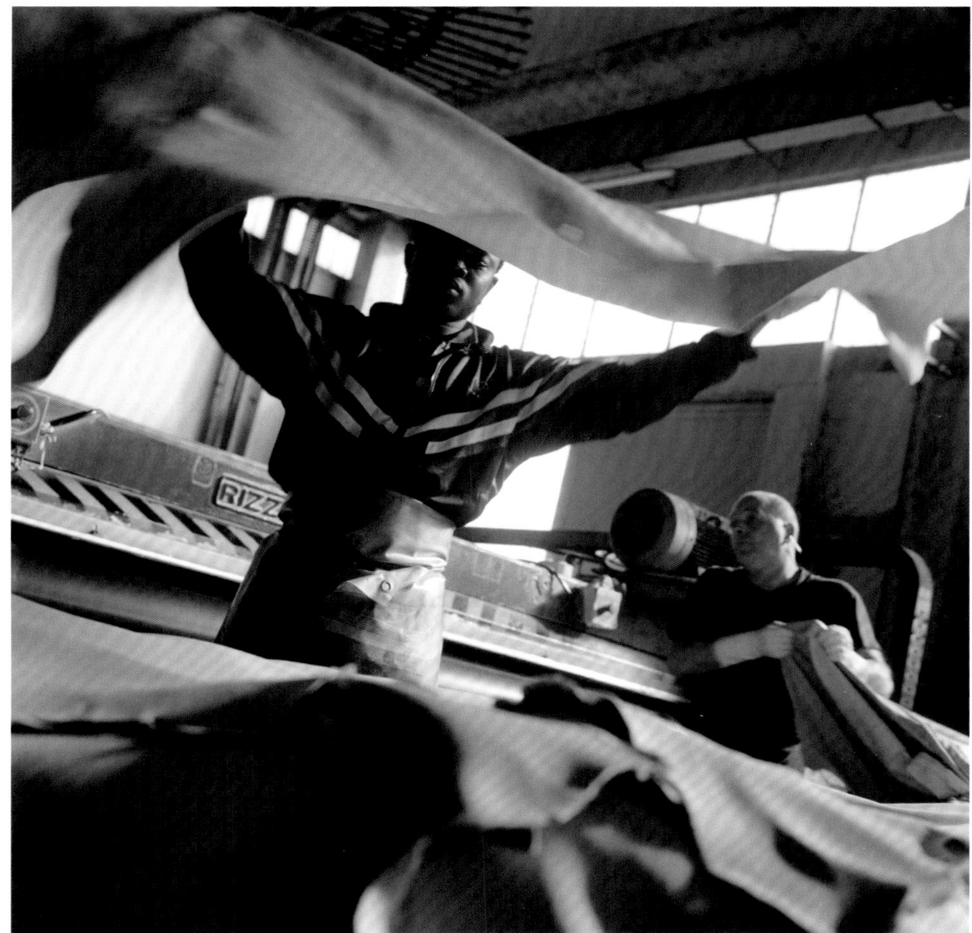

*Above and left* Tannery district, Arzignano, Vicenza, March 2005 (MB)

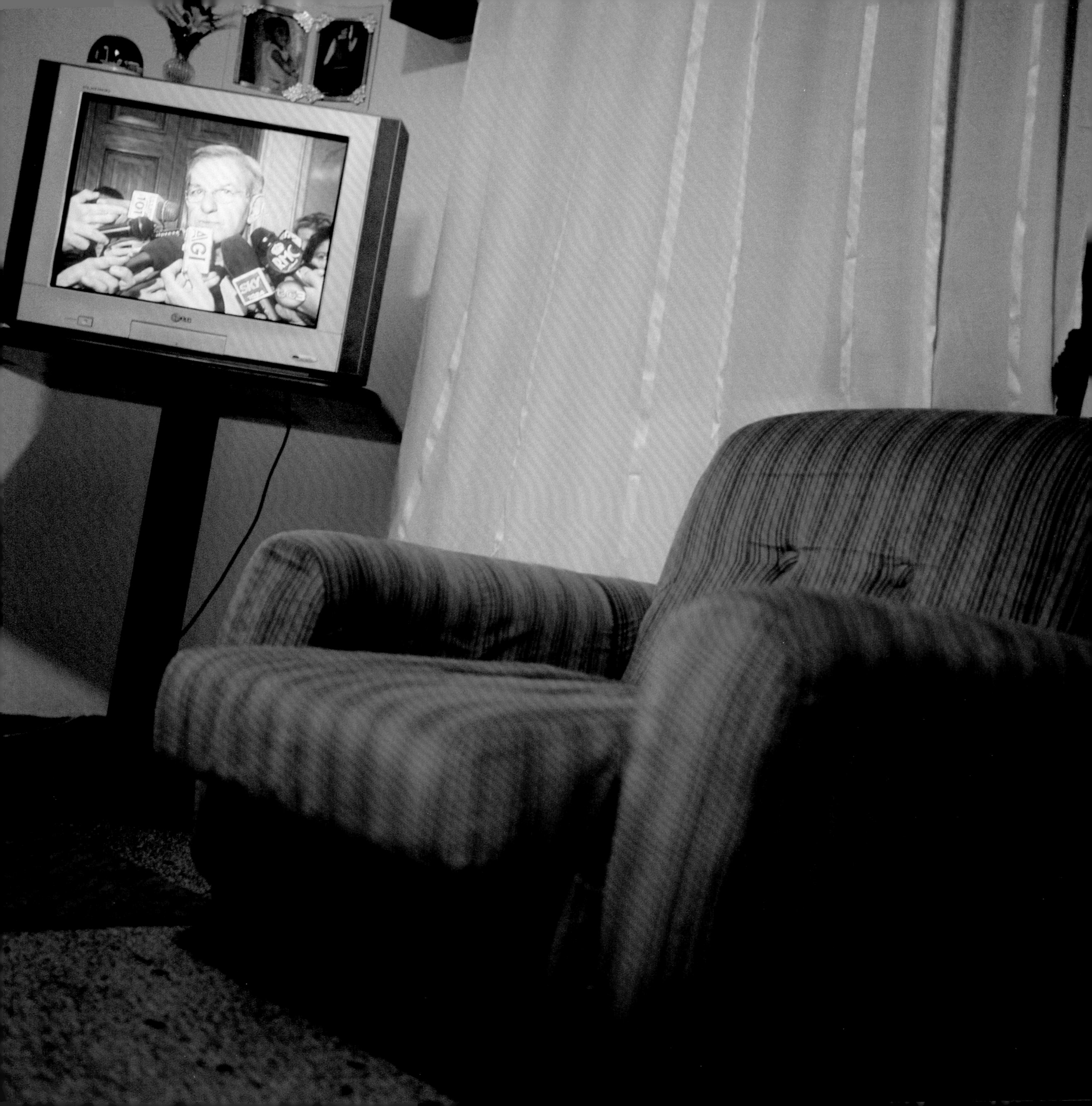
101
AGI
SKY

Inflation in Italy between 2002 and 2004 cost
employees 1.269 to 1.380 Euros.
About 6,5 milions workers earn less than 1,000 Euros per month,
and about 10 milions less than 1,350 Euros.

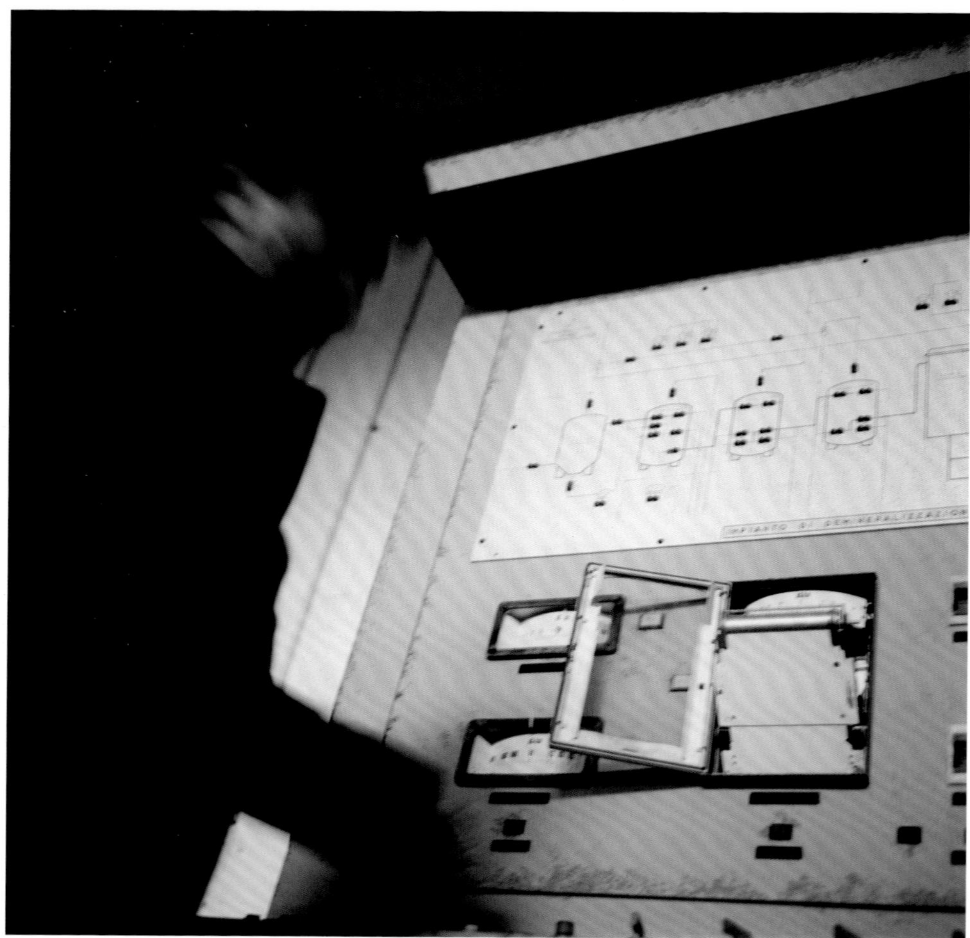

*Above and right* Porto Marghera, Venezia, December 2004 (MB)

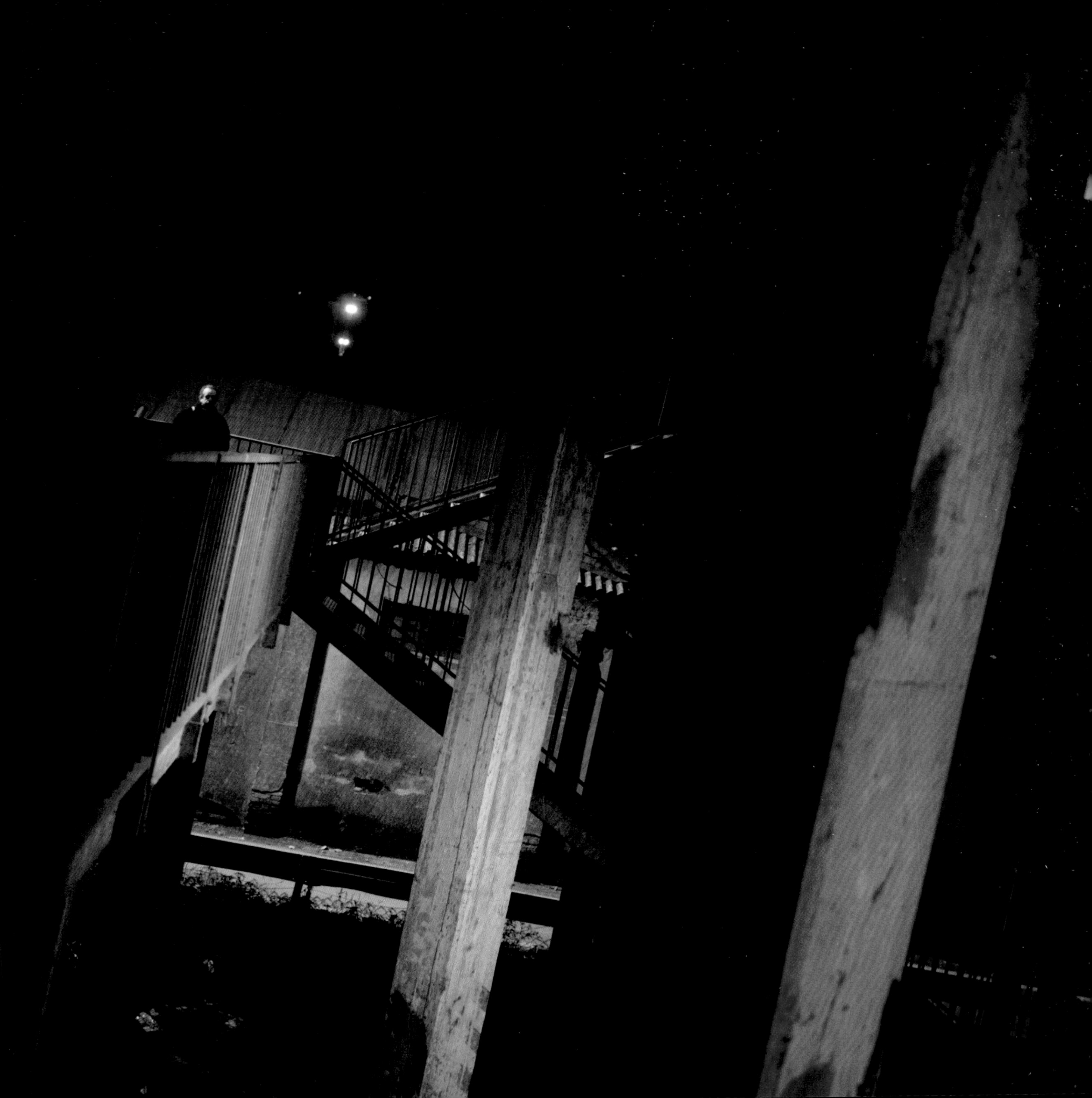

Between 1995 and 2000 the labour costs per unit decreased by 4.2%, and in 2004 by 2%

ufficio economico Fiom-Cgil

*Right and following page* Porto Marghera, Venezia, December 2004 (MB )

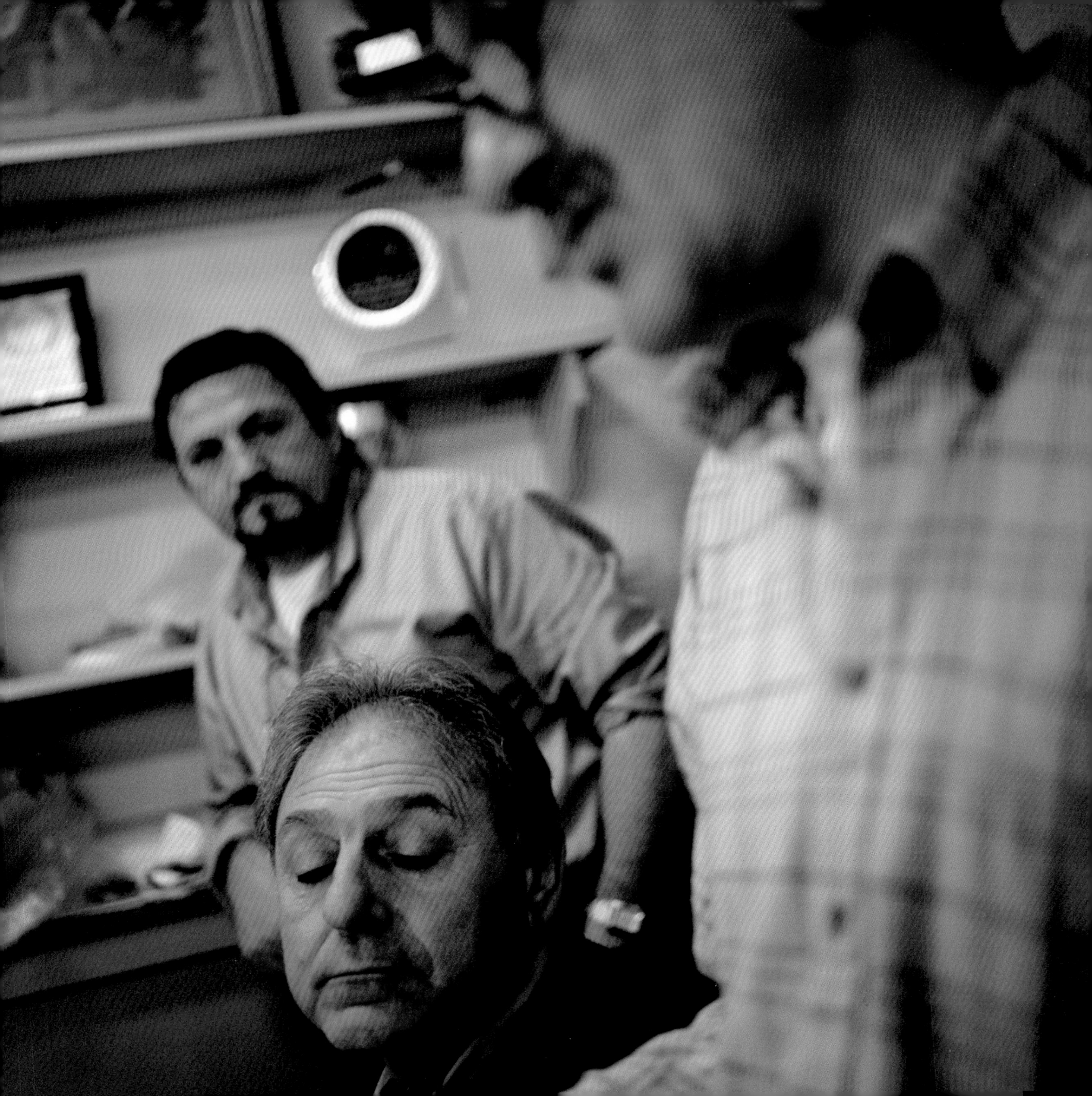

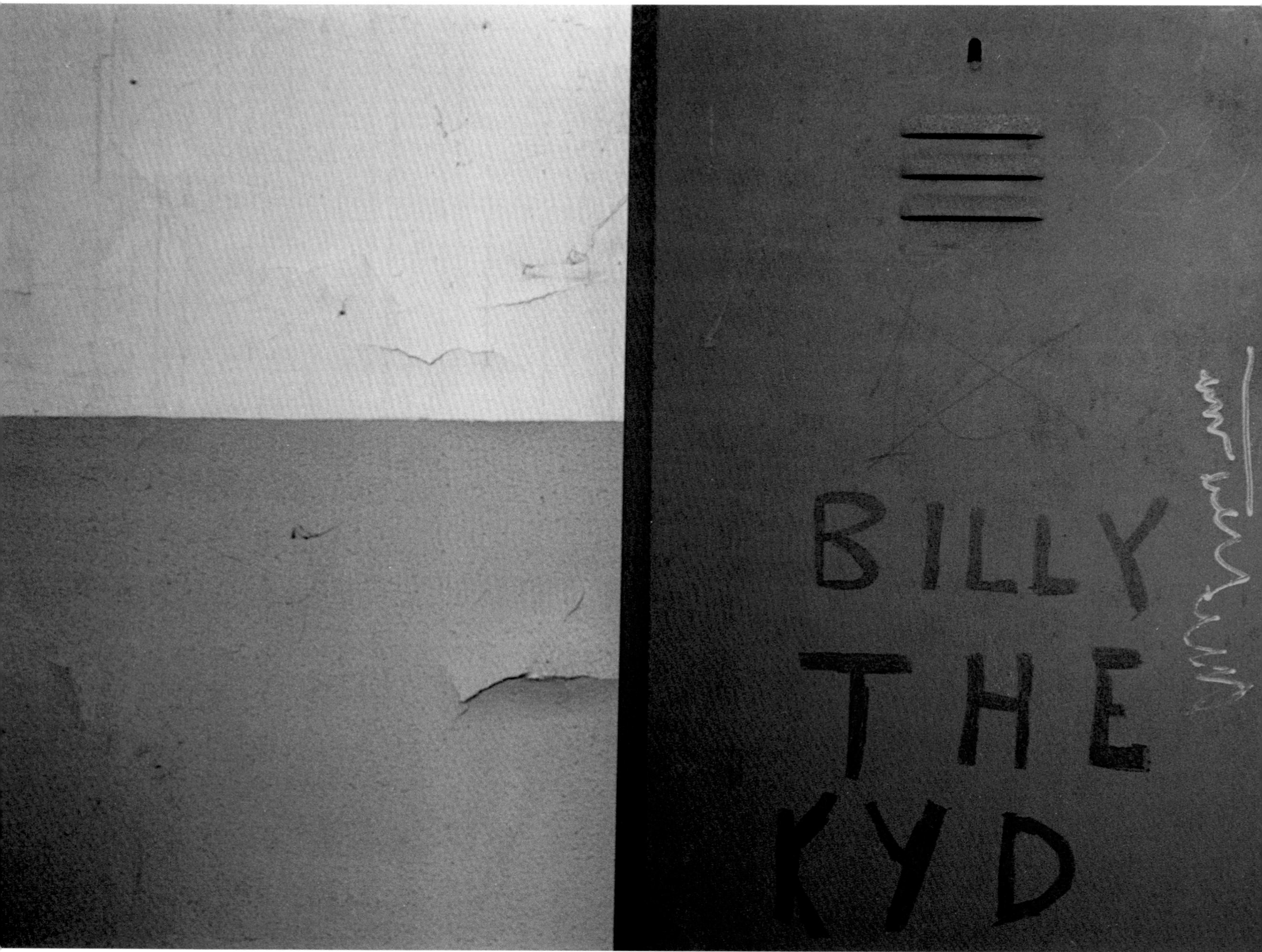
BILLY
THE
KYD

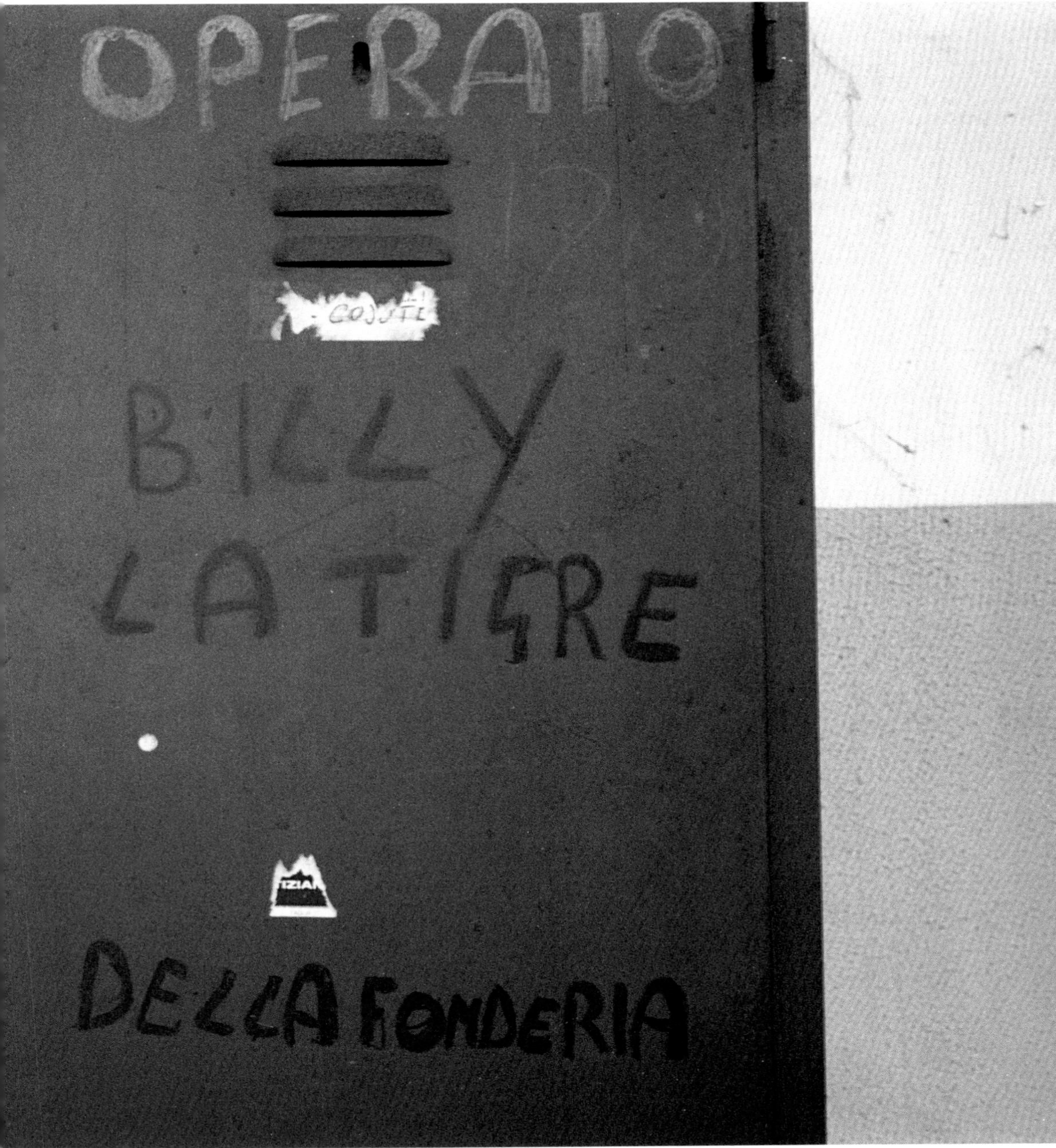
OPERAIO
BILLY
LA TIGRE
DELLA FONDERIA

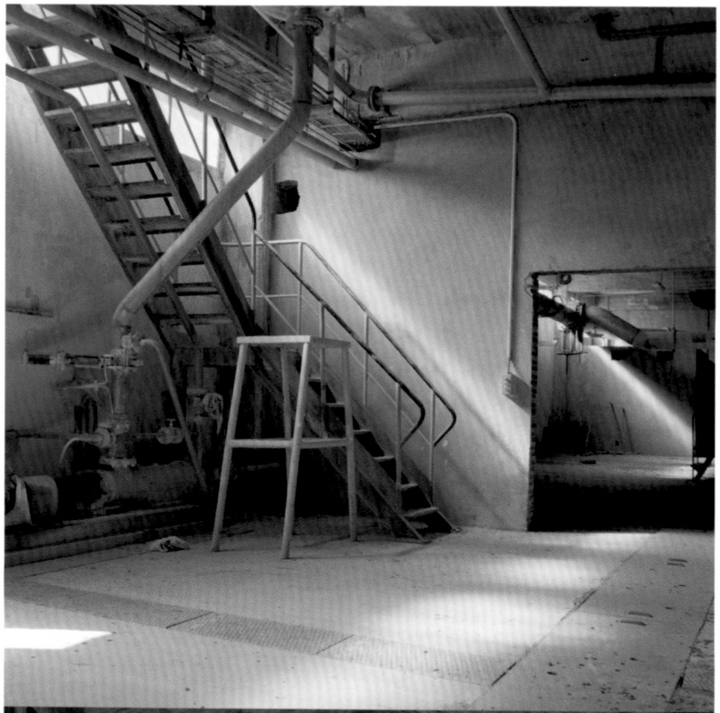

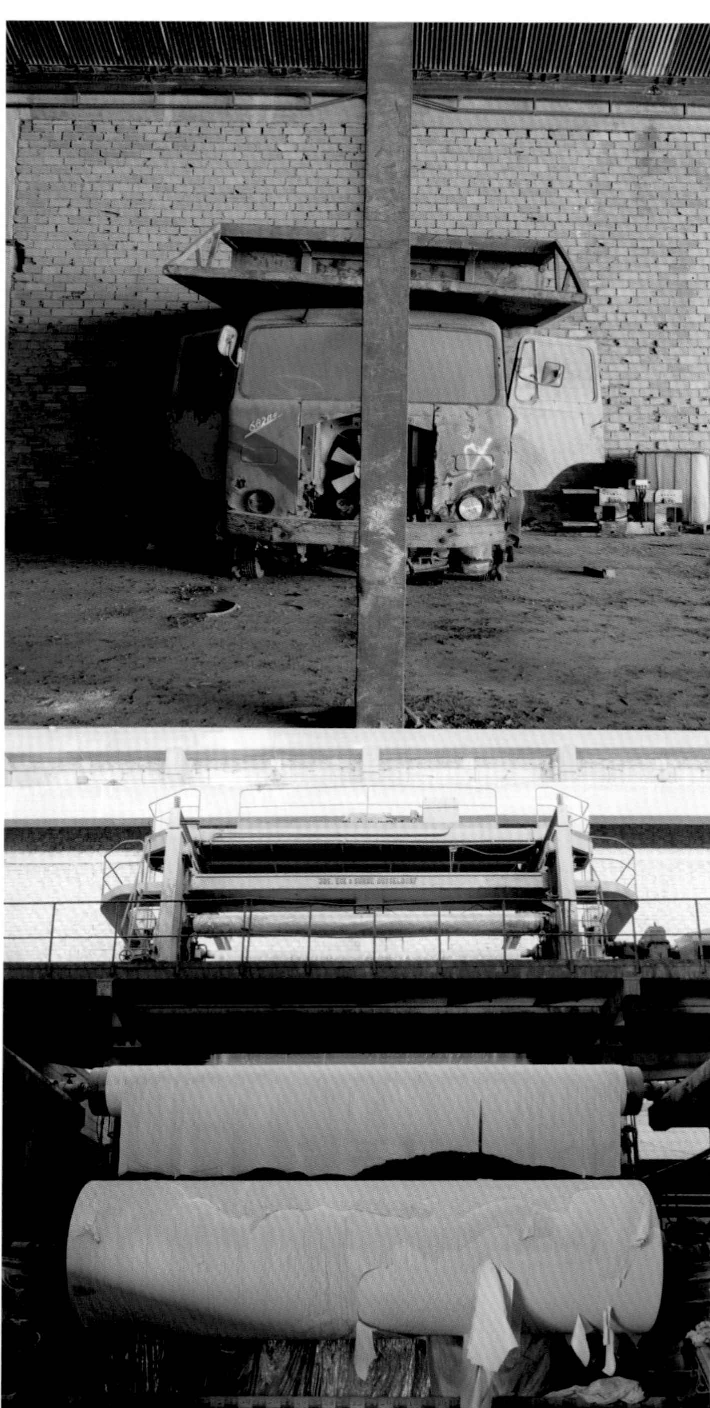

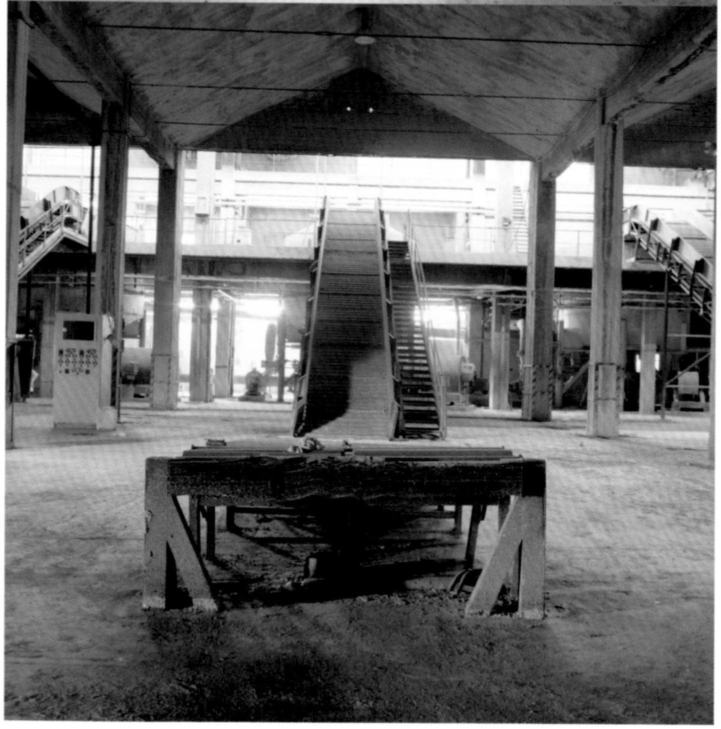

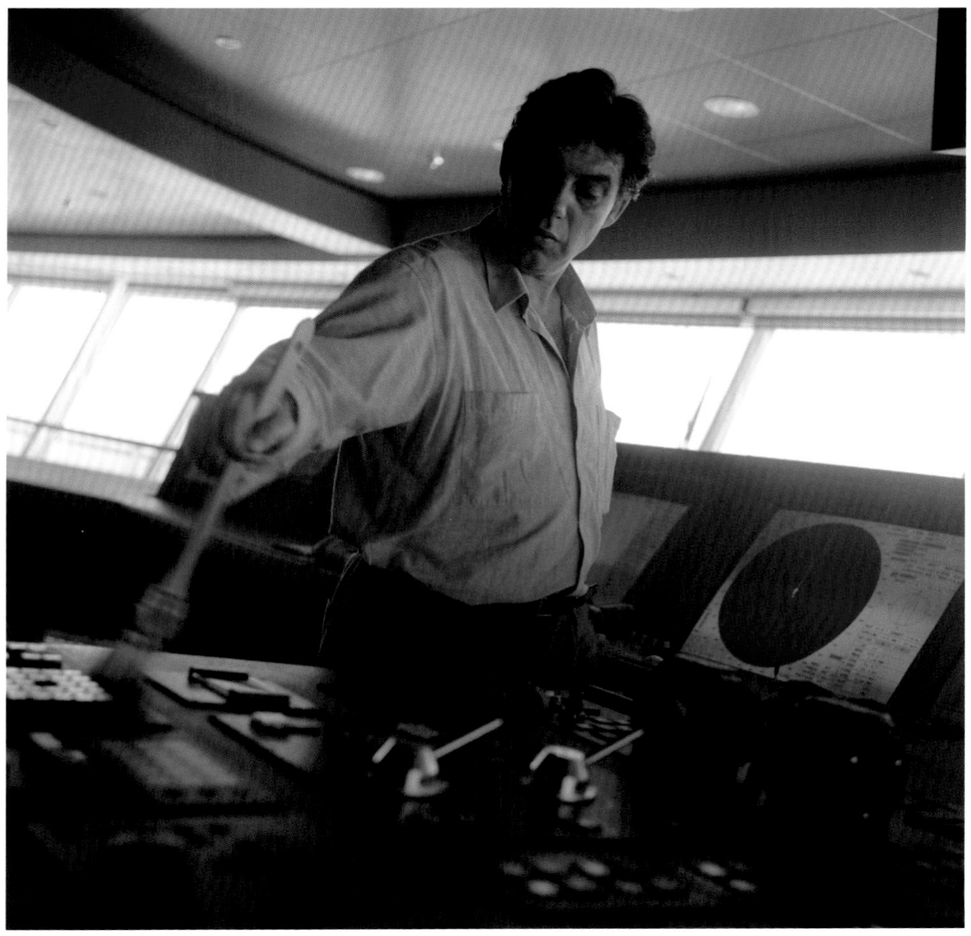

*Above* Genova – Olbia ferry, July 2005 (MB)
*Left* Papermill, Arbatax, Sardinia, July 2005 (MS)

Of the 500 European companies investing most in Research and Development, 149 are from Great Britain, 100 from Germany, 66 from France and 44 from Sweden. Italy, in eighth position, is represented by 19 companies

Genova , January 2005 (MB)

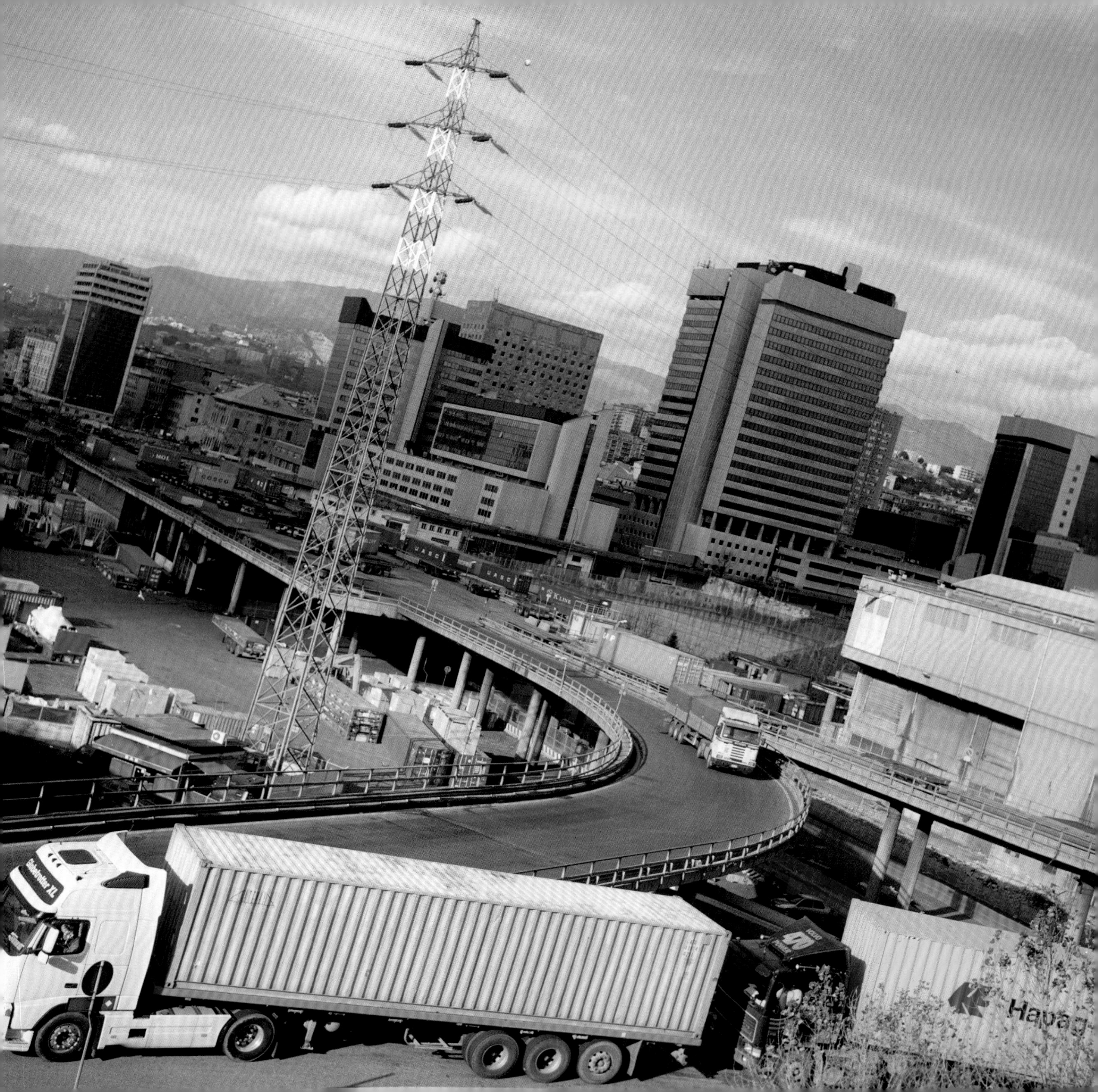
Globetrotter XL
Hapag

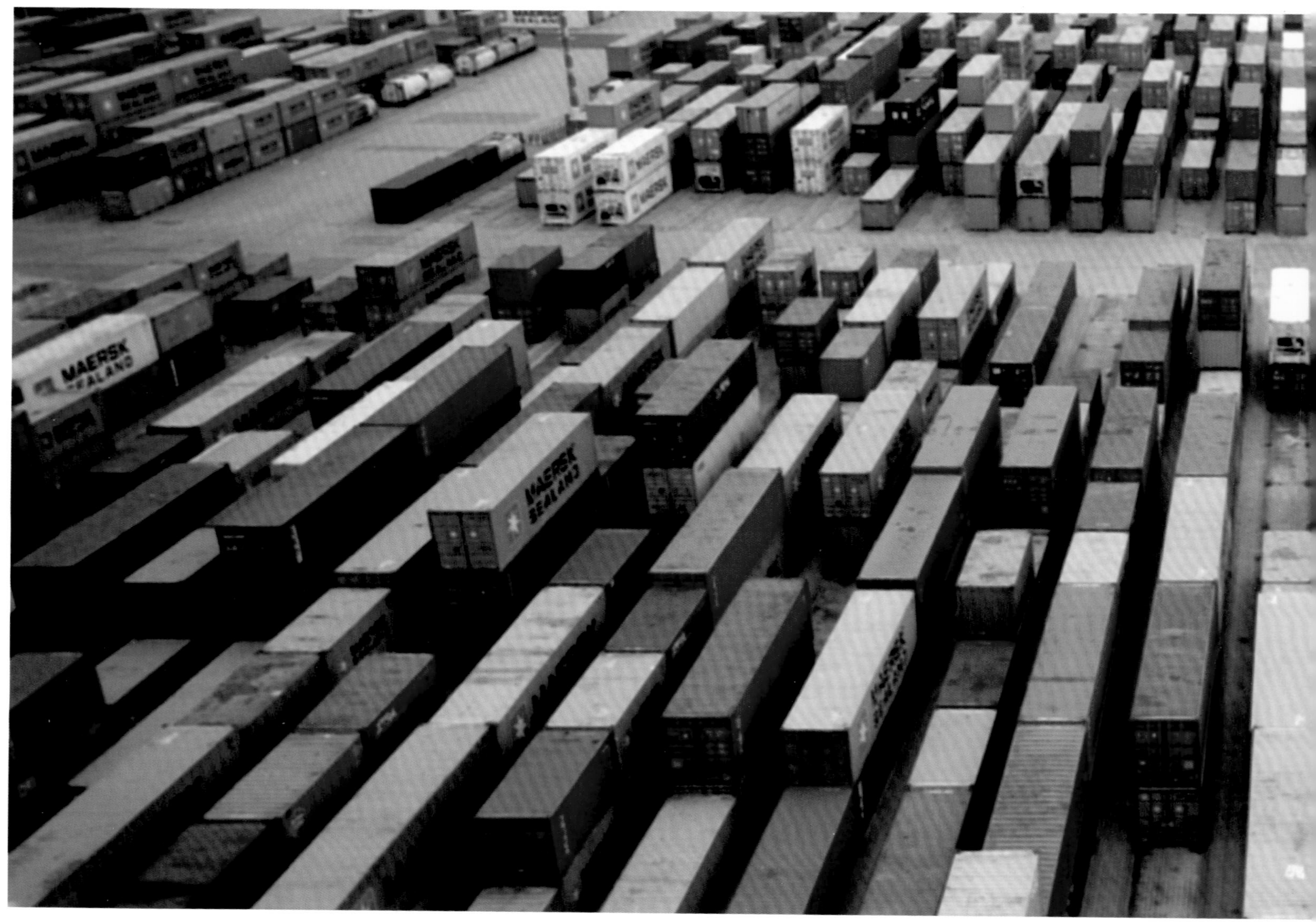


Port of Gioia Tauro, Reggio Calabria, January 2005 (GC )

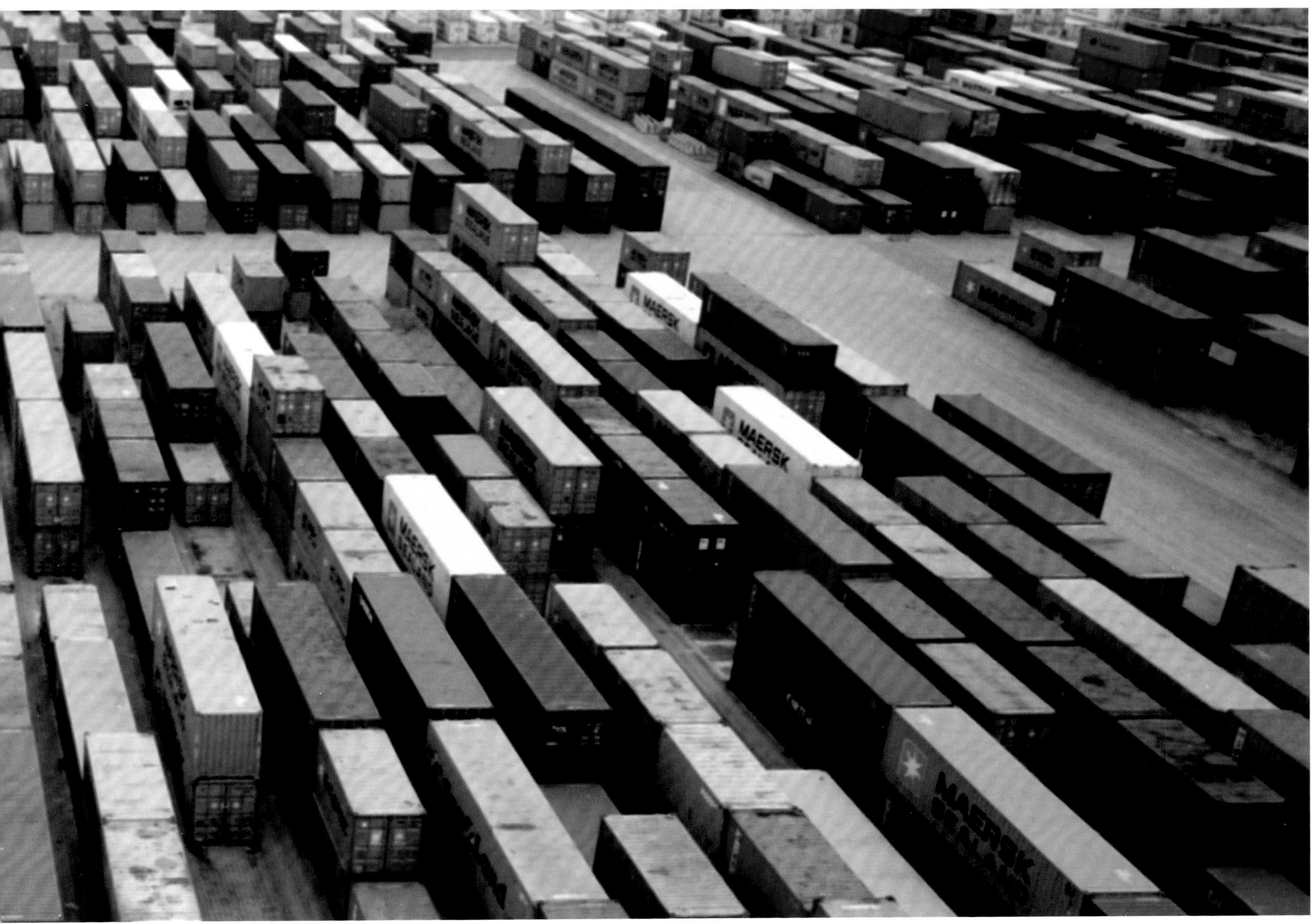
MAERSK
MAERSK
MAERSK
MAERSK SEALAND
MAERSK SEALAND

In Italy real wages grew by 0.2% between 1995 and 2004. In Germany they grew by 16.1%, in France by 10.5%

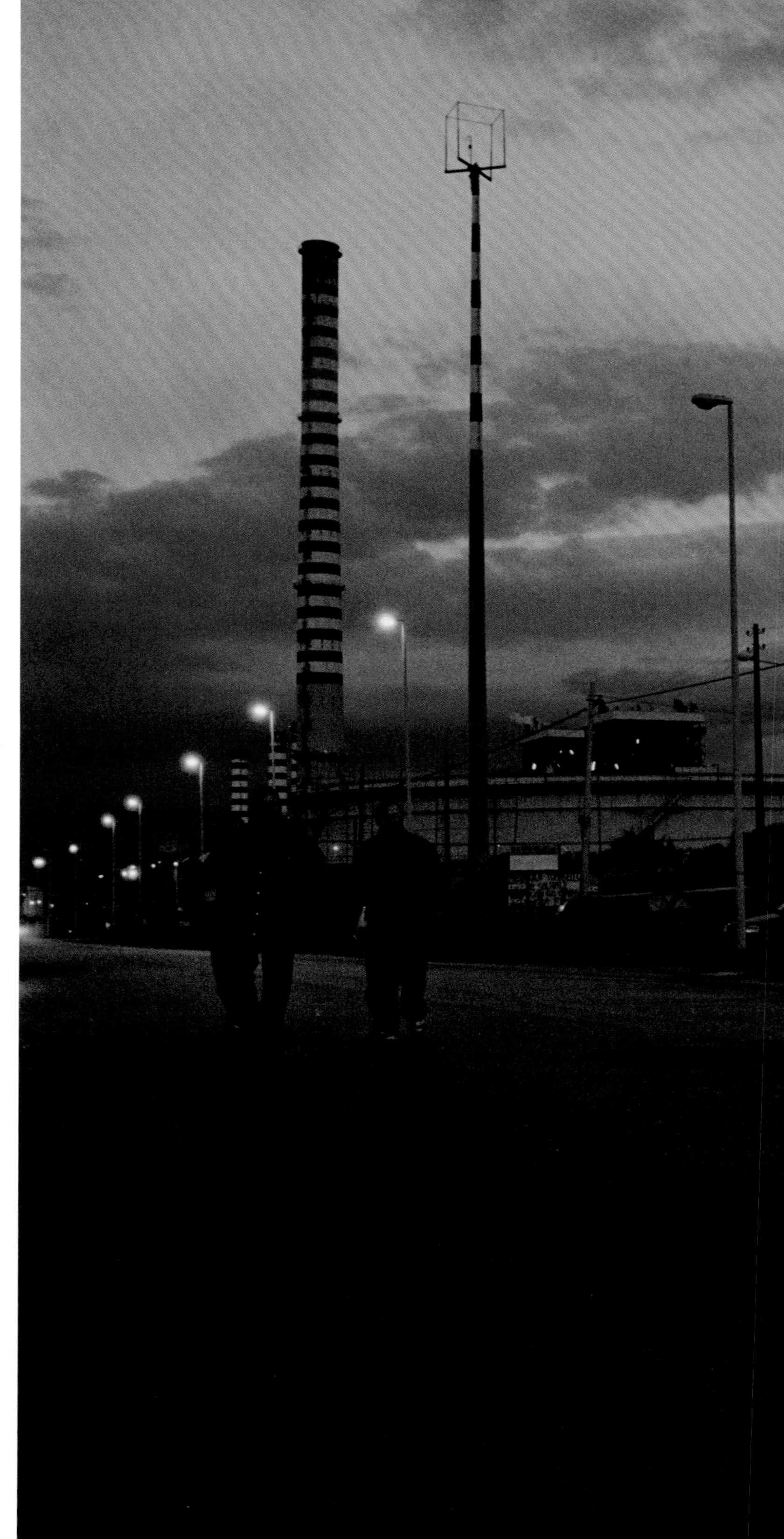

Workers' protest against the closure of the Fiat plant, Termini Imerese, Sicily, October 2002 (EM)

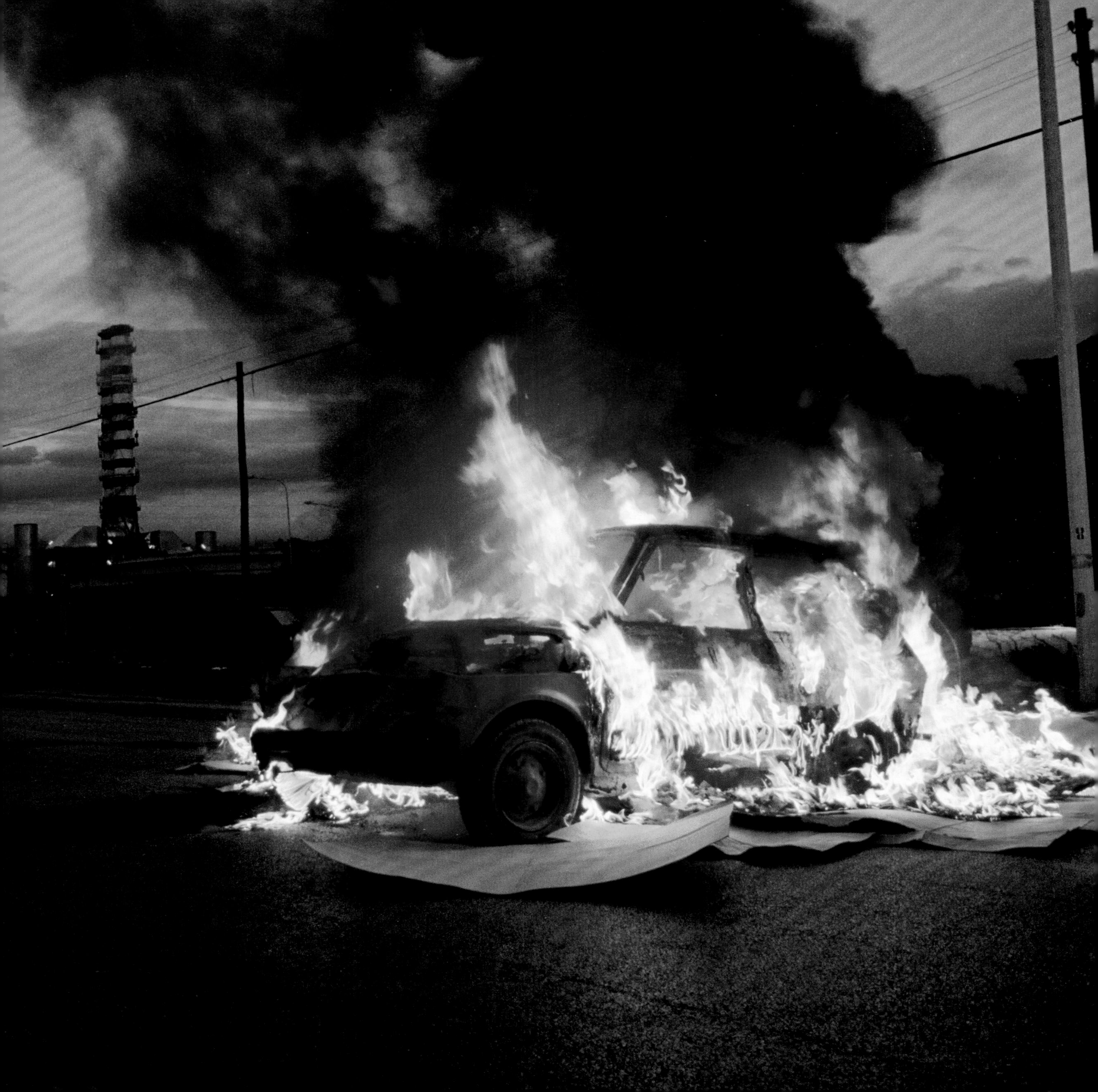

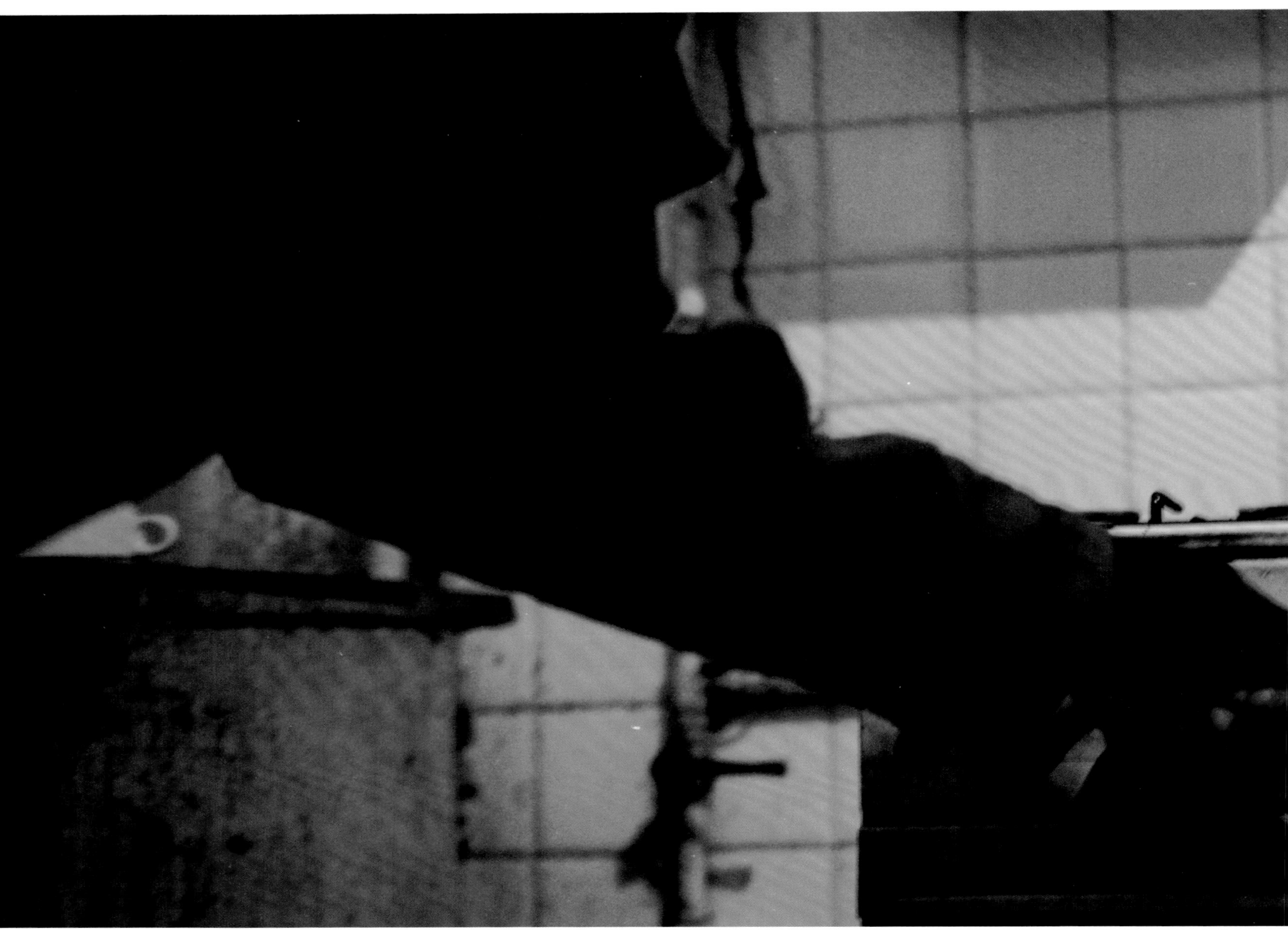

Immigrant home, Genova, October (2005 MB)

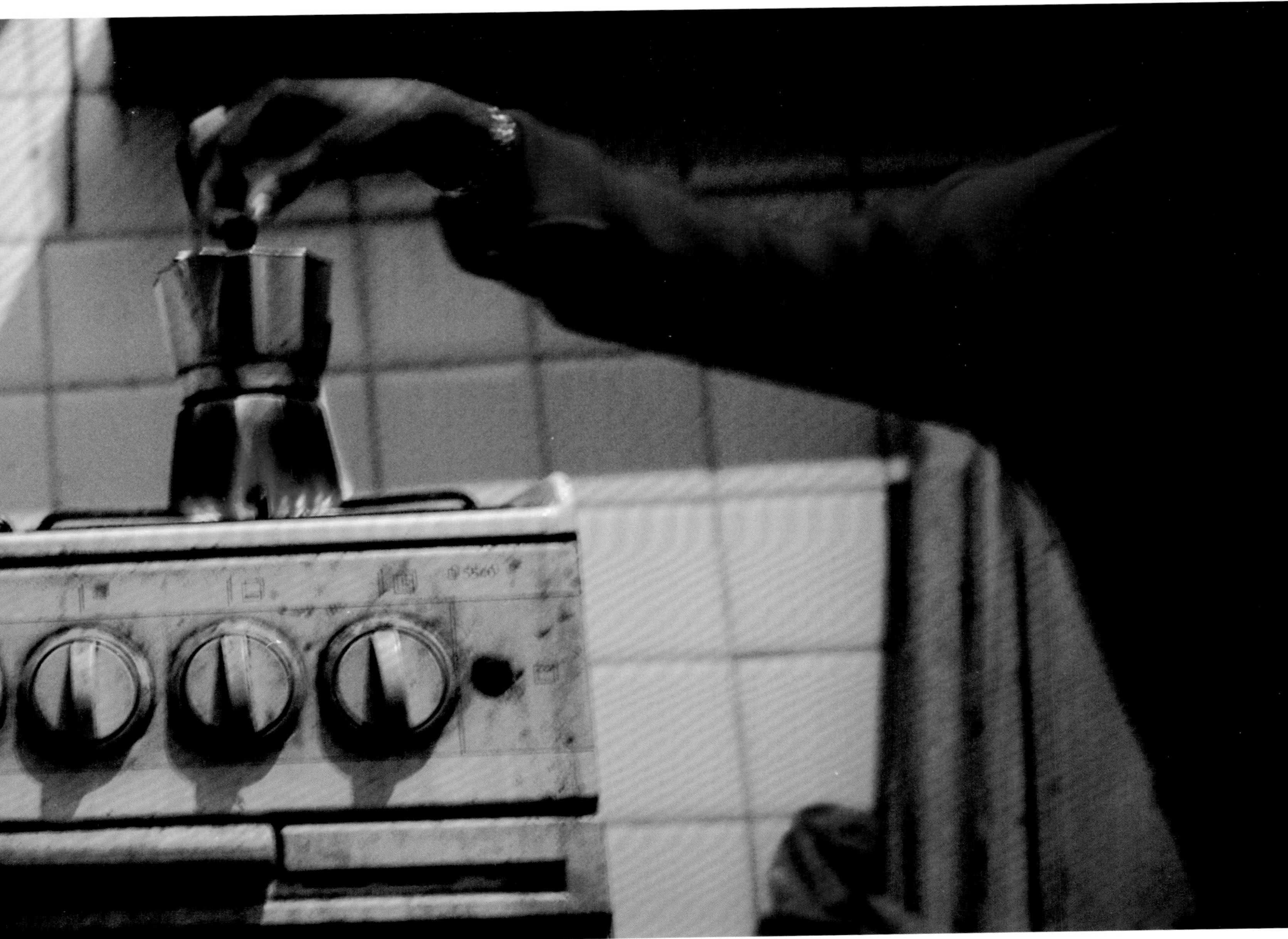

# THE GLOBAL REBELLION

## Umberto Galimberti

The rioting of ethnic minorities in Paris this winter is culturally dynamic and significantly represents three aspects of immigration of critical importance. The first facet of the immigrant's condition in a foreign land is the very powerful contradiction that exists thus: maintaining an identity means not to become familiar with the world in which the immigrant finds himself, while on the other hand becoming too familiar with that world means to forget his origins. Therefore the immigrant constantly finds himself in contradiction between fidelity to his origins and fidelity to the culture and mores of the host country. Consequently integration tends to be a sort of psychological betrayal process. These are the prevailing conditions for every immigrant, and they should be regarded as a basic tenet when considering immigration.

Secondly, in Paris the immigrants have congregated in the impoverished outskirts of the city, where a sort of agglomerate of various peoples without identifiable habits, customs and figureheads now live. In my opinion the outskirts represent the decline of the city. This is an ominous effect of globalization, as one of its more injurious aspects is what I call ‘deterritorialization”, which means the absence of a culture where relationships have been established, where people have grown up together, where commercial activity has allowed in part an ability to trust. Where the territory of that culture does not exist, because there is merely a random human heap in a non-urban context - the outskirts of a city are not social entities and are no more than human agglomerates - then relationships break down and individuals become suspicious and hostile.

The third issue to take into consideration is the fact that, as the French author Miguel Benasayag has evidenced in his ‘The Age of Sad Passions’ (Feltrinelli), not only immigrants but the whole youth generation face a future that is not a future of hope but a future of disillusion, a future of threat in which the realization of ambitions and dreams seems impossible. It is recognizable that young people today can engage themselves in studies until they are perhaps thirty, taking diplomas, degrees and doctorates, and still search for employment. In the immigrant world, where study is an all but forbidden luxury, there is virtually no prospect of fulfilling employment. When the future offers threat rather than hope, when possibilities are replaced by a pervading feeling of uneasiness, then the future proffers nihilism and, ultimately, destruction.

Without work, without the succour of everyday human relations with members of a class and culture beyond the void in which immigrants live, when practically the home is no more than a dormitory and genuine hunger is prevalent, then crime is unavoidable.

This is true not only of France and Paris, and it is a problem that will expand. Demographists say, although nobody listens to them, that in twenty or thirty years the great bulk of humanity is liable to be concentrated in no more than thirty to forty cities. If they are right then the future has already arrived, in the phenomenon of ‘deterritorialization”. The majority of humanity will therefore exist without hope, without a recognizable culture and with its activities reduced solely to feeding itself as best it can directly as a result of globalization.

I do not forget that the spirit of '68 was born in Paris, the city that brought the French Revolution. It has always pre-empted social crises dramatically and violently. Paris's conflagrations are an announcement of what will attend us. It is a prescient city. It is clearly time that we organized and developed our cities in such a way as to avoid the human agglomerations, ghettos even, that are beyond the pale of cultural intimacy and exploration, without expression, and especially without the rewards others take for granted.

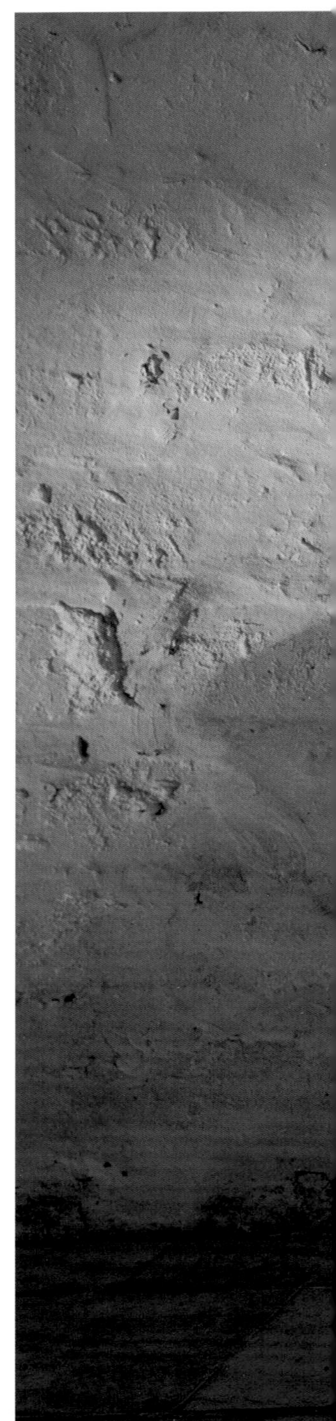

A refugee is a person in danger owing to a well-founded fear of being persecuted for reasons of race, religion, nationality, membership of a particular social group or political opinion, who is outside the country of his nationality and is unable or, owing to such fear, is unwilling to avail himself of the protection of that country; or who, not having a nationality and being outside the country of his former habitual residence as a result of such events, is unable or, owing to such fear, is unwilling to return to it.

Geneva Convention, 1951. Signed by 145 Countries subscribing to the Convention or to the1967 Protocol, or both.

Immigrant labourers, Borgo Segezia, Foggia, July 2004 (EM)

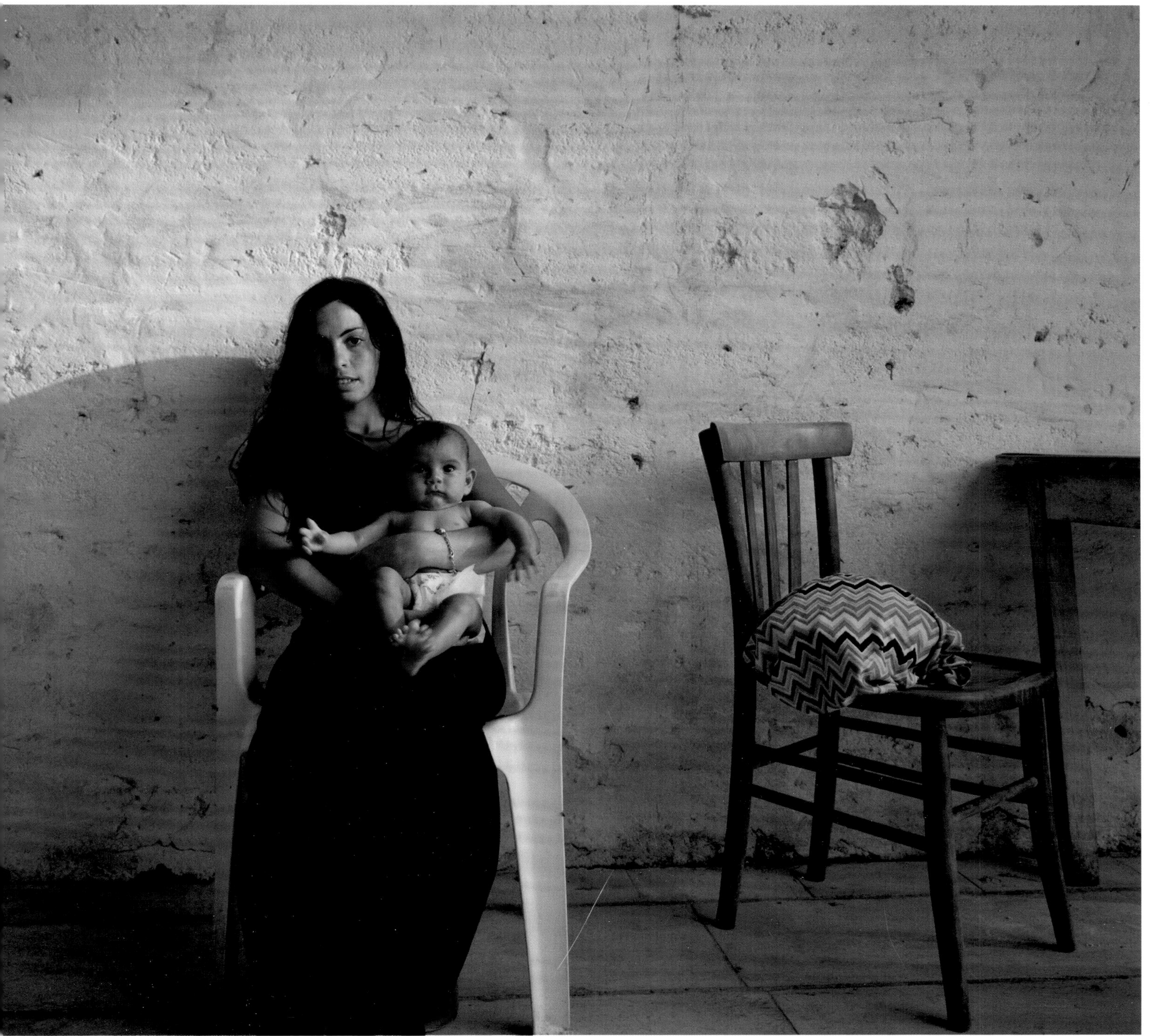

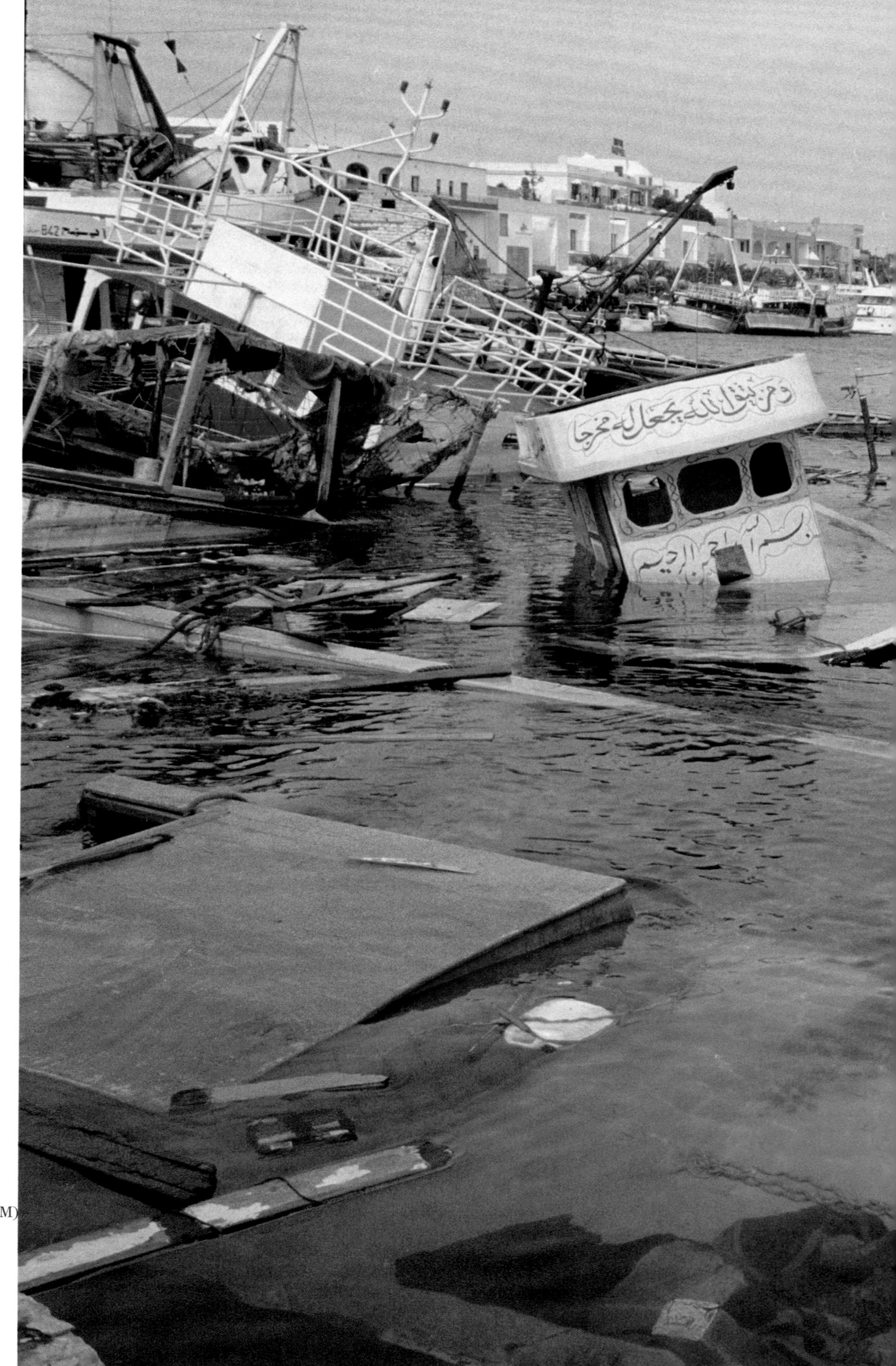


*Right* Illegal immigrant boats, Lampedusa July 2004 (EM)
*Following page* Illegal immigrant, Lampedusa, August 2005 (EM)

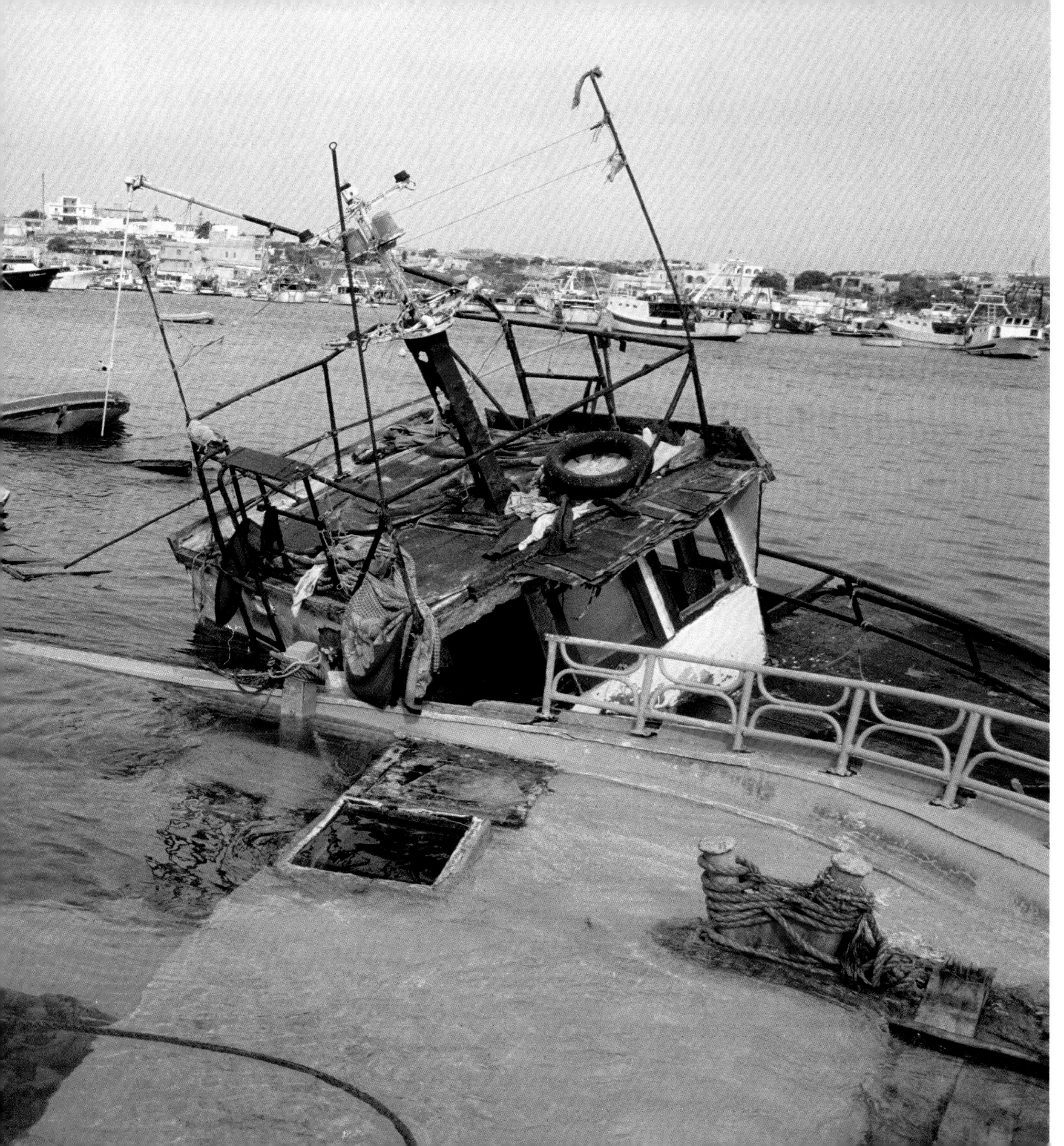

A foreigner, who in his own country is prevented from exercising the freedoms guaranteed by the Italian Constitution, has the right of asylum in the territory of the Republic, subject to the conditions of the law. Extradition for political crimes is not permitted.

Constitution of the Italian Republic, art. 10
[Official Gazette, 27 December 1947, n. 298]

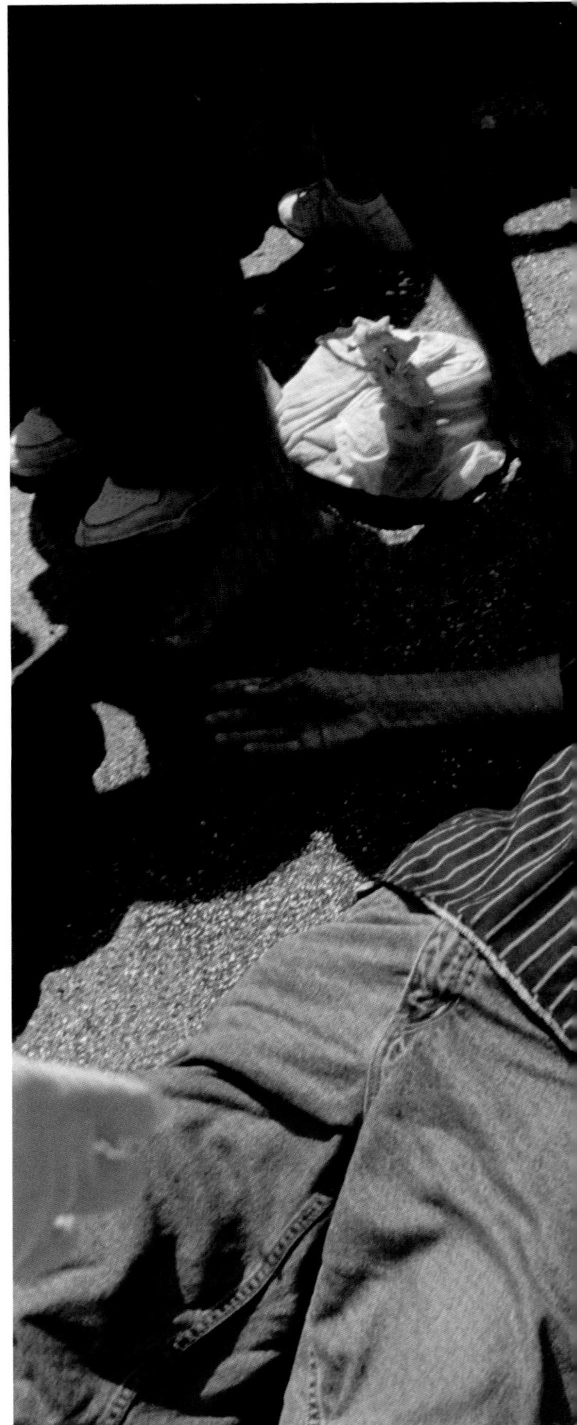

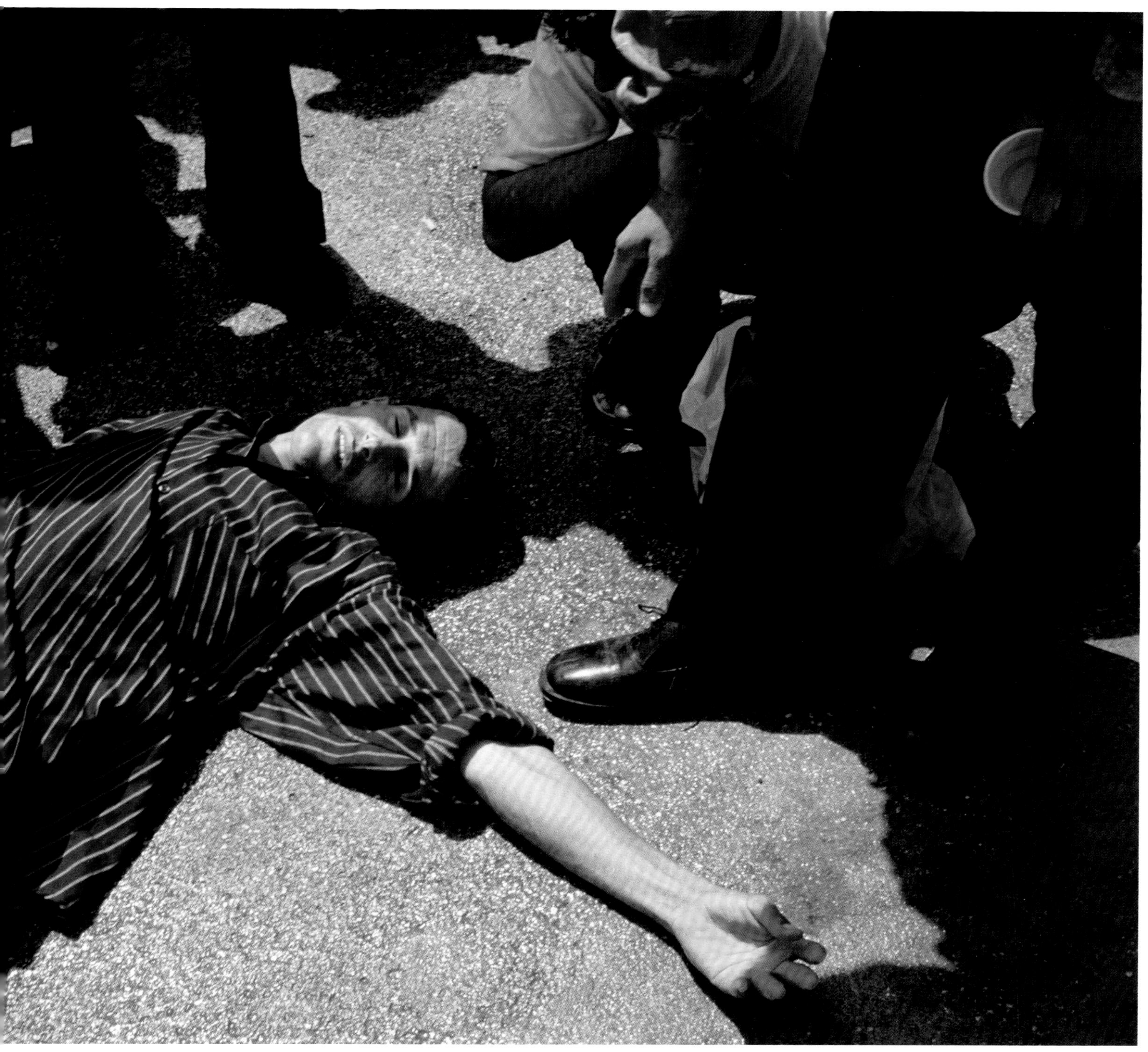

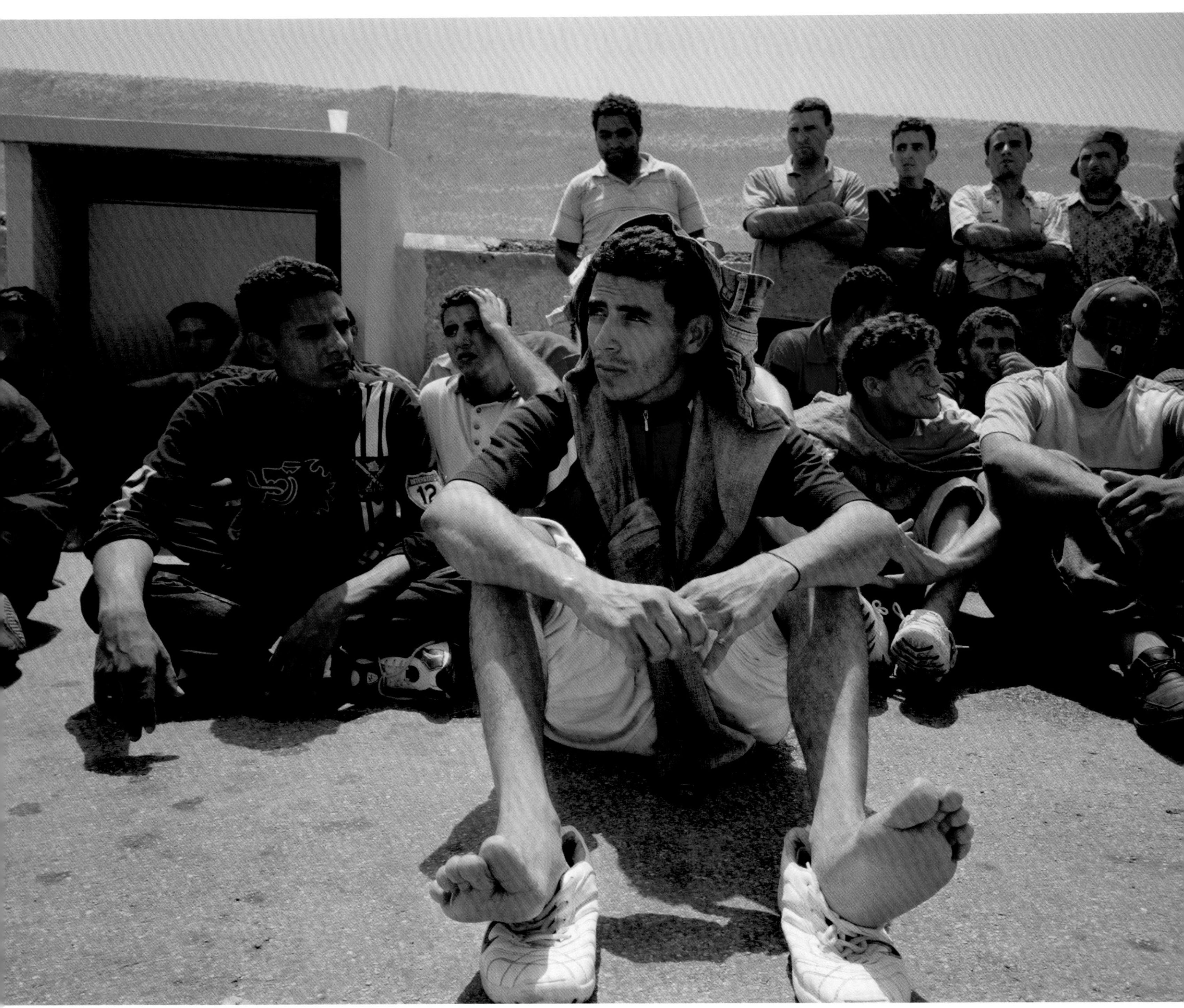

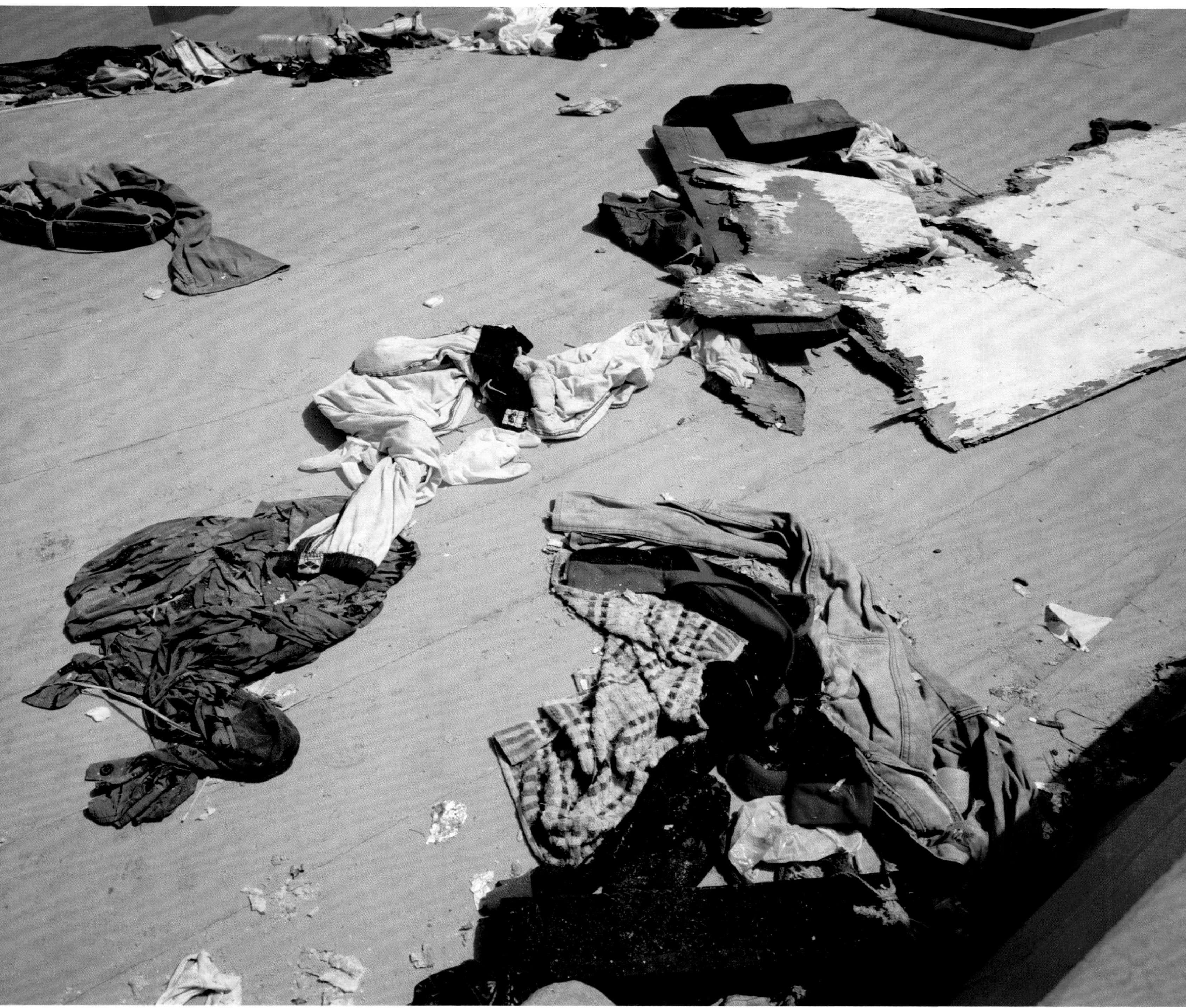

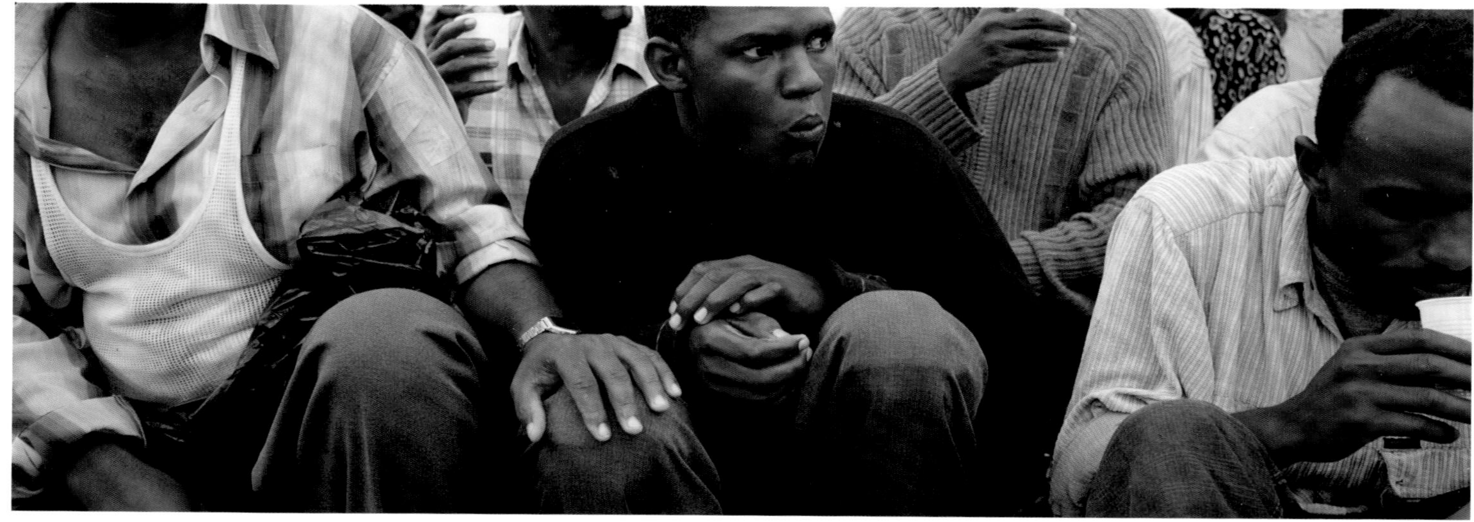

During 2004 12,737 illegal immigrants arrived in 231 boats that landed at Lampedusa. Close to 2,000 died during the attempted sea crossing

*Above, right and previous pages* Illegal immigrant, Lampedusa, August 2005 (EM and GC)

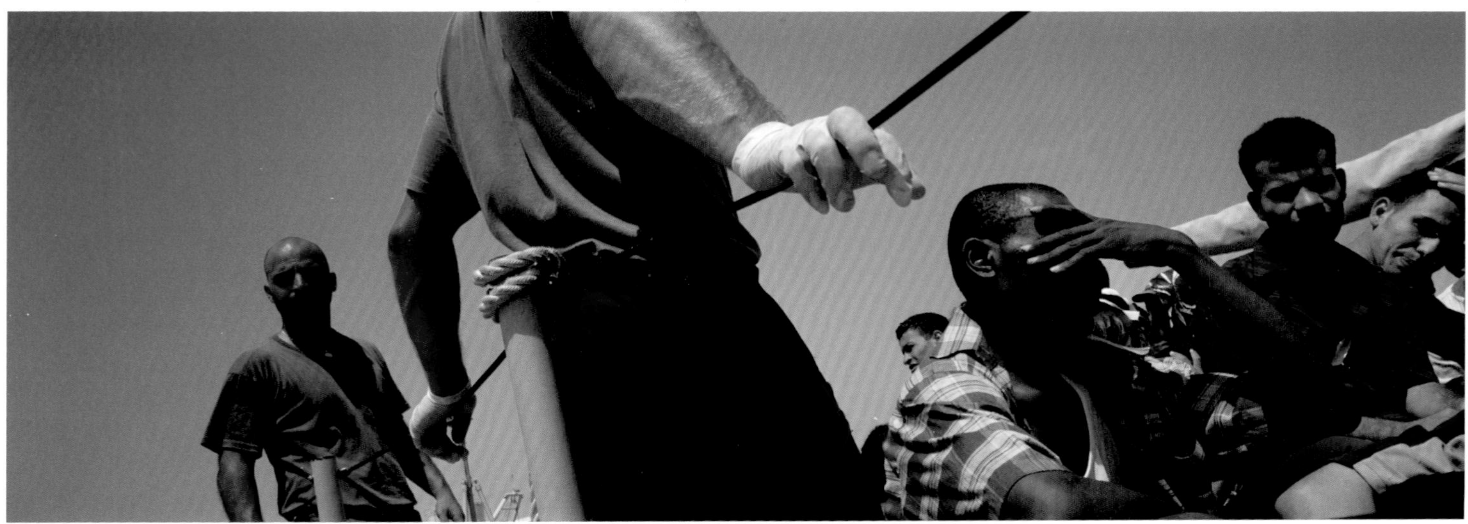

During the period from October 2004 to March 2005 Italy began a policy of collective expulsion and several hundred migrants were deported by Italy to Libya.

# WHAT LAND IS THIS?

by Said Qassem

Who commands the waves to rear at the coast?
Who directs the wind to guide a sail to the coast?
Who conducts the drama of man's journey to the coast?
Who binds the wounds of the men flung on the coast?
Who salves the craving of man to reach that coast?
Who allays the fears that drive men to the coast?
The joy of the sun
The coast delights in the sun
Food is the right of every man
And security is a right for every man
Freedom is a gift for those who seek it
The coast the destination of the immigrant

My name is Abdel Khaleq Said. I was born on 17th December, 1970, in Jenin, Palestine. I ought not to have been born in Jenin because my family's home was in Nazareth. But that house isn't there any more.

I arrived in Italy when I was 19. I had already been arrested twice by the authorities before the first Intifada and before I was 16. But I finished school and got to Italy from Palestine with a student visa issued by the Italian Embassy in Amman, Jordan.

I changed my university courses several times, and ended up in Venice after trying for three years to complete a degree, frustrated by problems with my visa. I found a job as a bartender to pay for my studies. The money sent by my parents was scarce, since I had three sisters also studying at university. In 15 years in Italy I've never had a problem with the law.

In 2000 I left Italy for my father's funeral in Palestine, but had problems when I got back. My permission to stay in Italy was running out and I didn't have a regular job, which I needed to renew my visa. By 2003 I had managed to find myself work in a pizzeria, and it was then that the police finally withdrew the *permesso di sorgiorno*. My Jordanian visa had also expired, so I decided to apply for a Palestinan passport. For the first time in my life I thought I could have an identity.

My Palestinian passport arrived after more than a year of bureaucracy in Rome, since they needed testimony from my mother and the permission of the Israelis to release the passport. It was at that point that I was fired from the pizzeria. I don't know why.

I took my passport to a lawyer friend to see where I stood with regard to my permission to stay in Italy. We discovered that my application had been shelved with the excuse that I had failed to attend a meeting at the police station, a meeting which I had actually attended with my two former employers. Then on 7th of July I was stopped by the police in a bar in Santa Margherita in Venice and my odyssey began.

They took me to the police headquarters and I slept there because the immigration department was closed. The morning after they took me to Santa Chiara for photographs and finger-printing. Later they took me by police van to Marghera on the mainland, to the immigration department, where they issued a deportation order. All this, probably, because of a mistake of some employee not recording that I was present at my

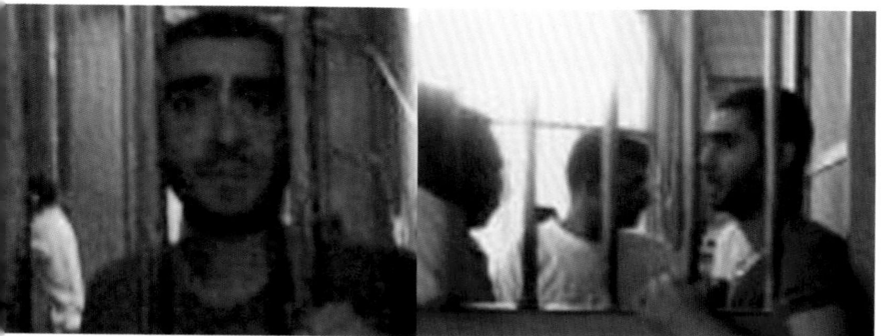

appointment at the police station. I tried to appeal to the judge, but he had no interest in my case. It looked like the beginning of the end. Considering the risks of returning to Palestine, my only choice was to ask for political asylum.

The law now said that I had to go to prison in Trapani, in Sicily, identified as an illegal refugee, as if I had just arrived in a rubber dinghy. That was it, 15 years in Italy cancelled. Two police inspectors loaded me on a plane and I arrived in Palermo that afternoon. I came down the steps of the plane to find an armoured police truck waiting for me. They loaded me in, with nowhere to sit, and we set off along the road from Palermo to Trapani. It's a familiar road to me as I had visited friends in the area in 1996. This time I was travelling as a deported person, with a life behind me and a frozen one in the future, in spite of the Sicilian heat.

Around 4 pm we arrived at an enormous gate that opened to let us in. I lit a cigarette and saw the prison for the first time, the high walls, the smashed glass. I wondered: what will happen to me? The Venetian police delivered me to their Sicilian colleagues. I saw a soccer pitch encircled by barbed wire, inside twenty prisoners pretending to play football. Perhaps they imagined the ball.

I went up the stairs and through a door of slabs, more stairs and another door of slabs. They searched me. Later they searched my suitcase, and confiscated a CD, my shampoo, my medicine, the belt, the razor, the scissors. I began to understand that this place could be dangerous. They left me my books, two notebooks, one pen and my change. They gave me number 885. I didn't have a name anymore.

Another gate opened. There was a corridor with four cells on one side and a blank wall on the other. The prisoners were thrown together. They watched me and I watched them, trying not to cry. I felt history heavy on my chest. A door was opened and there was number 8, my cell. There were eight other prisoners, criminals, refugees, drunks, you name it. I was lucky. You could see the sea from one of the windows, and I asked them to close it. I had almost drowned in that sea nine years before, when I was free.

My telephone rang continuously. My friends in Venice had begun to collect signatures. In ten days they collected 2000. There were interviews on the radio and in the newspapers. They testified to my good conduct over 12 years, a bit of a student, a bit of a bartender, fun-loving and a poet.

Some prisoners thought I was Italian, and in some way I entered the place as an Italian with Palestinian blood, or vice versa. For this I suffered a little more. The food was awful, horrible, my phone rang constantly, there were shouts in strange languages, rows, fights, sometimes stealing, sometimes crying in silence, but they also knew how to laugh. Often they explained things simply with their eyes.

There was a guy from Togo who seemed to be able to tell me everything about his country with his eyes. He had travelled for 23 days with his friends, losing one of them and all their money, just to end up in this prison. I knew already a little about the situation in North Africa, and of Chad, when Idris, an Arabic-speaking guy seeking political asylum, told me about Sudan and Senegal, China, Serbia and the great Egypt and its pyramids. Now he had been arrested by the Roman empire.

Then there is the story of the angry Nigerian because his wife, alive in his feelings and in his thought, is in the same prison.

Here there were people with university degrees and arrested dreams. Outside the stone-slabbed walls was the heat of Sicily. Ten cigarettes a day of poisonous tobacco were not enough. Coffee and tea could be bought from small machines through workers or the Carabinieri.

There were fights in the baths - how could baths like this exist in Italy? Italians would rather die than enter these baths. I had asked for political asylum after 15 years without even a fine in this country, and now I was suffering for 15 days as if I was paying a tax, a day for every year. For those 15 days I didn't call my sick mother so as not to worry her.

They didn't treat me badly, rather they ravaged my mind, my sensibility, my culture and my pen, because all inside me stopped, became inarticlulate, except for my nervous system and my patience, which was all that could get me out of the place sane.

Once I refused Friday prayer, but not because I'm a non-practicing Muslim. It's beautiful to pray. But I didn't want to receive instruction from the Imam there who didn't care about religion. He'd been sentenced to eight years for larceny. Truly I had to choose between two hells: the first was the one I was living in and the other was the humiliation of my faith, confirmed by this prison.

Continuously phone calls, fax, lawyers, stress. I didn't lose patience, not even when I begin a five-day hunger strike. I did it not for food but rather in order not to stay in that place anymore; on Monday I was shaved by a racist Sicilian barber who charged me 1.50 euros. Shall I scream? My stomach ached for medicine from the infirmary. Still today I do not understand who was the doctor and who was the nurse.

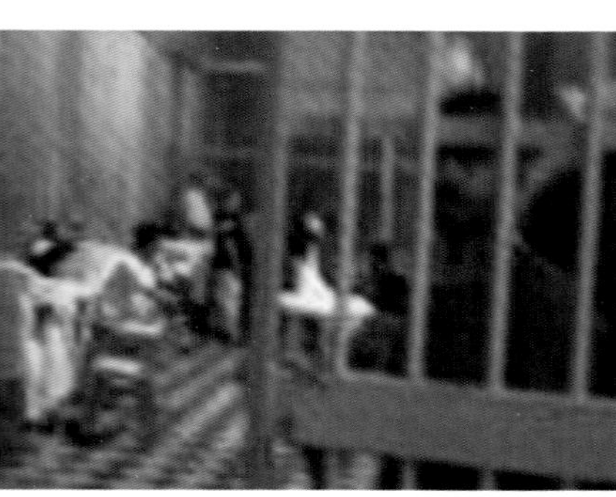

Nor did I then understand the

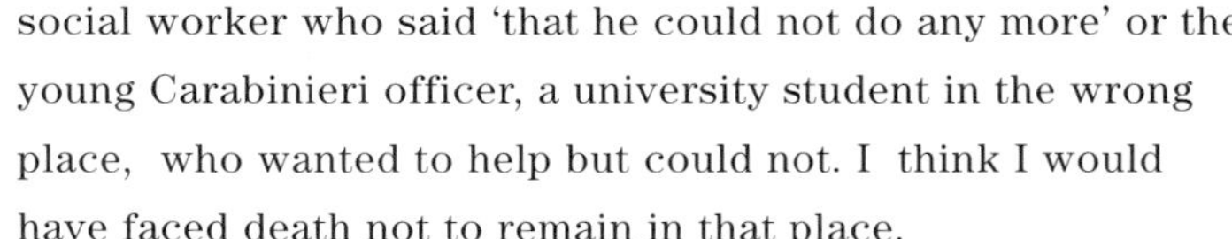

social worker who said 'that he could not do any more' or the young Carabinieri officer, a university student in the wrong place, who wanted to help but could not. I think I would have faced death not to remain in that place.

These are small memories of that laager. It is very hard to write about the boy from Kurdistan who talked about his country in poetry and who lost his brother to the sea. His grave reads like this: Sex: M. Race: Black. I don't want to write about the pregnant women or children who died trying to reach the coast.

An American friend of mine, who has lived for some time in Italy without a visa, told me that he himself wanted to change his skin so he could feel like a normal citizen. Wherever the immigrant comes from, this is his real drama.

Enough.

Who stops the sea to find themselves at the beginning of their coast?
To die of thirst in the water.

Enough.

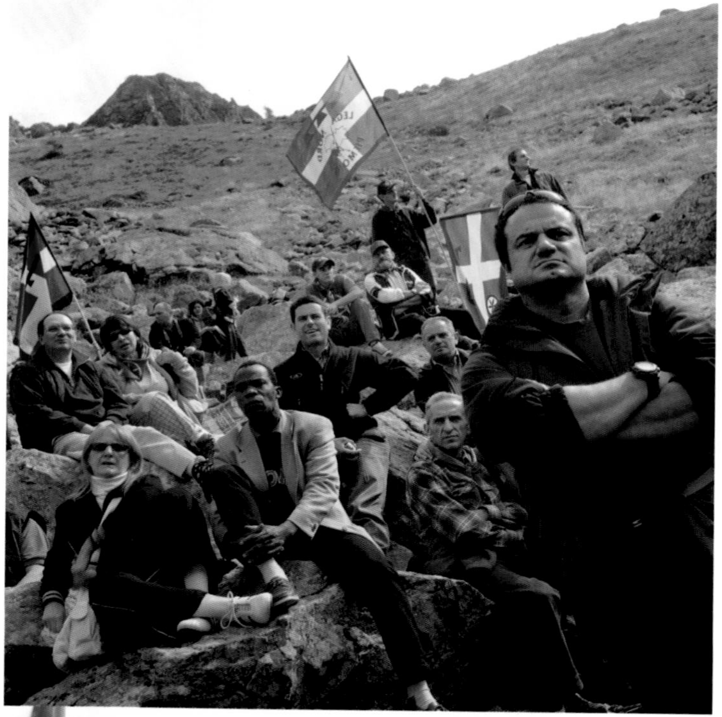

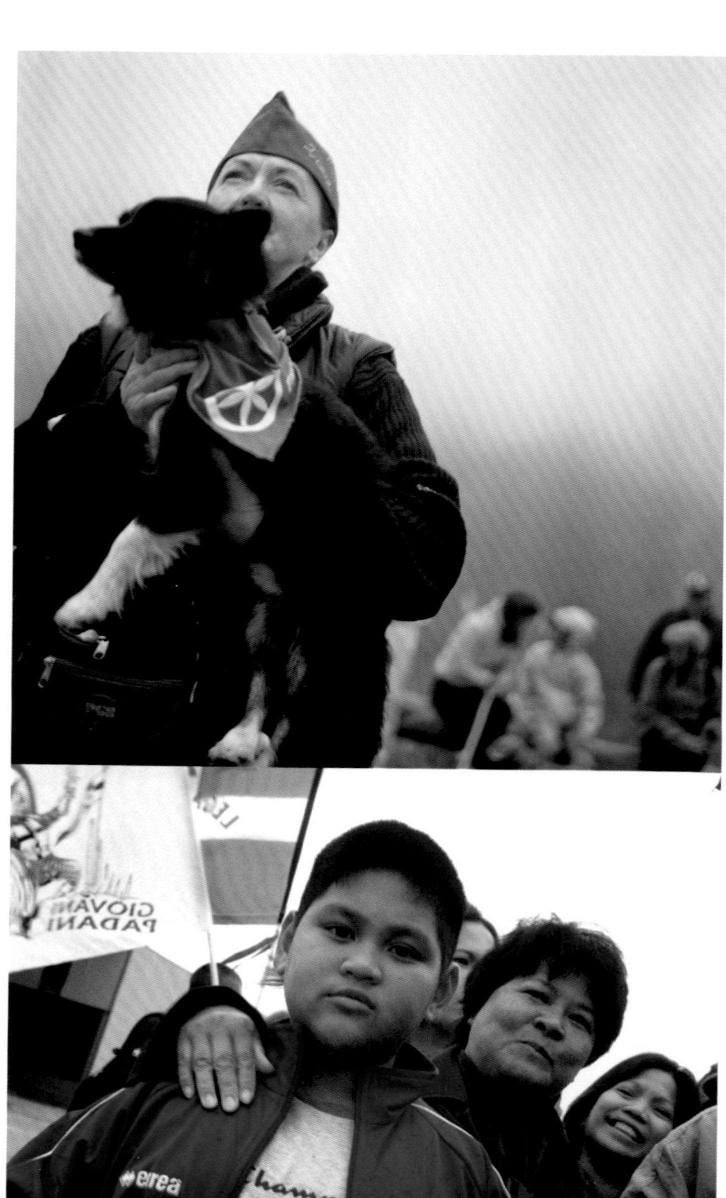
LEGA NORD
LIGA VENETA

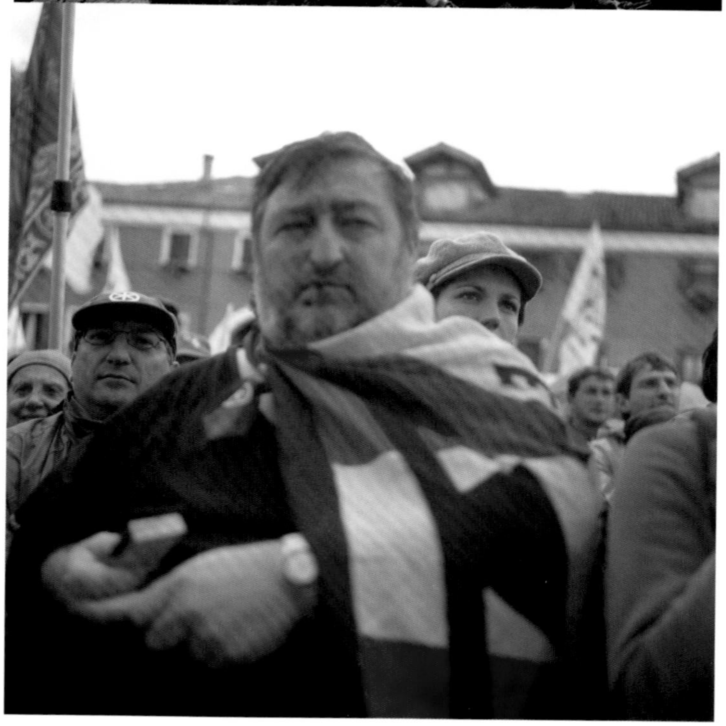

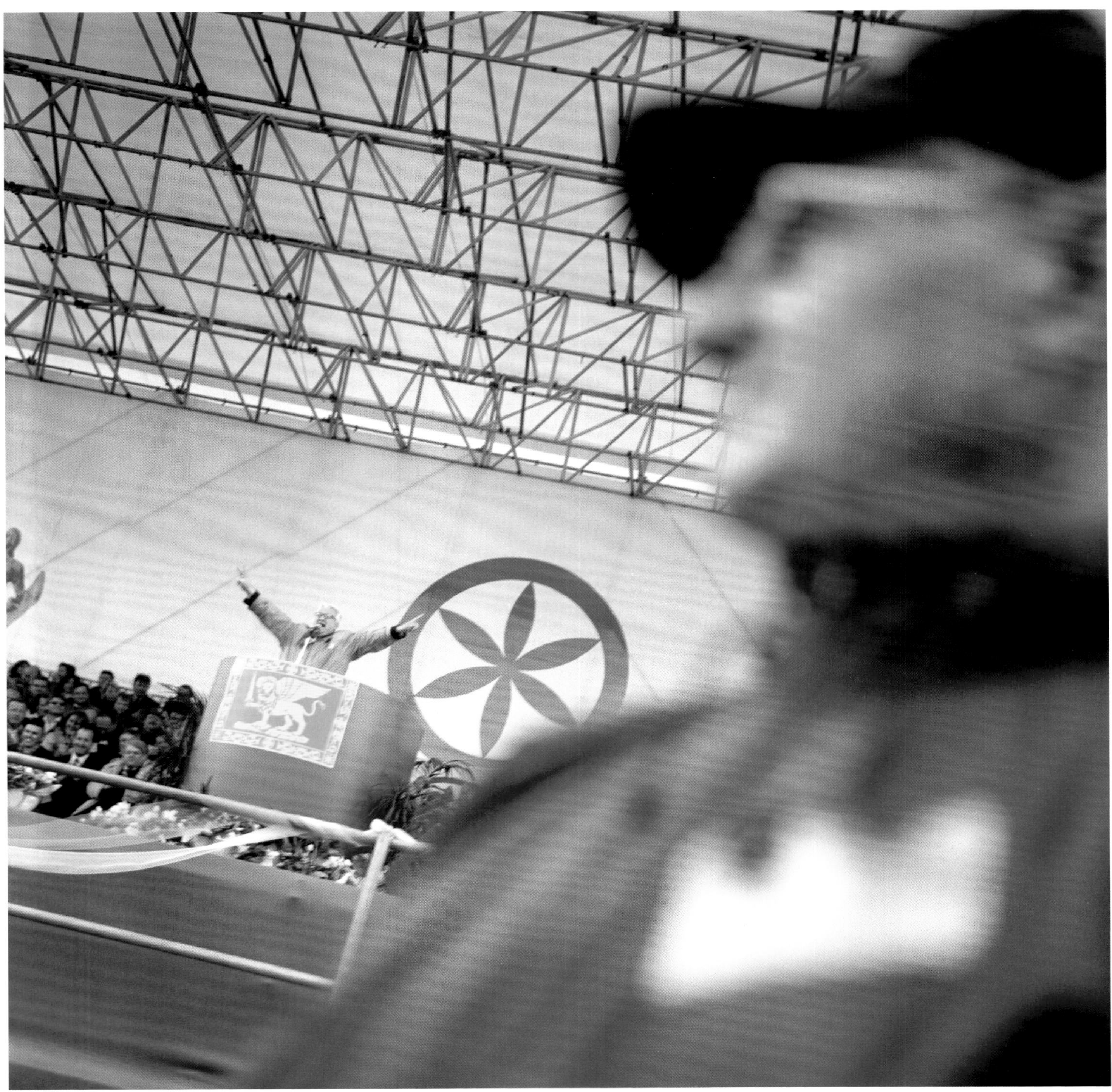

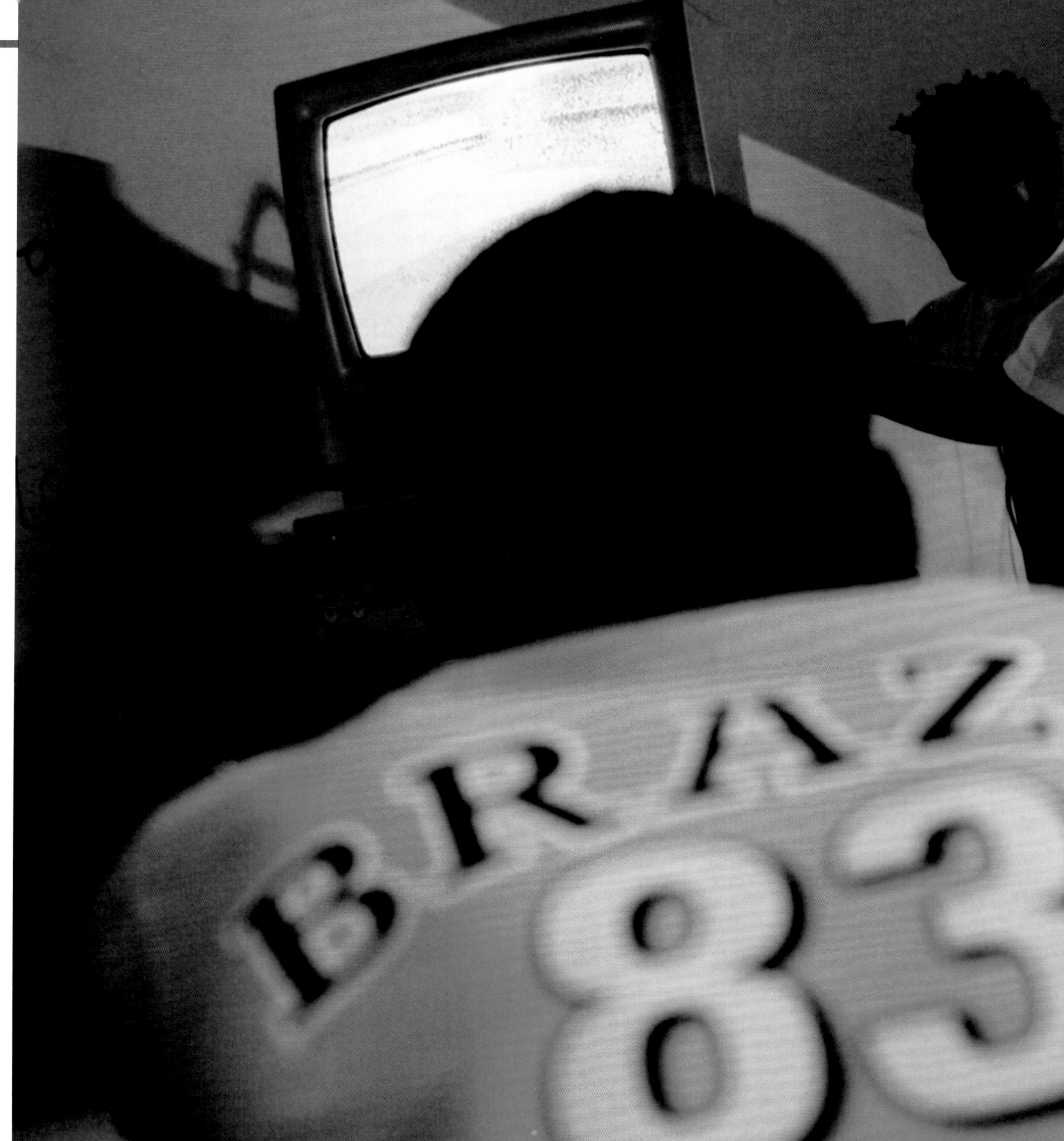
BRAZ
83

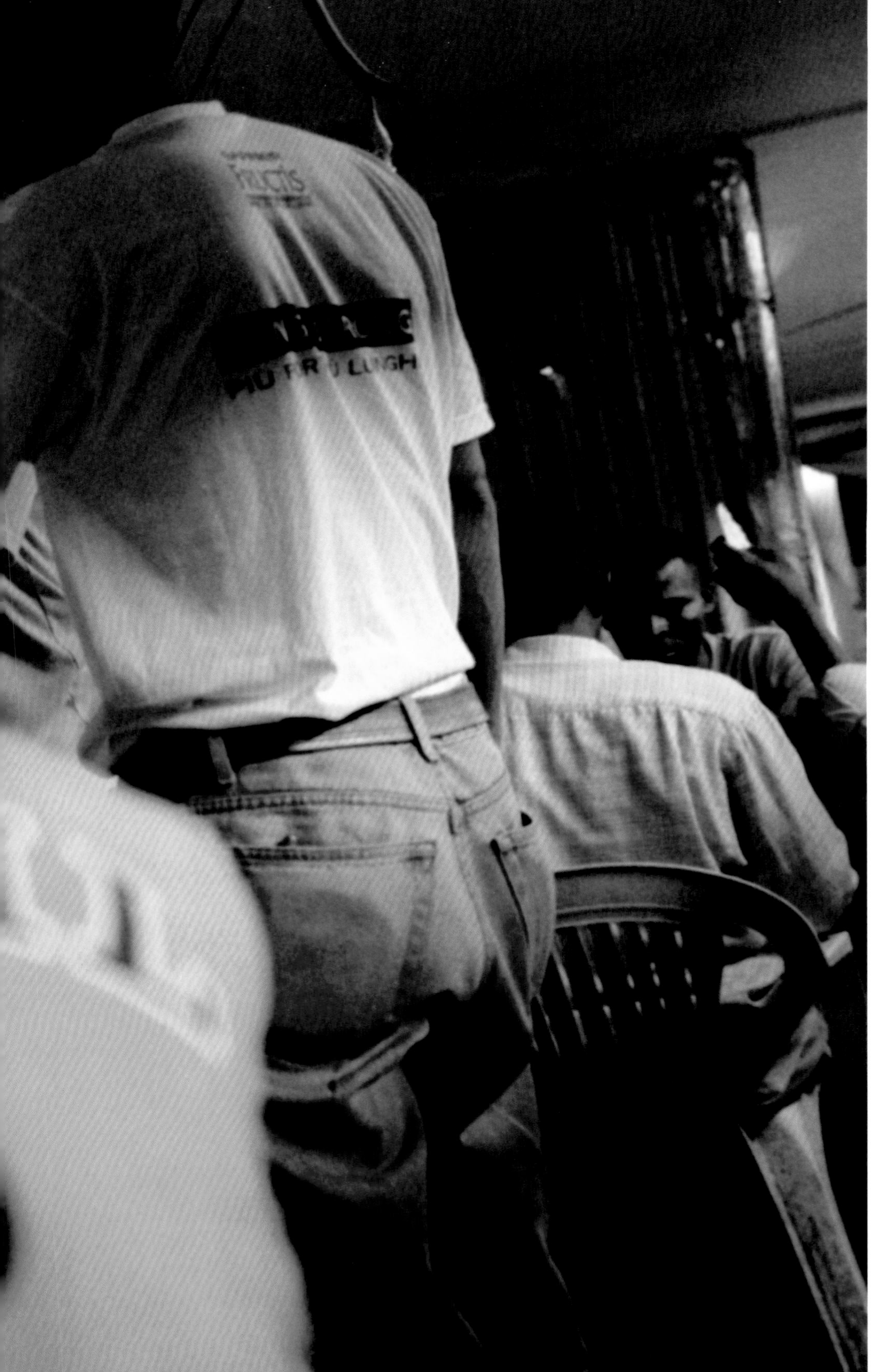

*Previous Pages* Pian del Re, Torino, Lega Nord water ceremony, September 2005 (MB )
Lega Nord rally, Venezia, September 2005 (MB)
*Left* Immigrant internet point, Arzignano, Vicenza, March 2005 (MB)

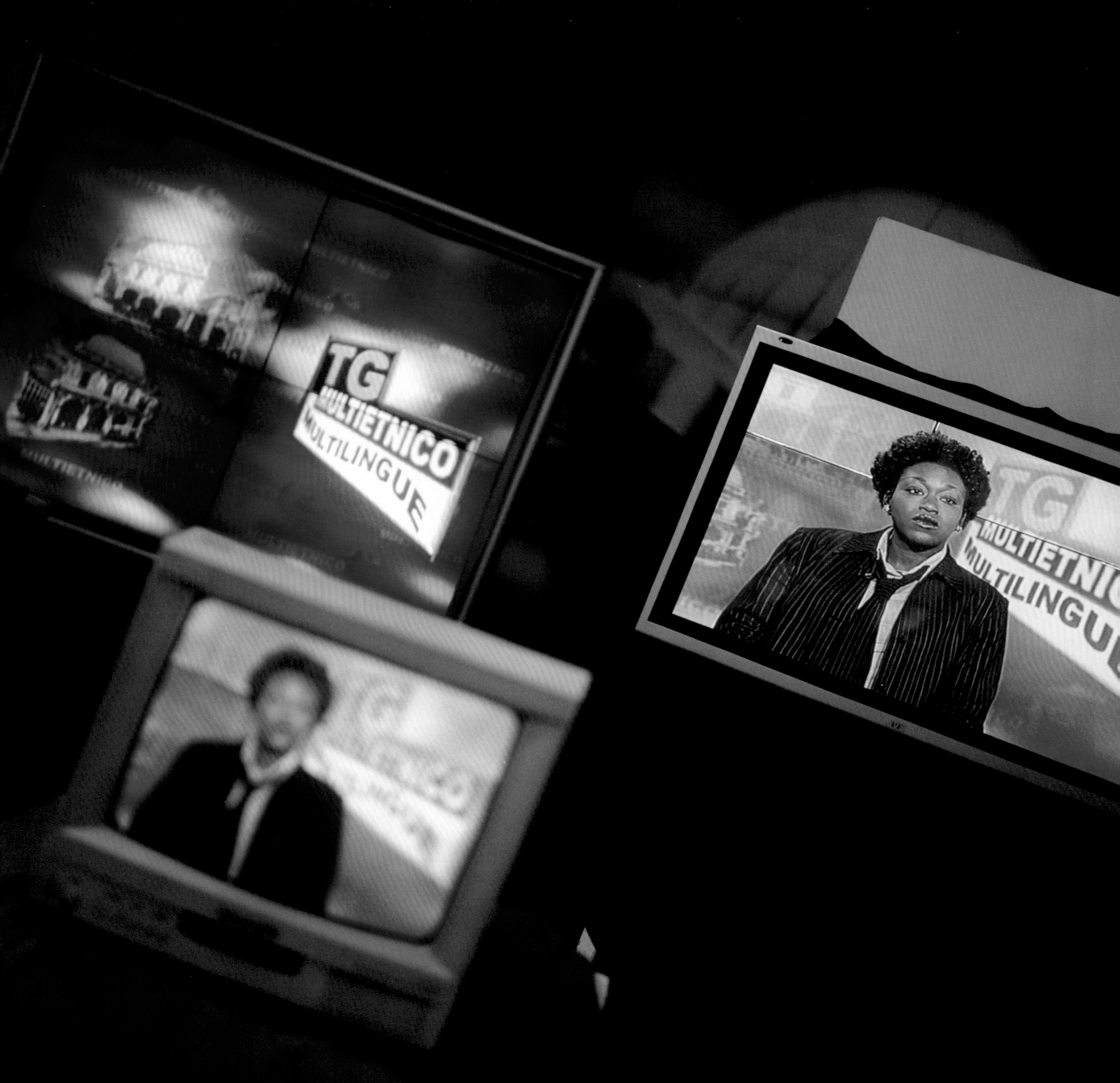
TG
MULTIETNICO
MULTILINGUE
TG
MULTIETNICO
MULTILINGUE

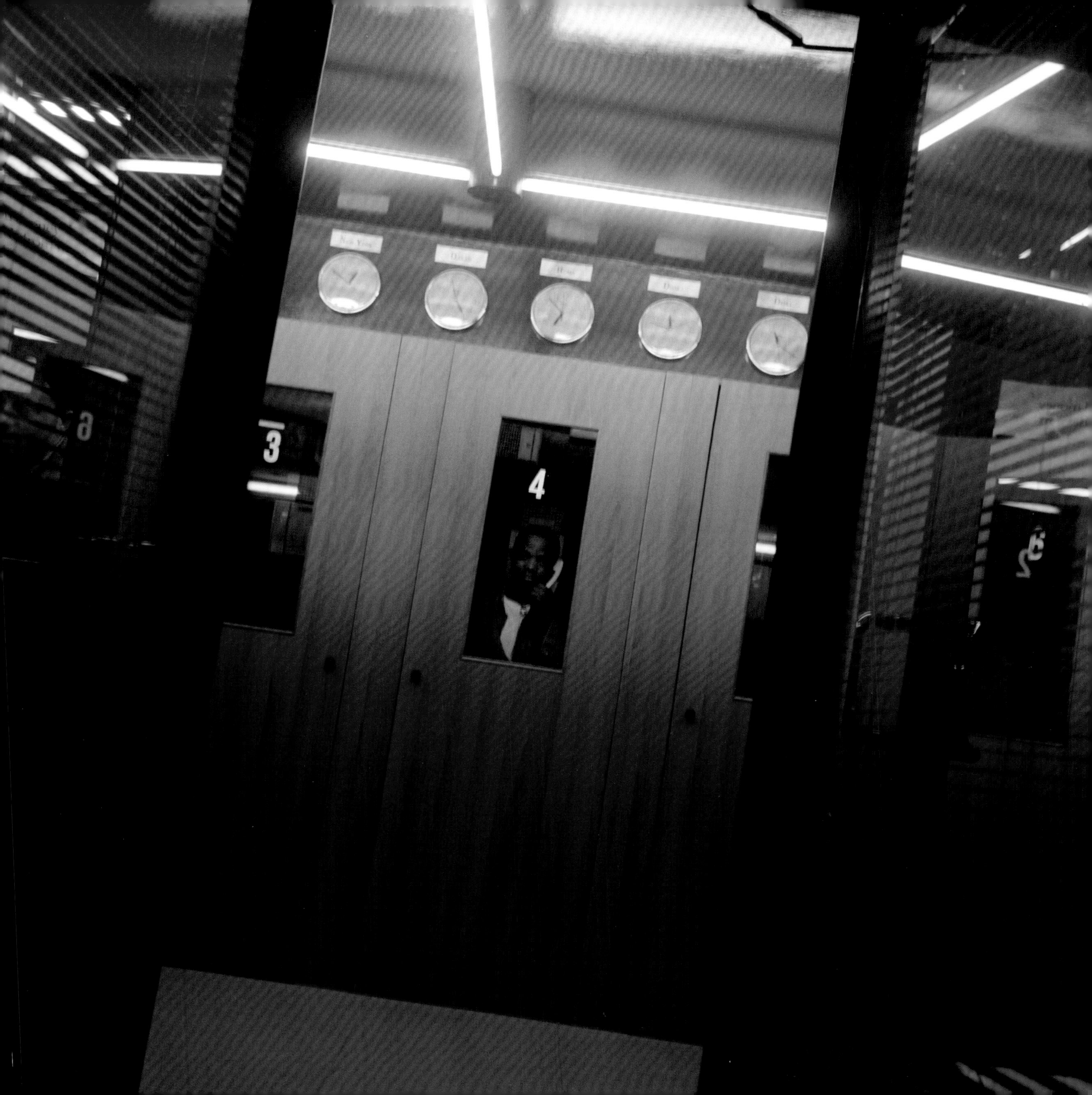
3
4

By 2000 foreign workers registered as National Insurance contributors and employed by Italian companies numbered approximately 226,000, more than double than in 1995

*Previous page* Multi-ethnic TV news, Brescia, May 2005 (MB)
*Right* Mixed-race wedding, Brescia, May 2005 (MB)

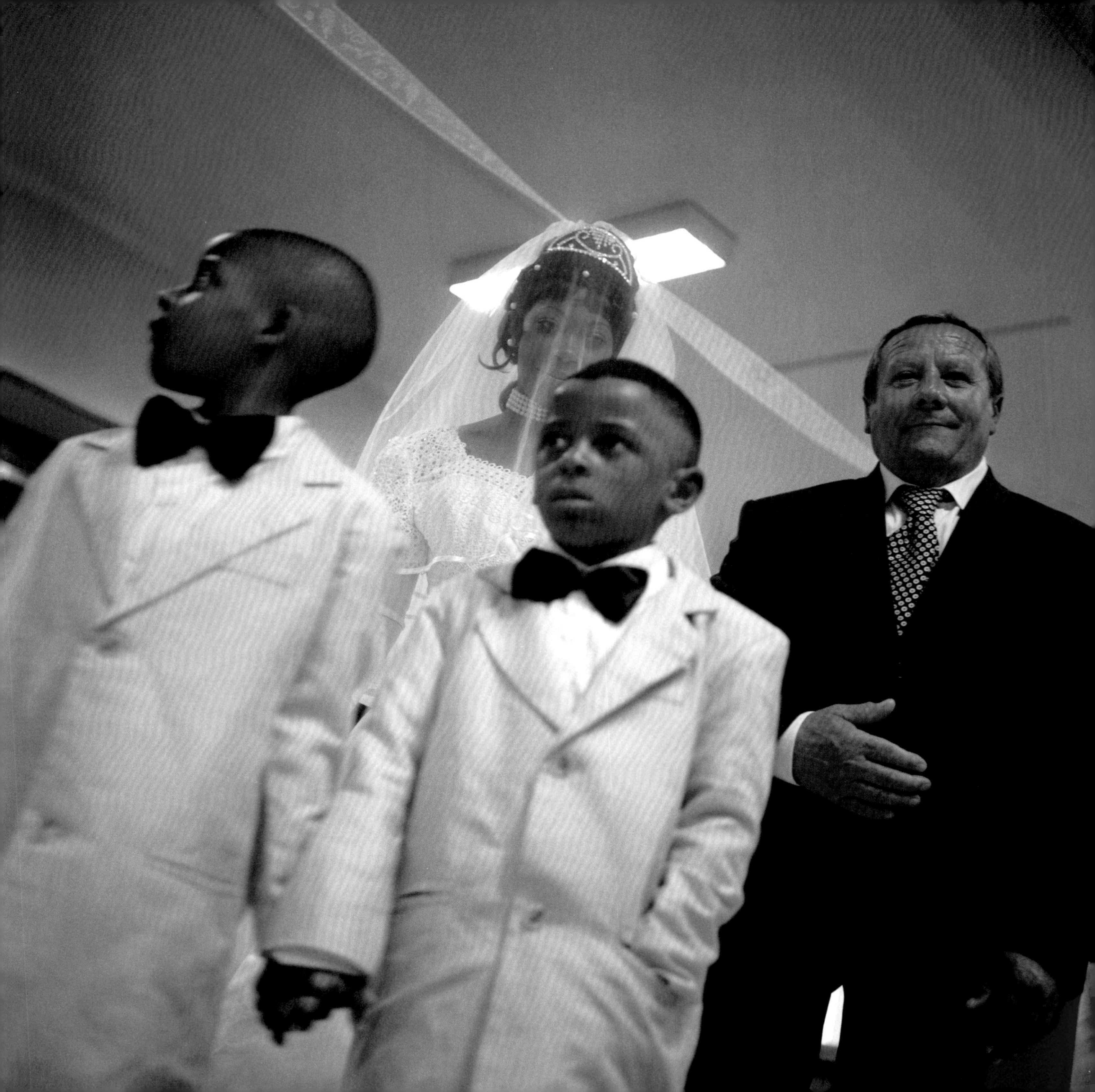

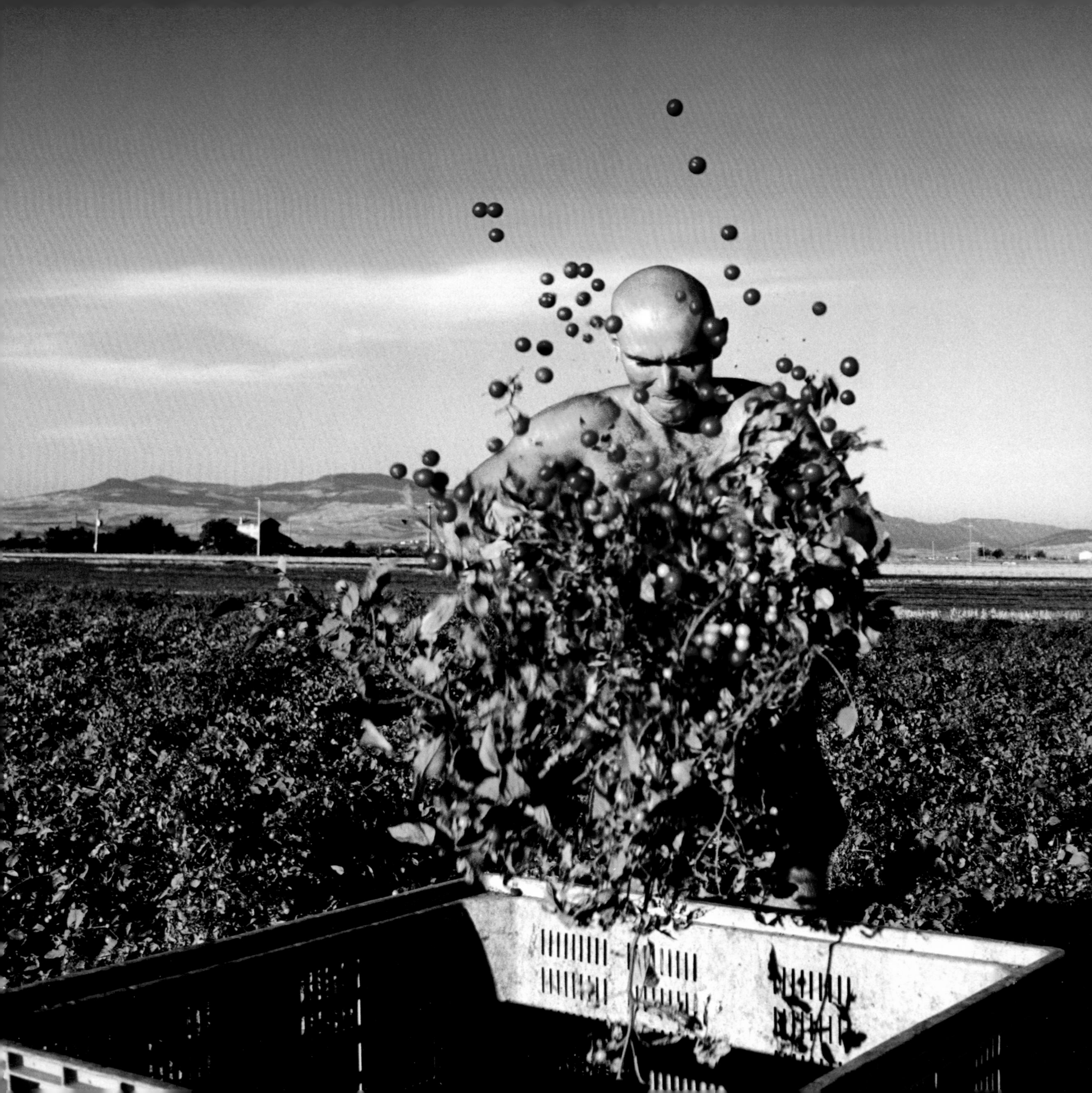

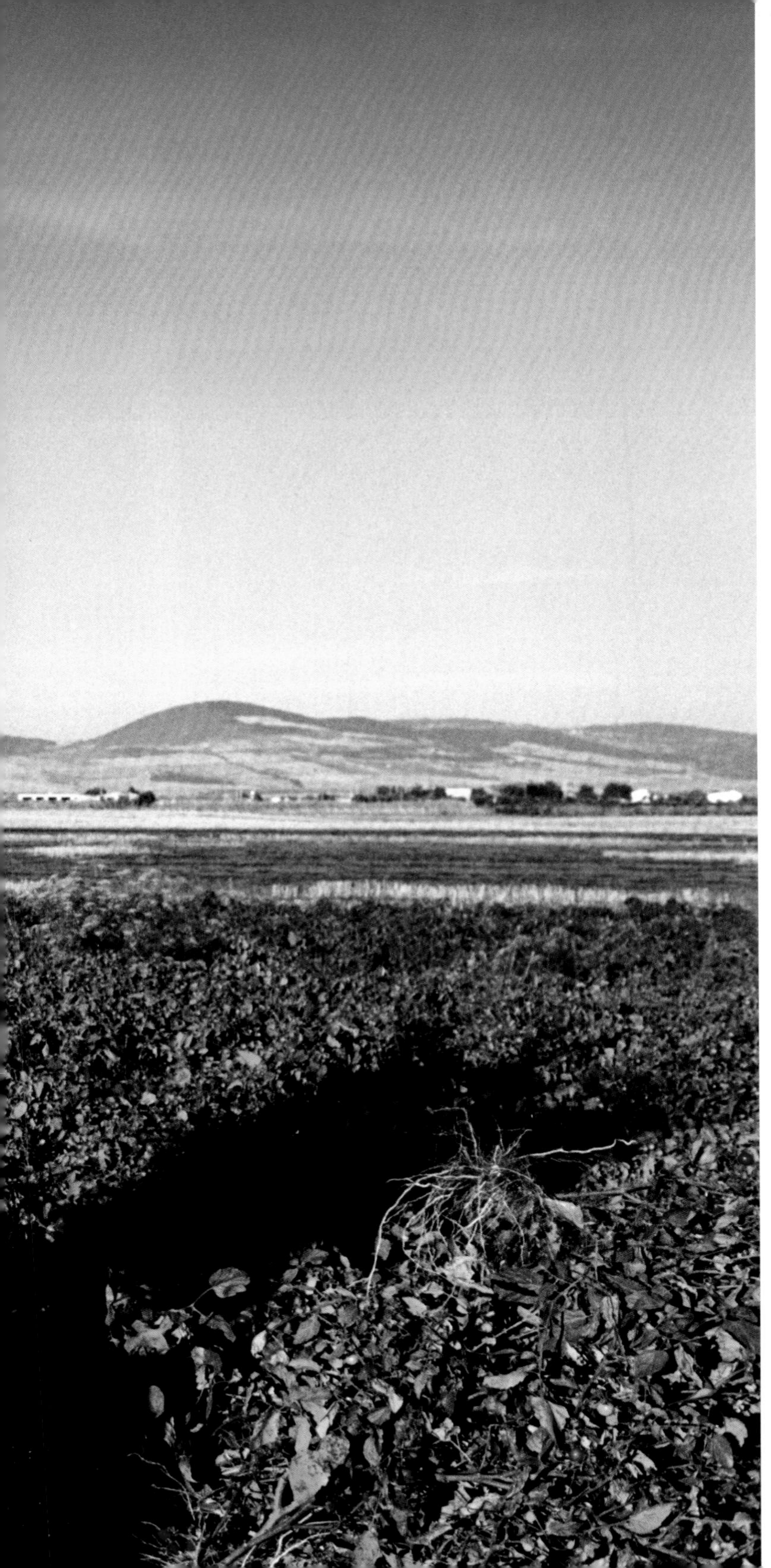

62% of immigrant labourers work in the industrial sector; 37% in the service sector

*Left* Harvesting tomatoes, Borgo Segezia, Foggia, July 2004 (EM)
*Following page* Palermo, August 2004 (RS)

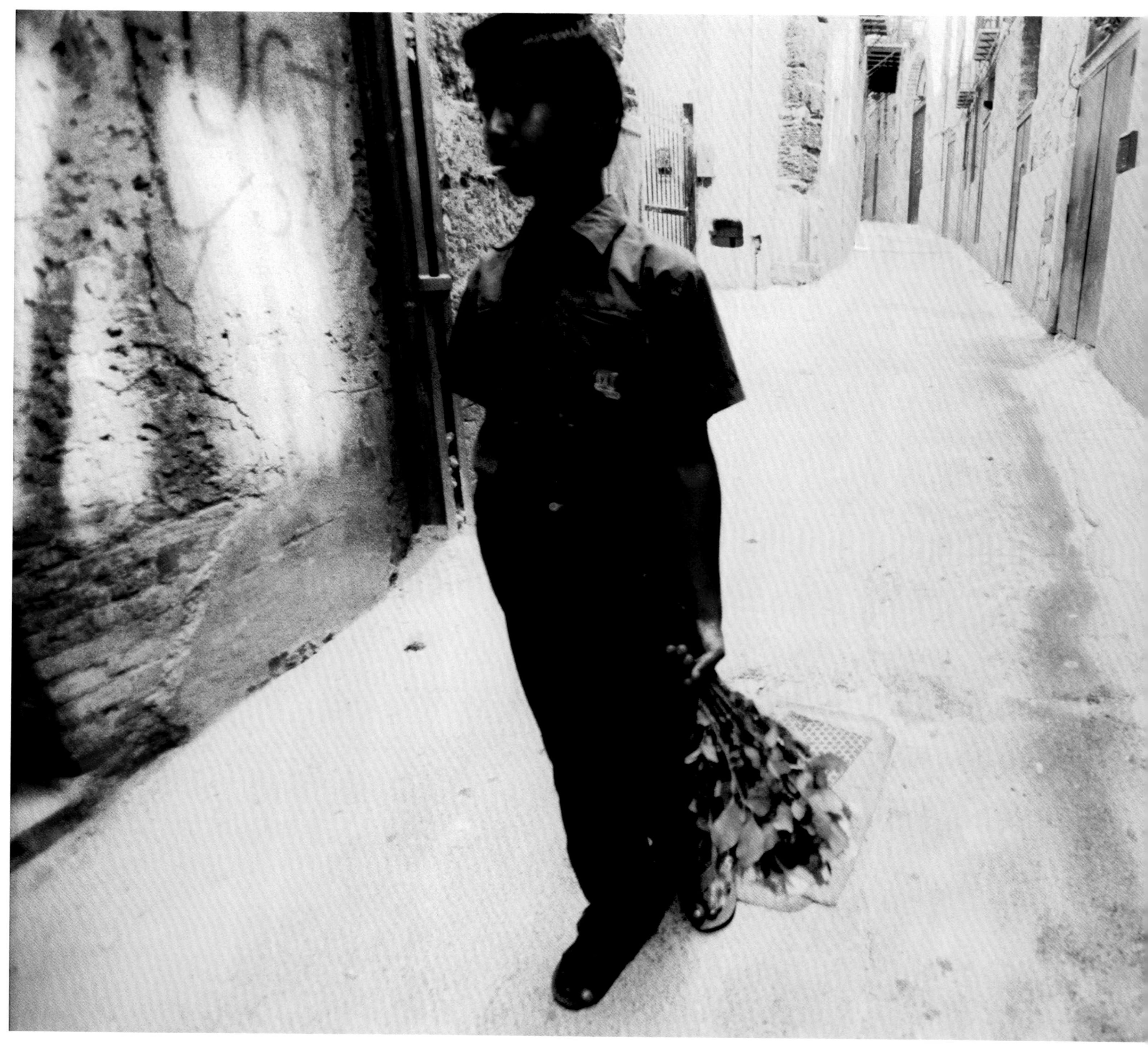

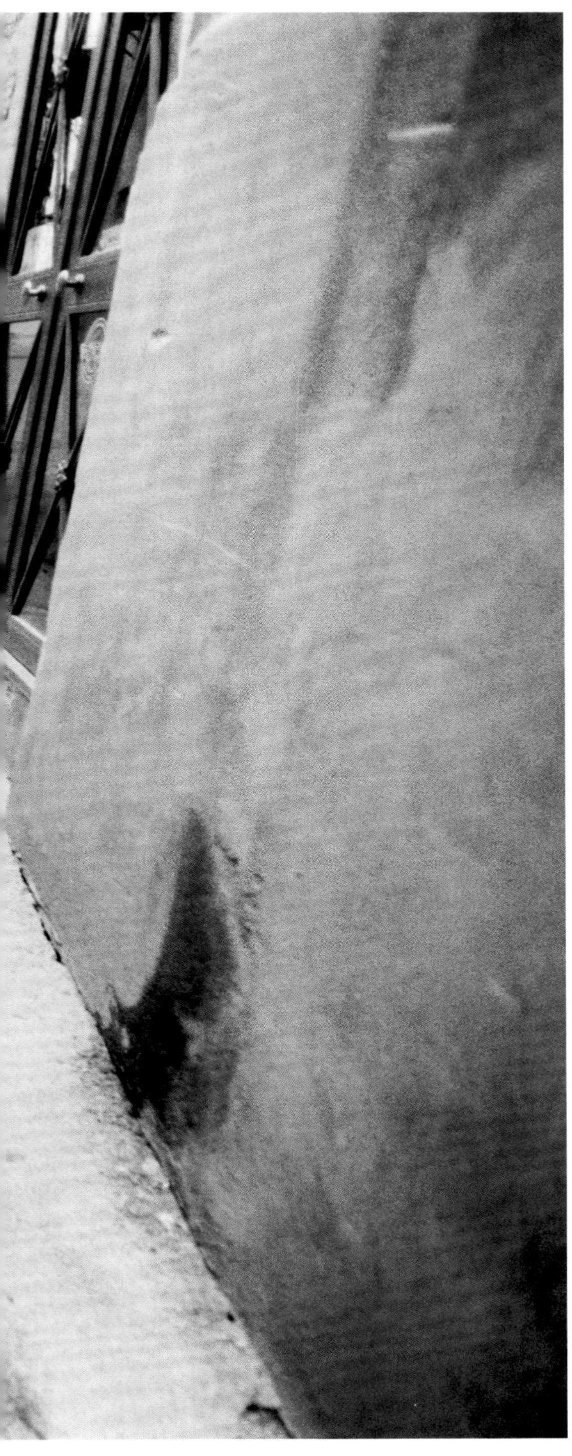

Immigrant labourers not registered
are categorized as follows:
85% with expired permits
15% with no permit

They find employment:
34% through immigrant friends or acquaintances
32% directly at places of employment
11% through Italian friends or acquaintances
6% through employment agencies
7% through a Trade Union or Voluntary Organization

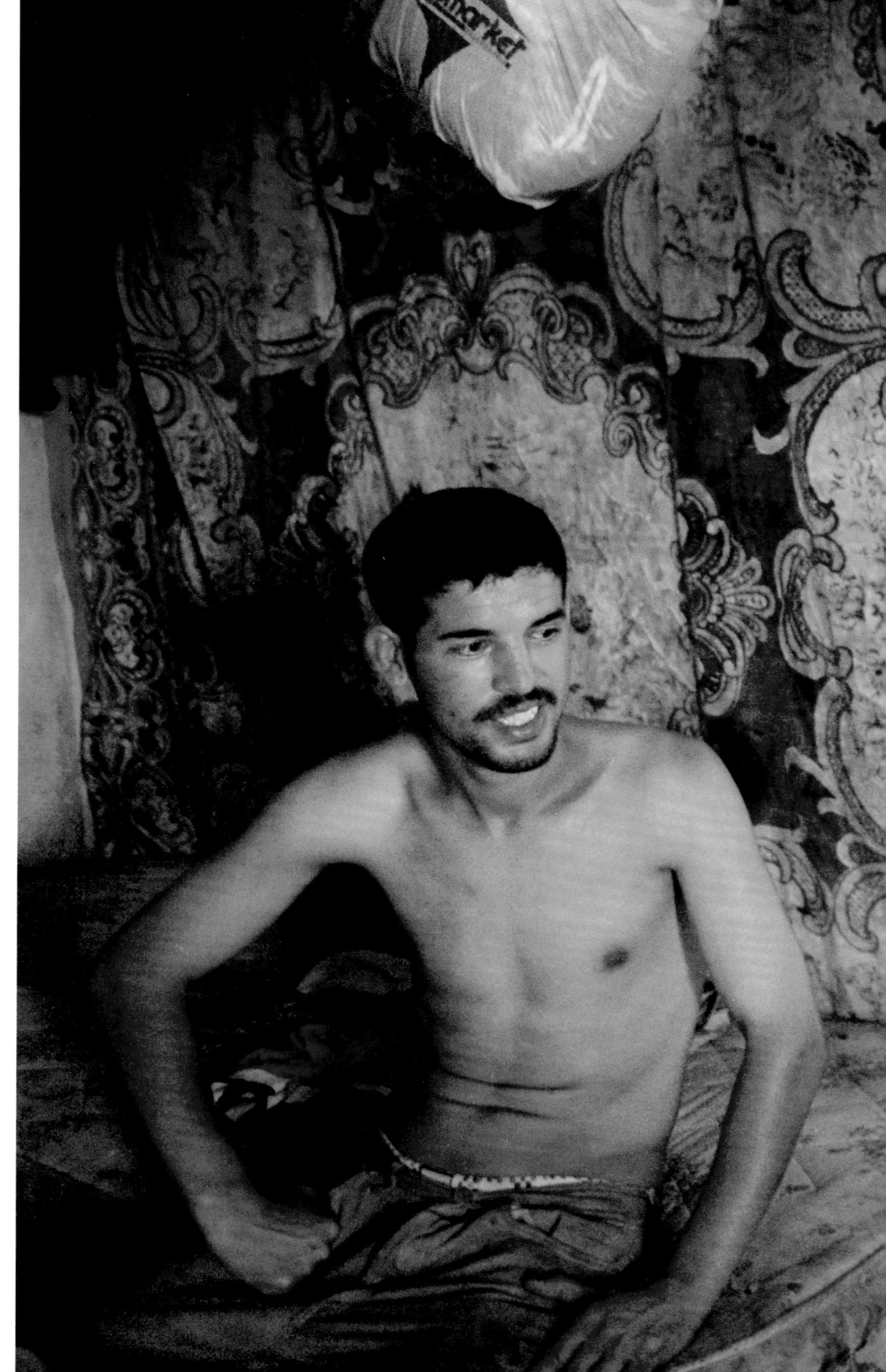


Illegal immigrant labourers, Eboli, Salerno, July 2004 (EM)

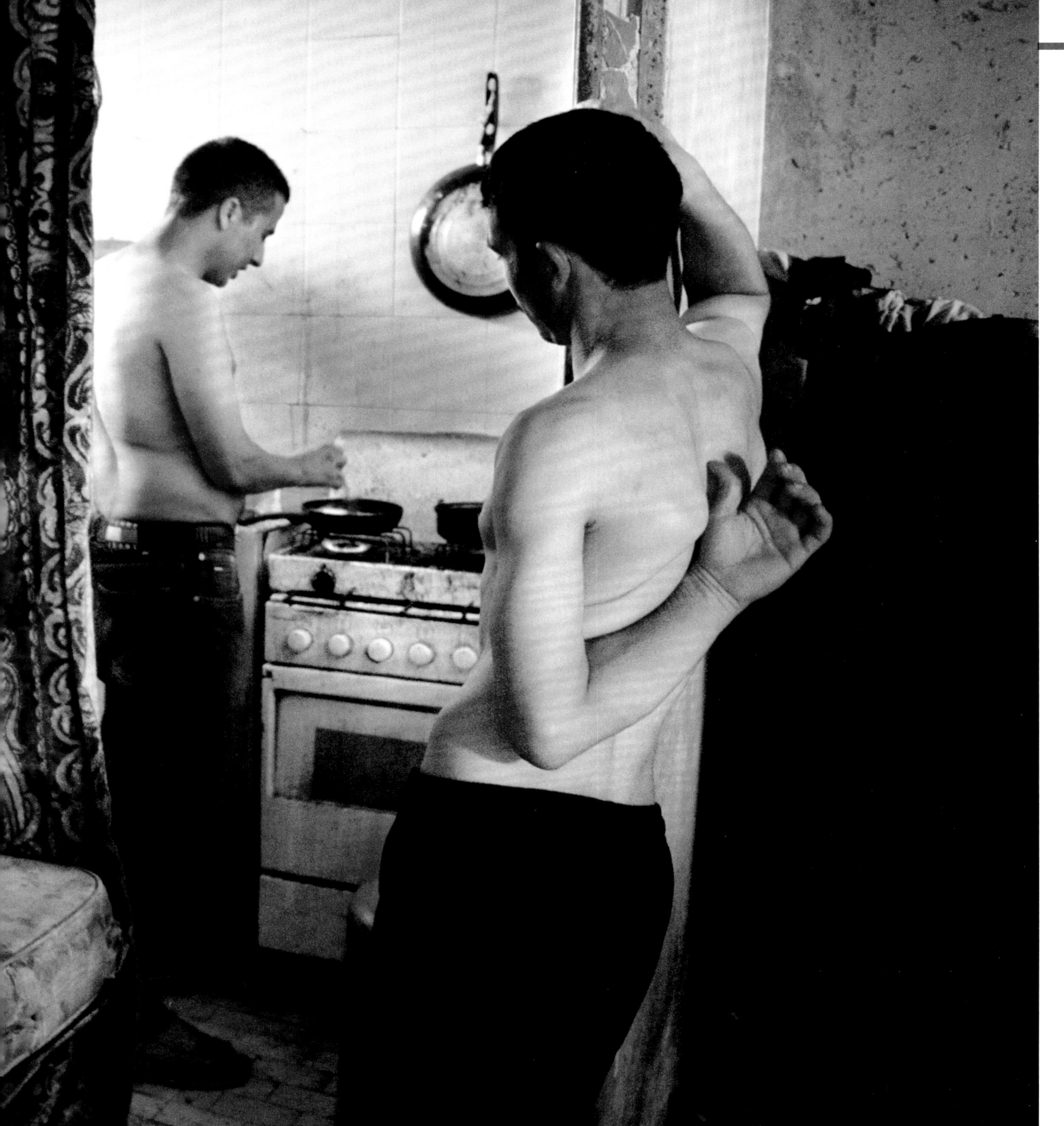

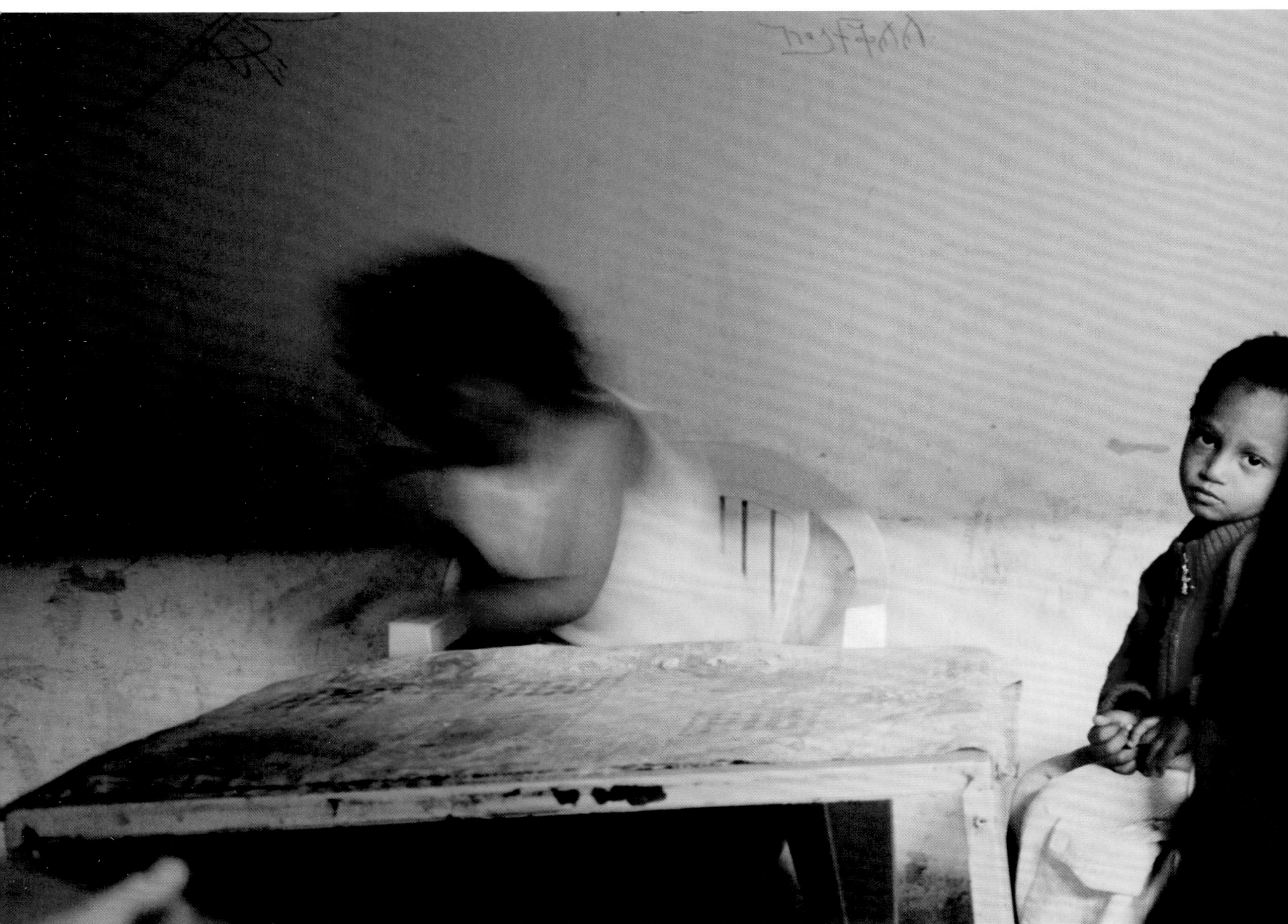

Hotel Africa, Roma, June 2004 (MB)

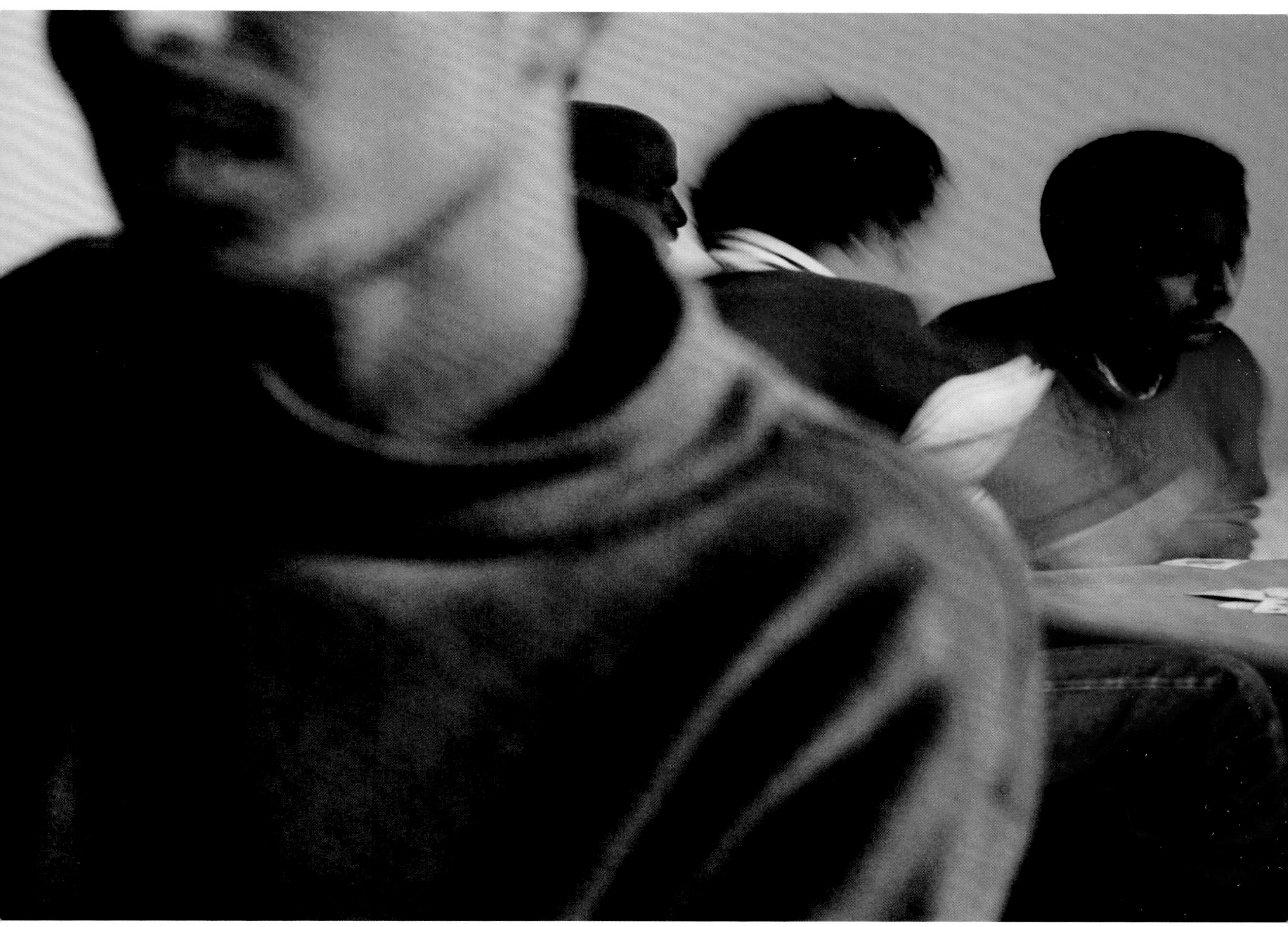

Registered immigrant workers: 536,604
Subscribers to the Trade Unions: 45%

75% of immigrants rent flats by themselves,
with their families or with other immigrants;
9% are housed by employers as a form of income;
5% have bought homes, individually or with other immigrants;
2% are homeless

Immigrant home, Genova, January 2005 (MB)

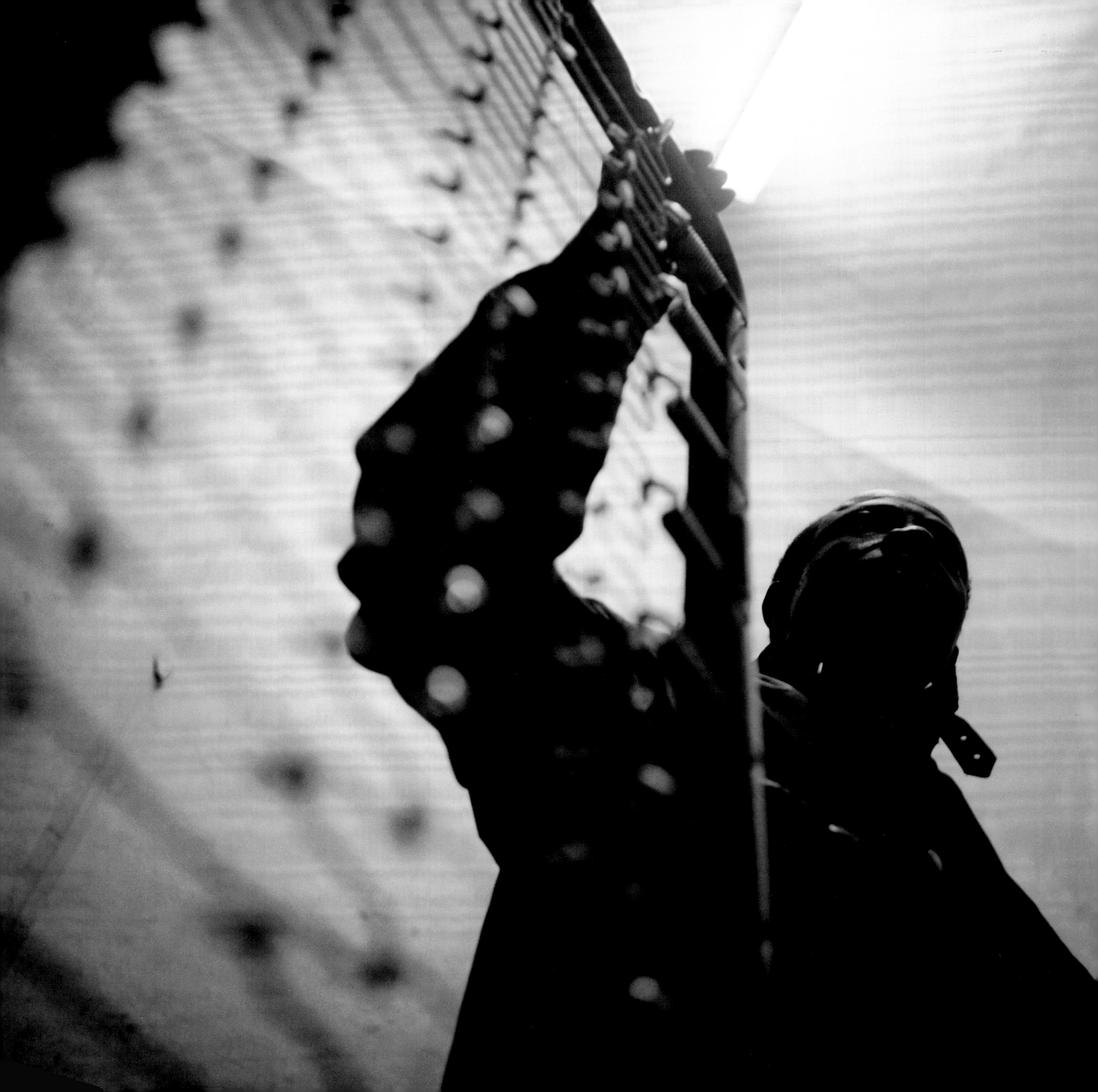

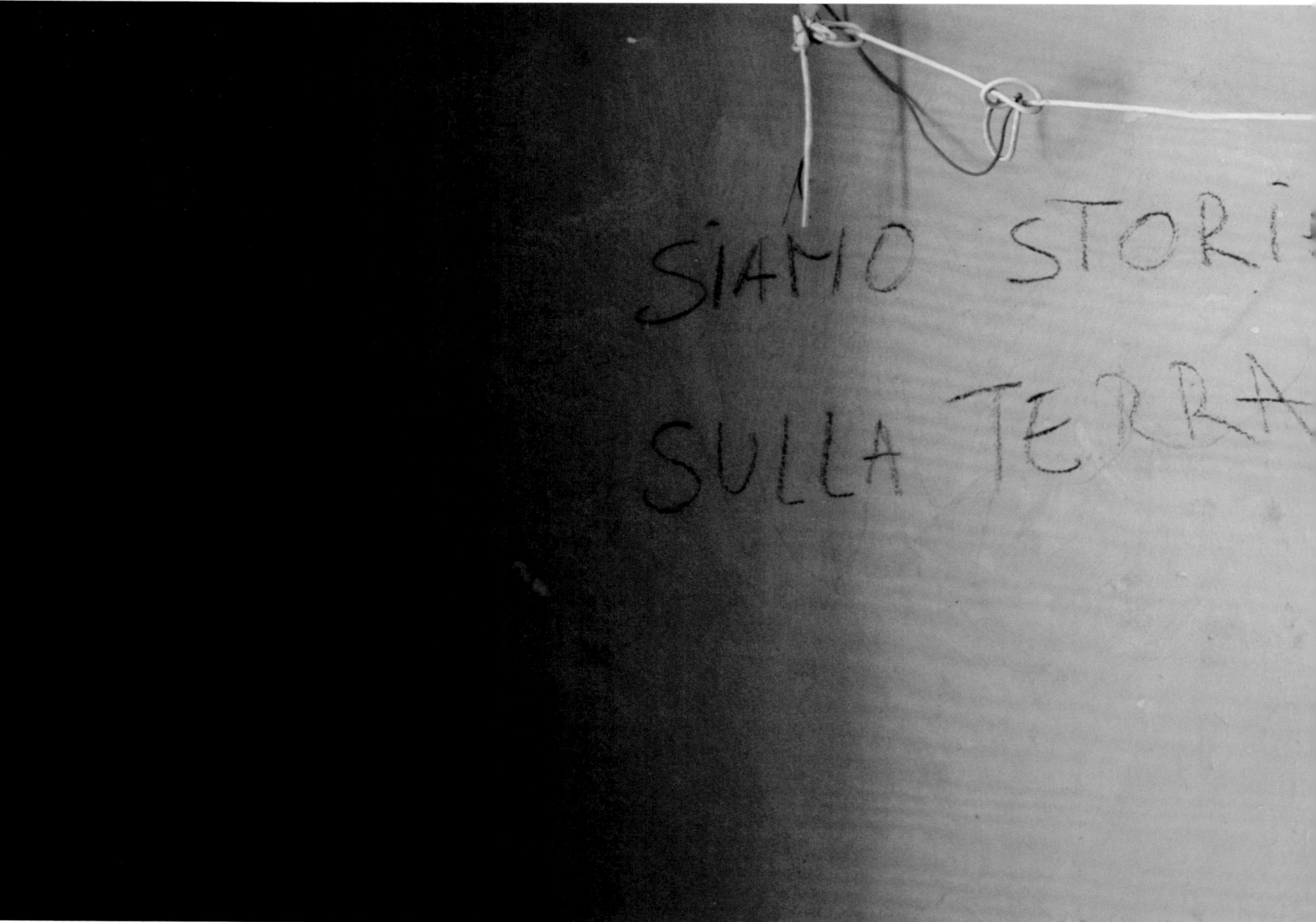


Hotel Africa, Roma, June 2004 (MB)

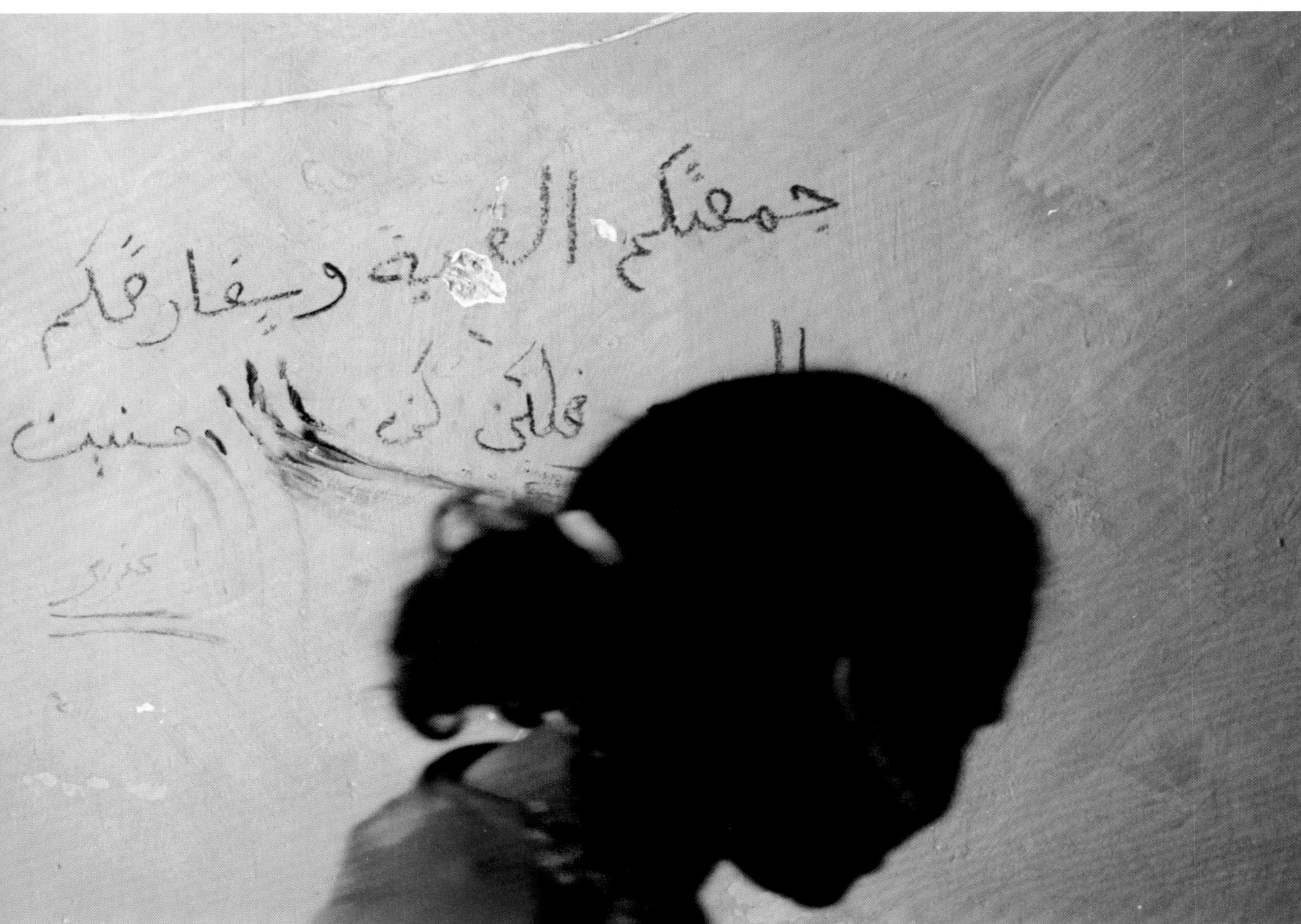

# THE INDIVIDUAL AS A COMMODITY

Umberto Galimberti

In January 2006 the Italian parliament approved a new law that stipulated an individual was entitled to defend himself and his goods, if necessary by force, were he to be threatened. The law went further - should the individual merely feel threatened then he was entitled to pre-empt any act against him, again with force. It is as if the state has abandoned the responsibility of protecting its citizens, indeed cannot do so, and that henceforth the individual must assume this responsibility.

We have returned to the mentality of the Middle Ages. In the 17th century Thomas Hobbes identified the state as being the guardian of justice in the affairs of men since, for example, revenge is a subjective reaction to events and therefore inadmissible as a form of justice. Justice must be objective, and consequently should be administered by the state, which cannot be led in its actions by the personal vanities of the individual. Thus the concept of justice being the sole province of the state has simply been left by the wayside, as if it were no more than the litter of an otherwise unoccupied population.

In 1842 Karl Marx addressed these concepts of law and justice when describing the philosophical consequence of a new law in Germany which allowed for imprisonment and even capital punishment for the theft of firewood. He observed that such punishment of the thief, who has embezzled the owner of the firewood, can only be regarded as a legitimate judicial consequence of the theft when the owner of the firewood is entitled to the protection of the law exclusively because he is the owner of the firewood. The punishment becomes legally correct, though nevertheless inhuman, only if the individual is the sum of his assets. Thus if his assets are removed from him by theft then the owner of the property is grievously diminished. Logically the thief must be mortally punished. But if the value of our humanity is understood to be beyond the possession of an individual's assets then the punishment cannot fit the crime. To regard it as just would be to reduce ourselves to what Marx calls greedy materialism. He wrote: 'The result of all our discoveries and our progress seems to be that goods have a spiritual life and that human existence has been reduced to merchandise".

Recently the Pope accused Communism of having reduced human beings to goods, and indeed accused Marxism of this crime against humanity. Marx in Das Kapital stressed the necessity for the redemption of humanity for its reduction to a merely material integrity by Capitalism. Clearly if the Pope maintains that the reduction of man to the value of his possessions is a Marxist event, when it is a Capitalist event, there will follow the confusion of ideas, ideas that justify that those who steal must pay with their lives.

Such confusion has to be avoided, independent of the fact that it will shift Italy into a world more conducive to the Wild West. Children will soon be going to school with guns to protect themselves, as they do in the United States. The blurring of the divide between the justice of the state and the individual's responsibilities and reactions will have disastrous, and fatal, consequences.

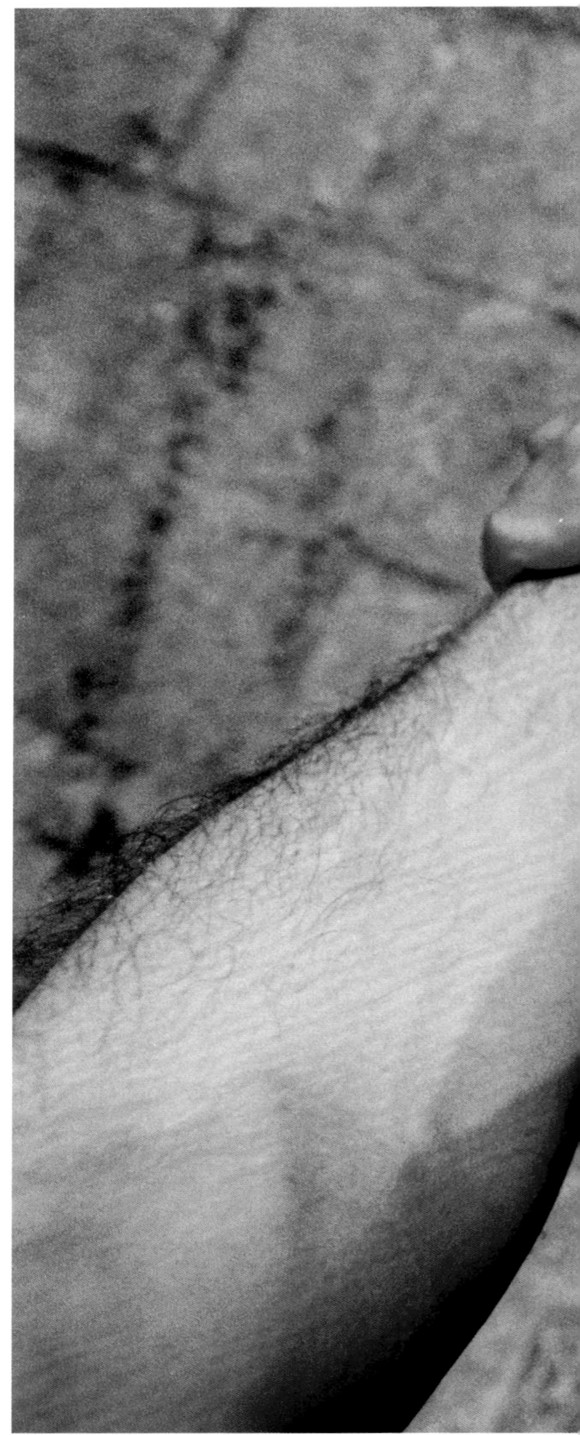

Palermo, June 2004 (RS)

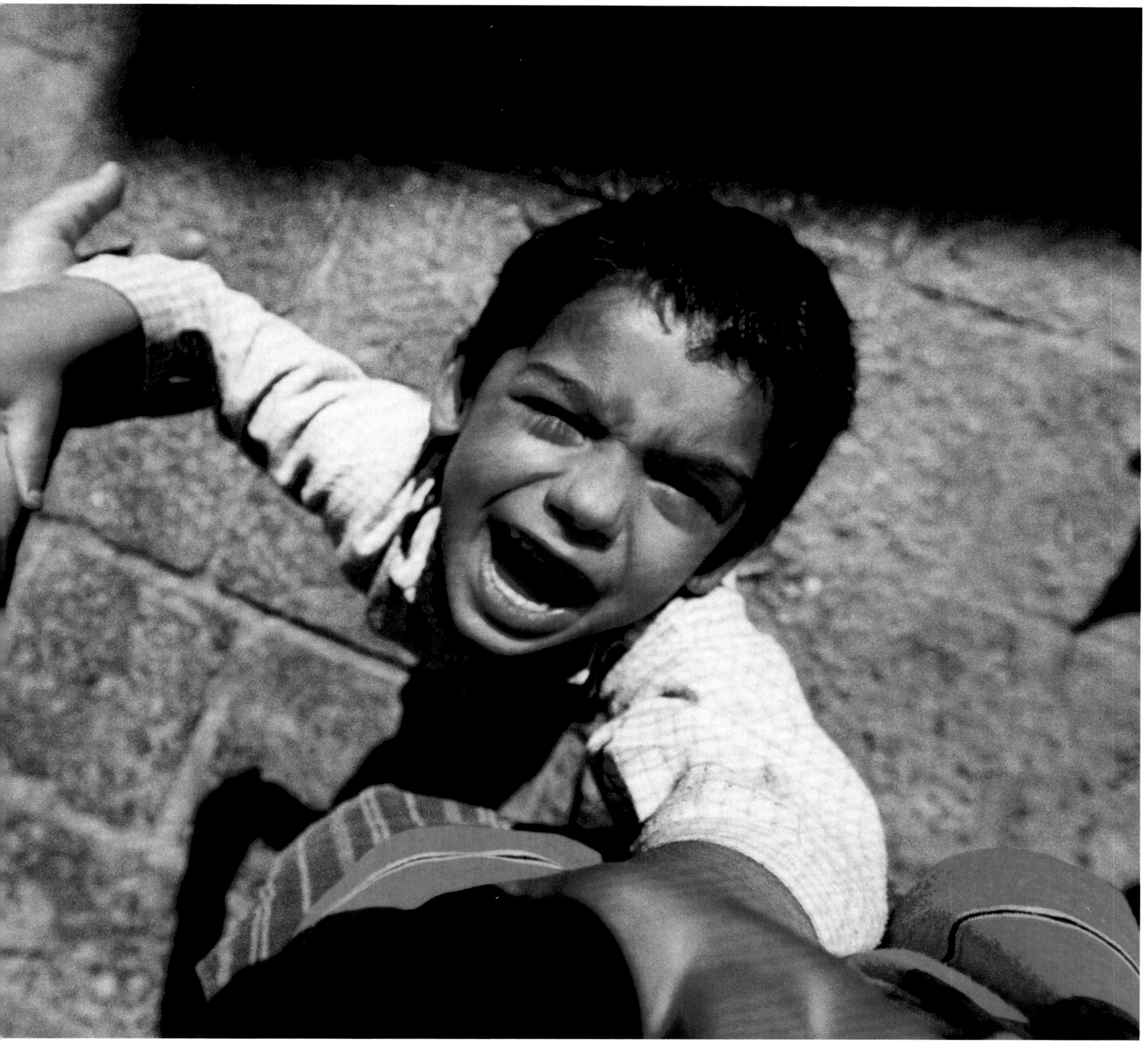

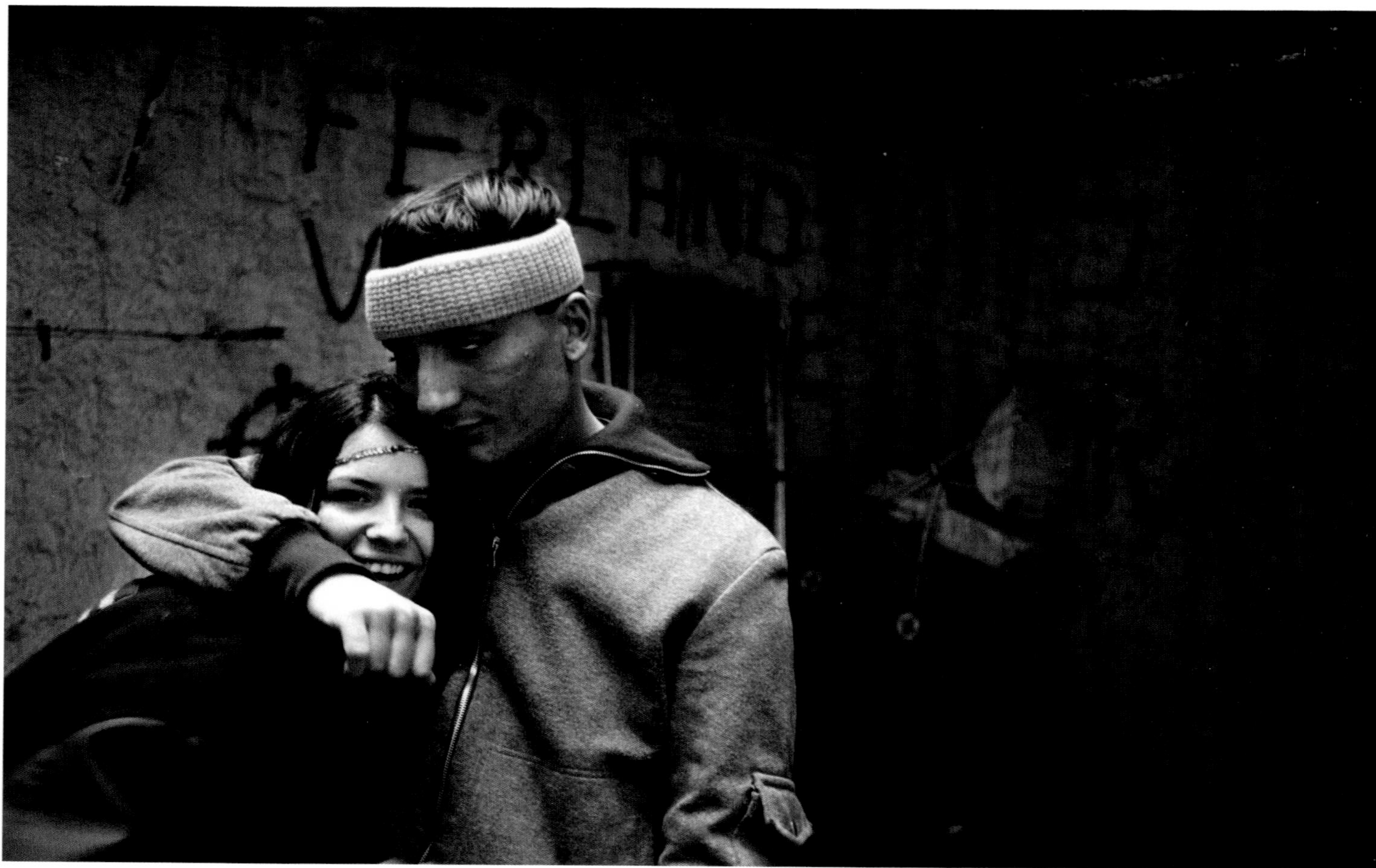

Hardcore football fans, the ‘Mastiffs’, Napoli, October 2002 (MS)

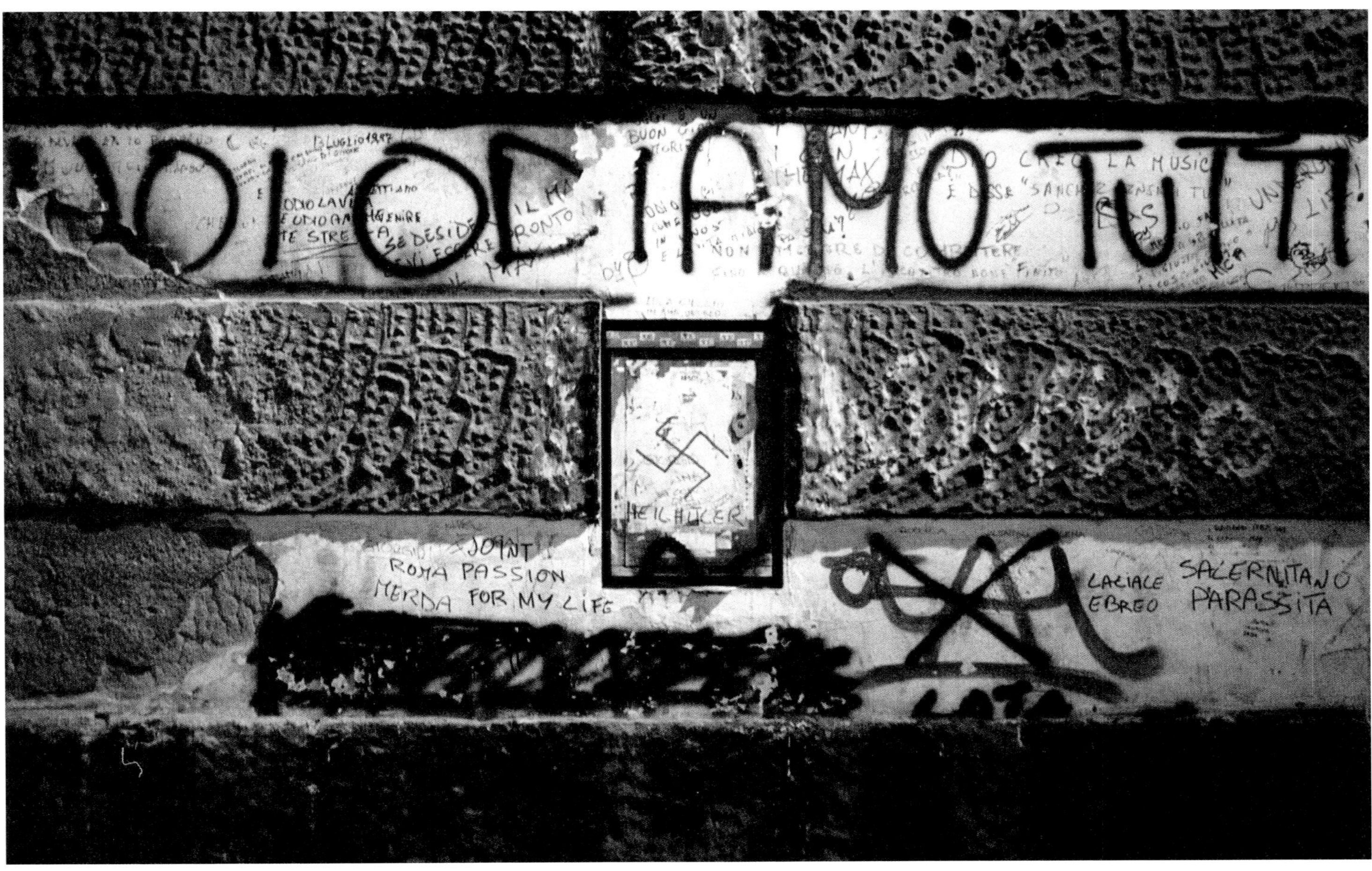


Graffitti by the ‘Mastiffs’, Napoli, October 2002 (MS)

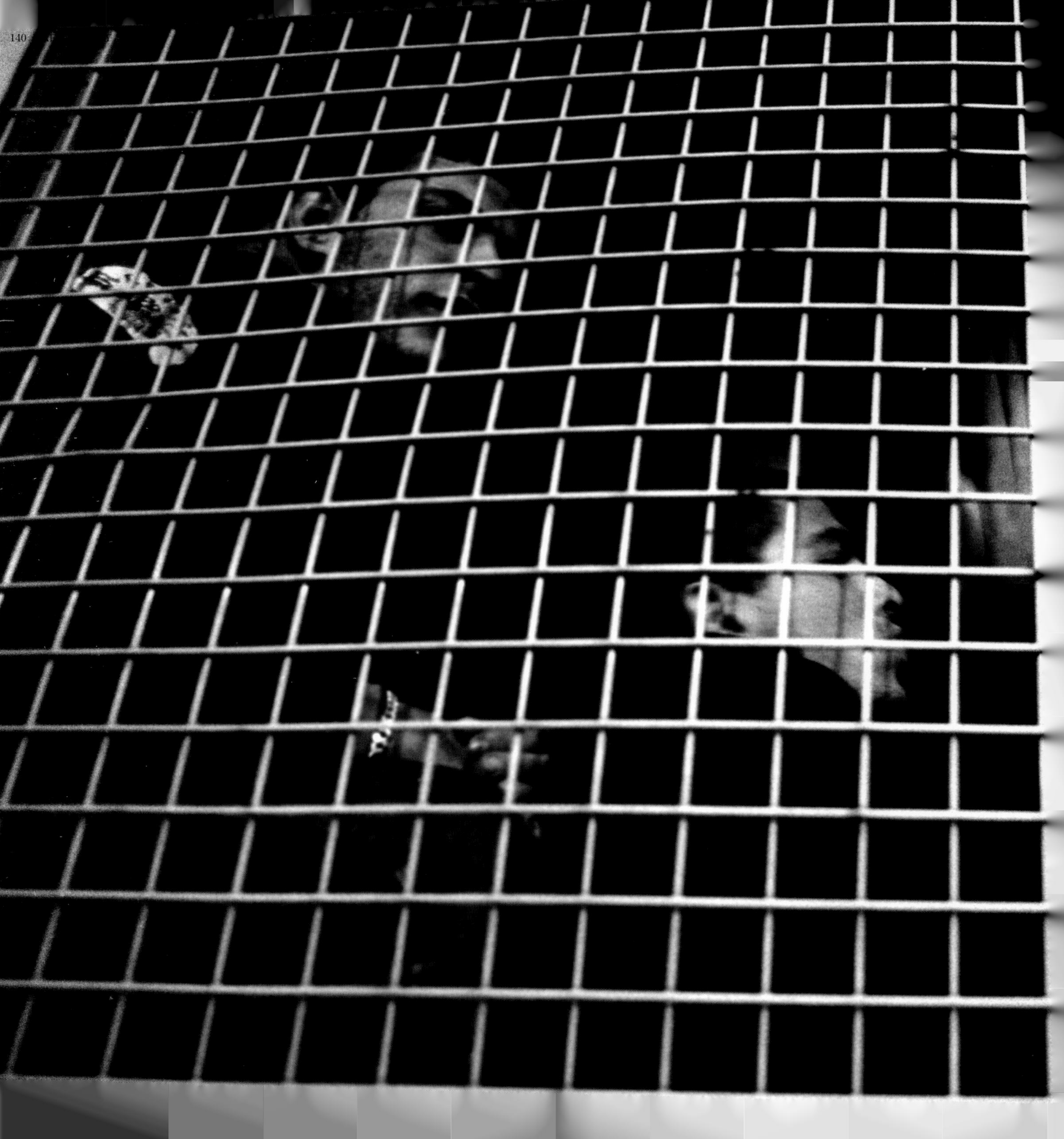

The 'Mastiffs', Napoli, October 2002 (MS)

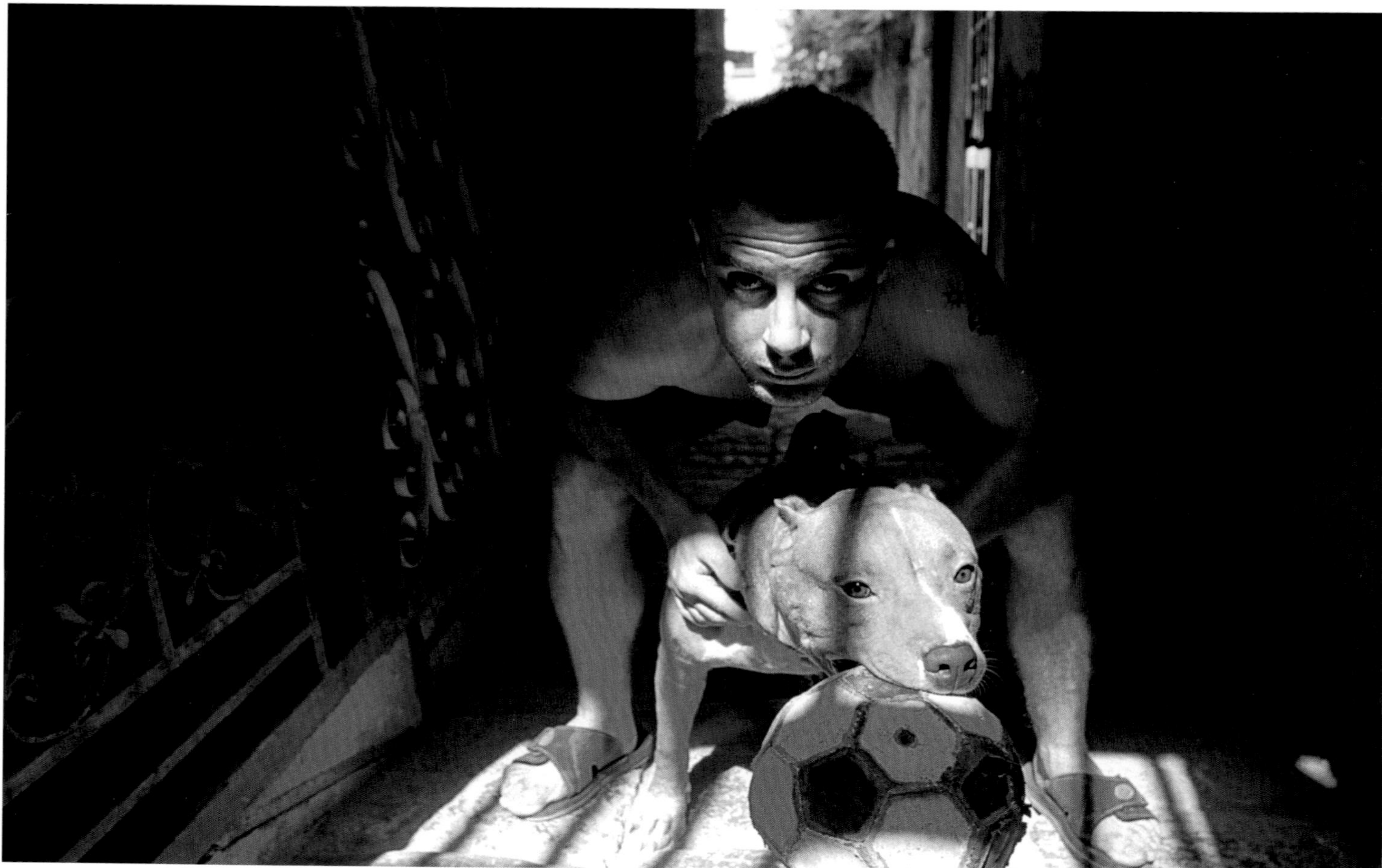

Napoli, June 2002 (MS)

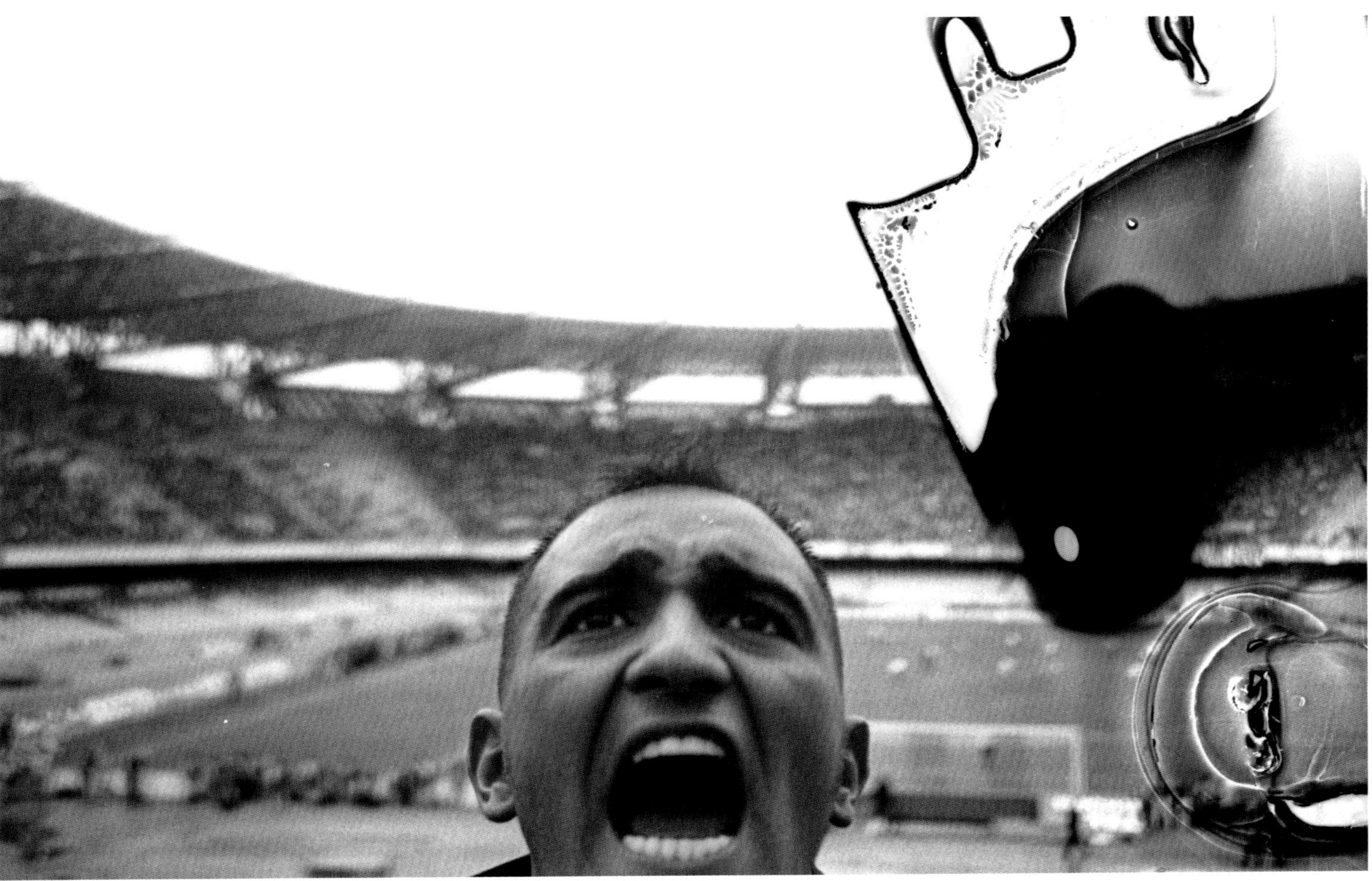

The 'Mastiffs', Napoli, October 2002 (MS)

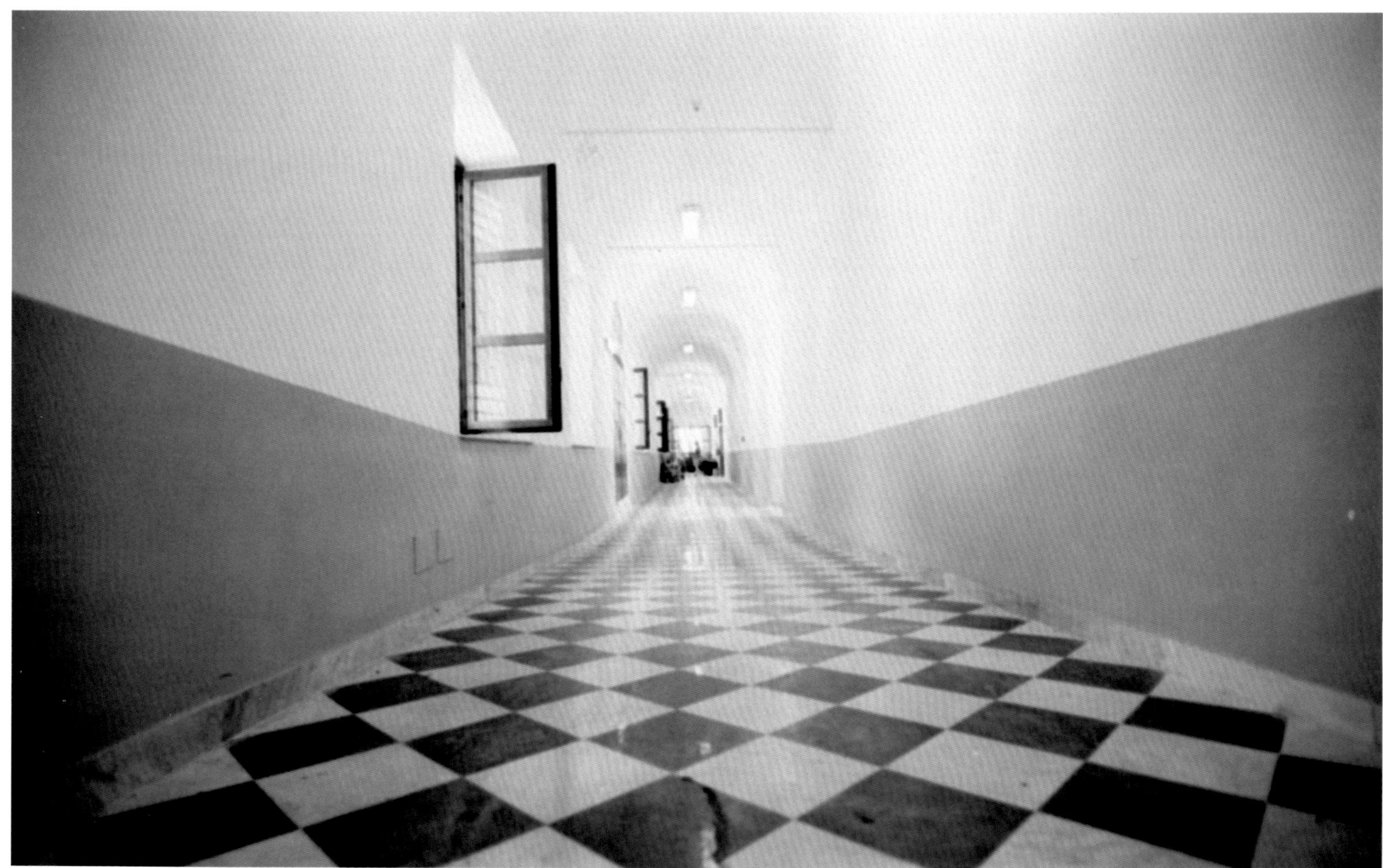

*Above and right* Malaspina Prison, Palermo, July 2003 (RS)

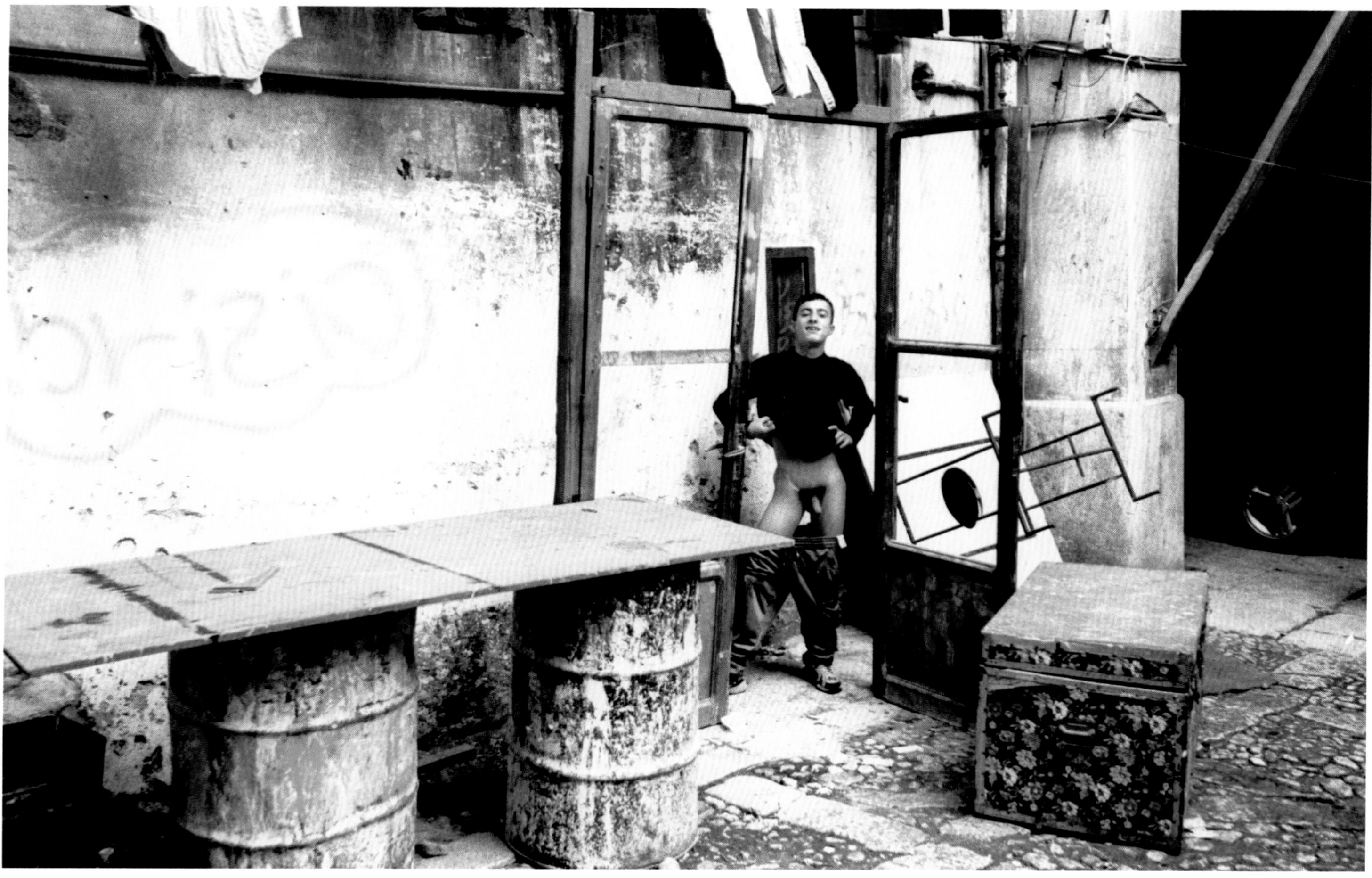

57% of Italians admit a feeling of impotence in the organisation of their lives because of the uncertainty of the future, compared to 47% throughout Europe

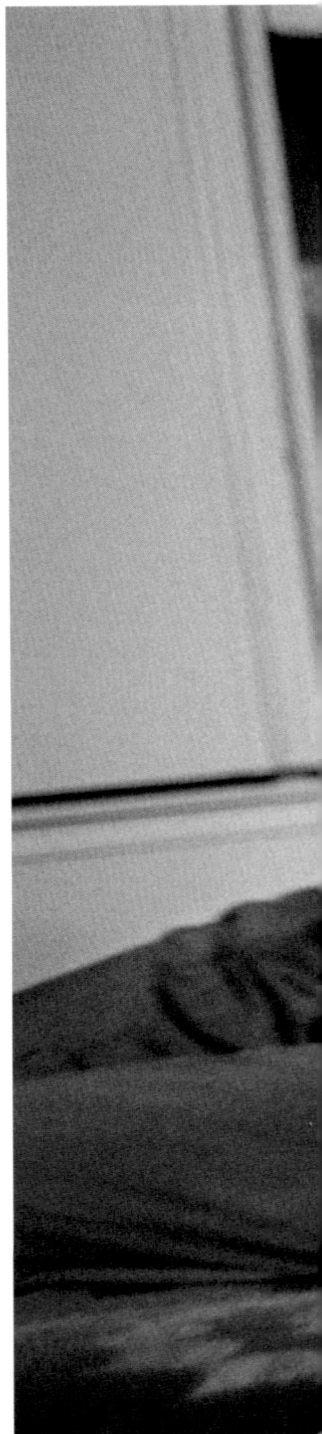

Napoli, March 2002 (MS)

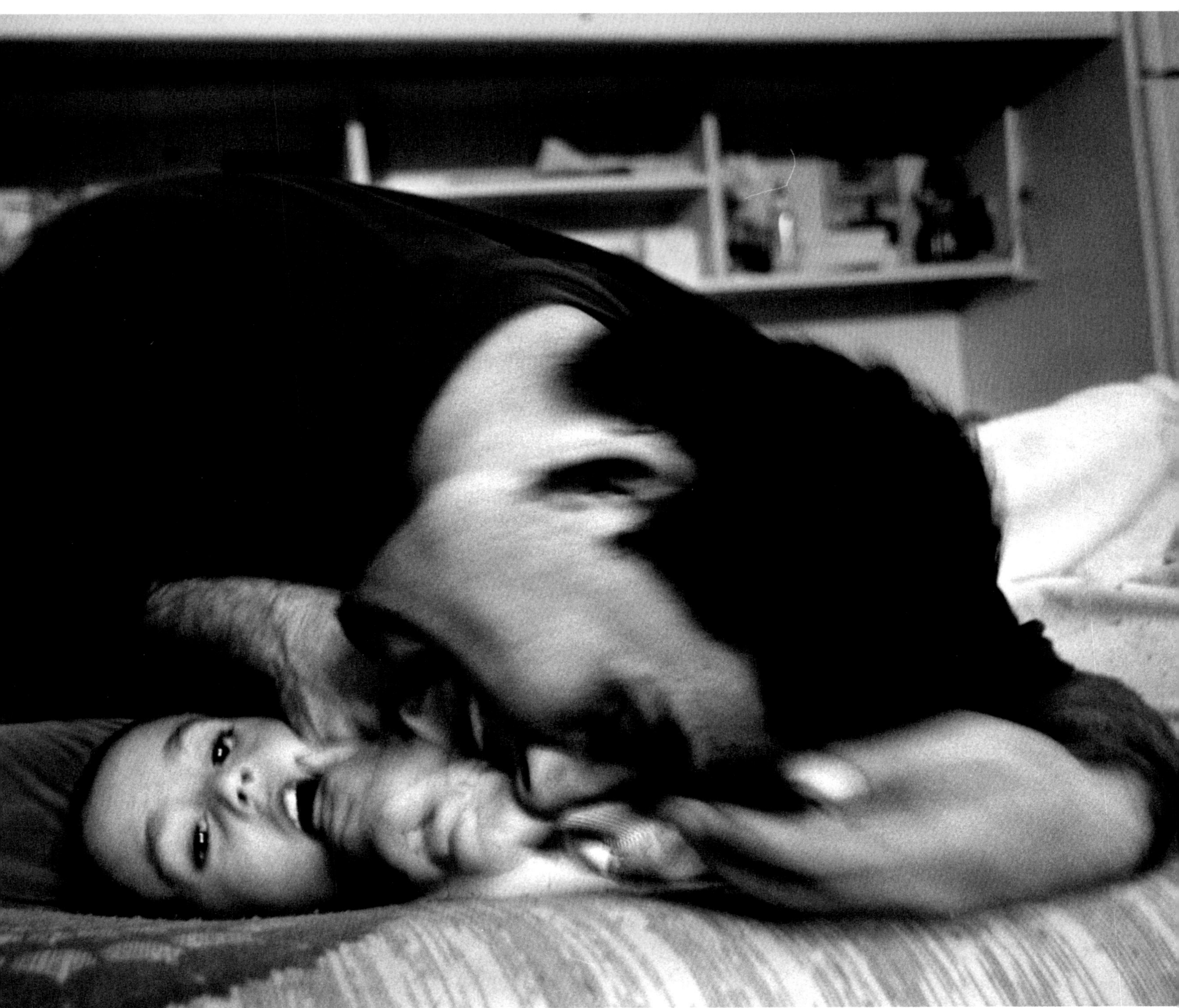

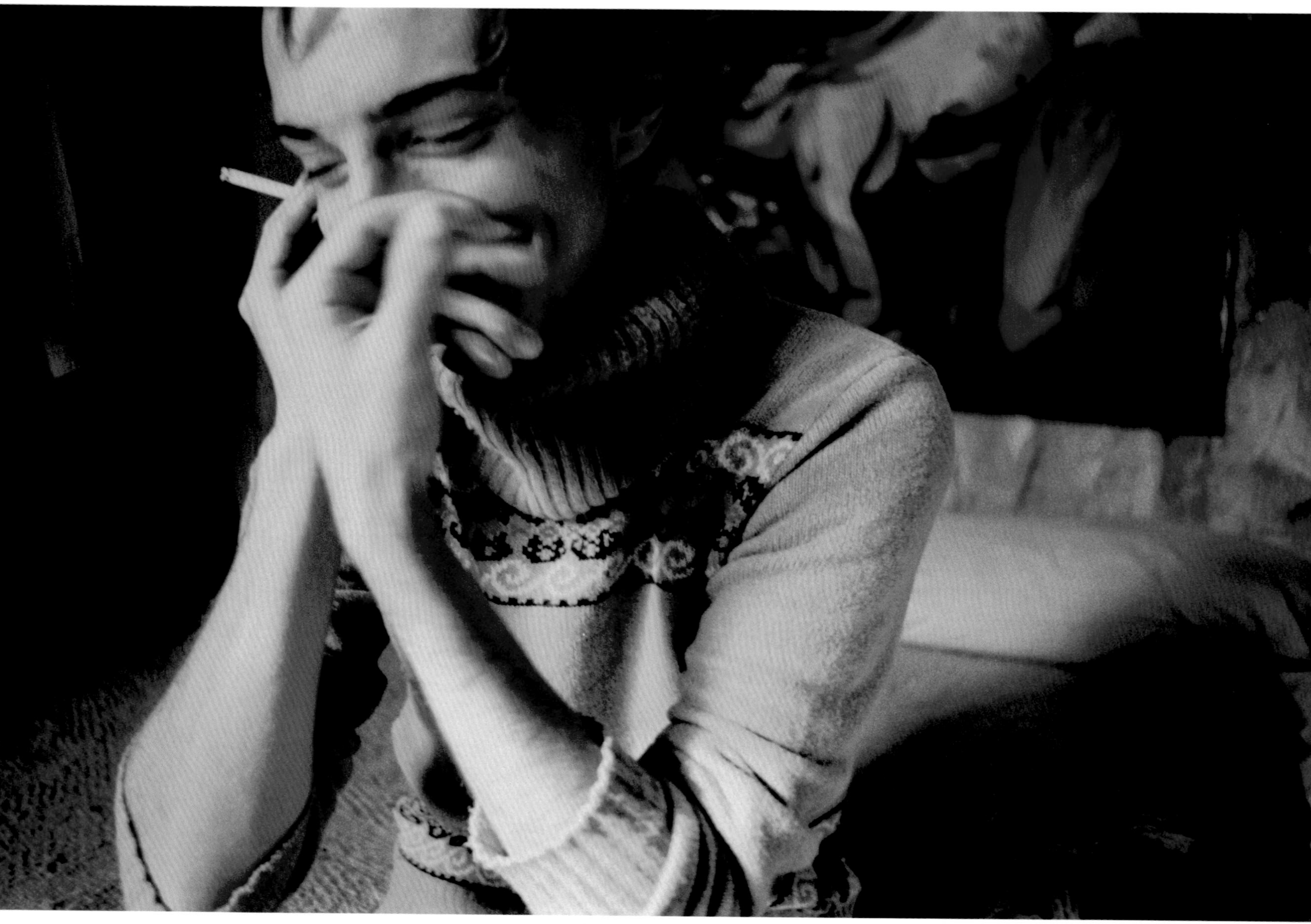

Palermo, July 2003 (RS)

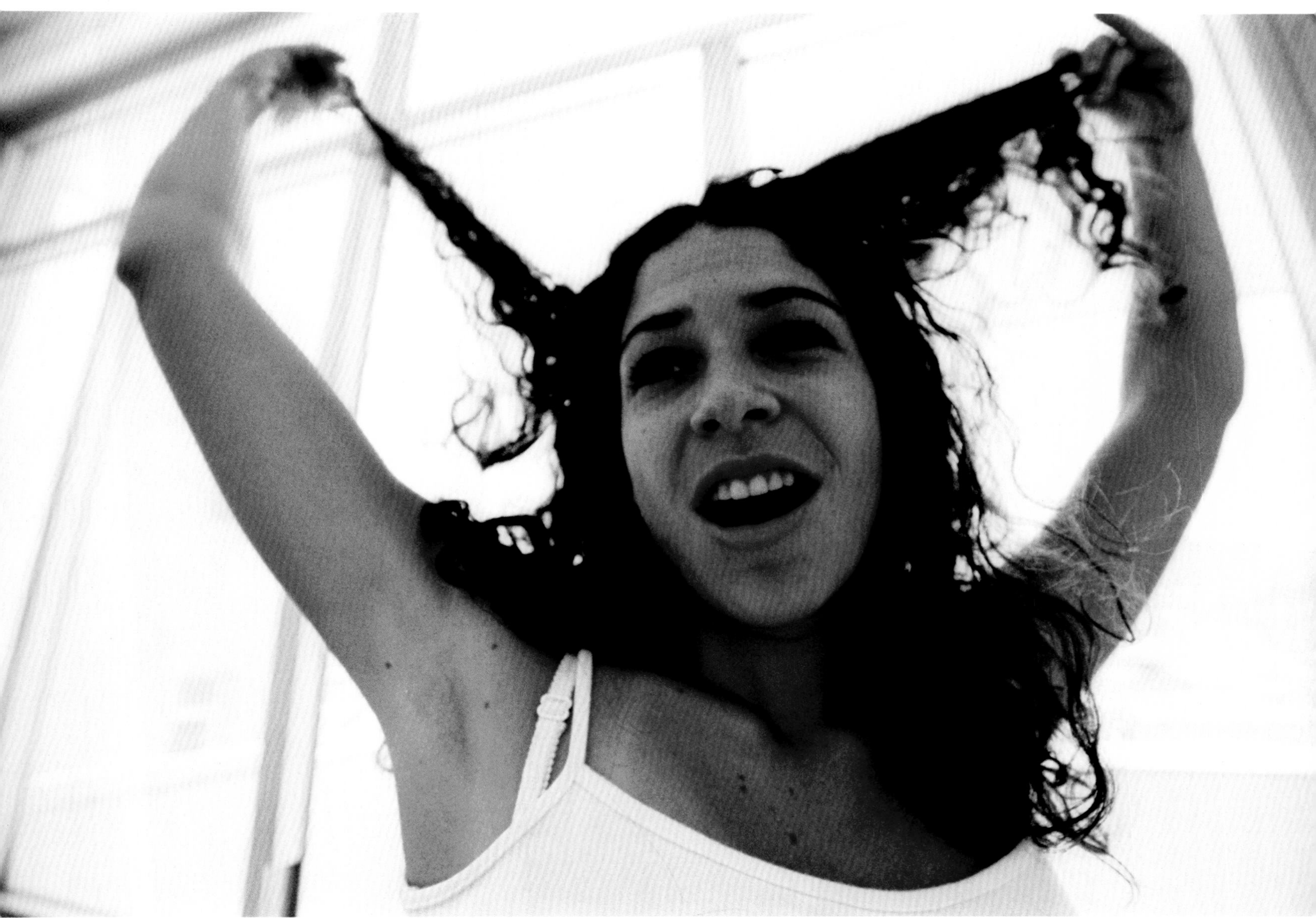

Palermo, August 2004 (RS)

Italians owing more than $1m
excluding their own property increased by 3.7%,
from 188,000 to 195,000

World Wealth Report

Sardinia, August 2005 (MB)

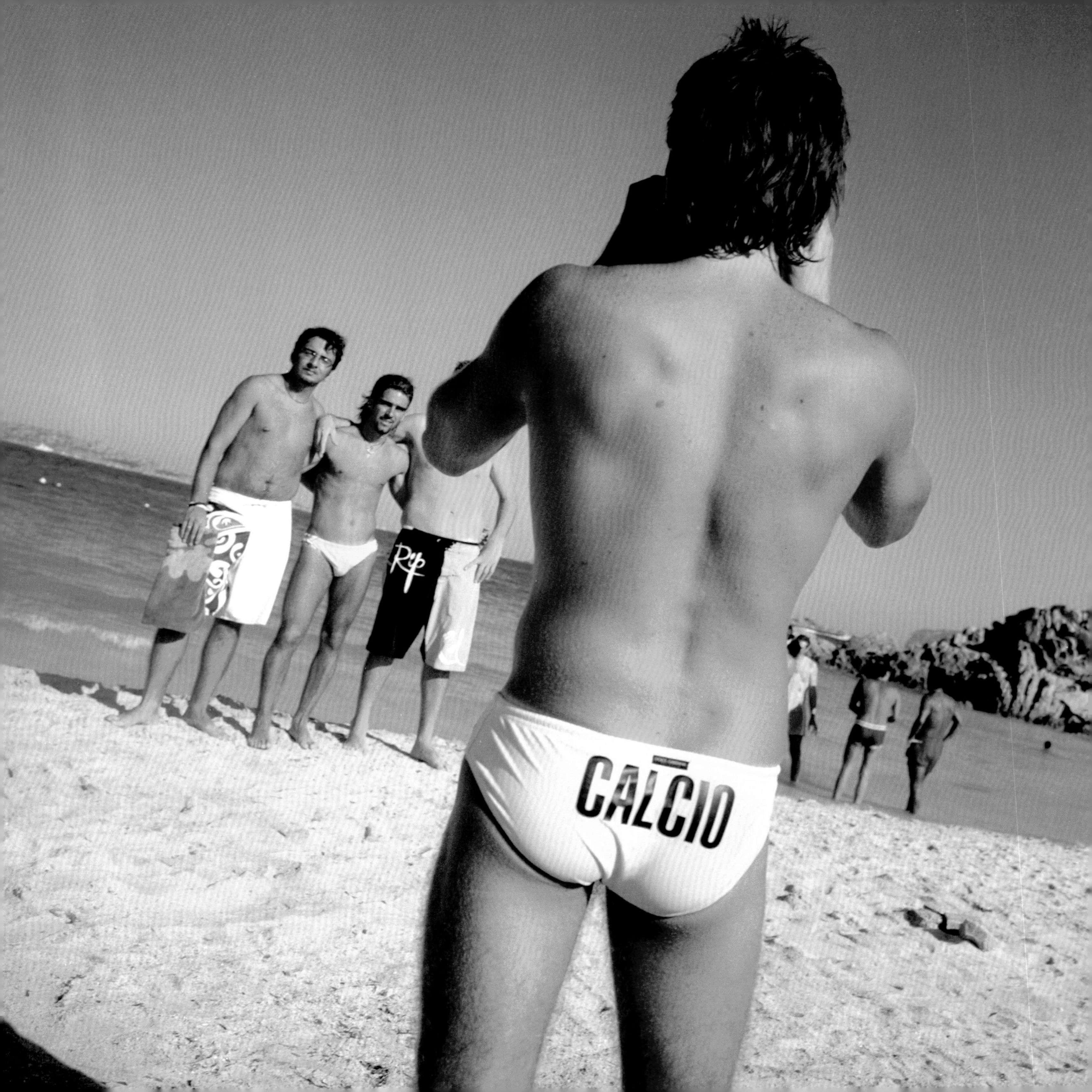
CALCIO

Post-graduate degrees, public and private,
cost respectively 101 million and 87 million Euros,
with an average cost per student of 2,651 and 7,500 Euros

Bologna to Lecce train, May 2005 (MB)

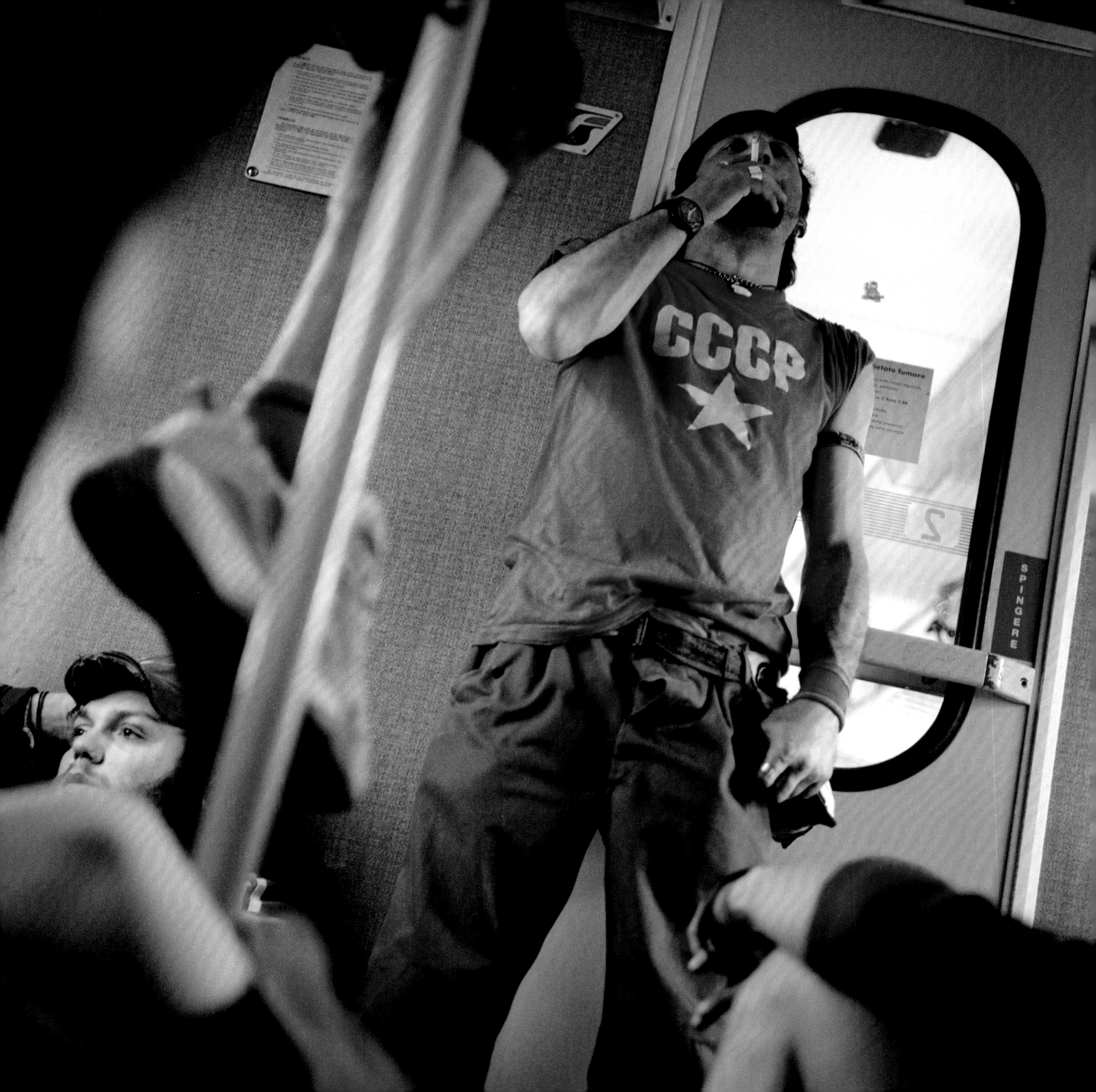
CCCP
SPINGERE

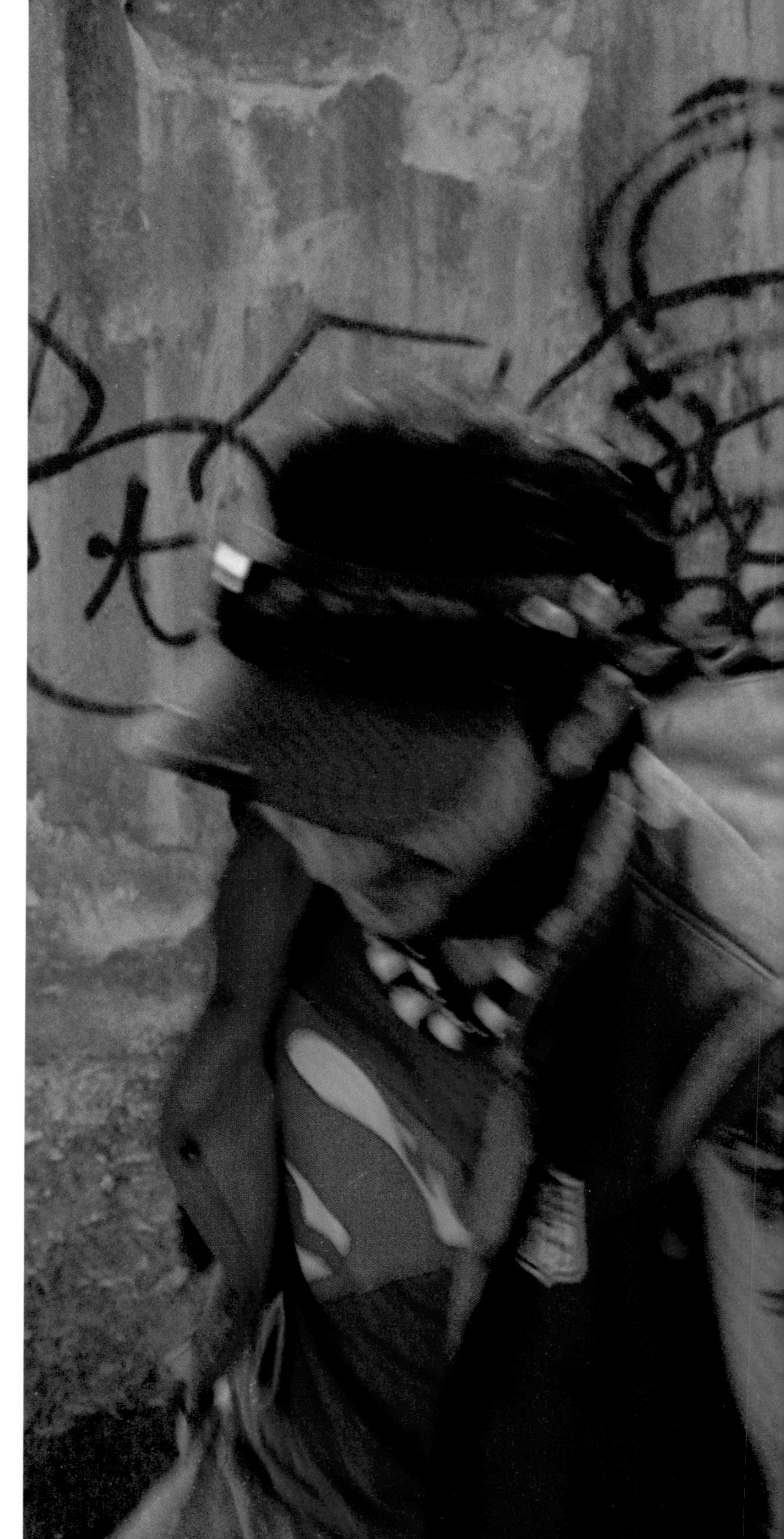

Bari, July 2004 (EM)

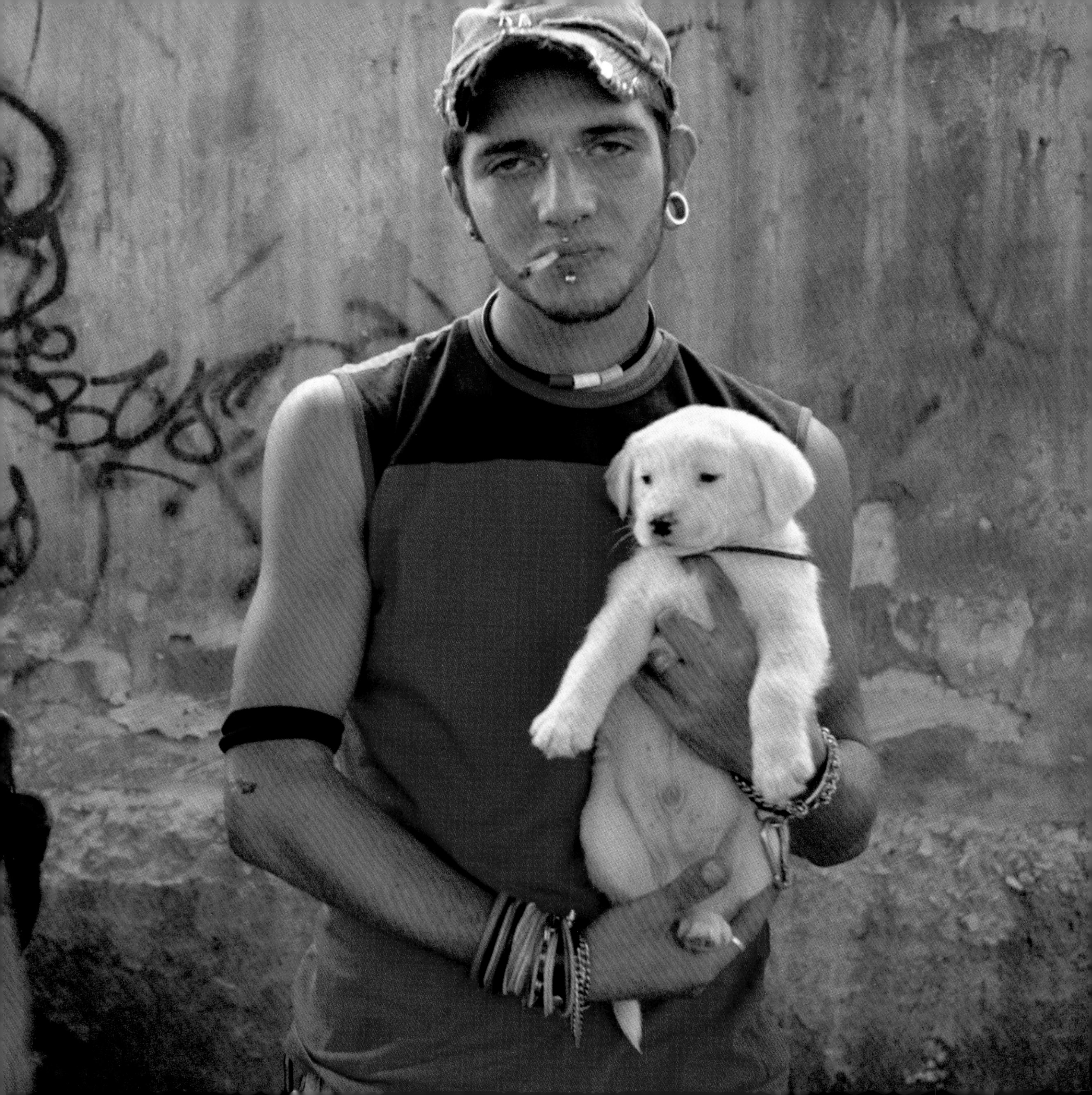

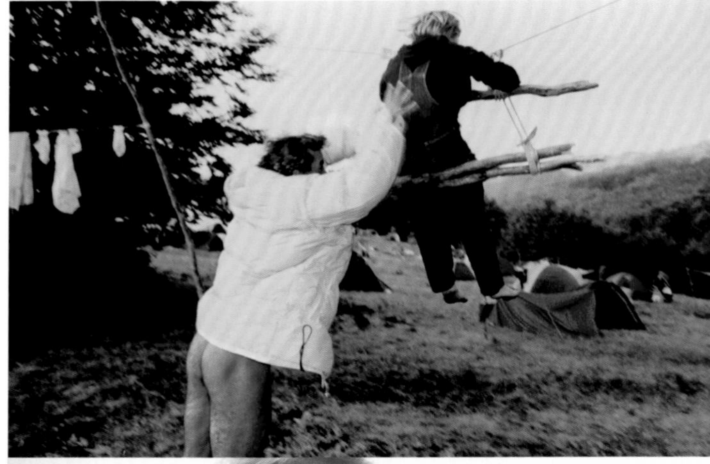

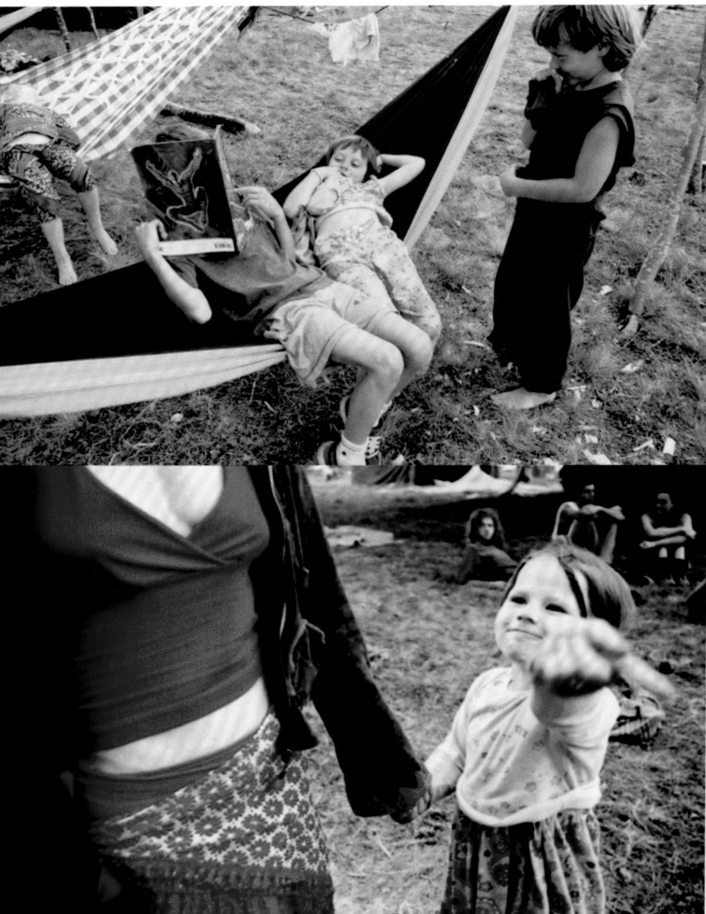

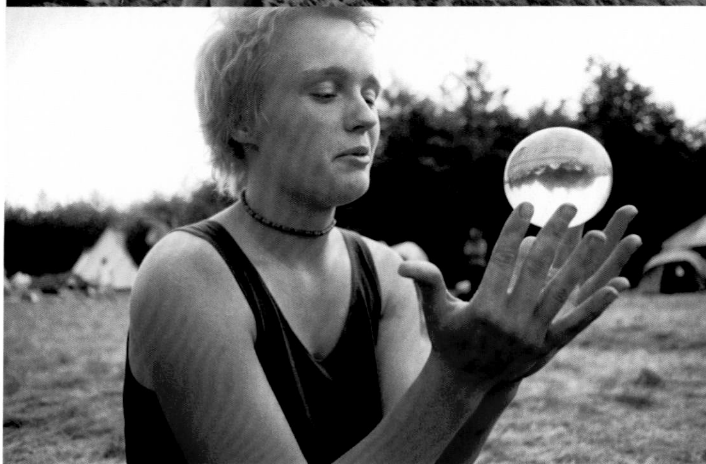

*Above and right* Rainbow rally, Abetone, September 2003 (RS)
*Following page* The Billionaire club owned by Flavio Briatore, Sardinia, August 2005 (MS)

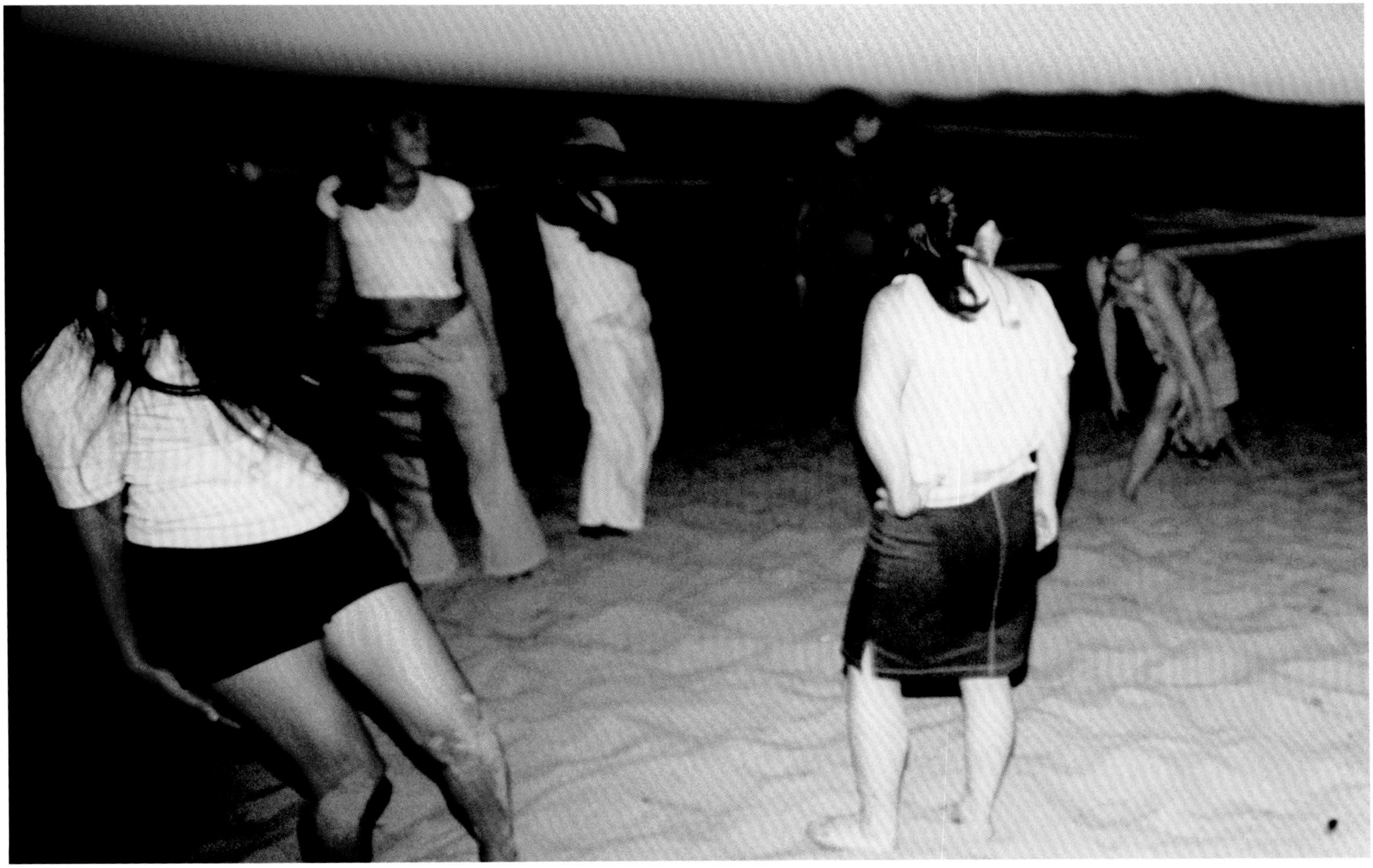

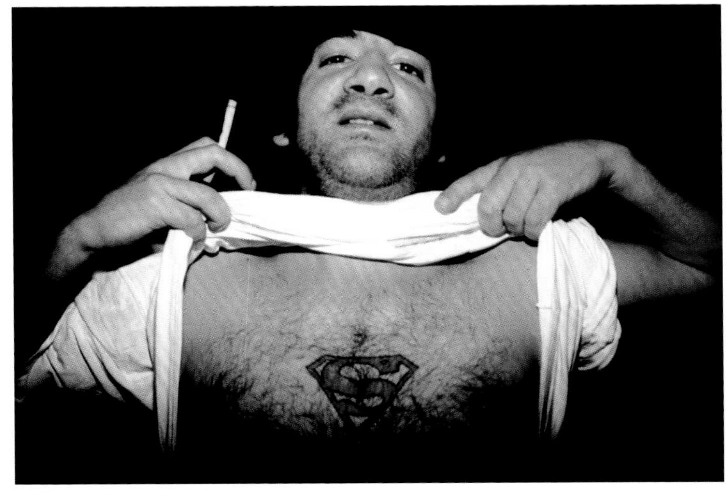

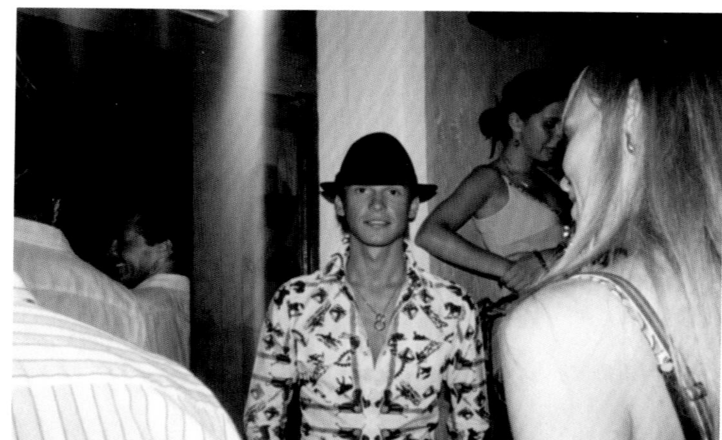

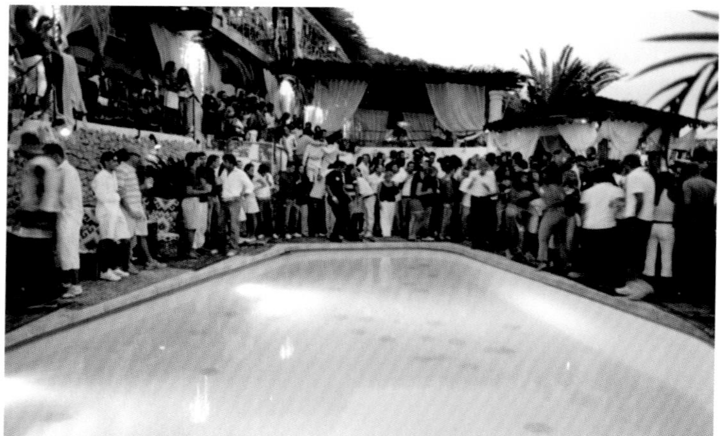

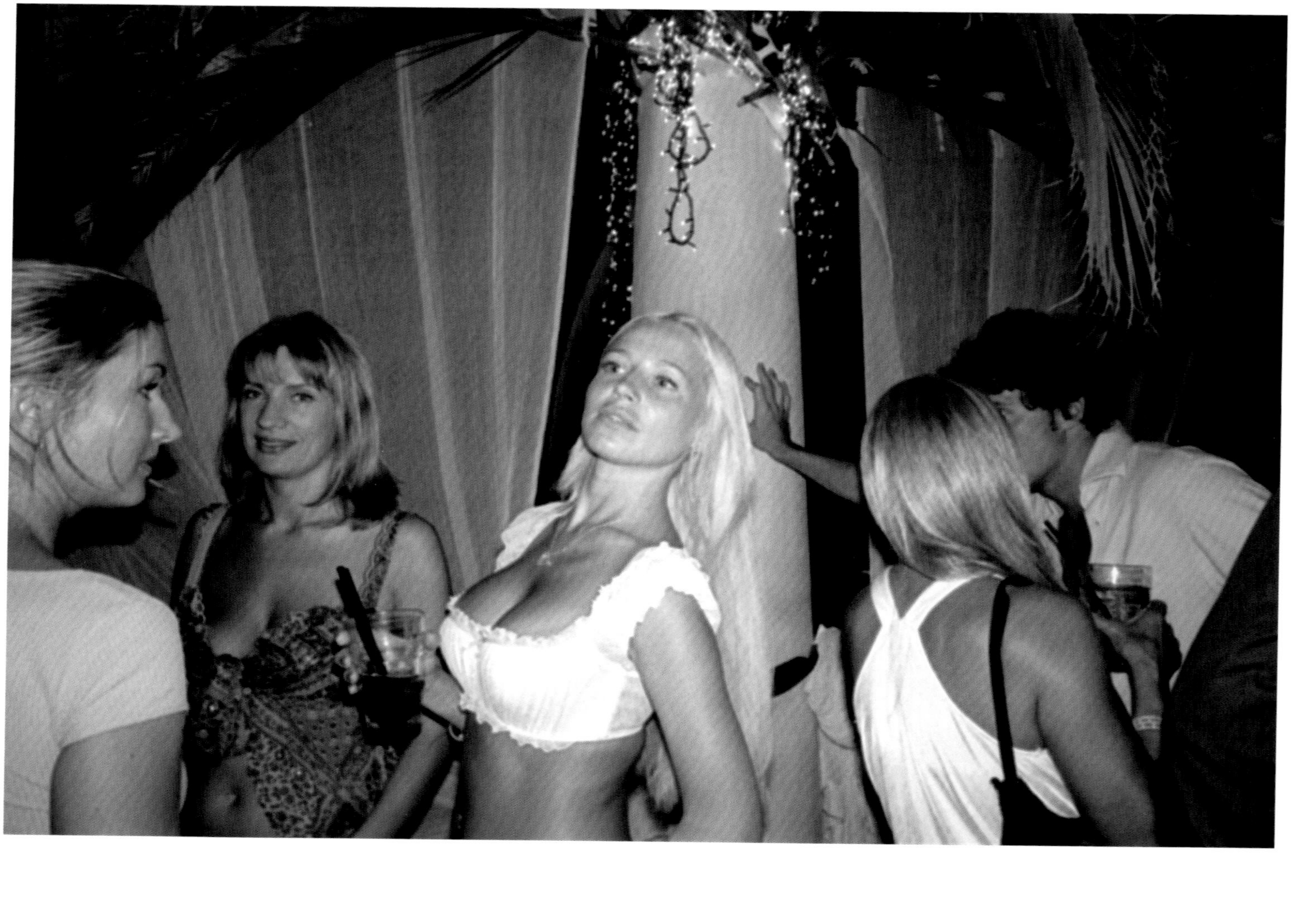

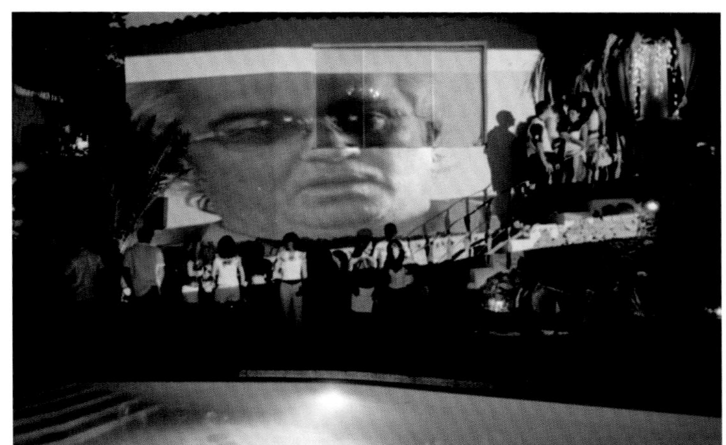

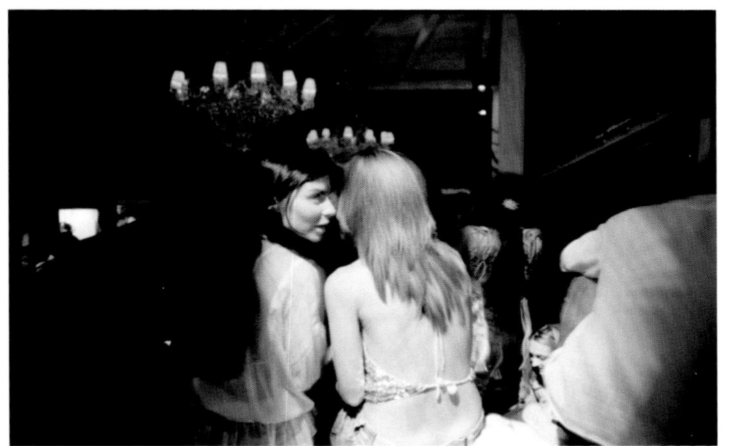

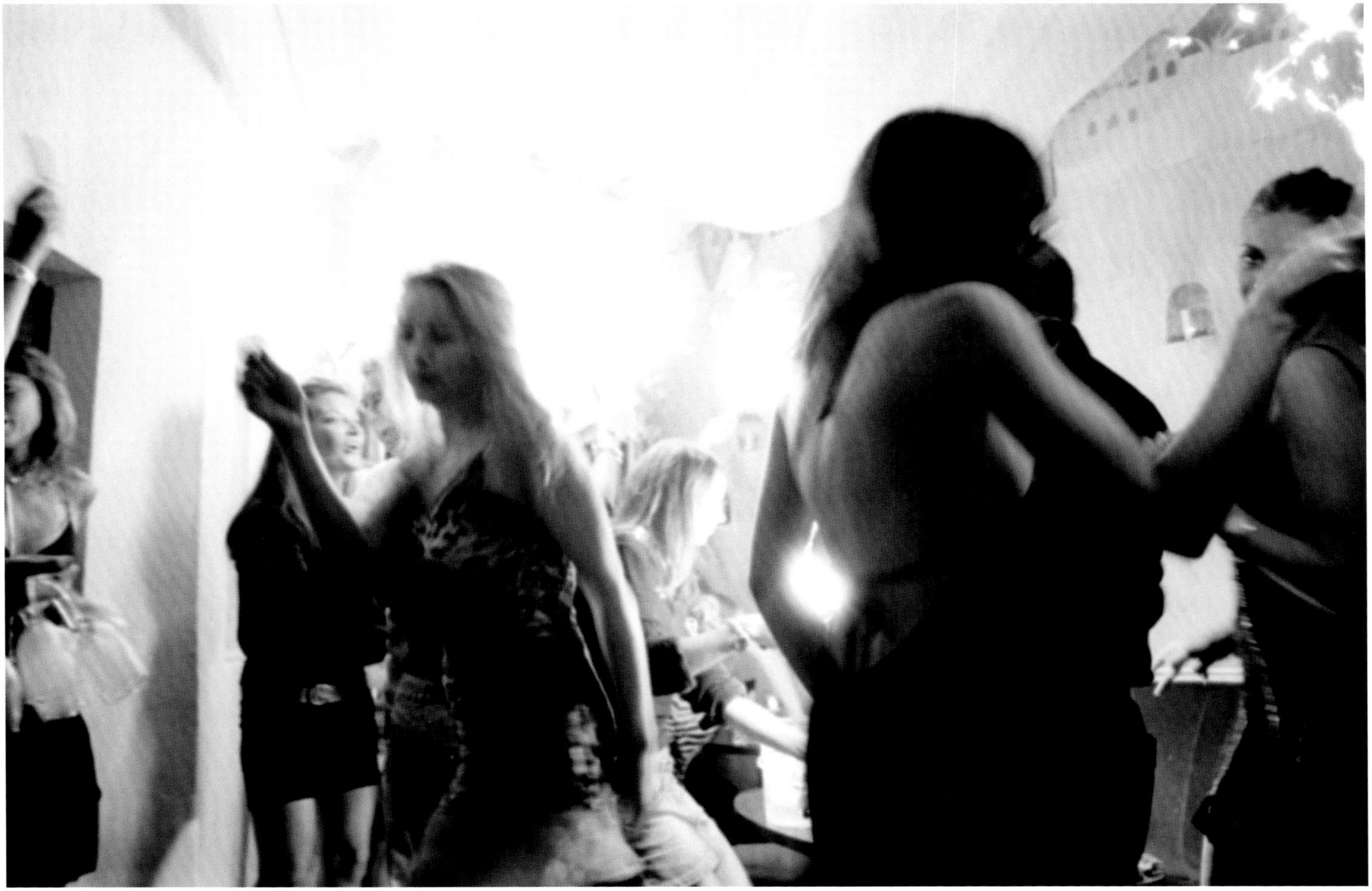

VIRUS

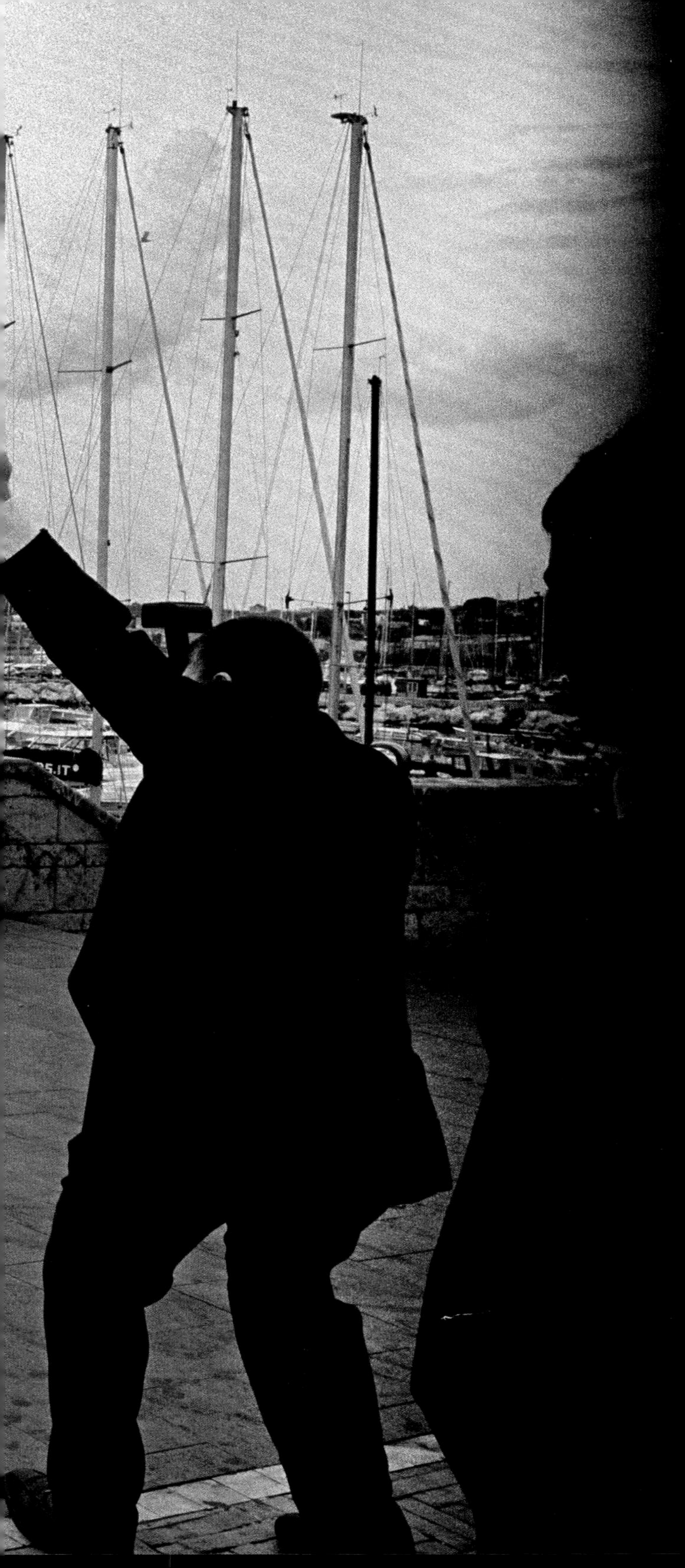

In the first eight months of 2005 approximately 6,000 new cars valued at 80,000 euro or more were registered, an increase of 12.6%

20.3% of Italians leaving education have a university degree, 42.7% have secondary school qualifications and 36.9% finish school with no degree

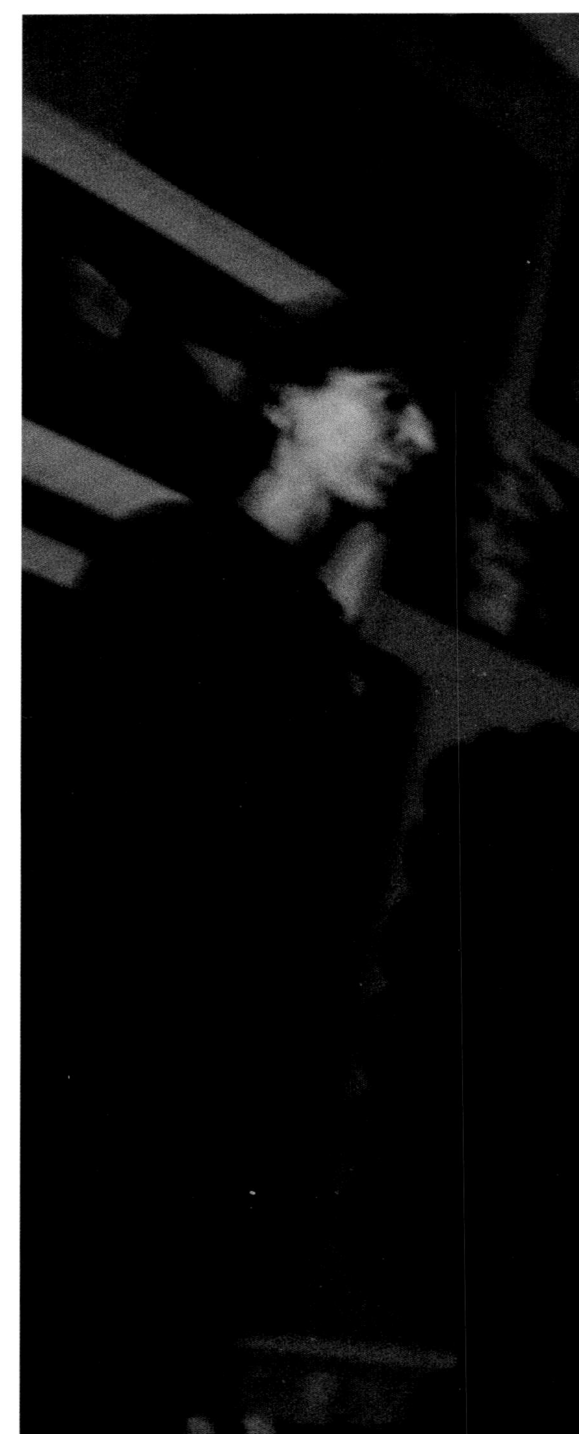

*Right* Napoli, October 2005 (MS)
*Following page* Capri, July 2005 (EM)

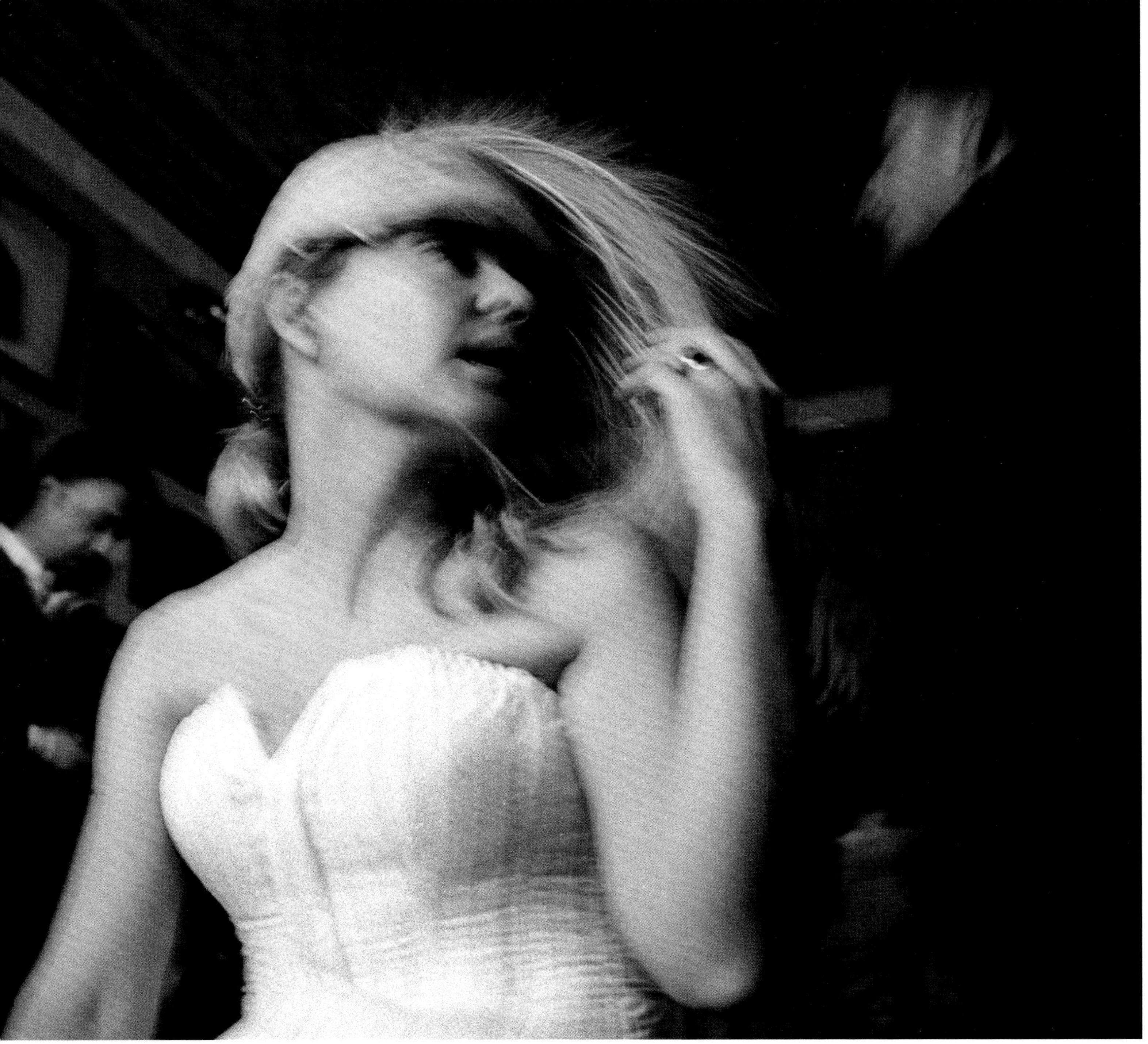

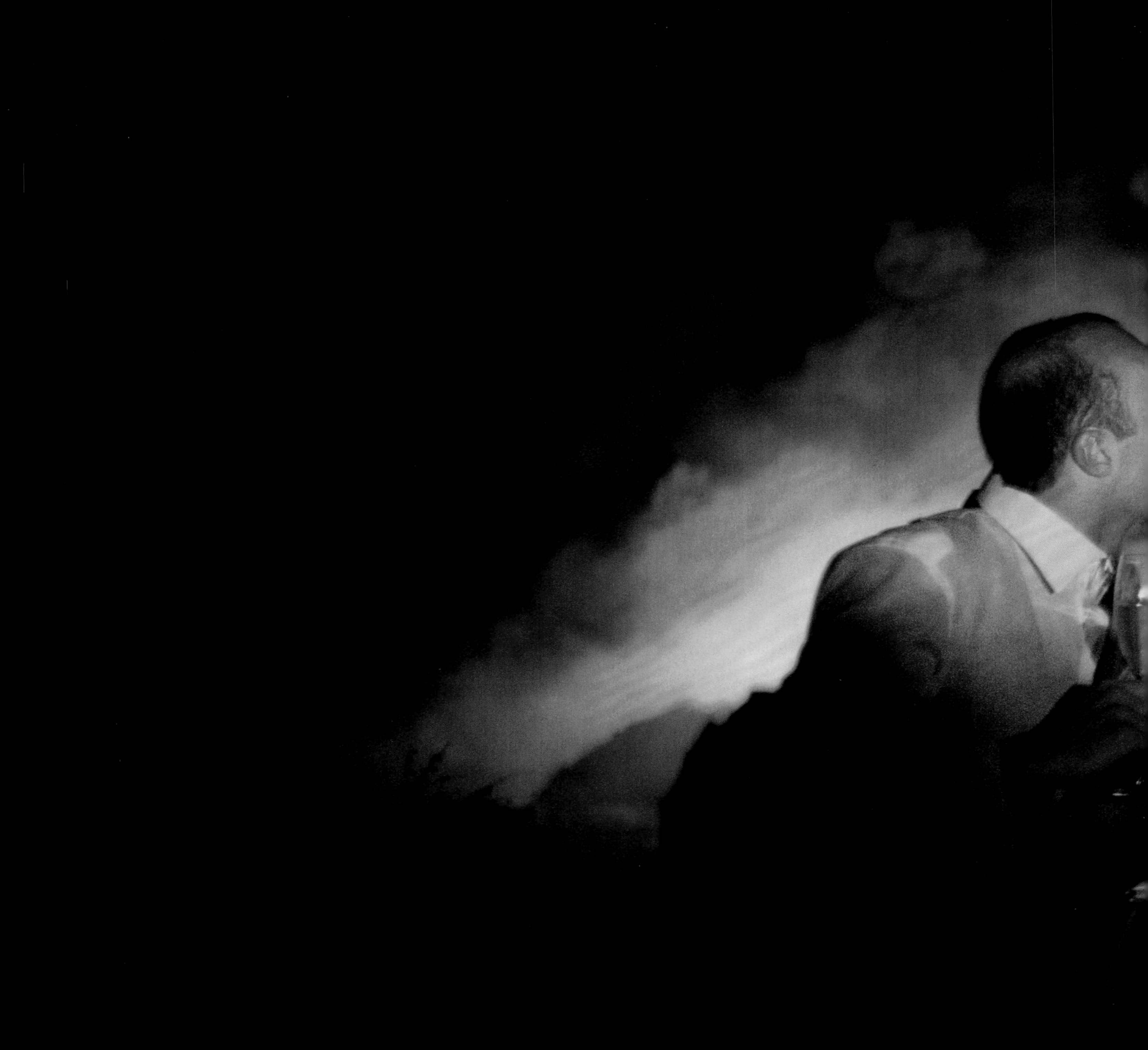

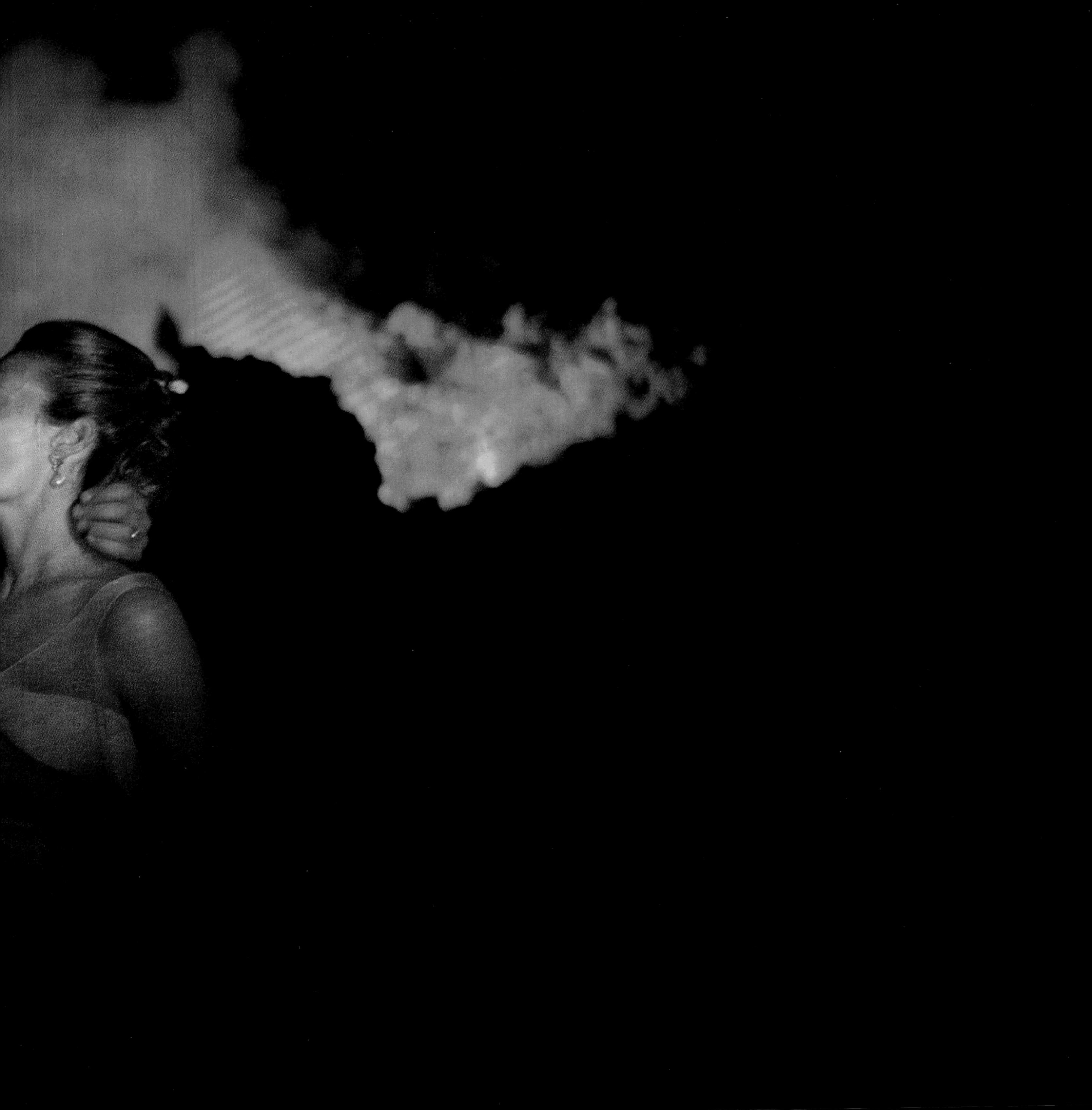

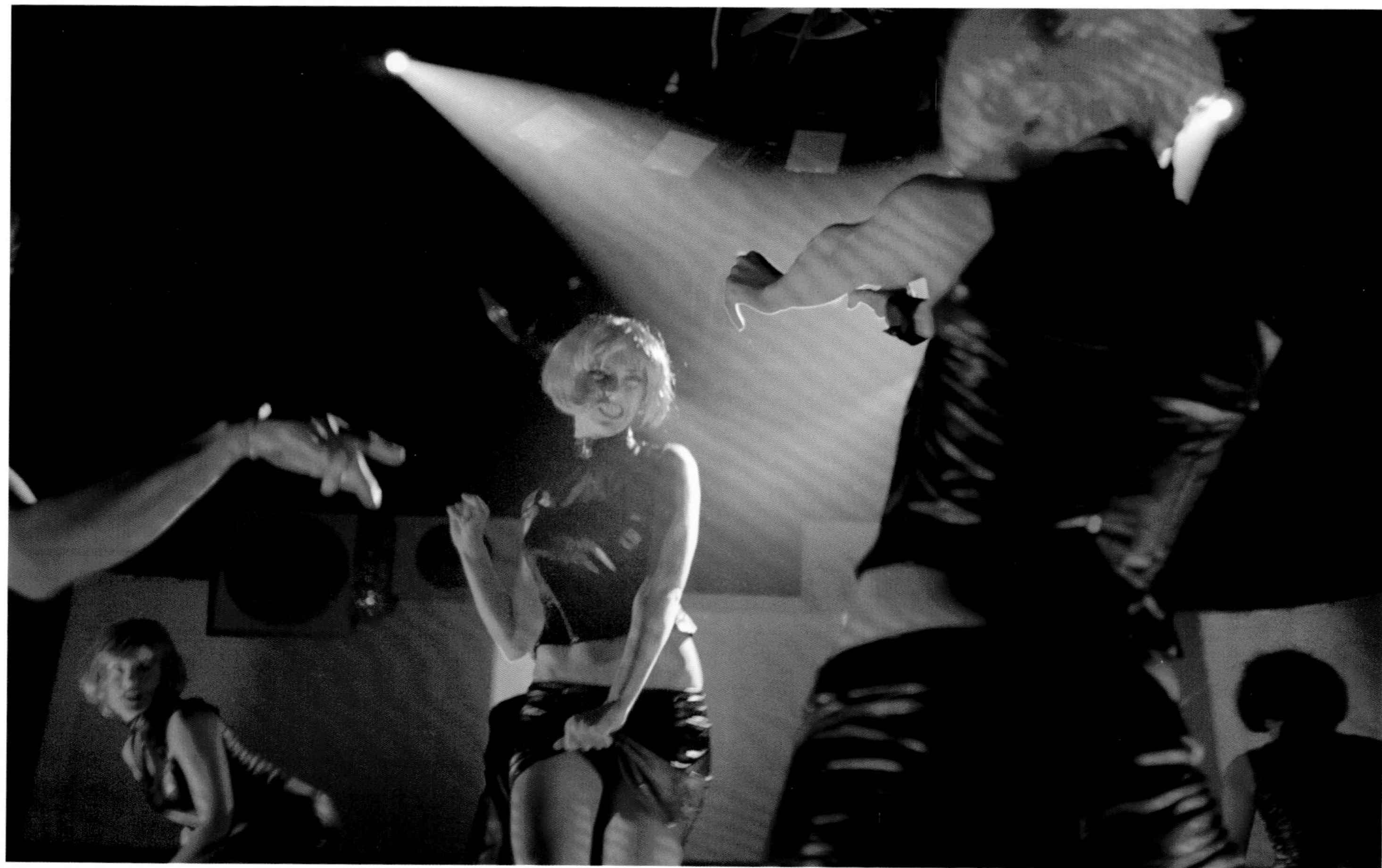

Milano, October 2003 (EM)

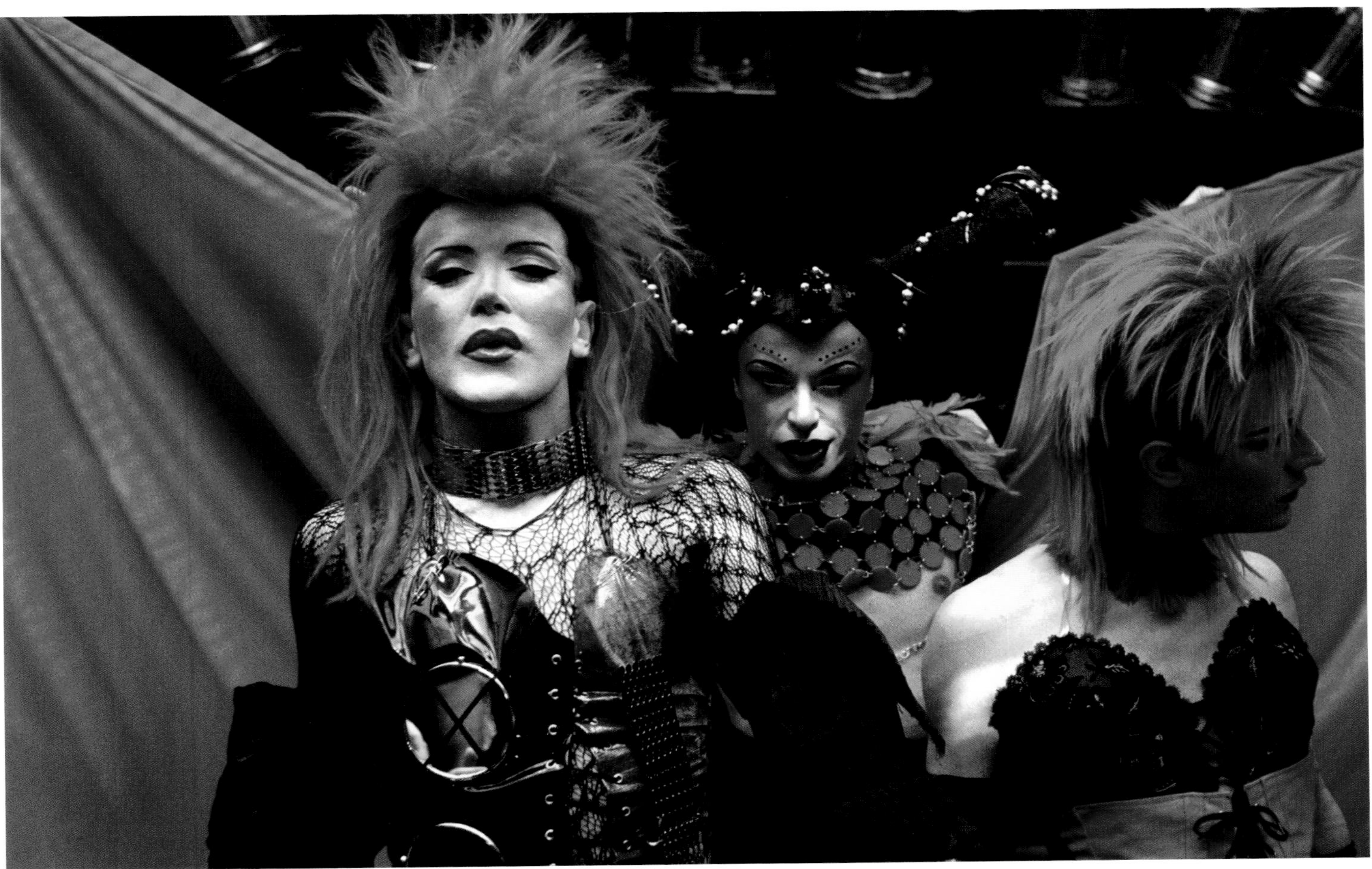

Roma, January 2002 (EM)

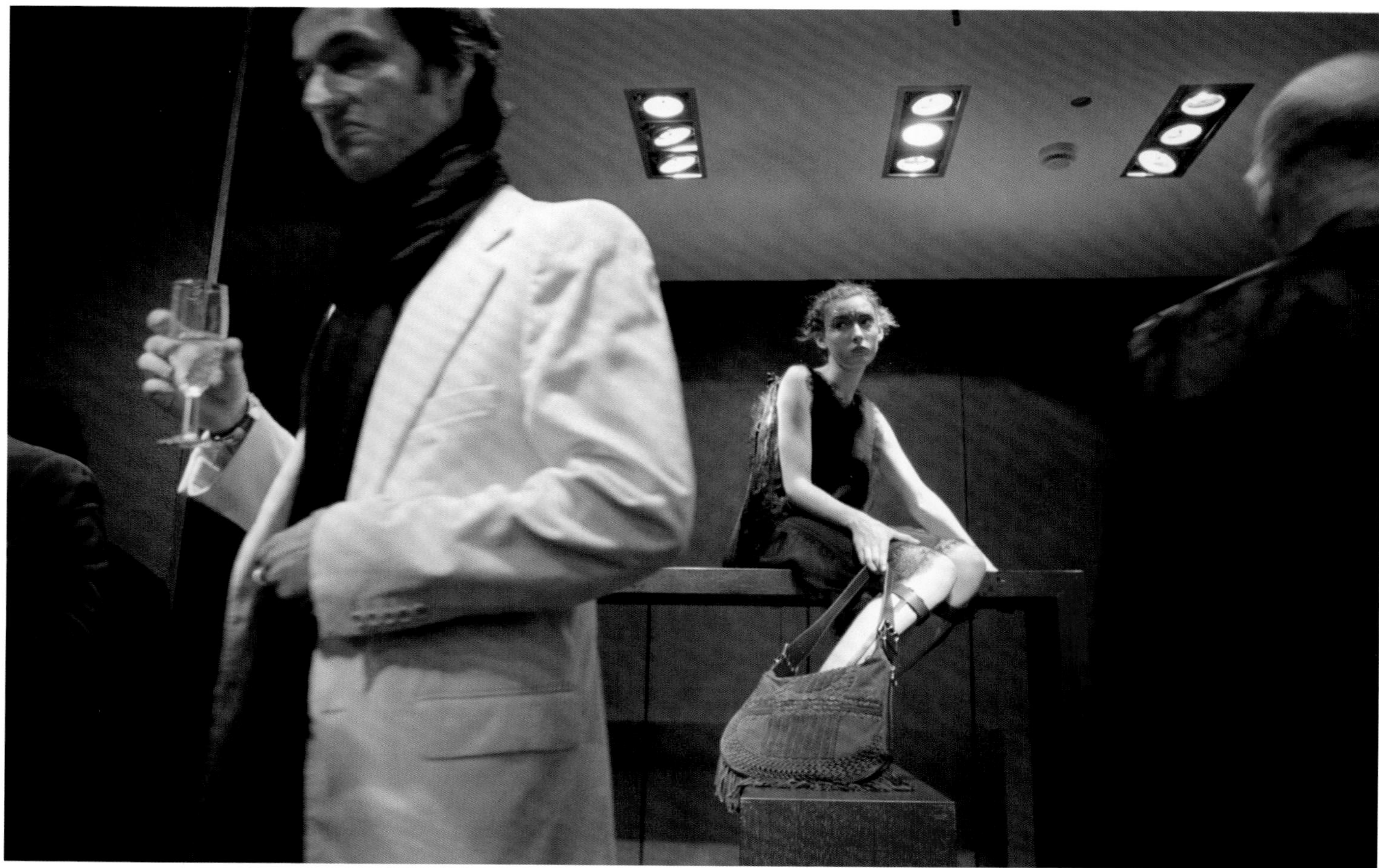

Roma, October 2003 (EM)

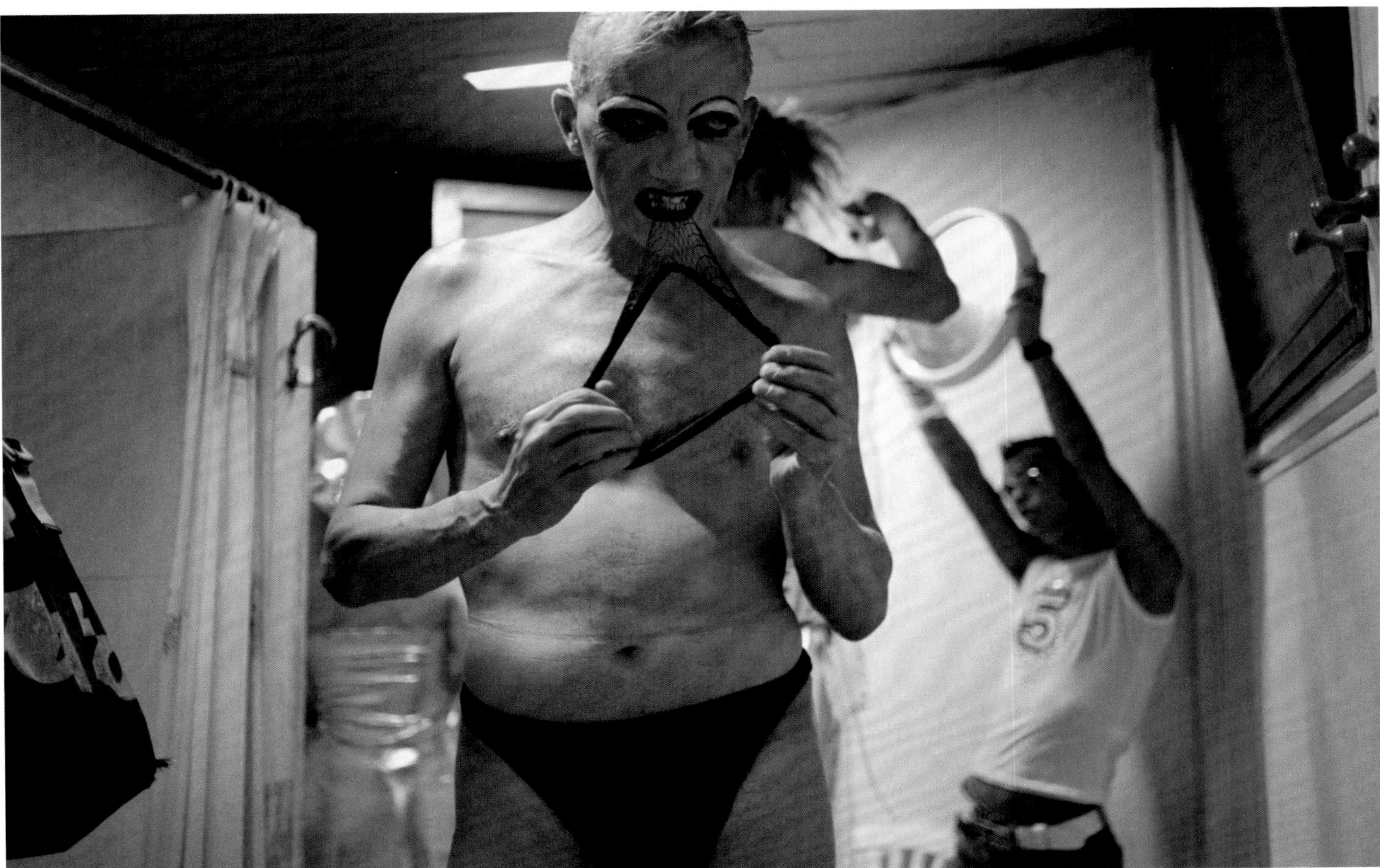

Roma, July 2003 (EM)

10% of the richest families own
almost half of net Italian wealth

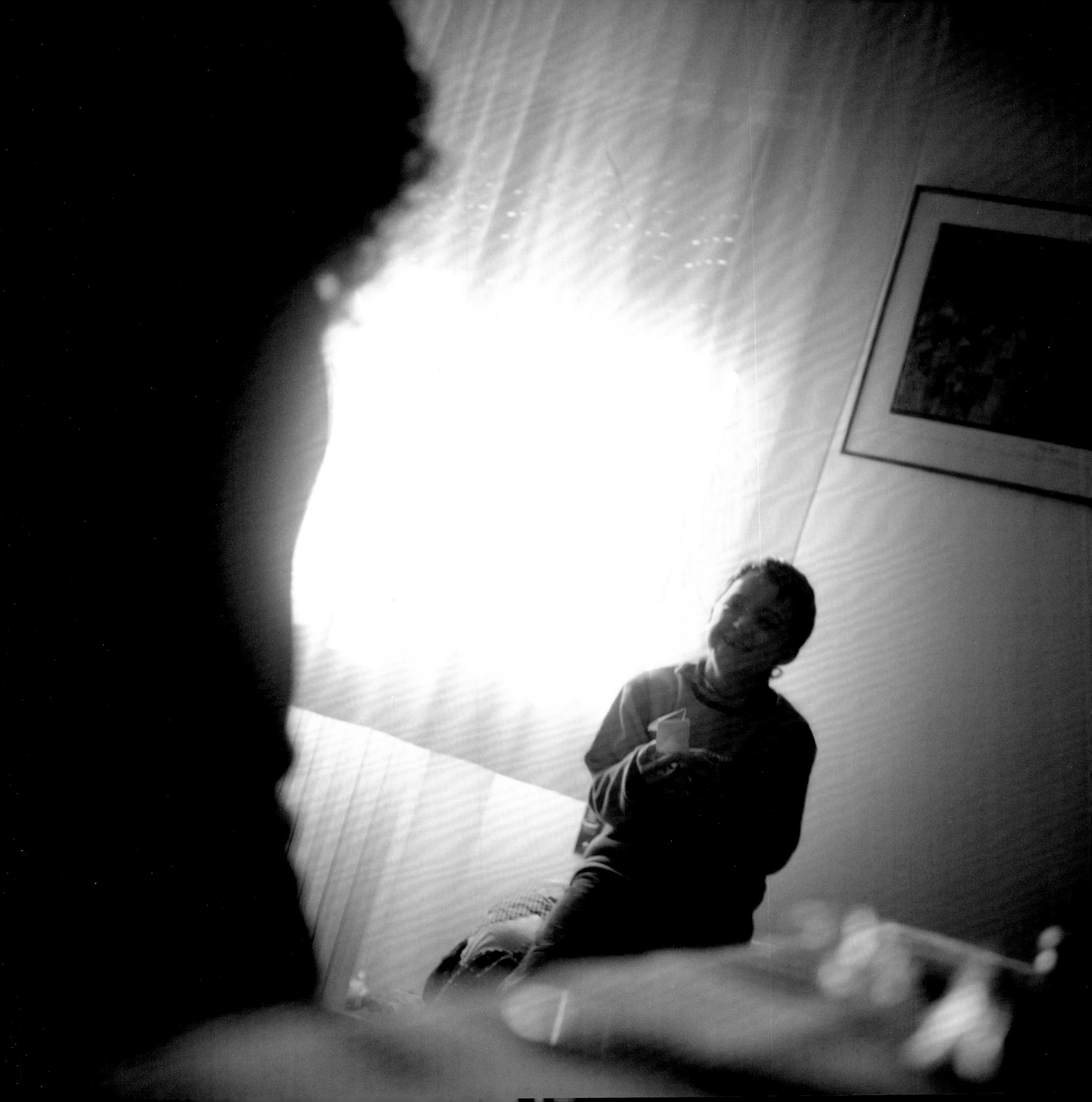

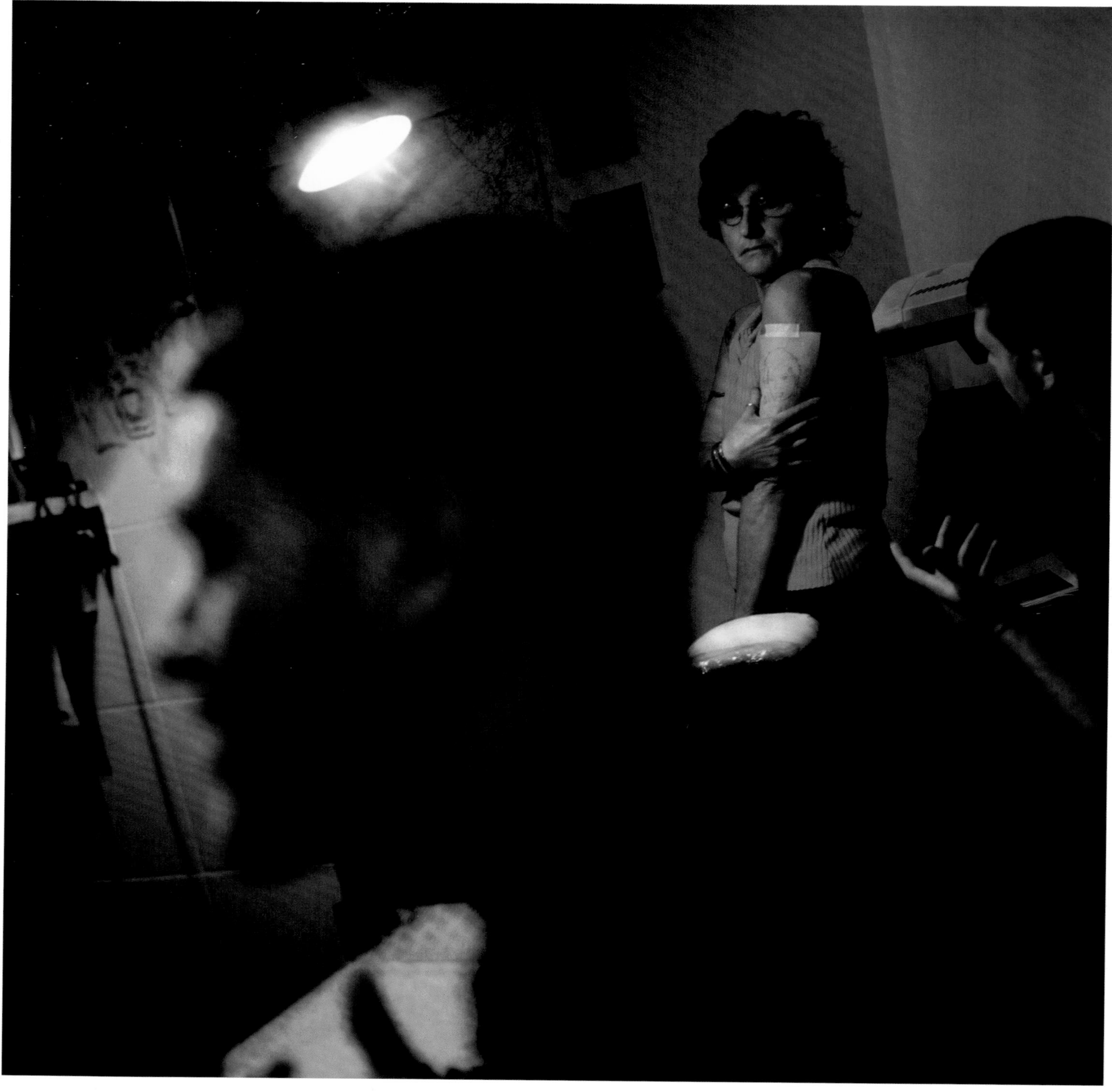

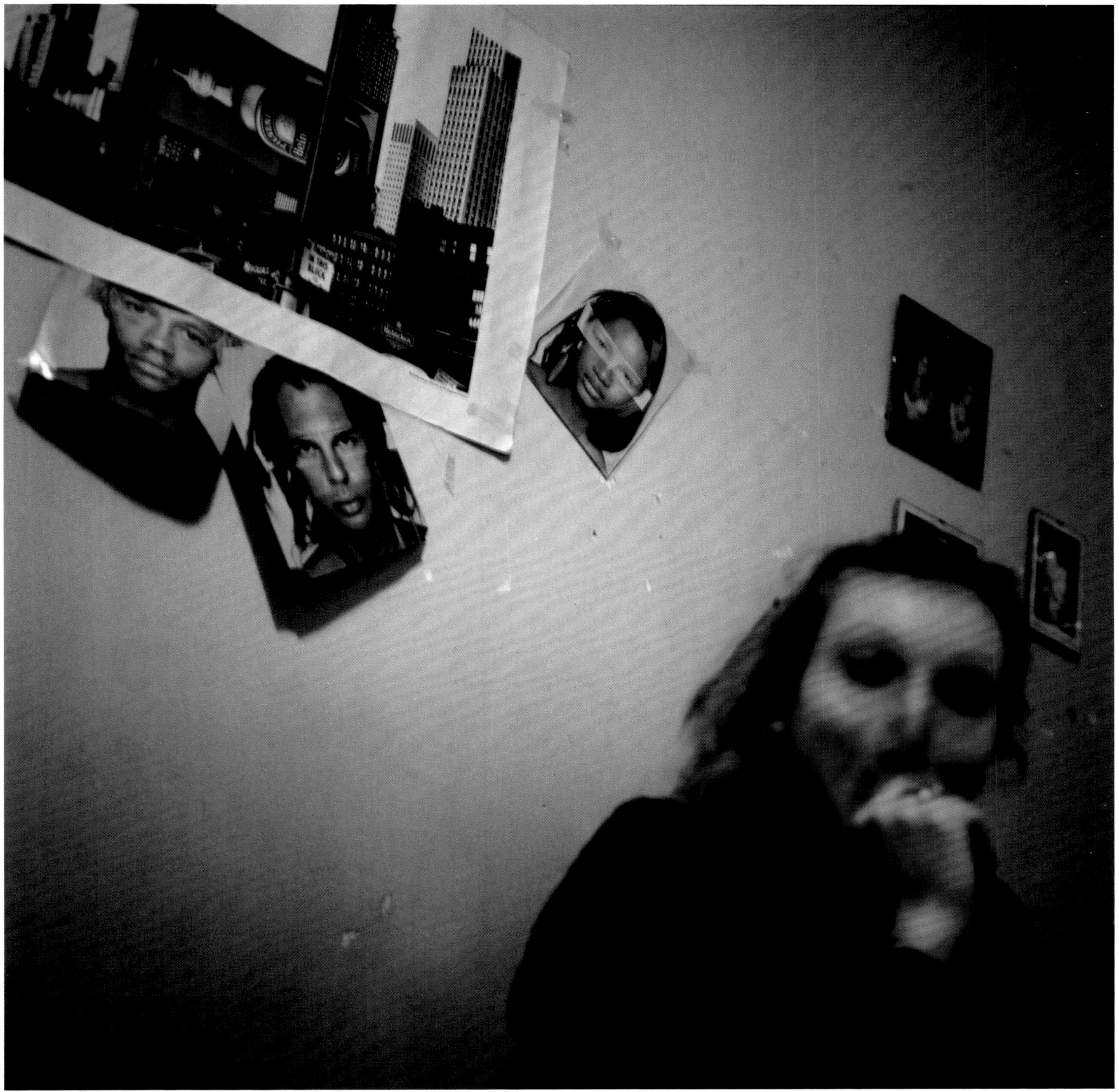

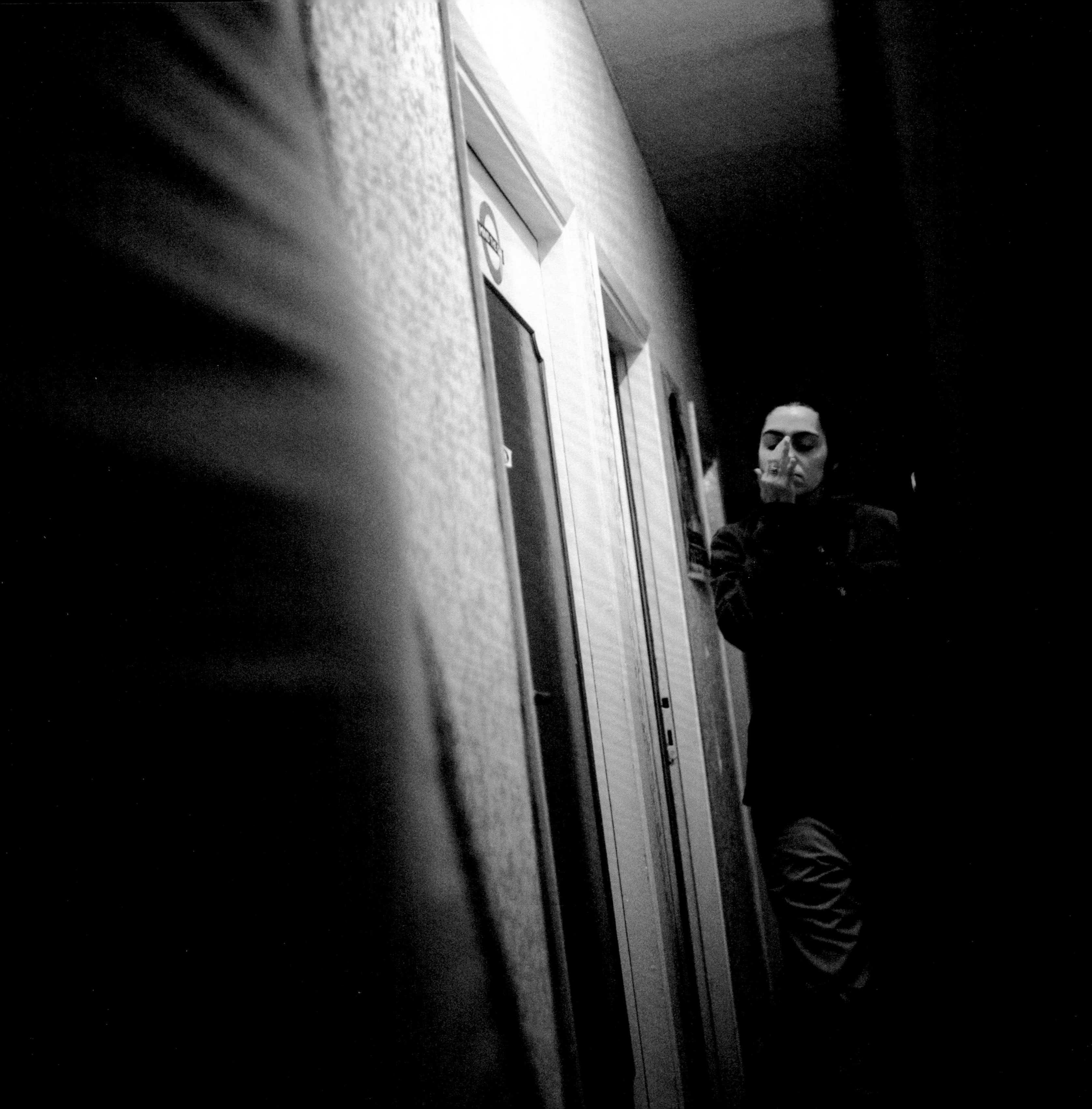

2,674,000 families (11.7%) or 7,588,000 people (13.2%) of the Italian population live in poverty

fonte Istat

*Page 170* Worker's house, Porto Marghera, December 2004 (MB)
*Previous page left* Corviale, Roma, September 2004 (MB)
*Previous page right* Quartiere S. Lorenzo, Roma, March 2004 (MB)
*Right* Ortigia, Siracusa, July 2004 (RS)

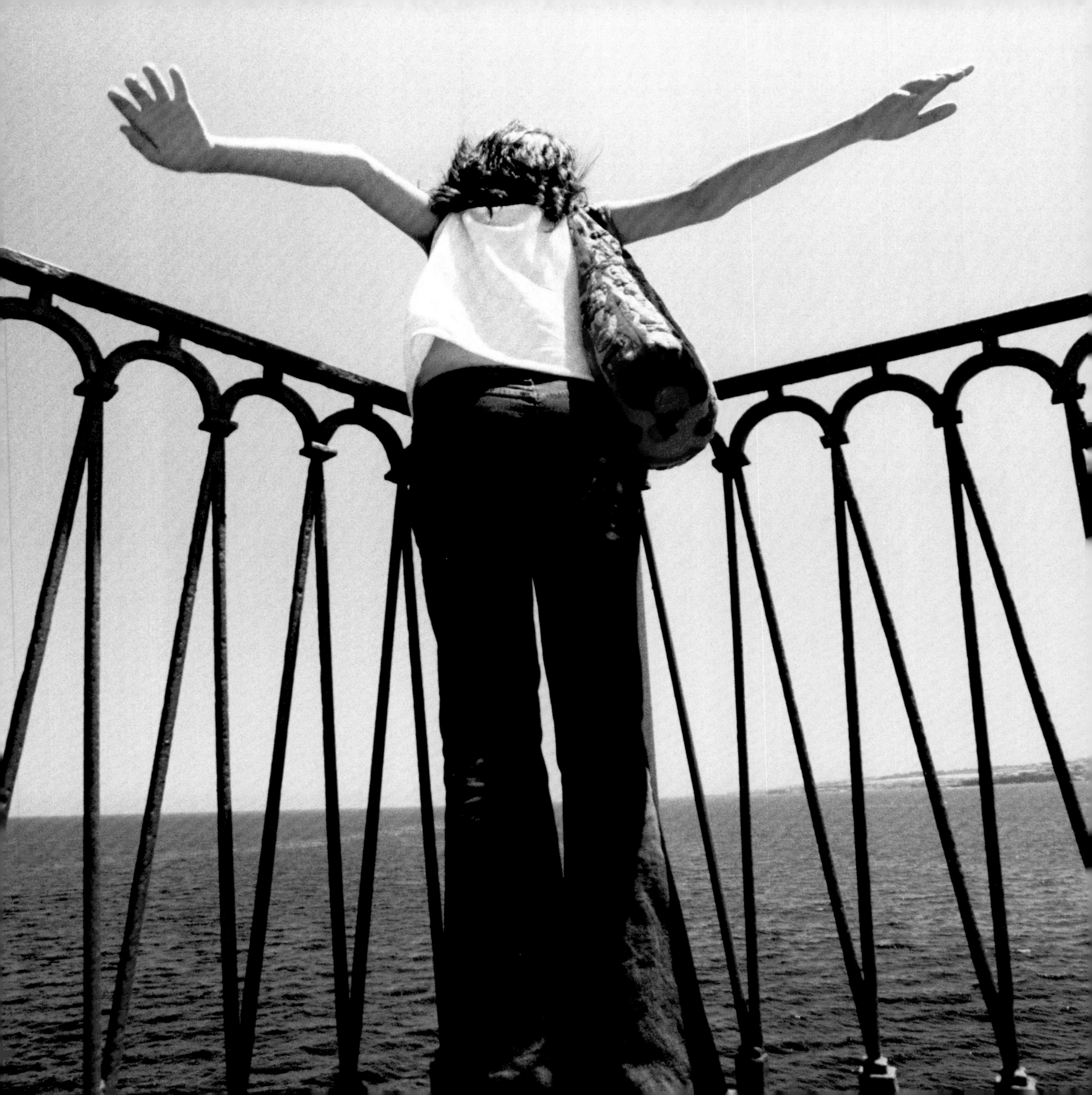

# LOVE AND THE POPE

by Umberto Galimberti

On January 20th the Vatican published the first encyclical of Pope Benedetto XVI.

His theme was that God is Love.

He provided no evidence to support his theory.

Tragedy is a commonplace of life. The Tsunami last year demonstrated to many that God's love is not all-encompassing. Similarly the Lisbon earthquake of 1755 persuaded Voltaire, and later Goethe, to investigate evidence of God's innate goodness.

If God is love then He surely encompasses passionate love, the love condemned by the Pope as a passion devalued by sexuality  and a love far removed from the adoration that transcends individual desires in order to attain a faith.
But why should passion be regarded as a negative influence for good?

Passion is undeniably a human expression of the body and soul. The Book of Genesis dictates that all human endeavour and expression is the work of God - and therefore good - and part of His design of the world in which we live.  Thus passion is a part of His creation.

But in order to relegate passion to a base instinct the Pope has had to define the erotic love of mortals, humanity indeed, as a commodity, in much the same way that Marx identified the ability of capitalism to reduce humanity to the consequence of commodities and their worth, when capitalism determines that money, and what it buys, is the sole arbiter of values.

The philosopher Emmanuel Kant was not a Catholic.
He understood that the purpose of human endeavour and activity was to recognise that humanity constituted society, and that social activity was an end in itself rather than a means to an end. He believed that one did not have to be a Christian to treat humans as individuals, with rights and freedoms, and not as integers.

The Roman Catholic Church has little problem with the practices of capitalism and its aims. The venom with which the Church has attacked communism is concommitant with its admiration of capitalism, while forgetting that the corruption of human values  comes not from communist ideals, which concern themselves with poverty, but from capitalist ambitions of wealth.

Such Christian love as demonstrated by the Roman Catholic Church, which has not hesitated to condemn the liberation of theology from the strictures of the Church - where it is possible to indentify genuine human love - has vociferously curtailed Franciscan support of established peace movements. So the choice is clear; the church of power, represented by the Vatican, or the church of love.

Benedetto XVI has taken the opportunity of reiterating Pope John Paul II's condemnation of Liberation Theology. In so doing he has reaffirmed his support for and belief in a powerful church that seeks to limit the range and expression of love. It is worth noting that John Paul II was the same Pope who chose to appear on a presidential balcony in Chile with the murderous dictator Pinochet. That seems to me a powerful indictment of the Church as presented in this encyclical.

A last reflection relates to Benedetto XVI's assertion that marriage, or holy wedlock, is the representation of God's unity with his people. Why then do priests not marry and refuse this unity? And if love is to be exalted why should it not be recognised between those who live together outside marriage, as in a civil union? This encyclical looks to me to be a manifest sign of the contradictions incited by the Church.

For elder widows, relationships with their sons represent
their most important resource:
more than 50% meet at least one son every day

Istat

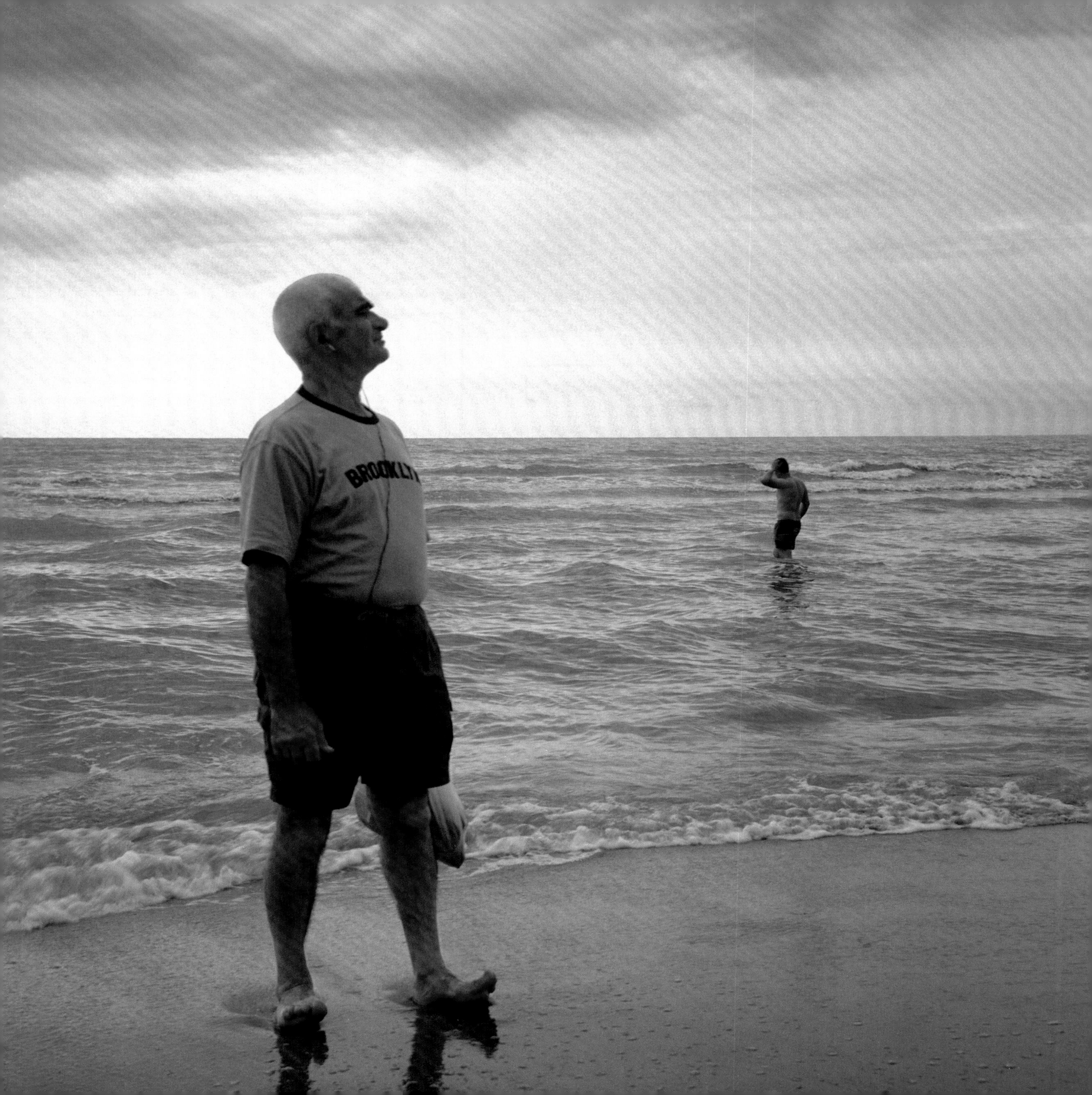

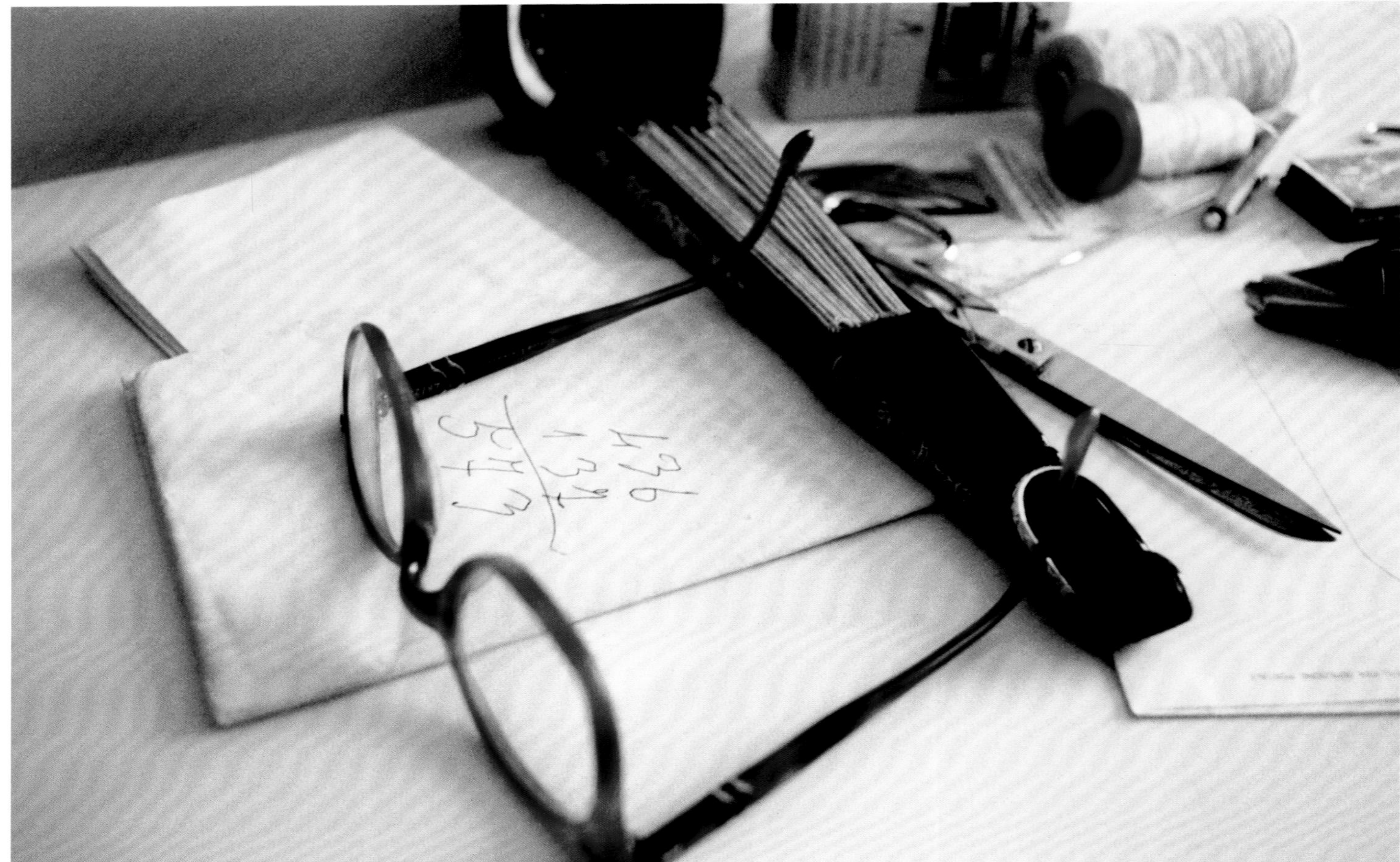

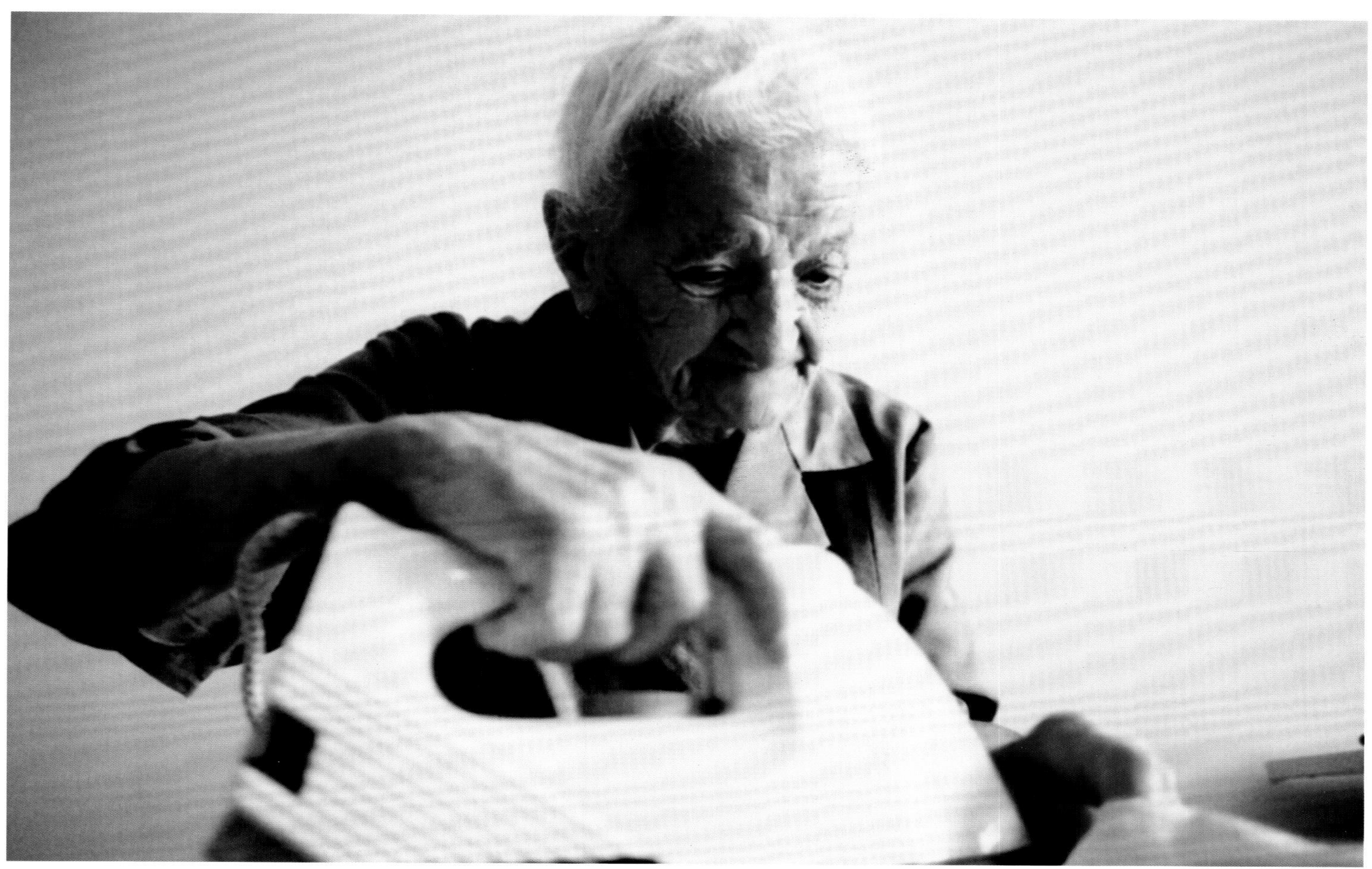

82% of Italian families own their homes

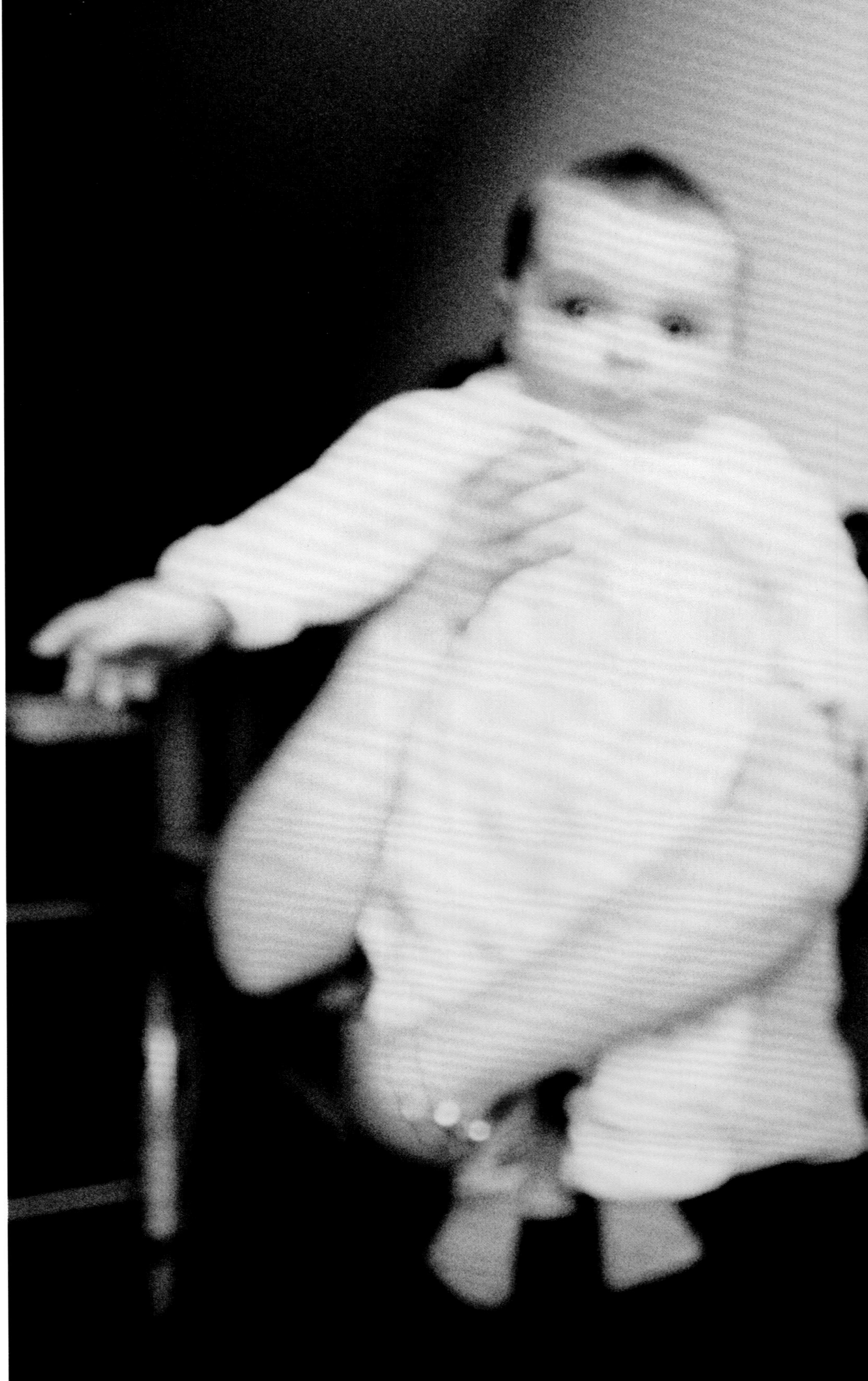

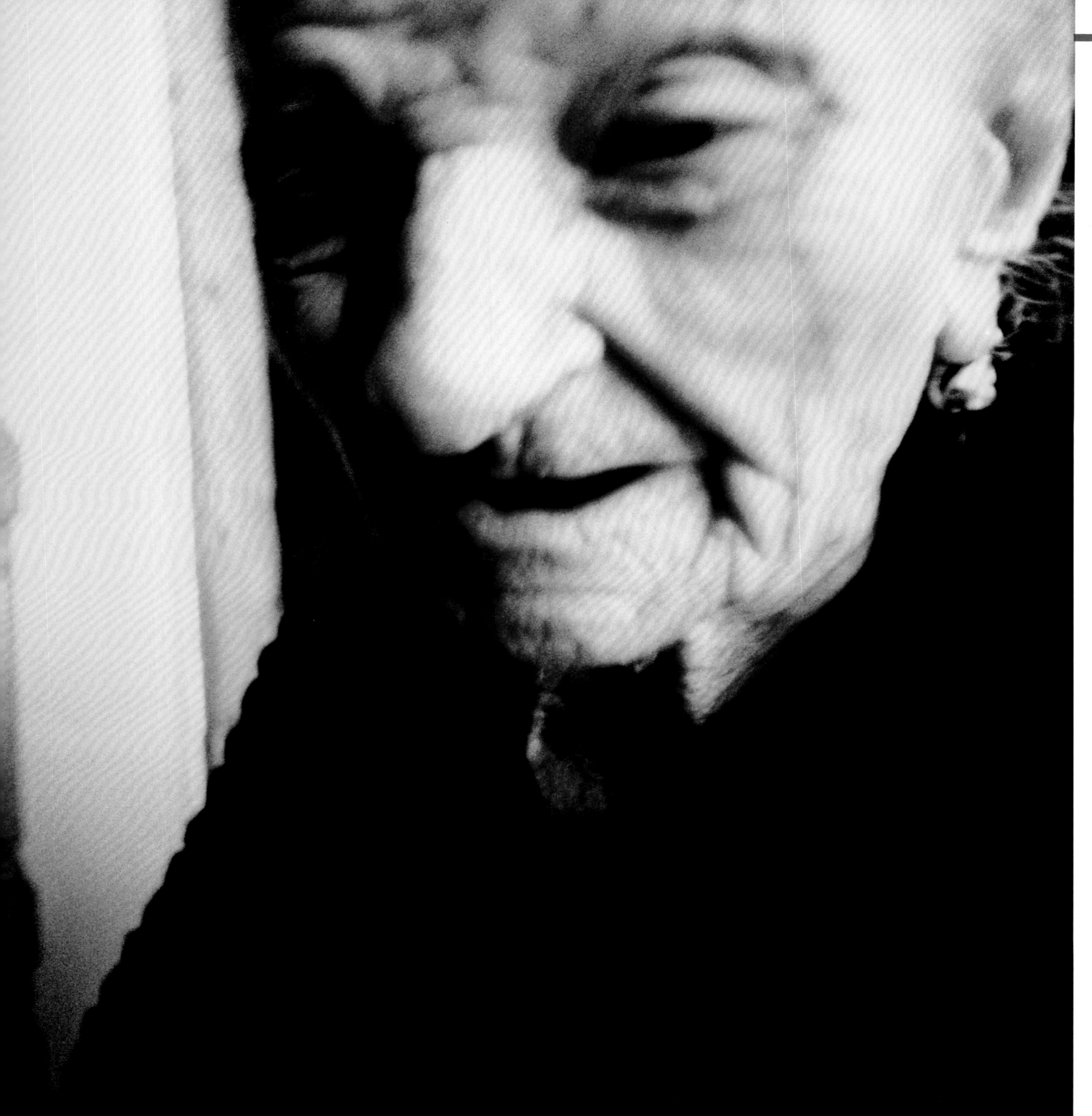

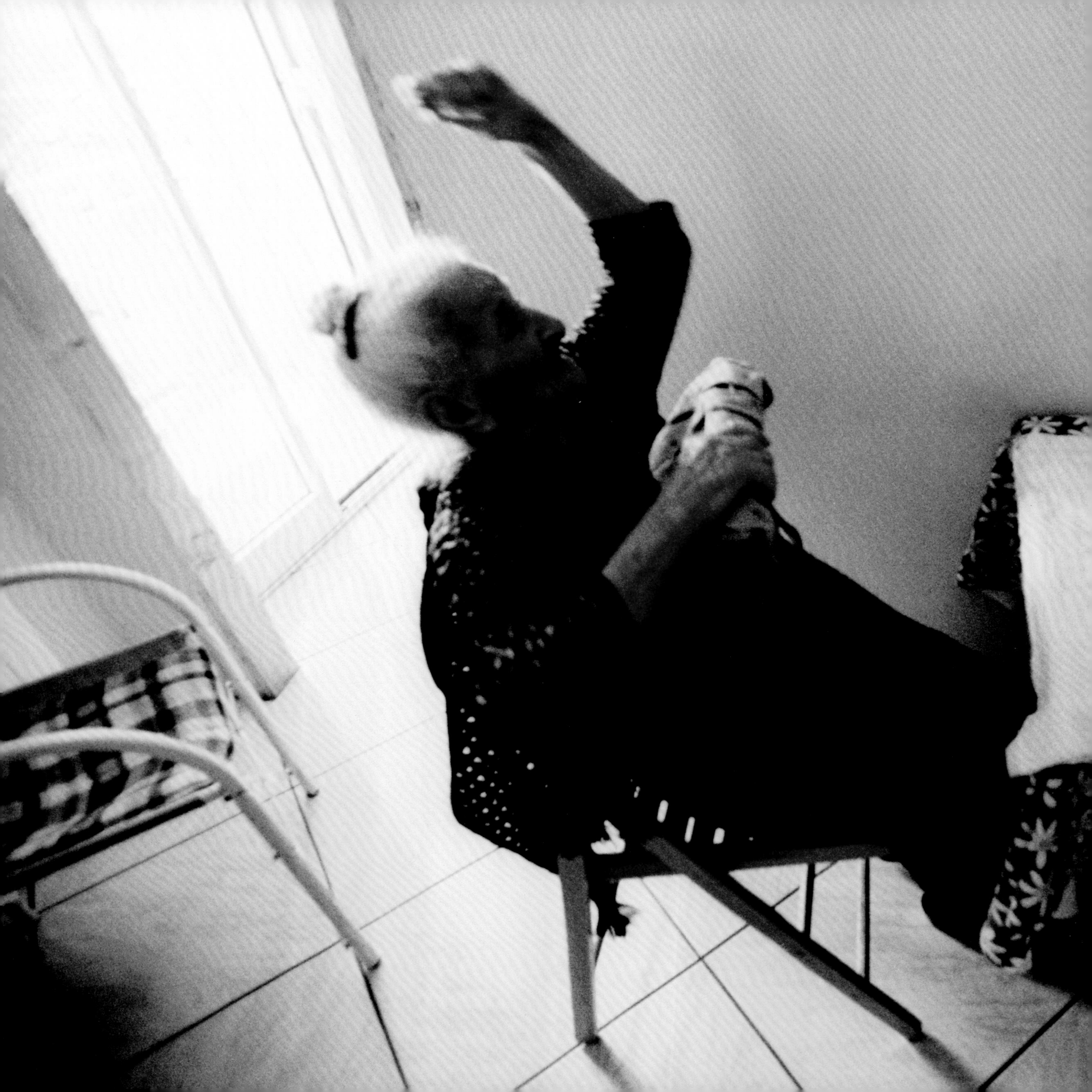

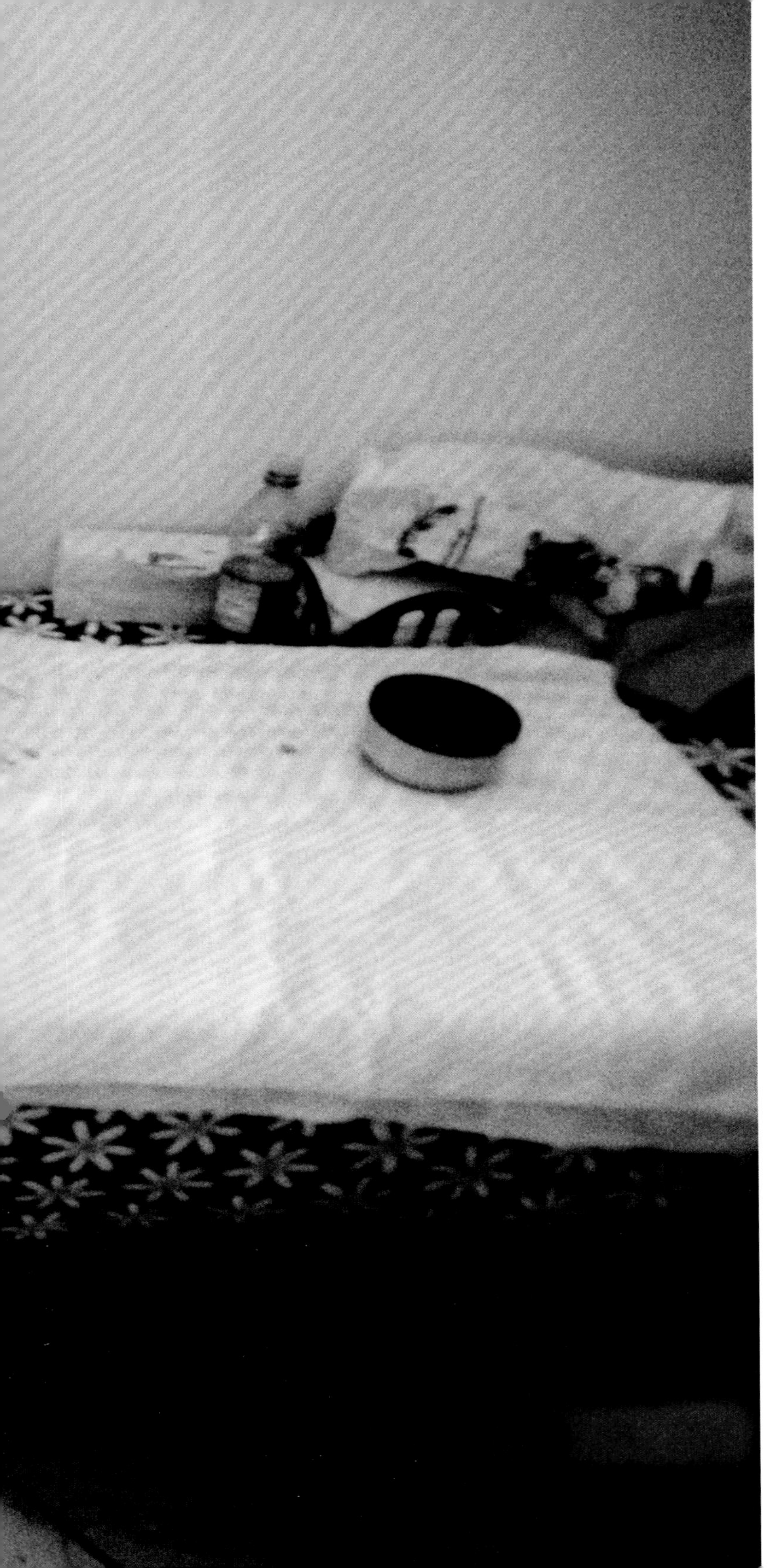

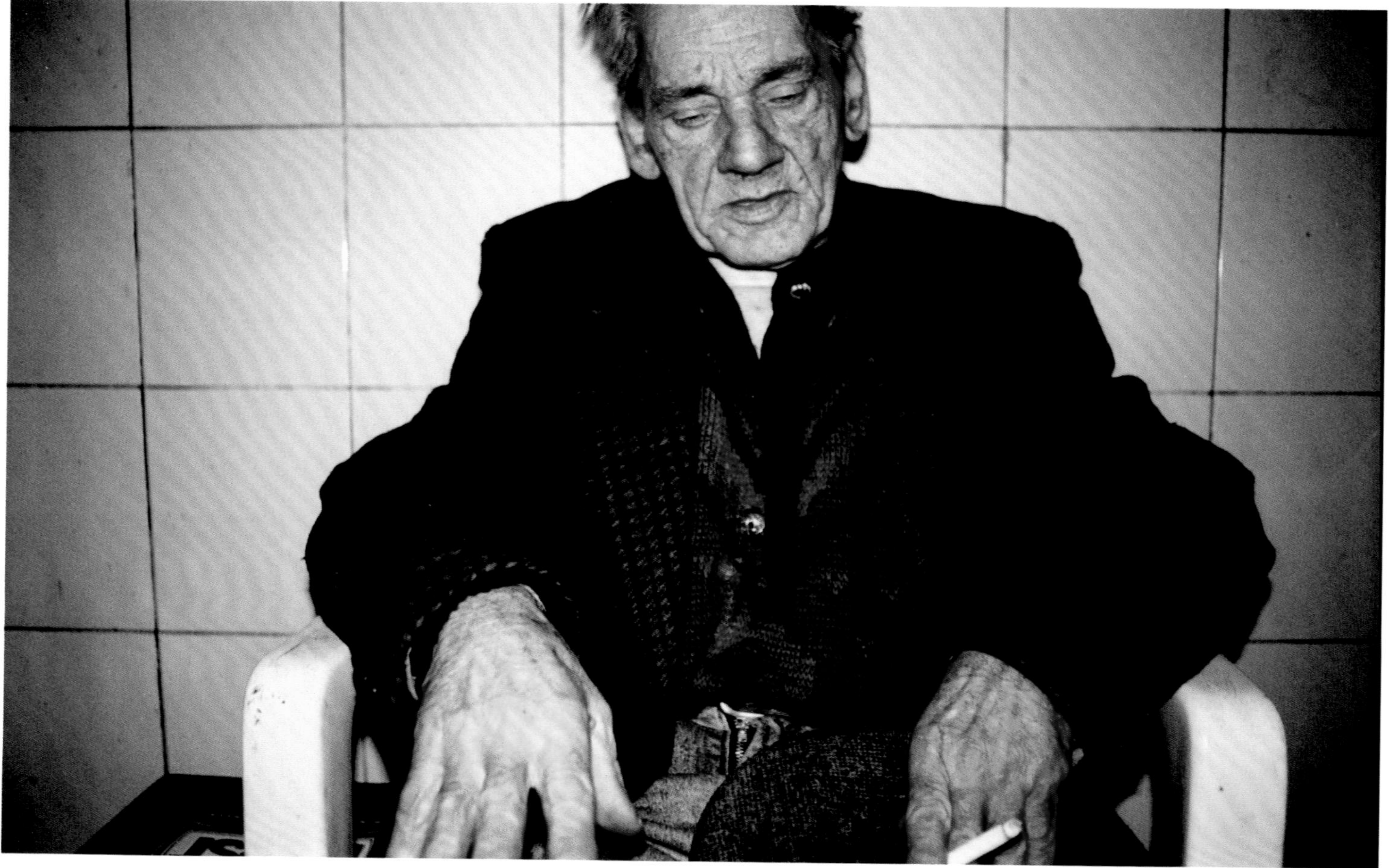

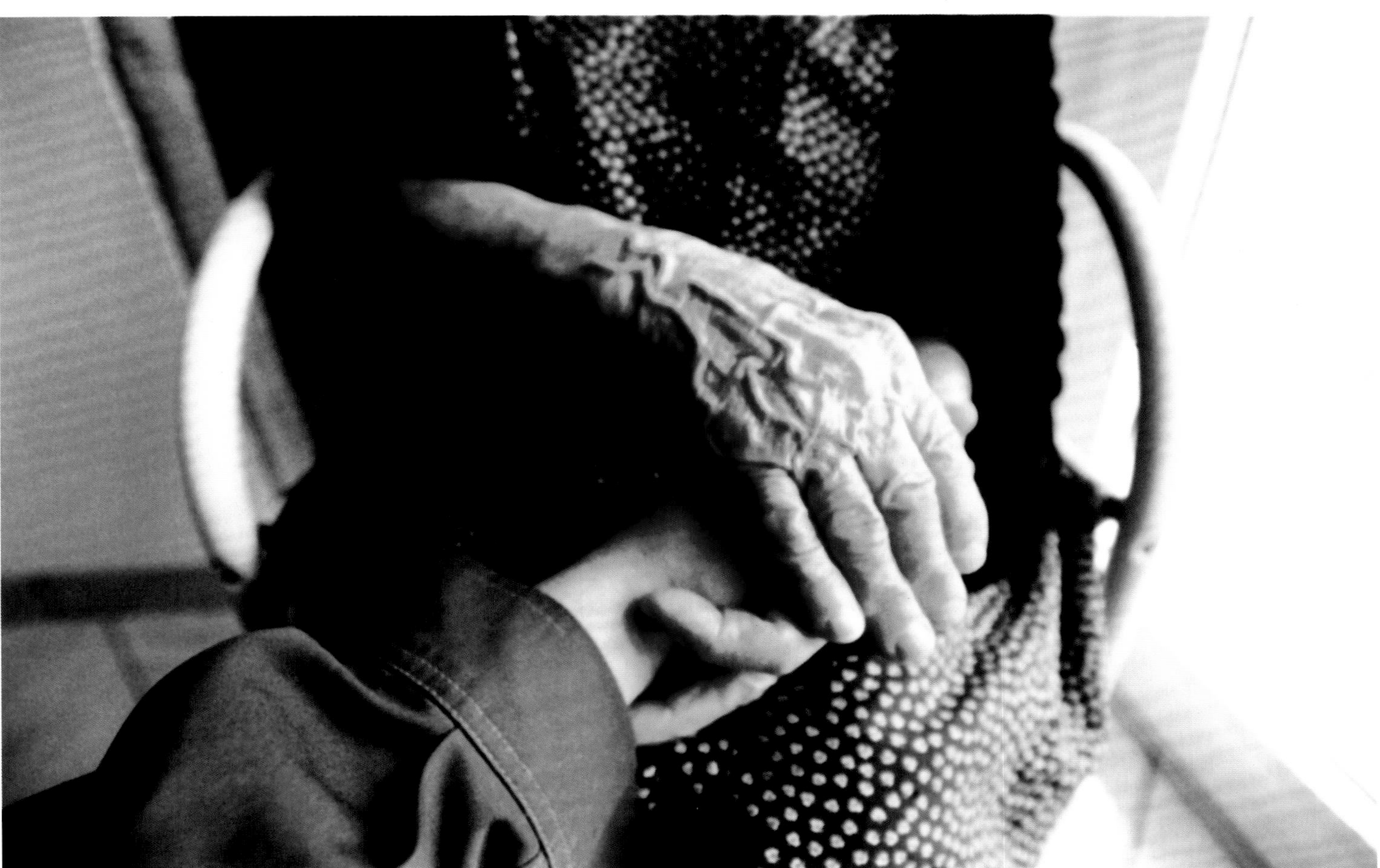

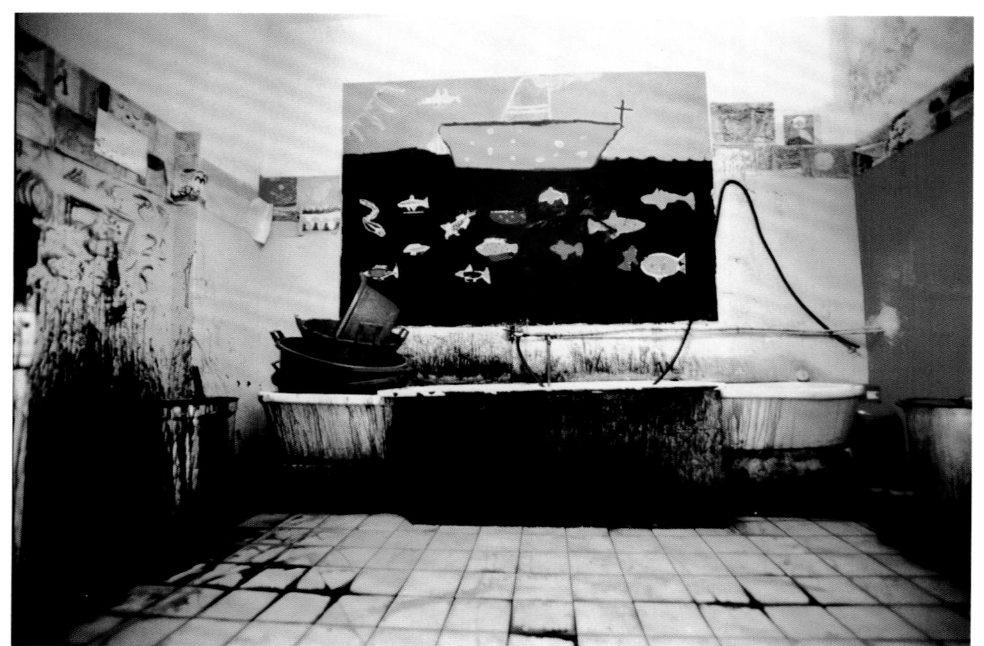

*Above* Palermo, March 2003 (RS)

*From page 182 to 189* 2001 - 2003 (RS), Cammarata, Agrigento

*Right* Corviale, Roma, September 2004 (MB)

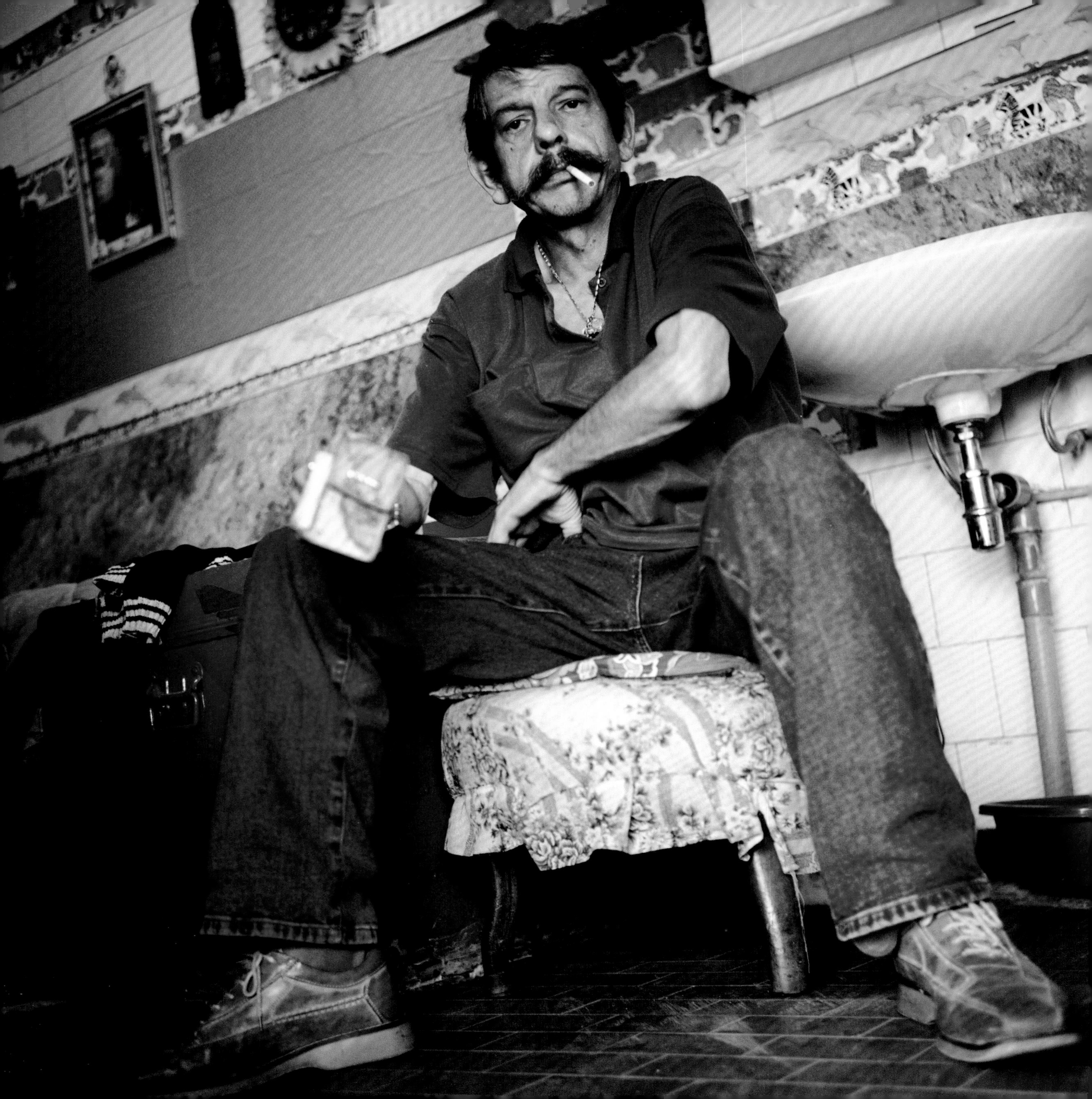

45.3% of tenants are on low incomes, 34% pay rents higher than 30% of their income and 13.4% pay more than 40% (sustainable rent is judged to be 20% of total income)

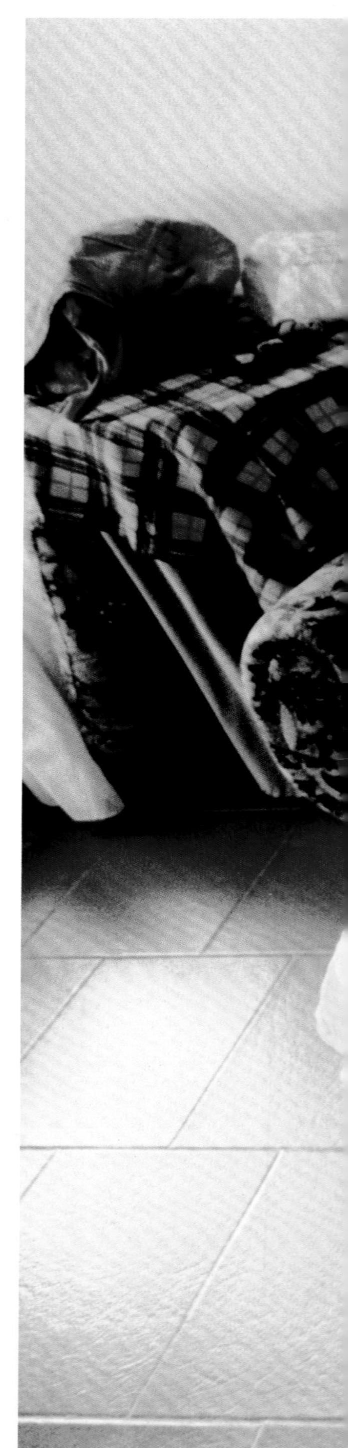

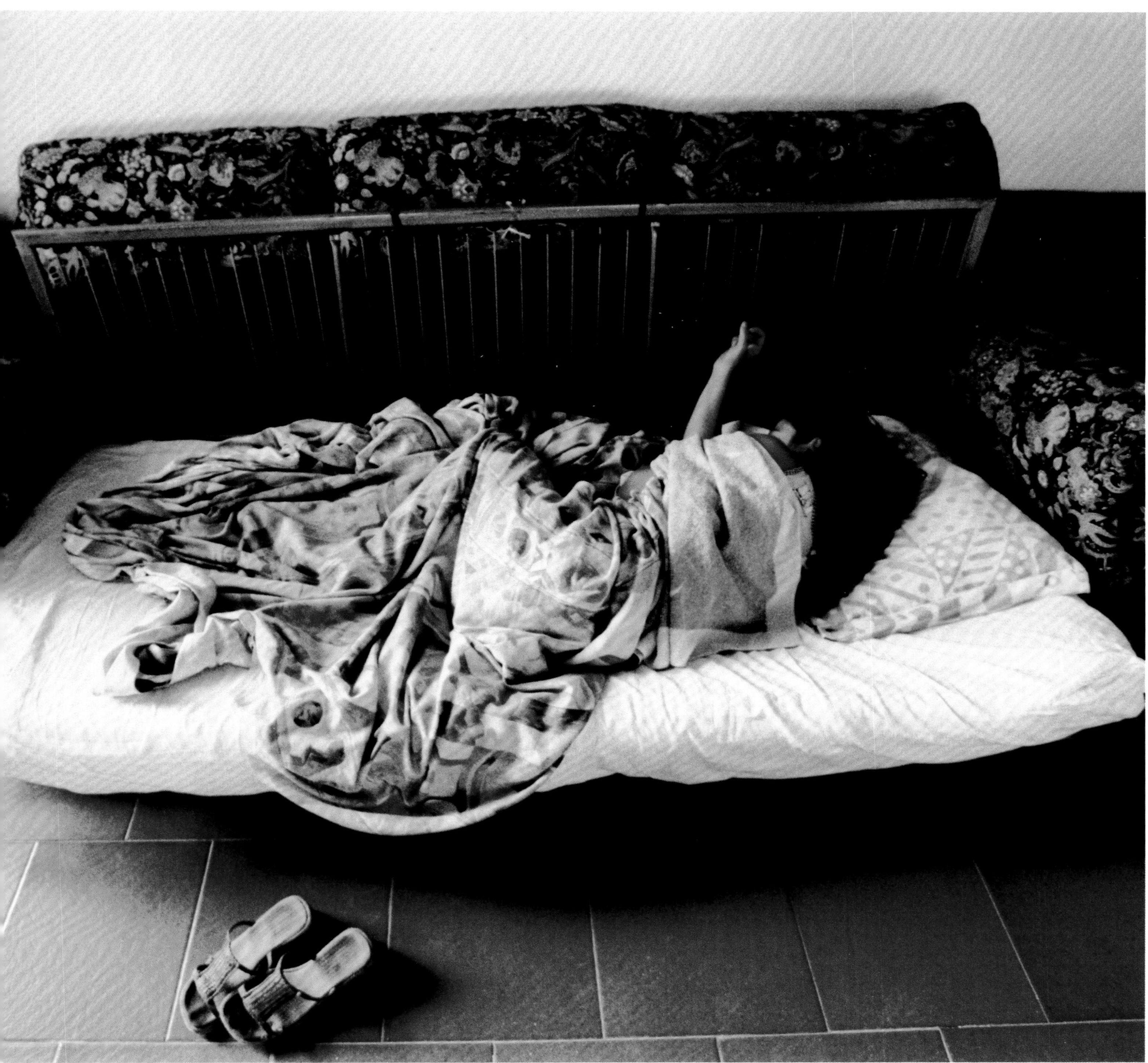

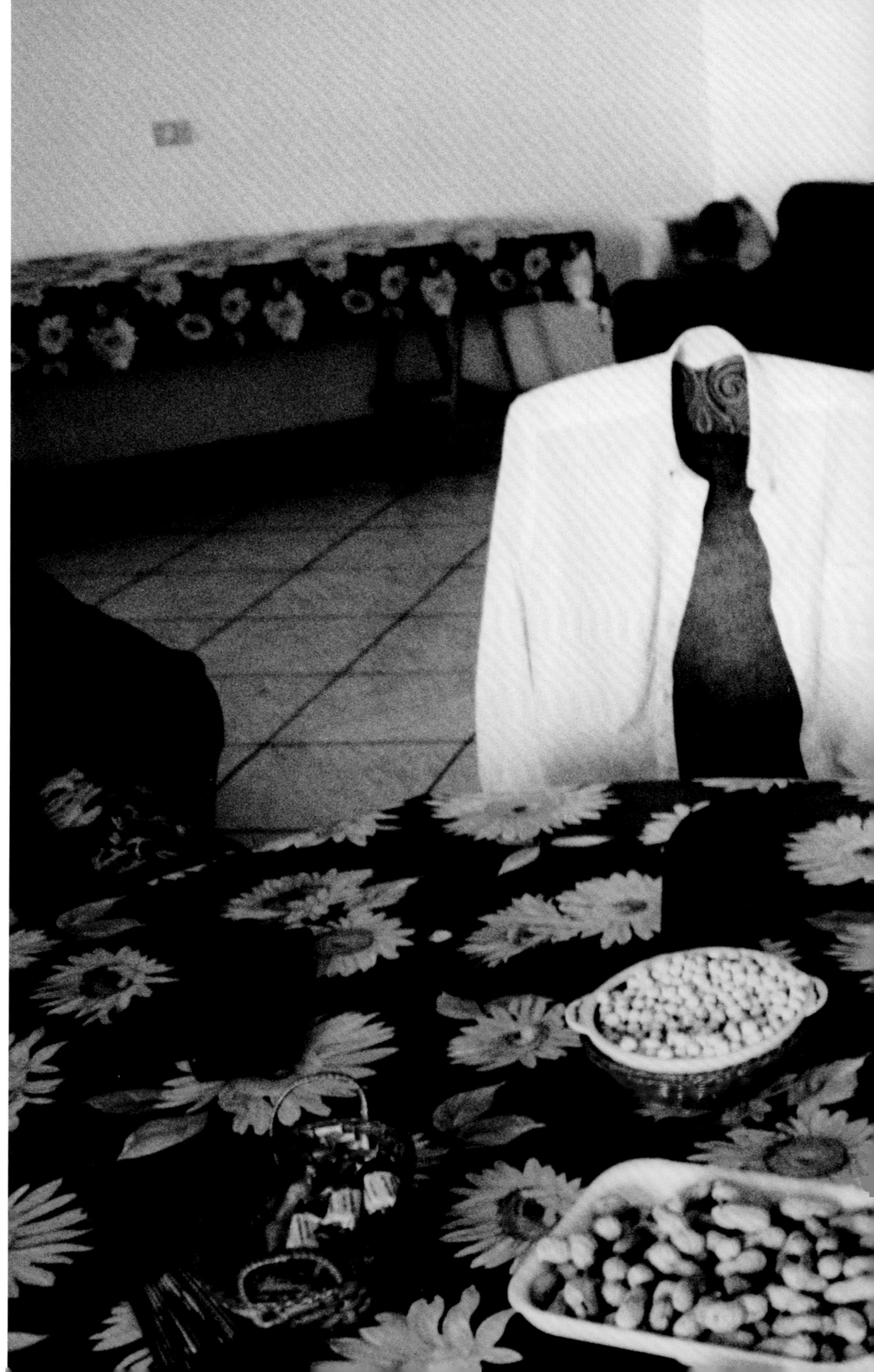

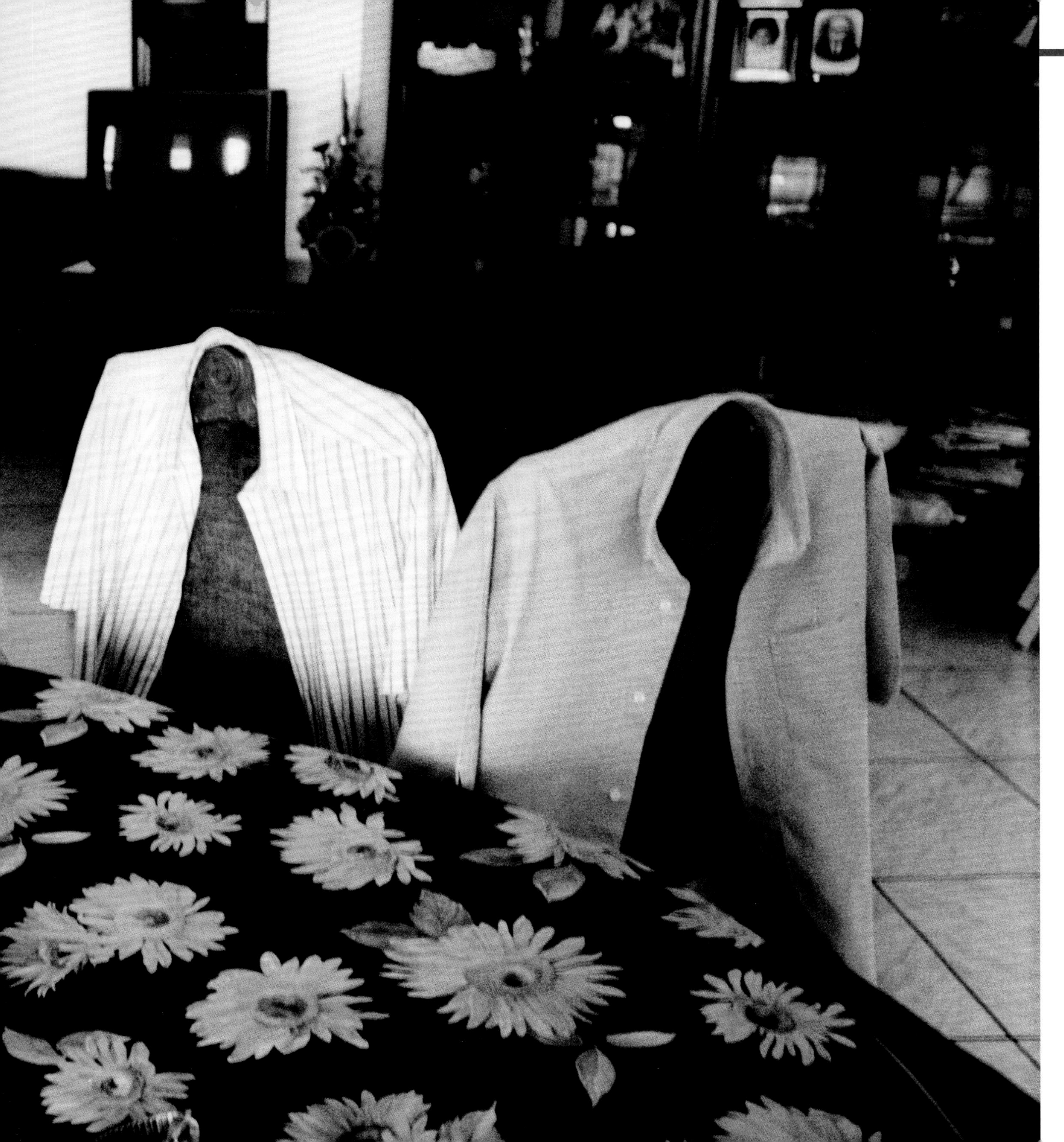

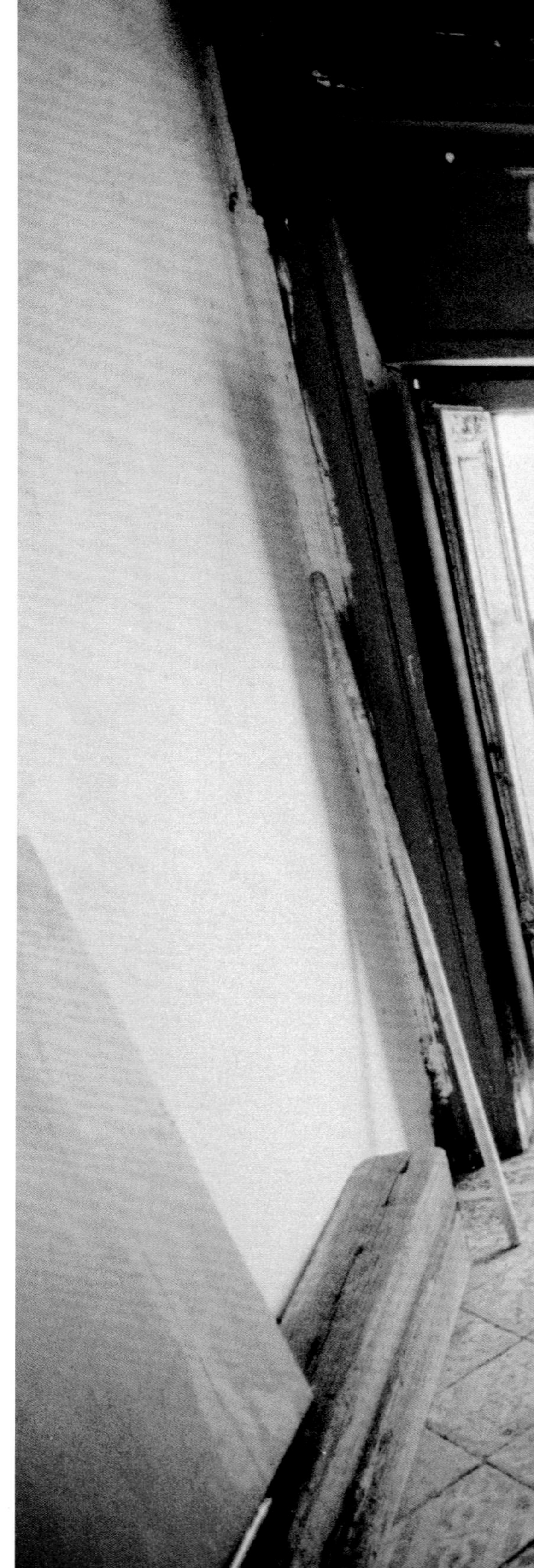

*From page 192* Palermo, September 2005 (RS)

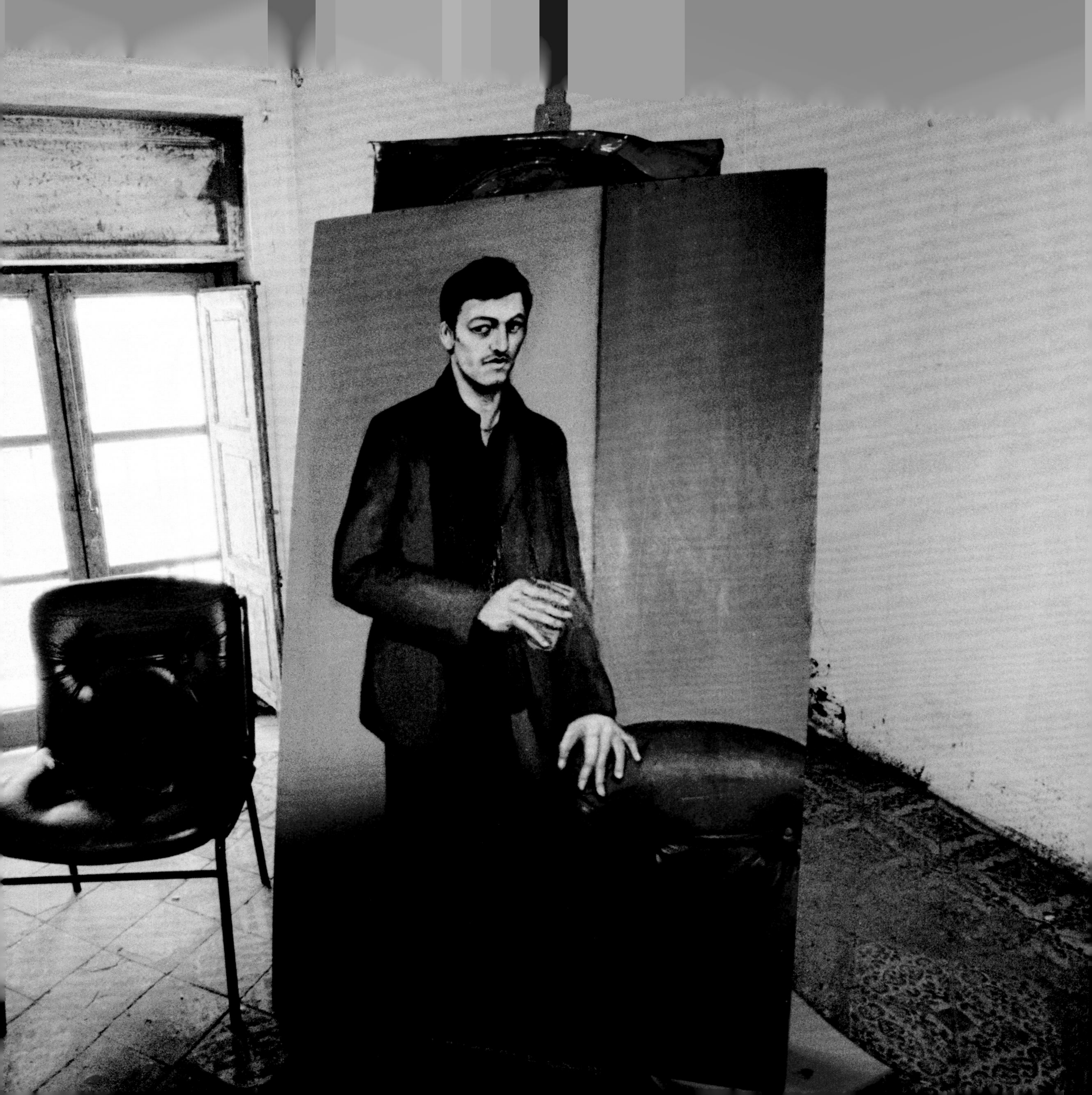

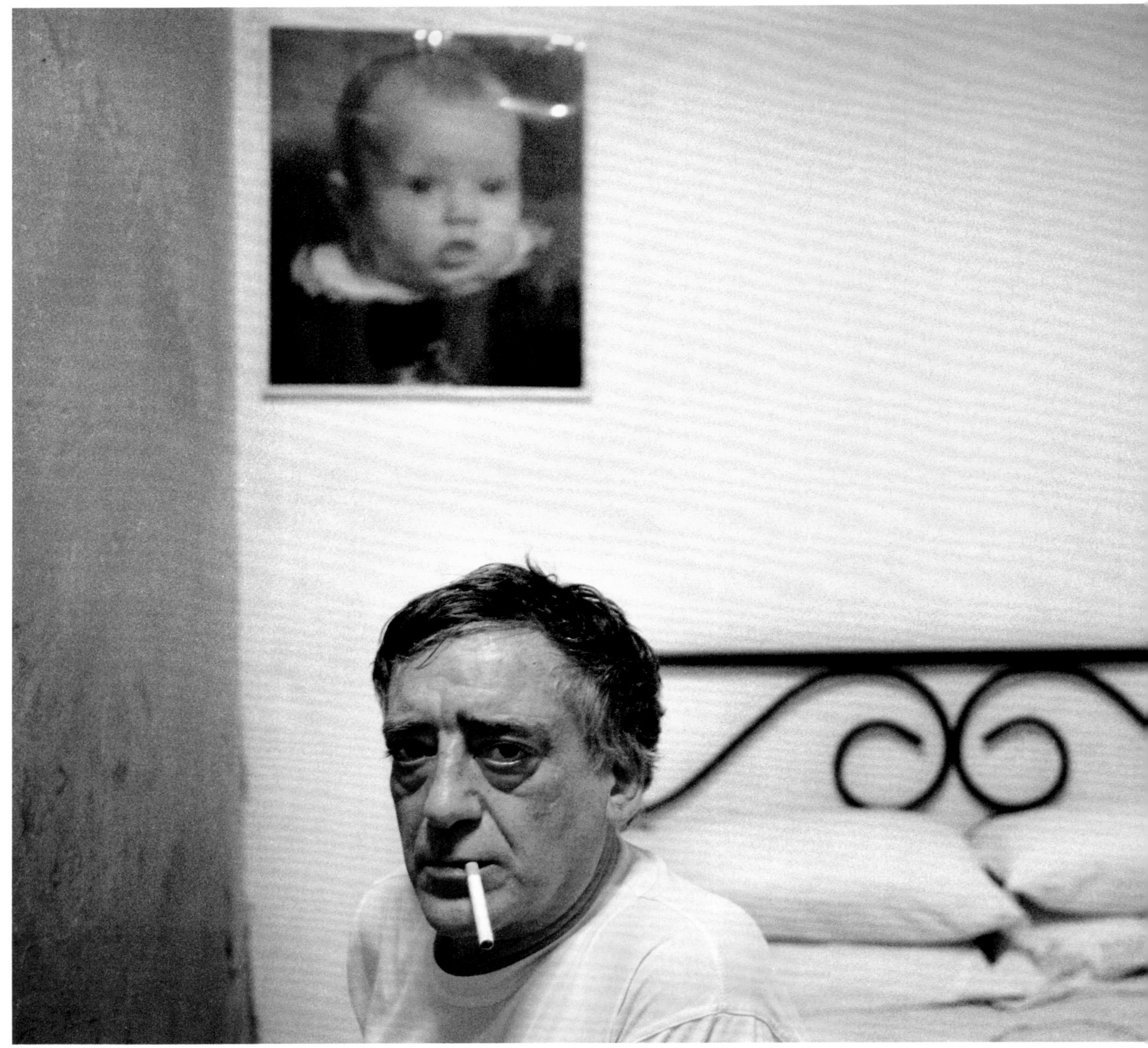

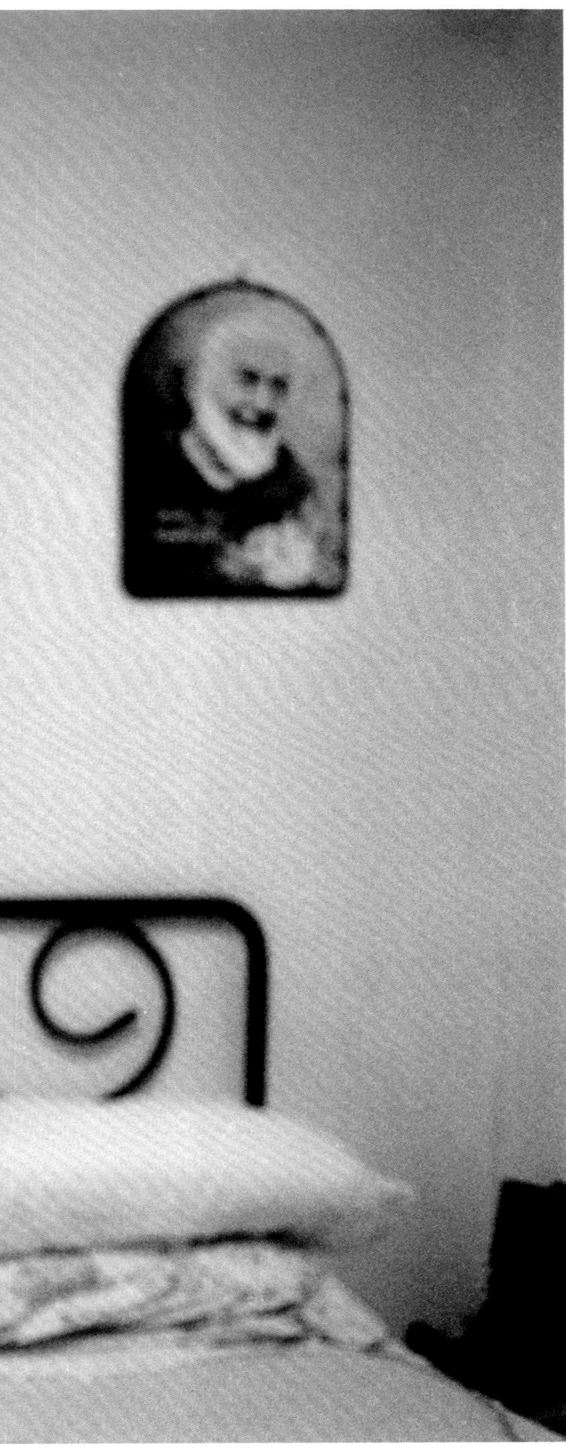

Quartiere Montesanto, Napoli, June 2004 (EM)

*Right page* Quartiere Montesanto, Napoli, June 2004 (EM)

*Following page* Corviale, Roma, September 2004 (MS)

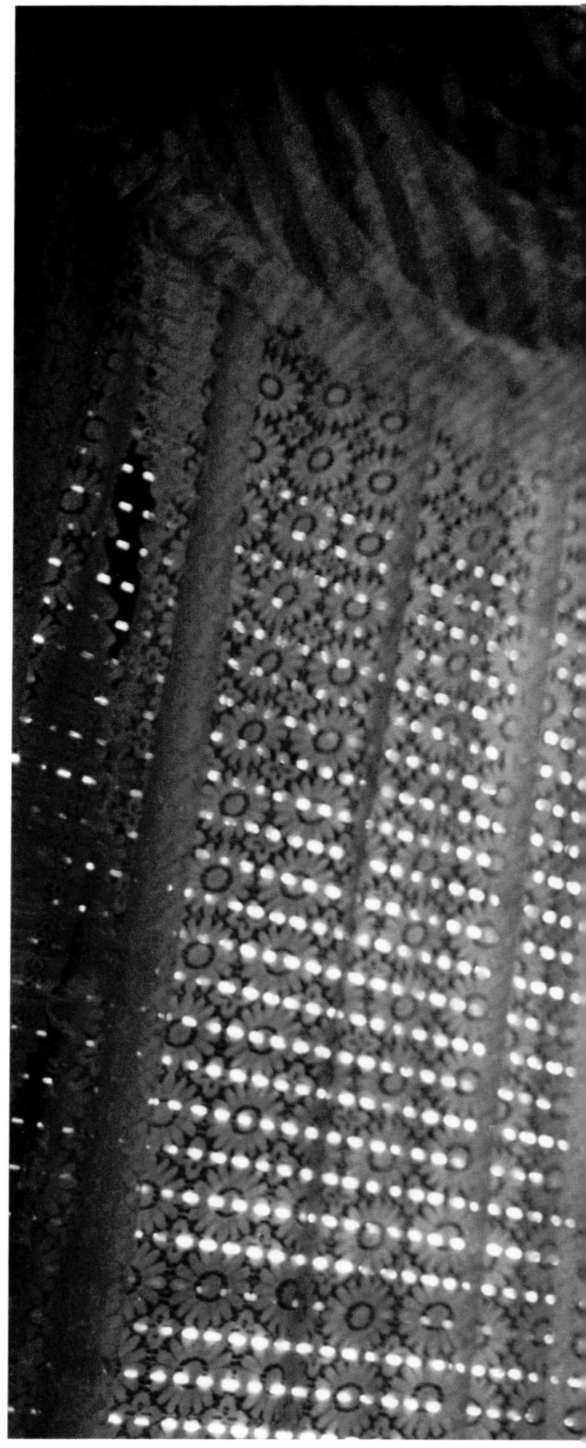

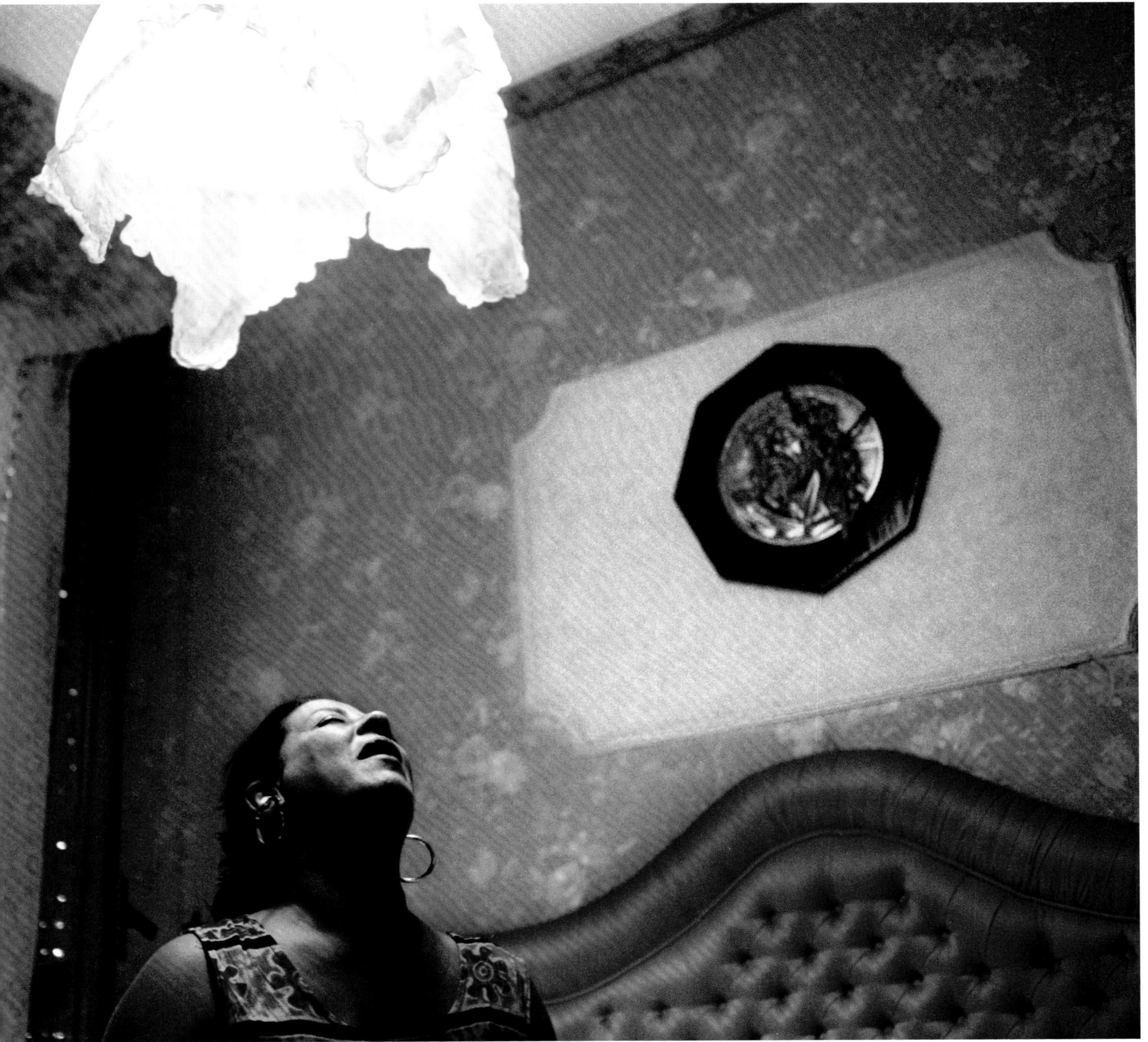

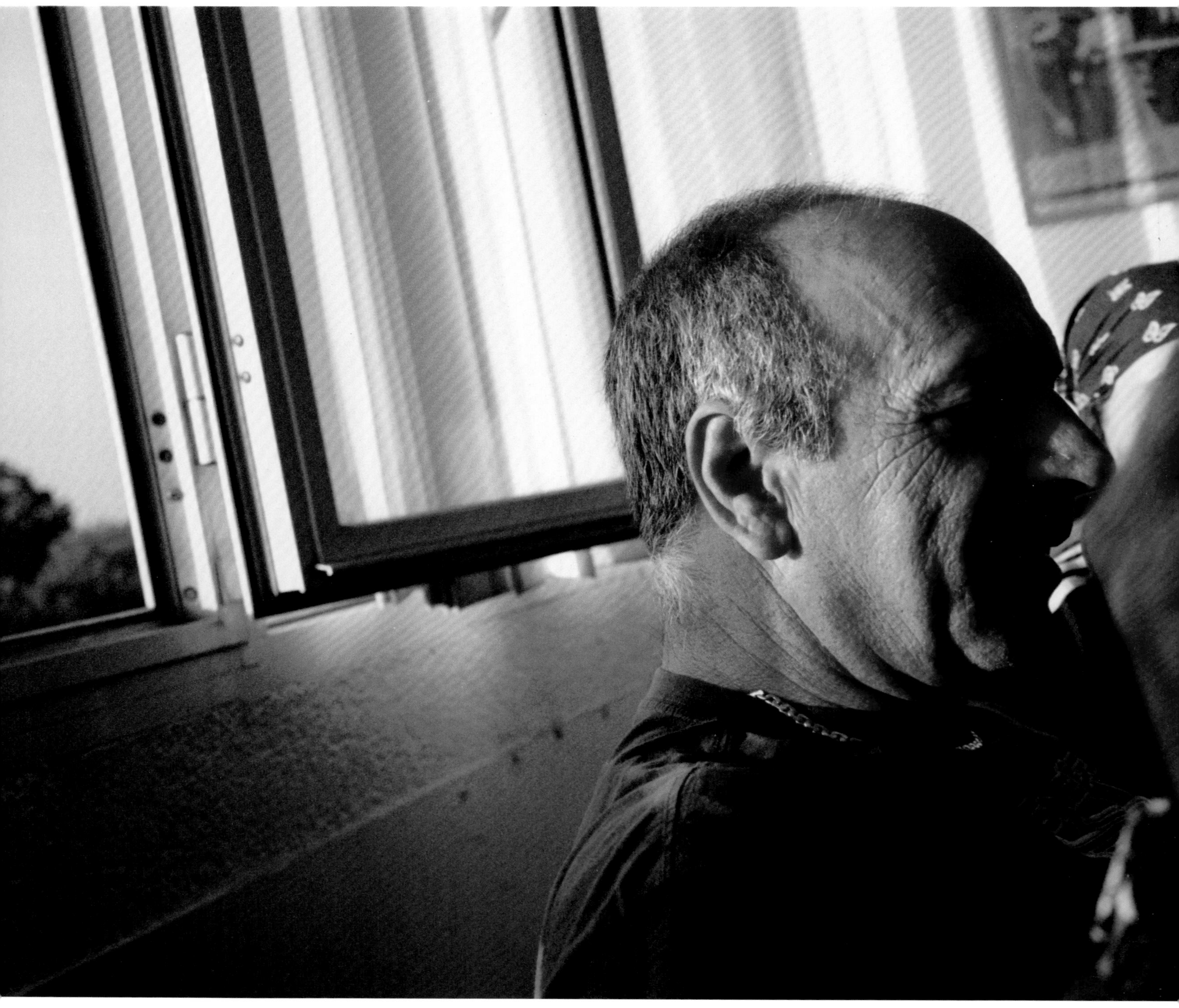

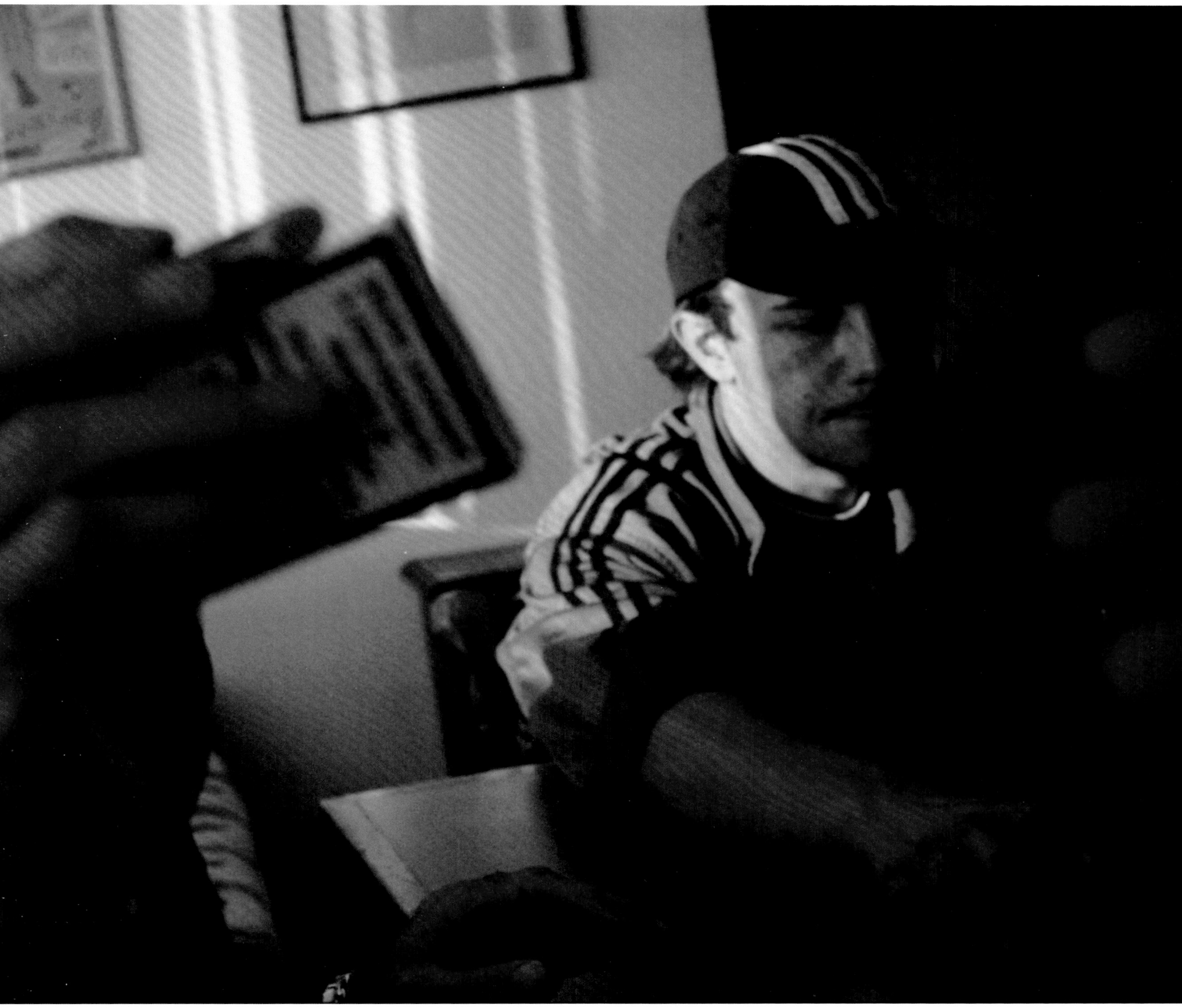

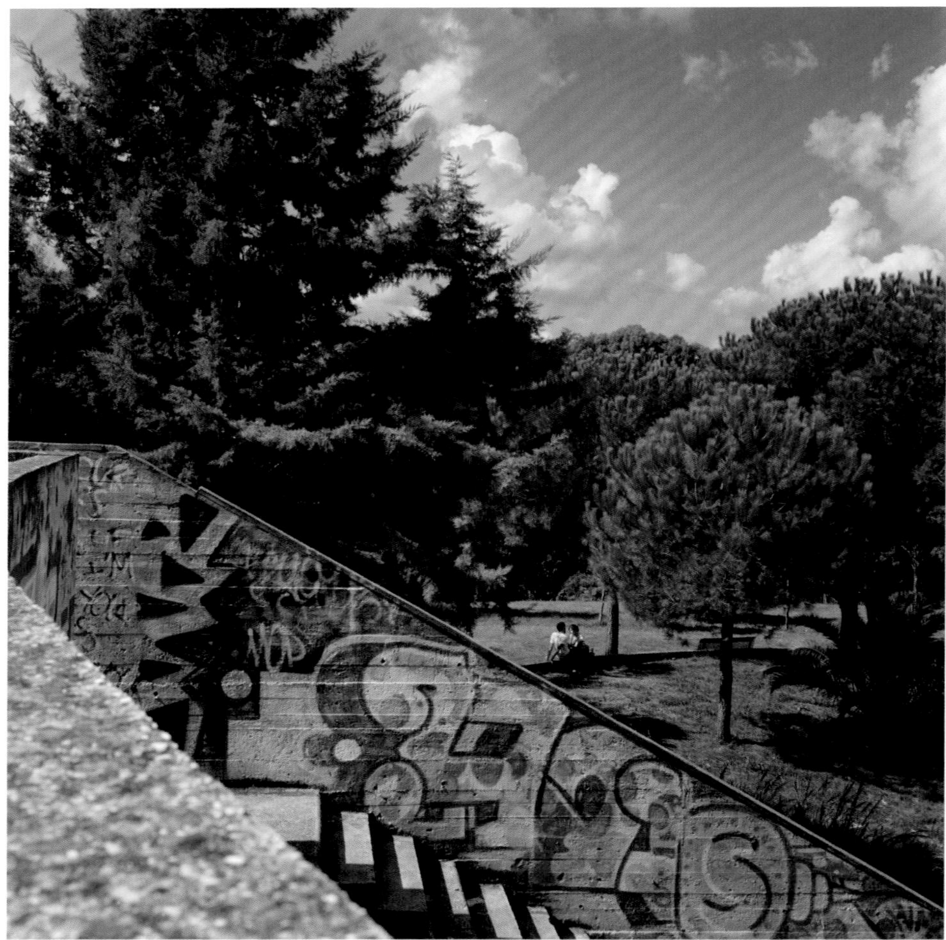

*Right and above* Corviale, Roma, September 2004 (MB)

# CENSORSHIP

## Umberto Galimberti

An innovation in Italian television recently occurred when the actor Adriano Celentano broadcast his show without being previewed by the T.V. network management, and therefore without the possibility of censorship.

The subject of his transmission was censorship.

The reality of the phenomenon of censorship is further sophisticated by the use of language, by the use of words and phrases that are in fact euphemisms but are intended as synonyms, in short by not referring to events as truths but as ideas connected to those events.

By not calling these events by their names it is possible to arrive at meanings that are more manageable, more malleable, creating effects that refer to the truth but are less explosive than the reality.

The English intellectual Stanley, who lived in South Africa with his rich family when he was a child, travelled with a retinue of 100 servants catering for their every whim. We shall not call them slaves even if they were very close to that.
He was sleeping in a comfortable hotel while all these people slept outside in the cold.
He had seen them from the window and the day after he asked his mother: "Why do they live outside while I am in here? Do they have a family as I have?"

His mother thought, "Stanley is a very sensitive guy".

Later on he reflected: "Did my mother see the same things I did? Did we feel the same way or did she feel something very different? Was my mother's understanding of the world we were looking at the same as mine?"

The answer he provided for himself was the following: she had denied herself the reality of what was obvious to everybody else. Out of this childhood experience he instituted a new university course in Oxford, a course of negation philosophy, where language plays a key role.
For example, if I define a massacre as collateral damage I do not obtain an emotional reaction from my audience as I would have had I called it a massacre. If I referred to a mass deportation as a population movement it is obvious that my words would obtain a mild and acceptable image and not the tragic picture that would be proper for a mass deportation. If I define war as a peace mission I am operating a negation effect, ameliorating the potential for disagreement, even rebellion.

If I then add that I am exporting democracy then my words become comical, as it would mean that I forget history, culture, and the generations that it took us to arrive at democracy.

I believe that censorship not only furnishes the media with a language of deformed information but that we need to beware of censorship as manipulation of language. We must refer to events as they are, however unacceptable the reality may be.

Palazzo dei Normanni, Palermo, December 2005 (EM)

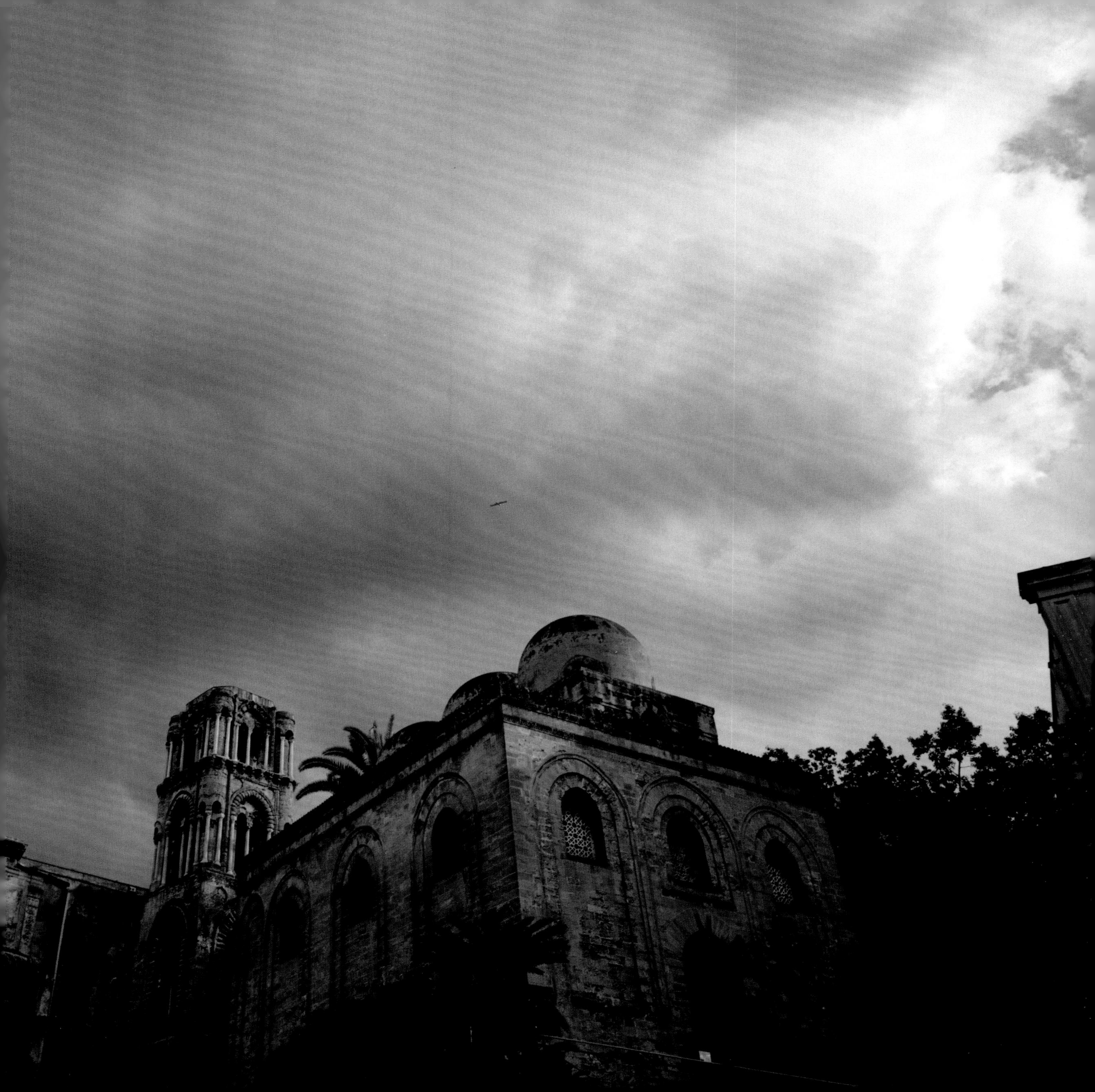

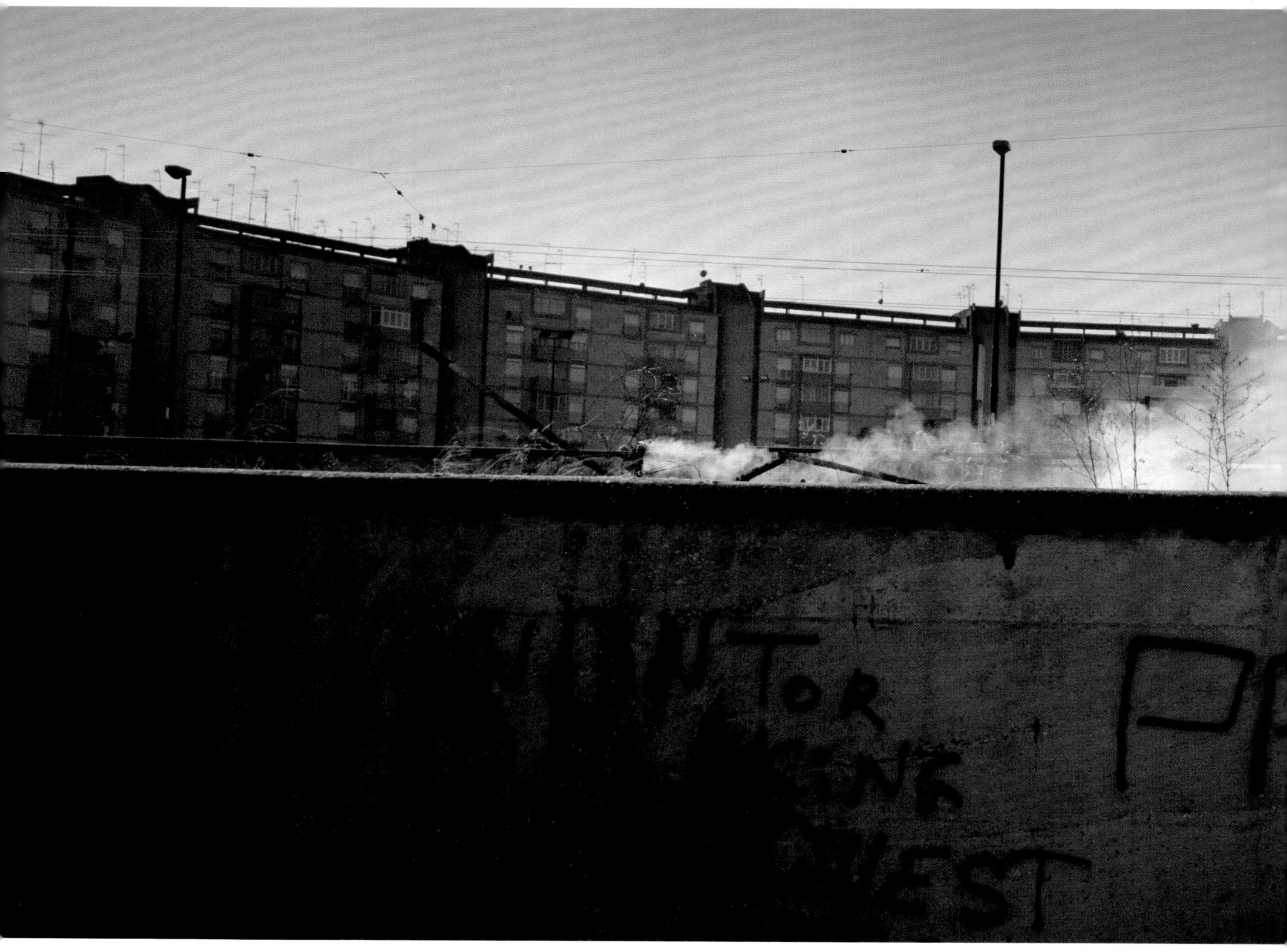

Vele di Scampia during the Camorra war, Napoli, January 2005 (MS)

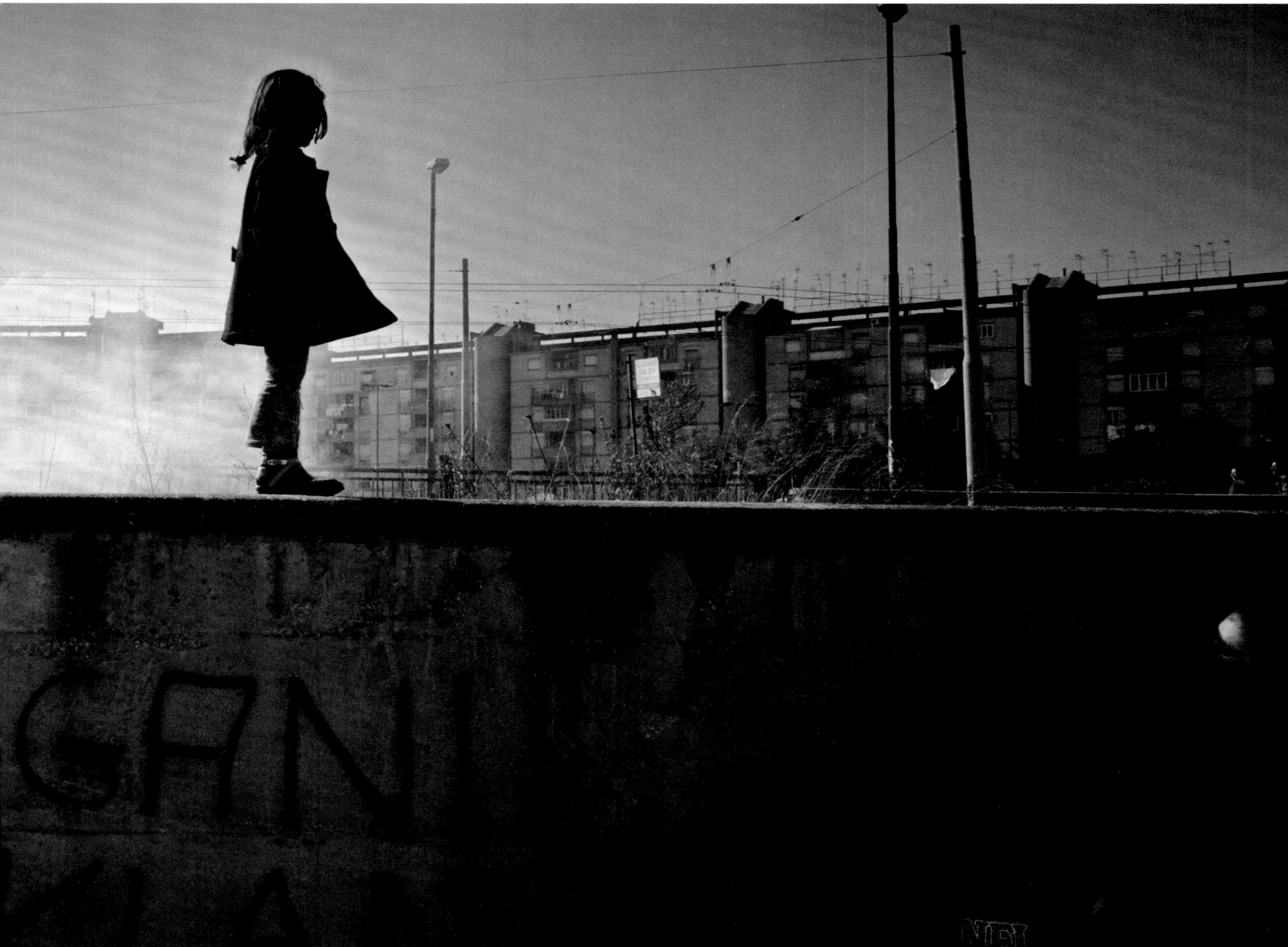

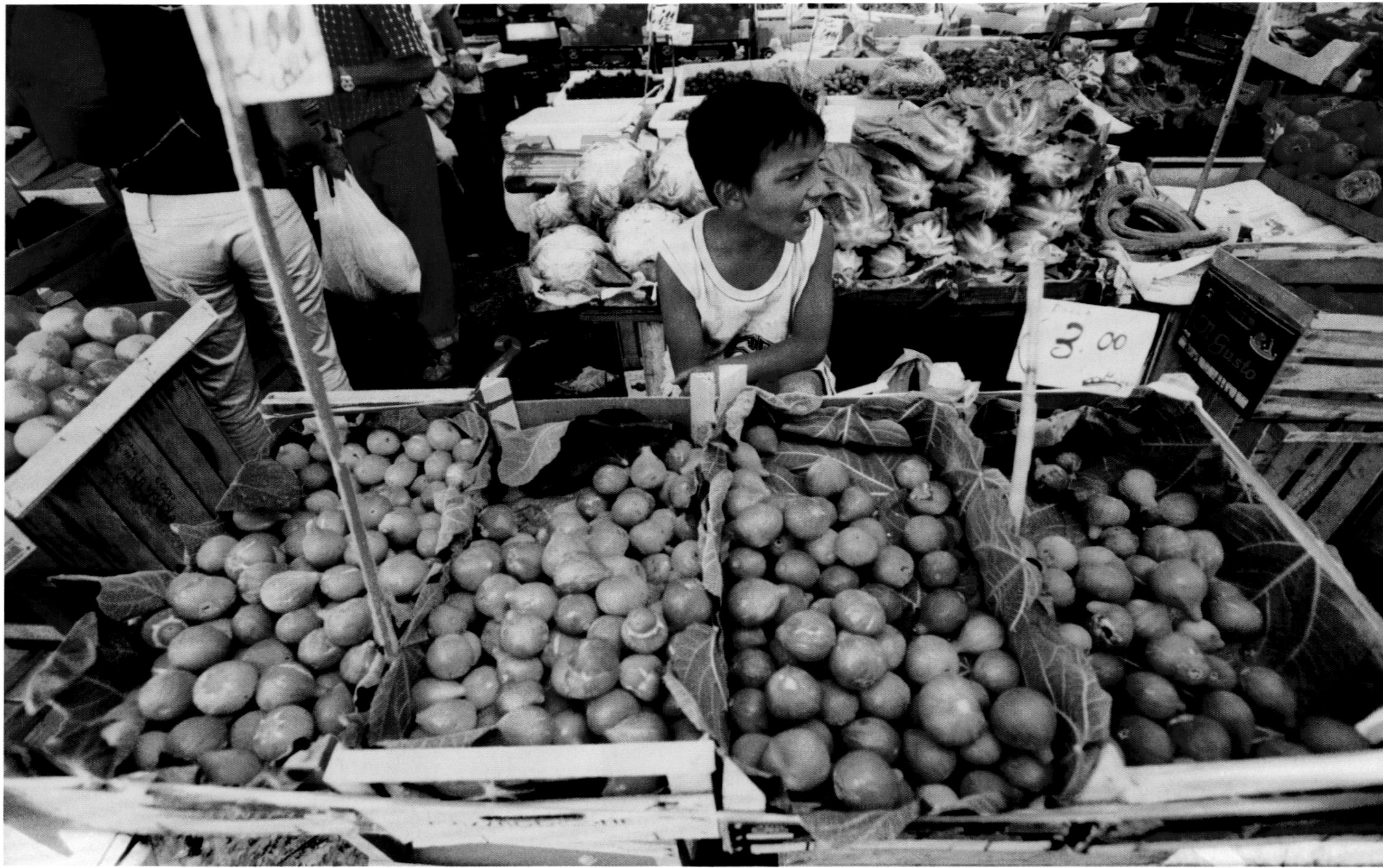


Capo, Palermo, August 2003 (RS)

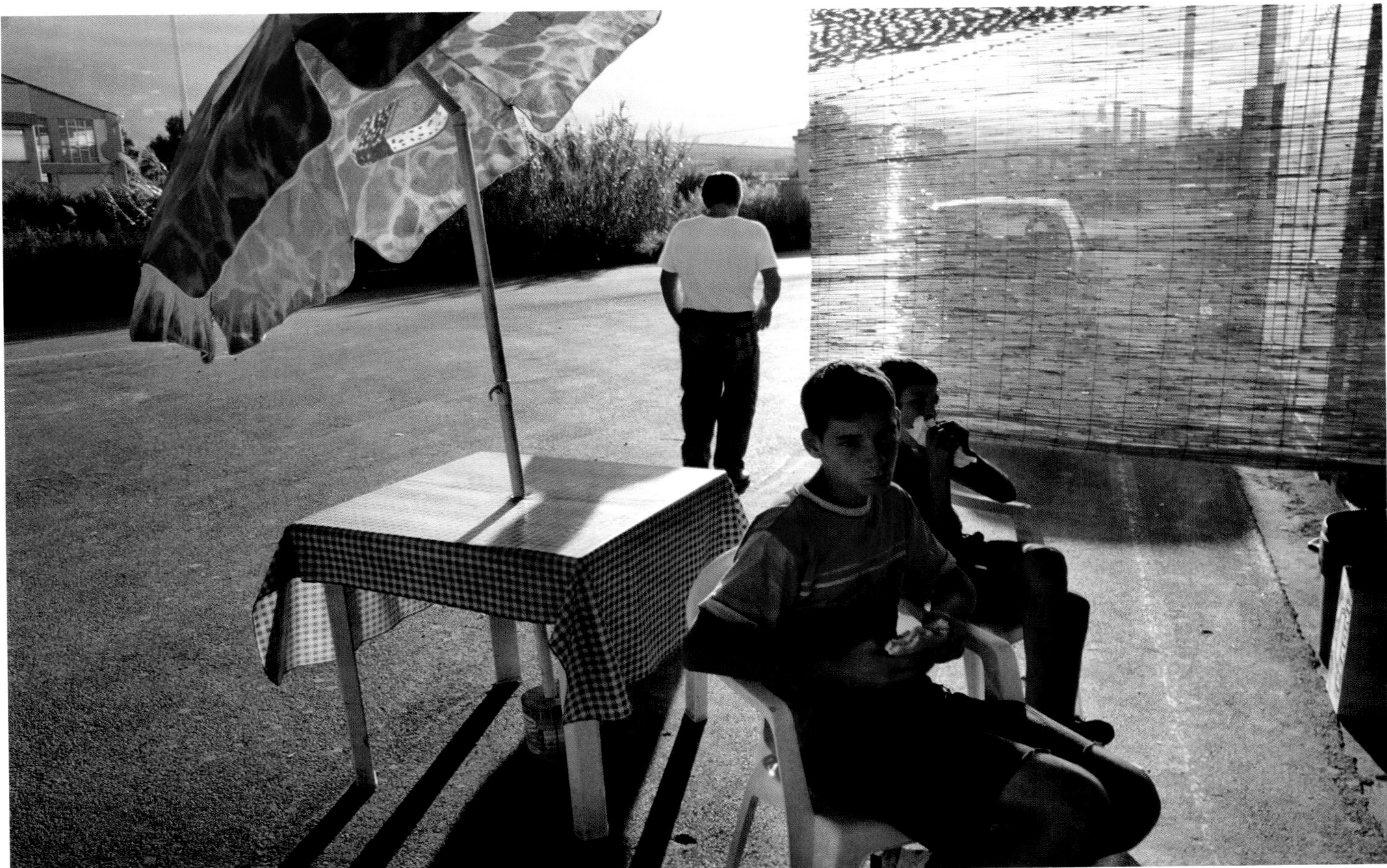

Termini Imerese, May 2002 (EM)

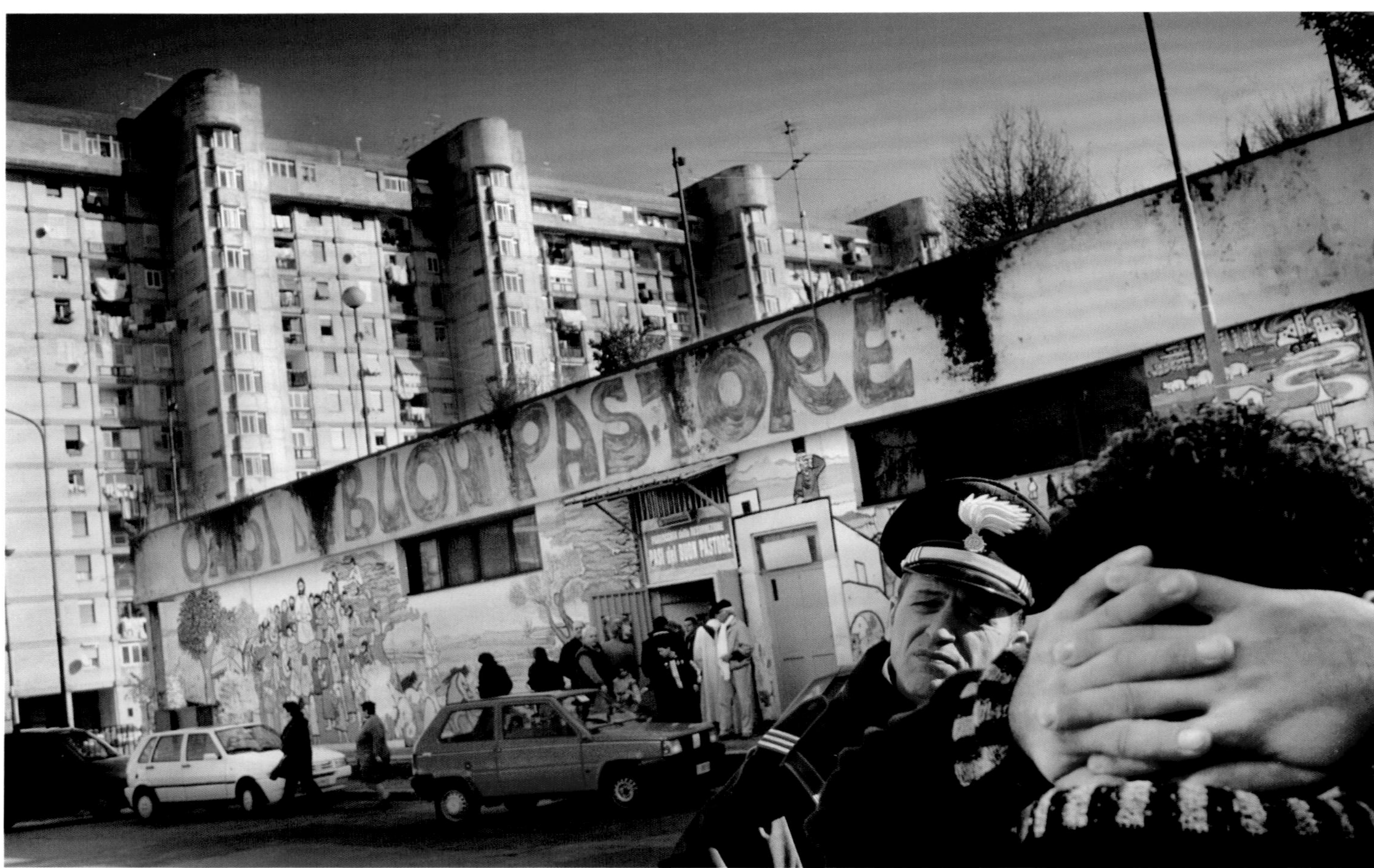


Scampia during the Camorra war, Napoli, December 2004 (EM)

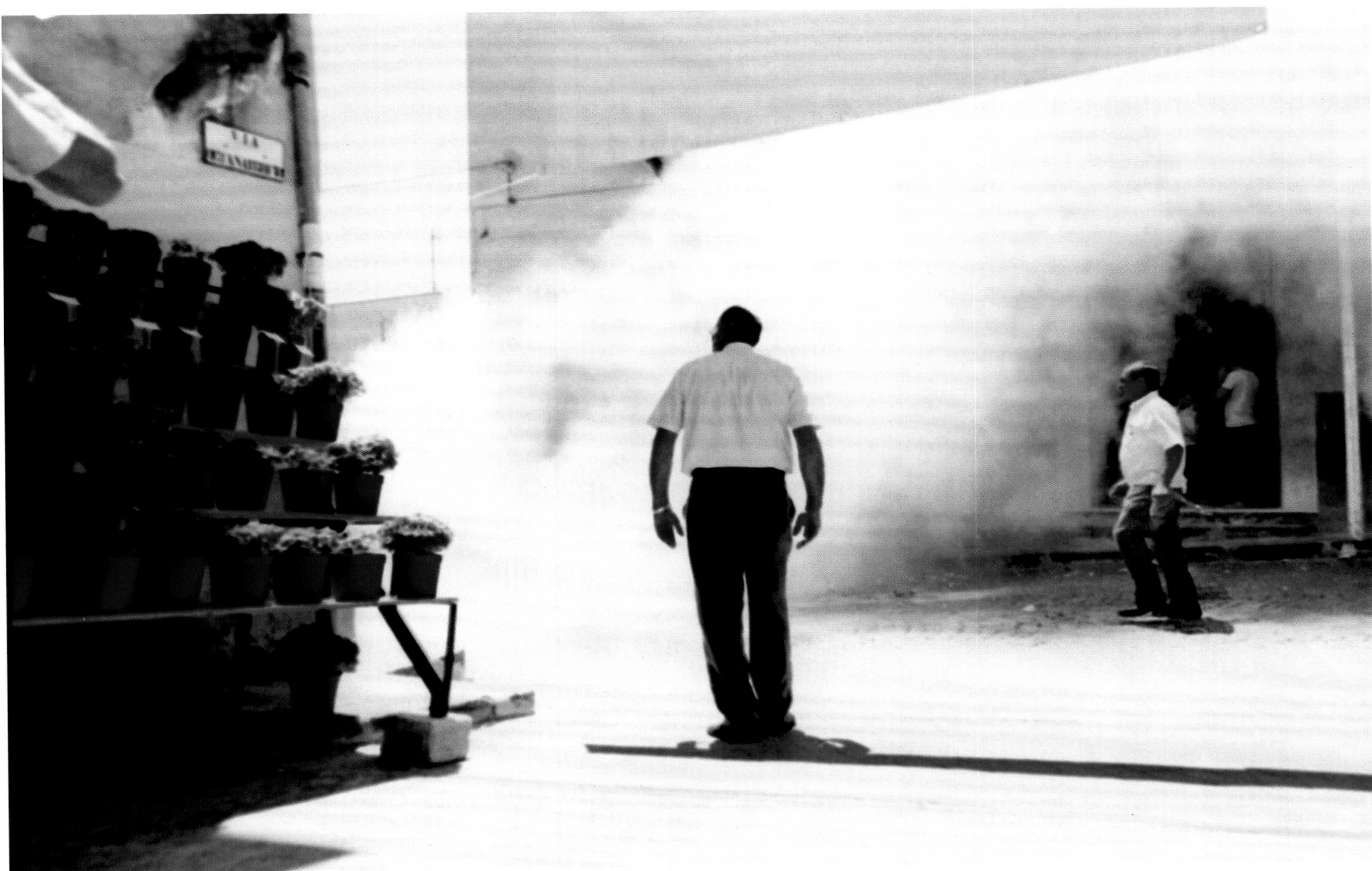

Festival of Gesù Nazareno, San Giovanni Gemini, Agrigento, June 2003 (RS)

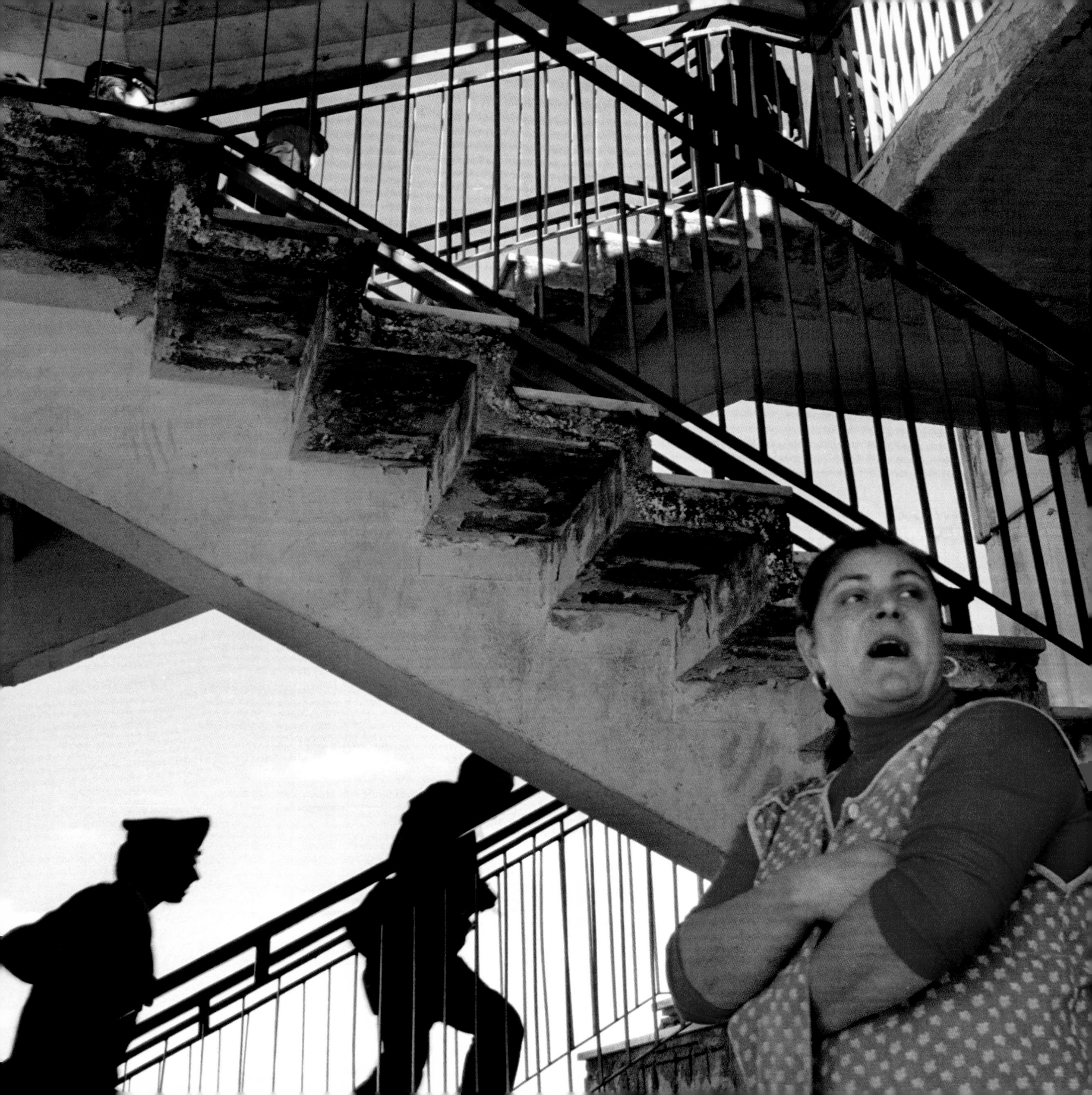

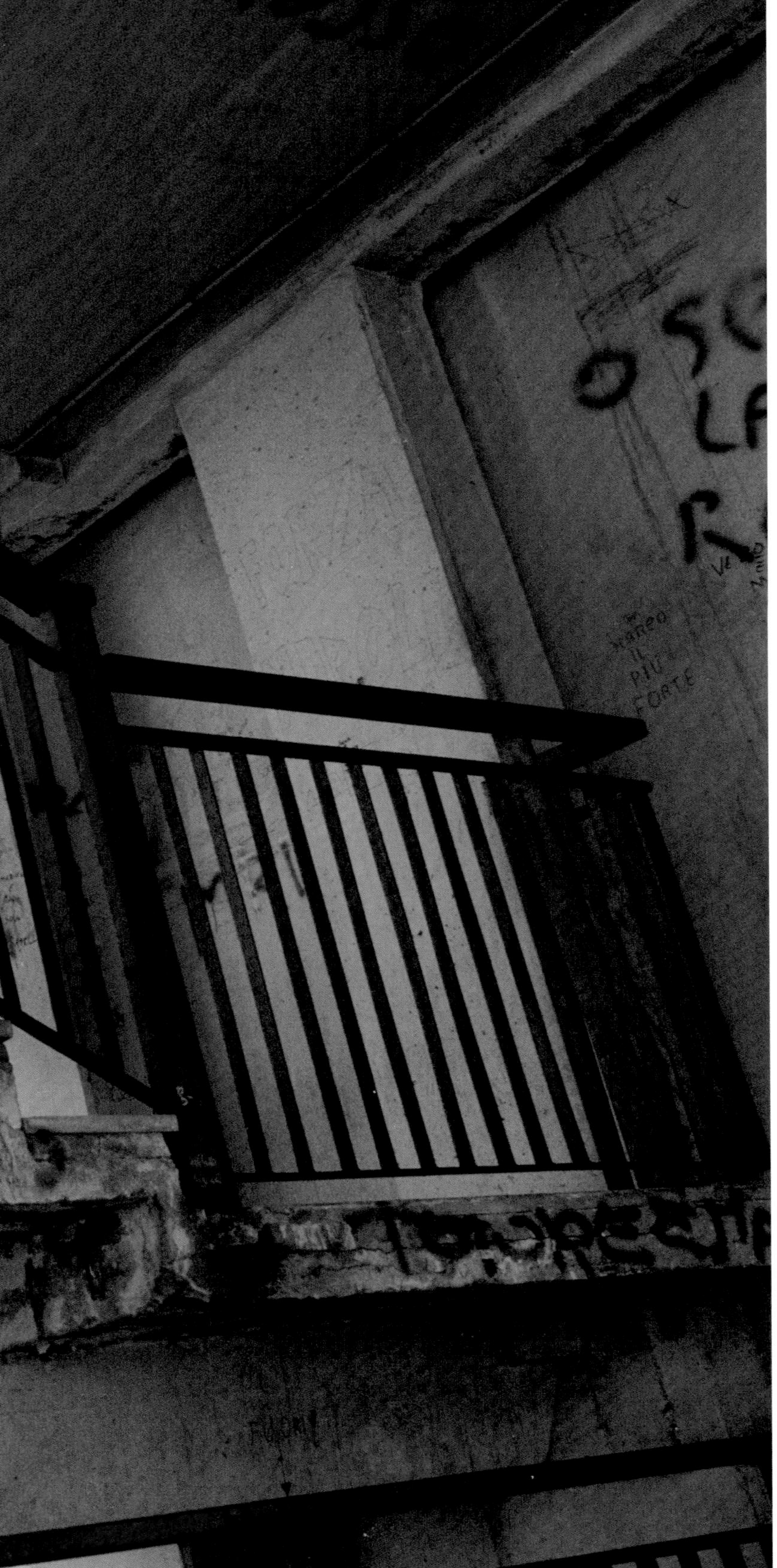

Scampia during the Camorra war, Napoli, December 2004 (EM)

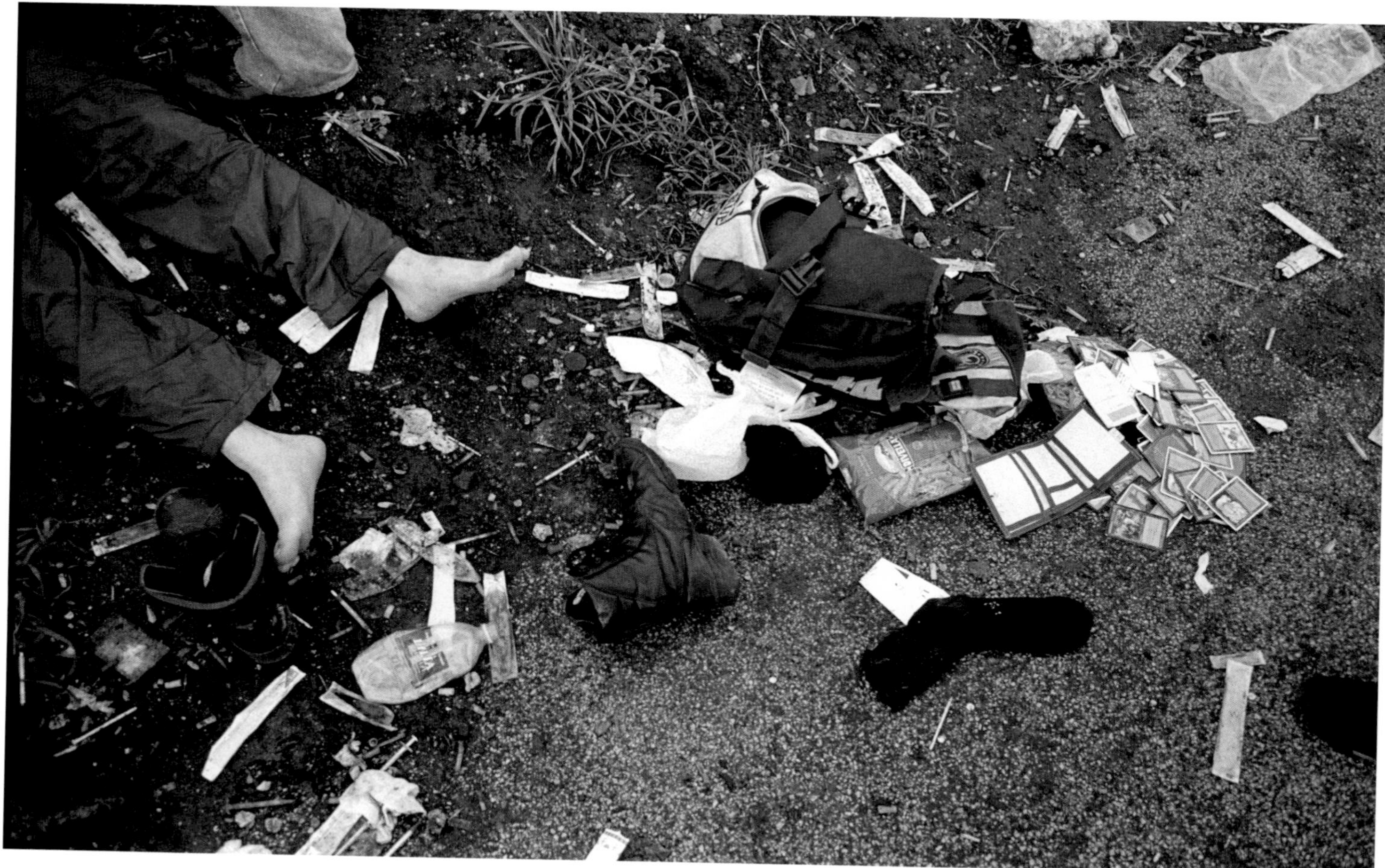

Scampia during the Camorra war, Napoli, December 2004 (MS)

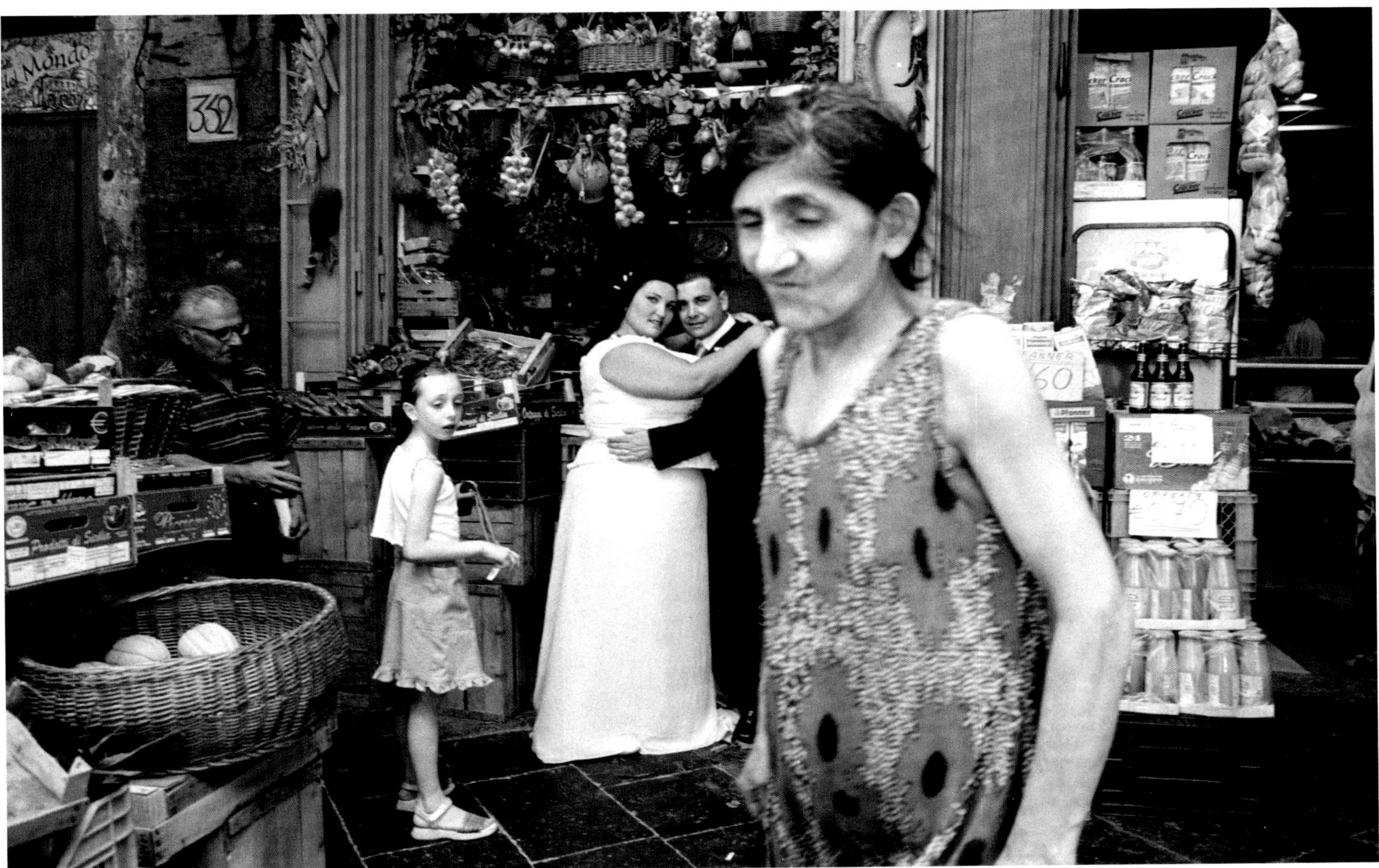


Wedding, Napoli, June 2003 (MS)

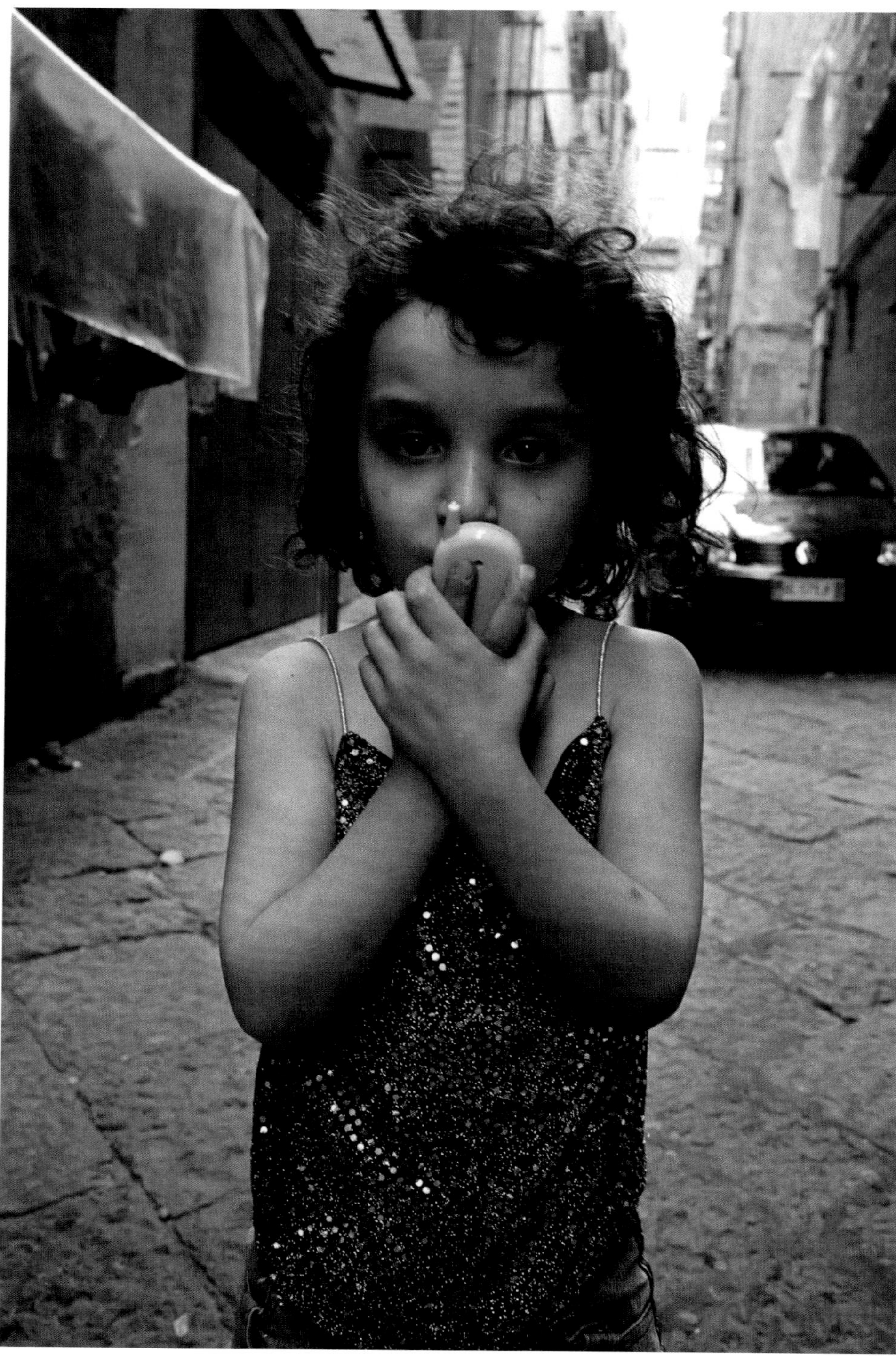

Napoli, April 2002 (MS)

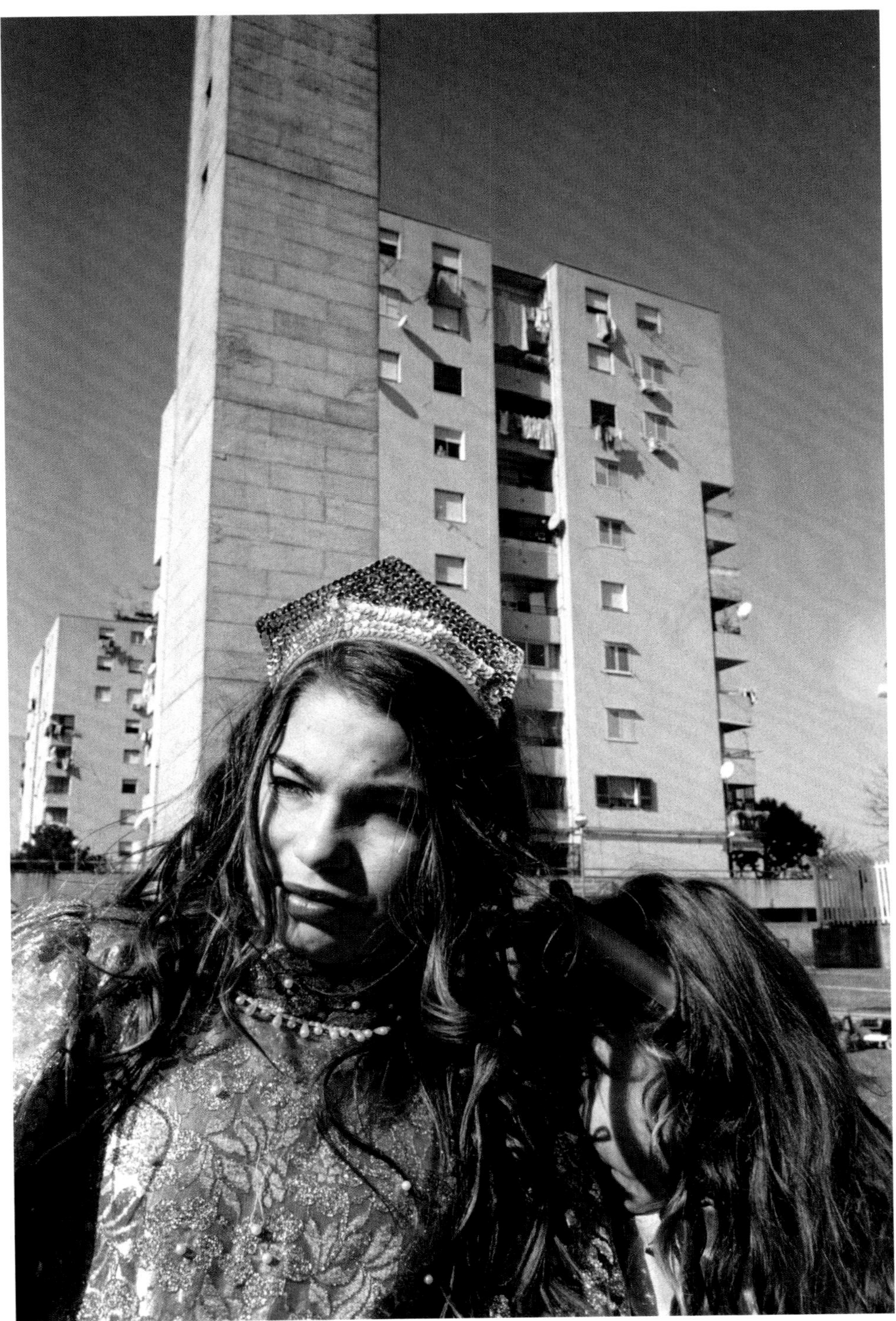

Scampia during the Camorra war,
Napoli, January 2005 (MS)

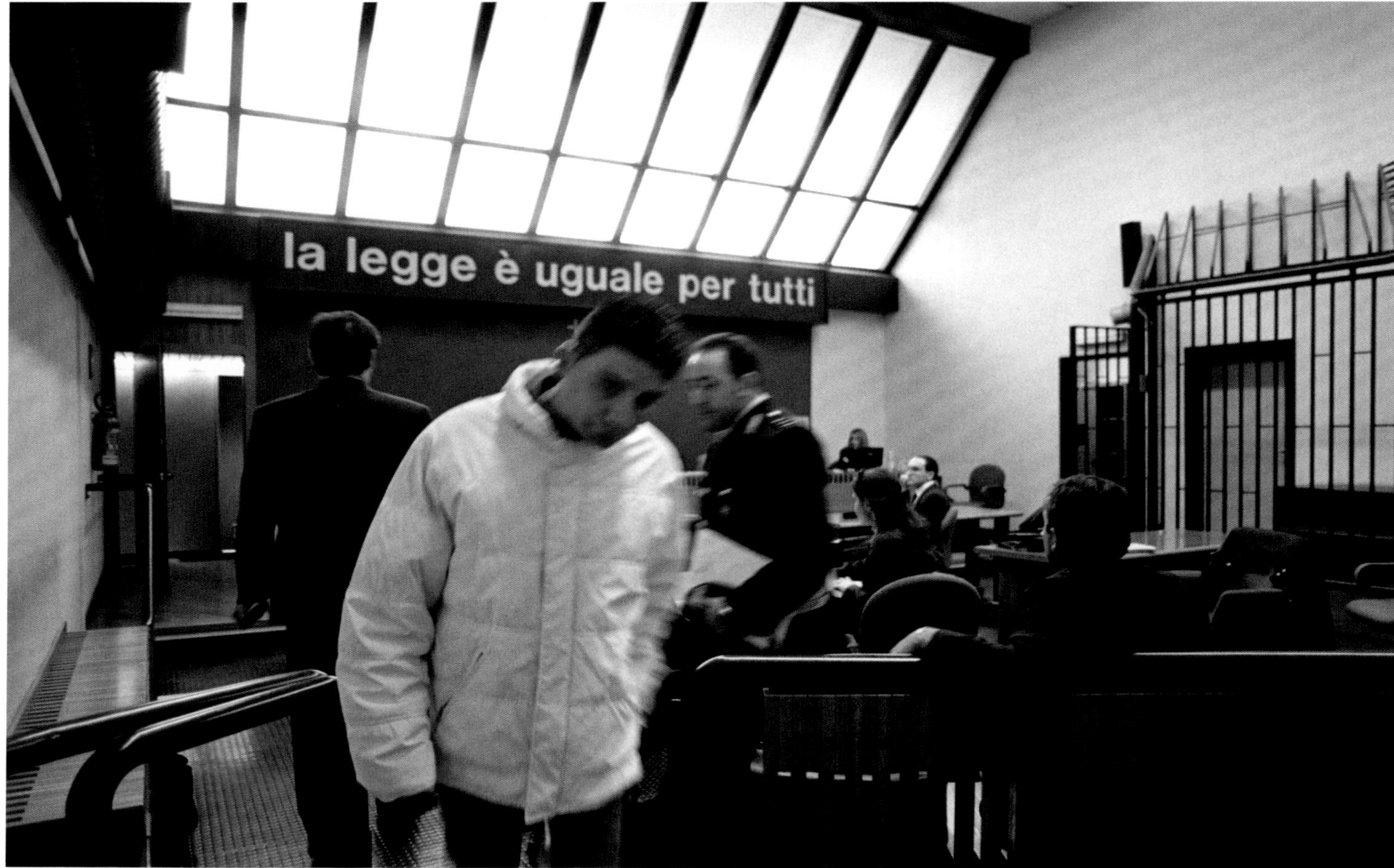


Napoli, May 2002 (MS)

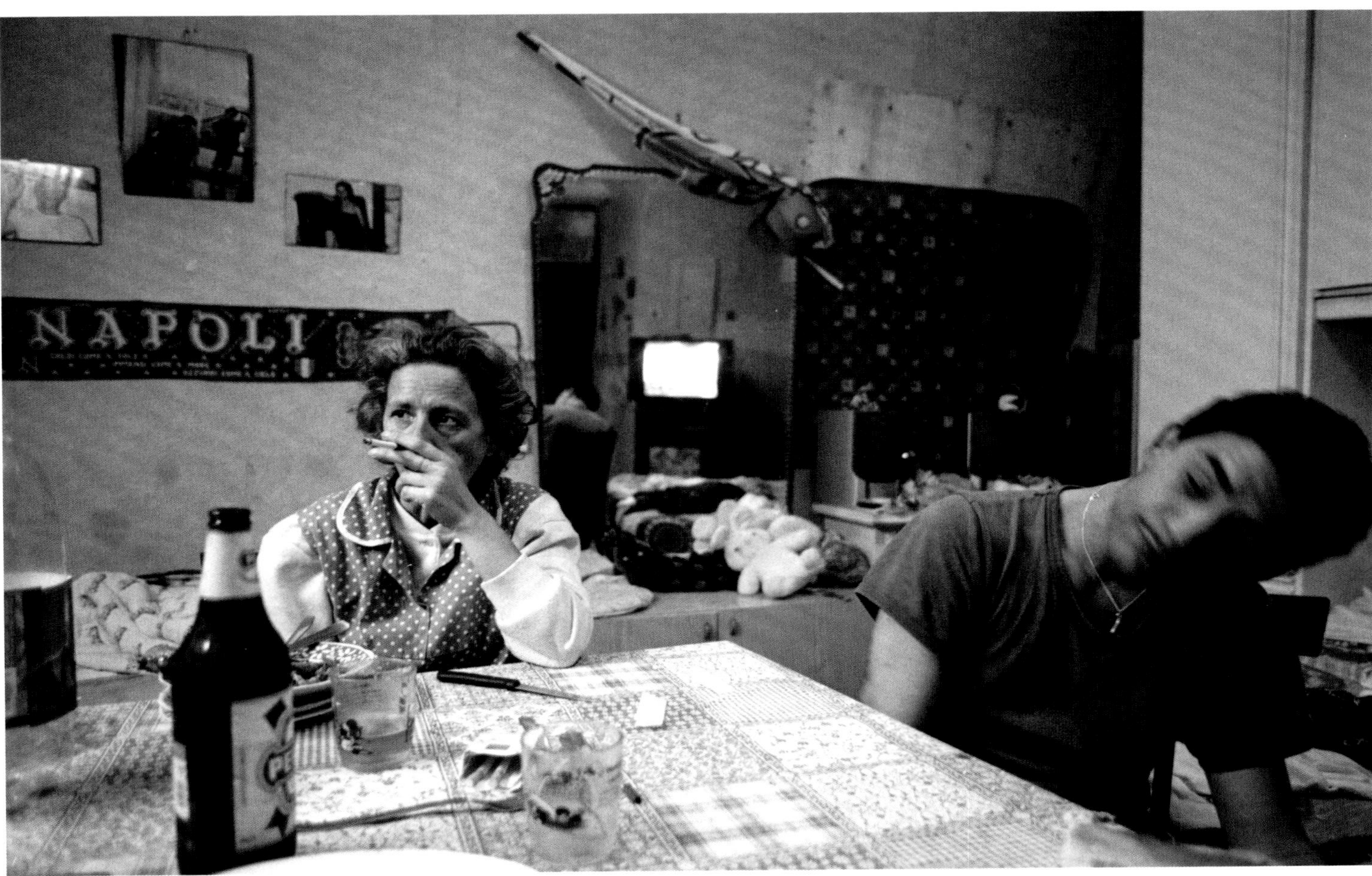


Napoli,April 2002 (MS)

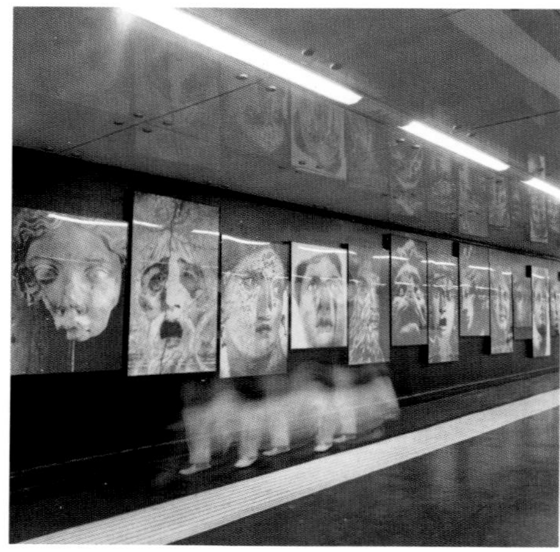

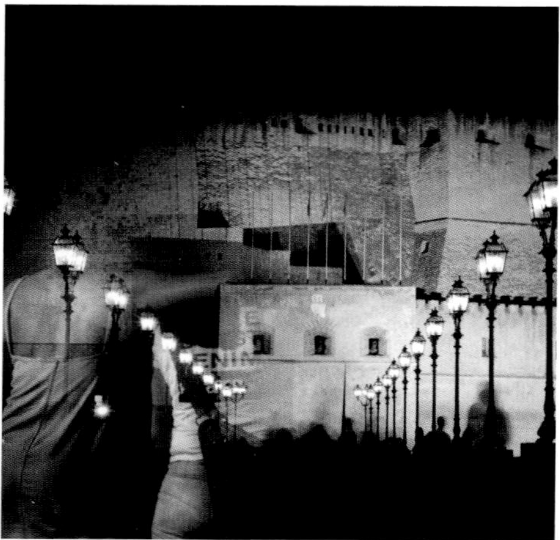

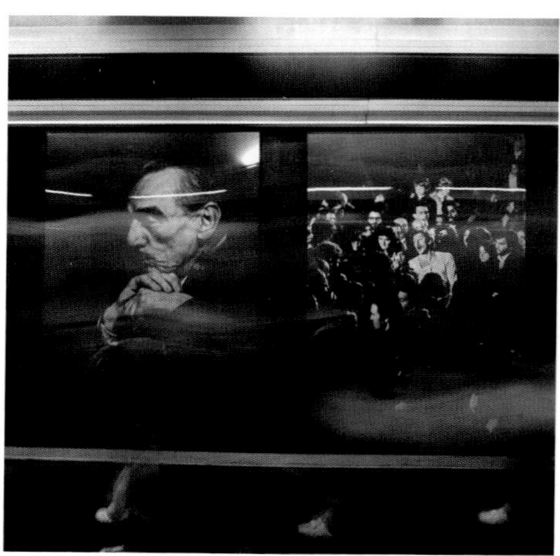

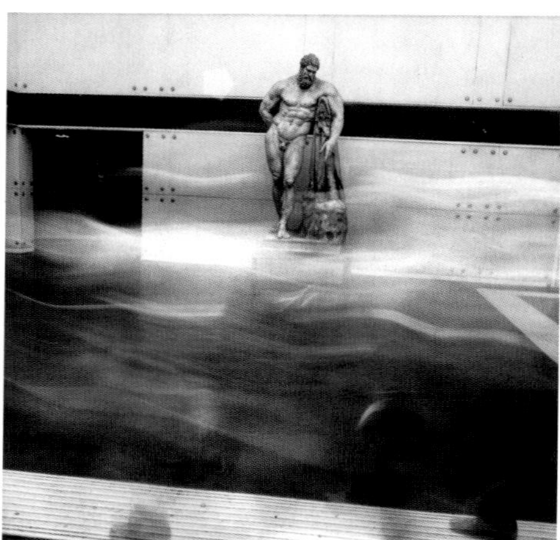

Metro, Napoli, October 2005 (MS)

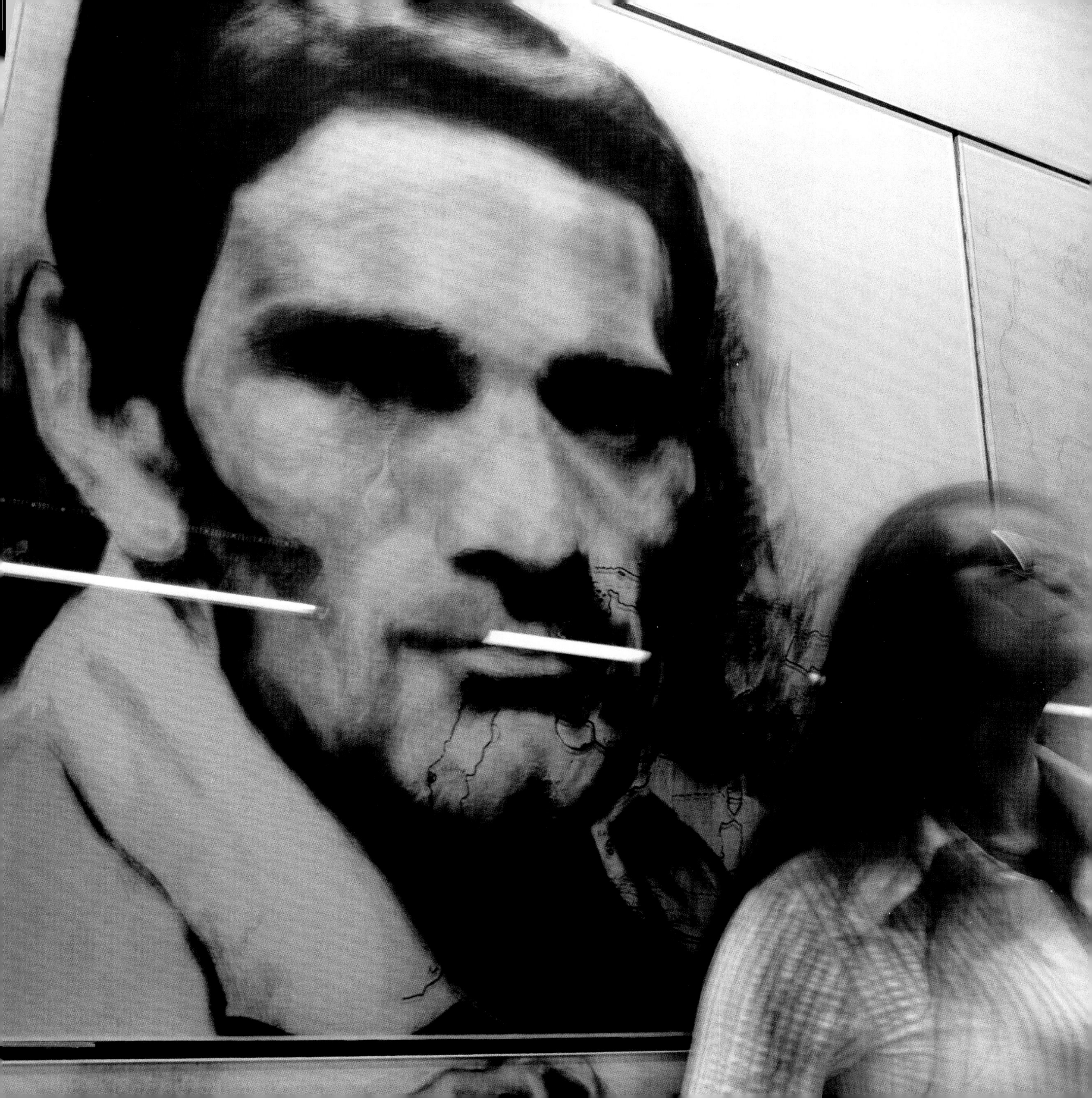

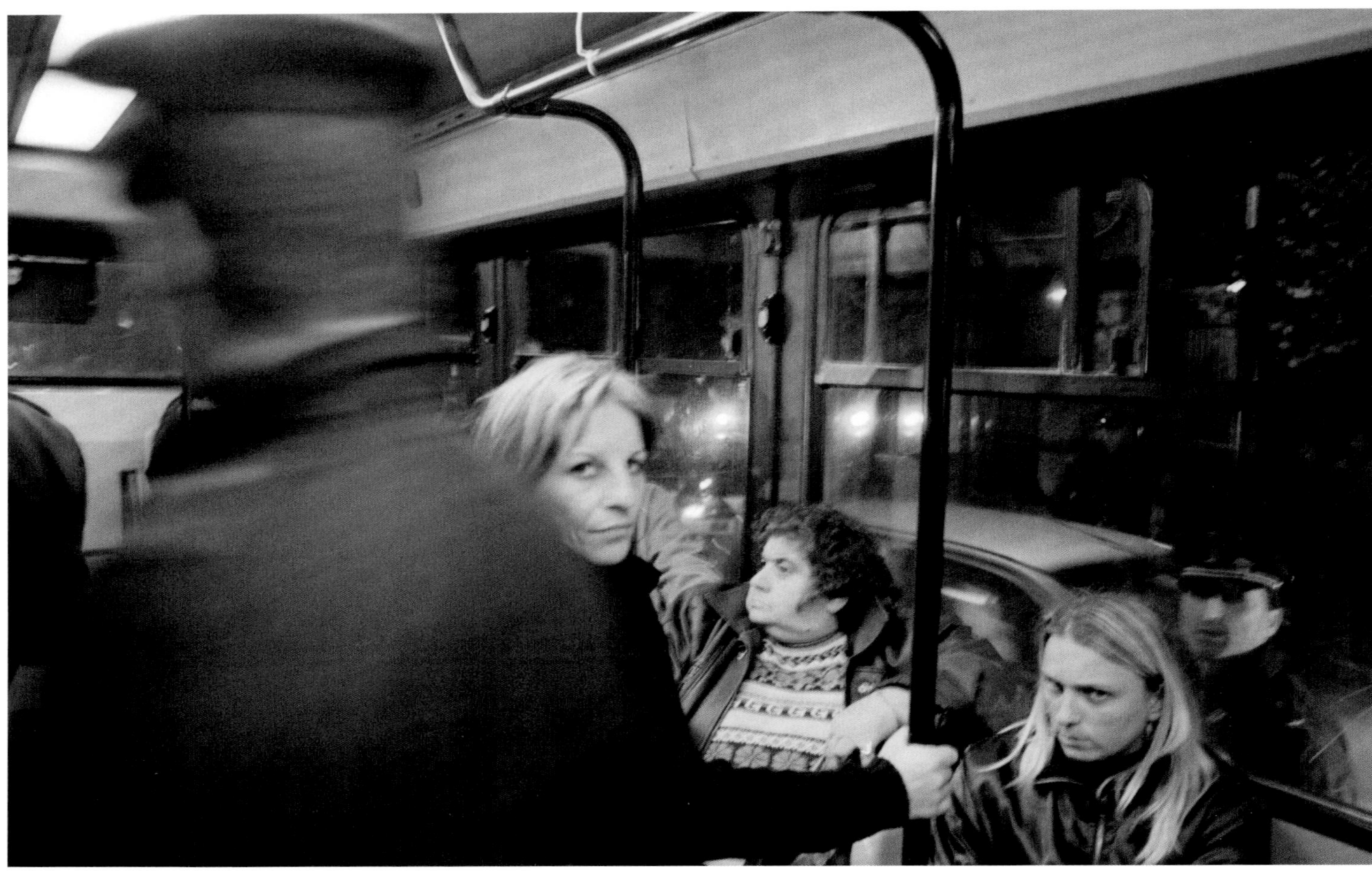

*Above and right* Scampia during the Camorra war, Napoli, December 2004 (MS)

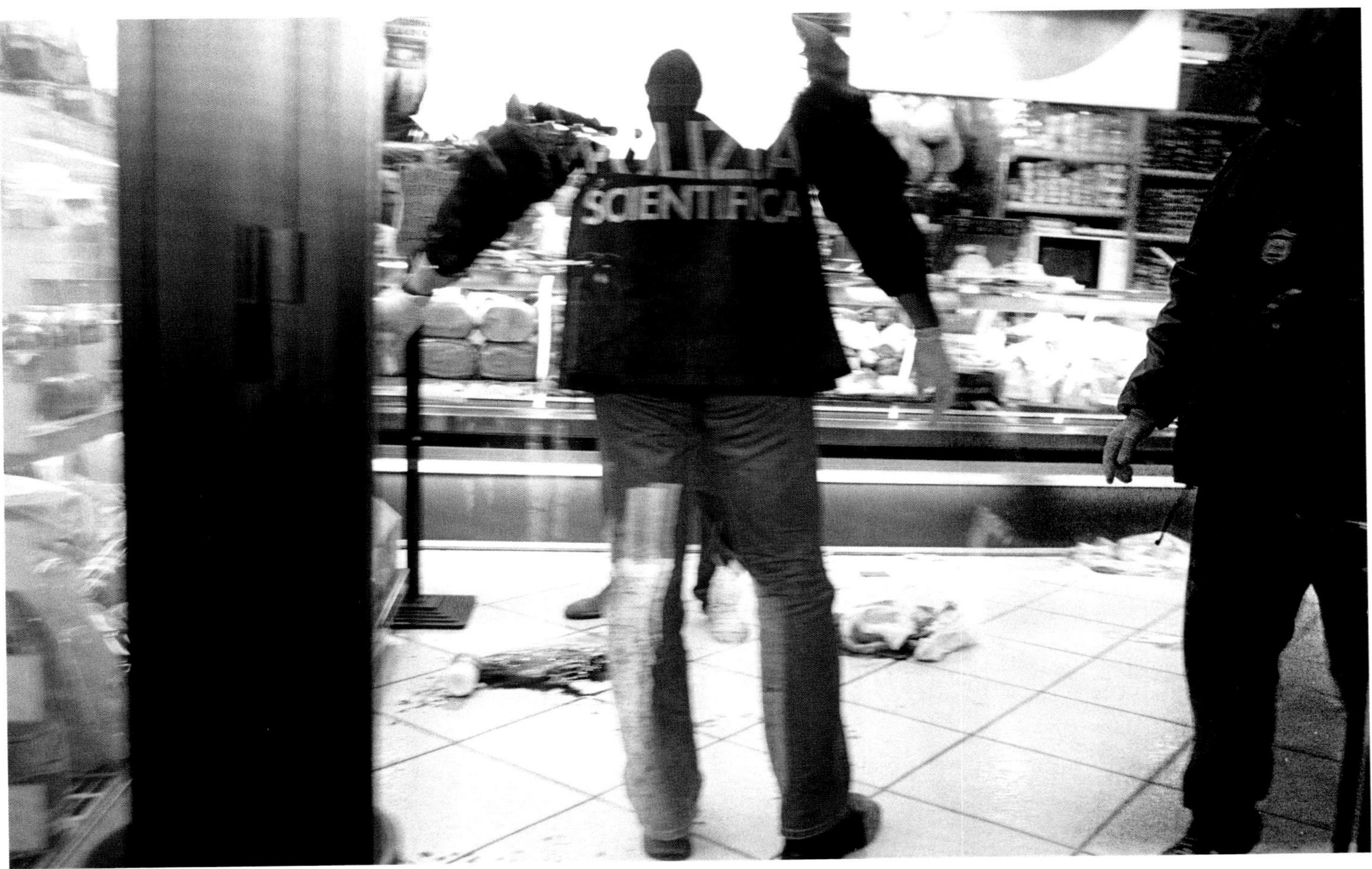
POLIZIA
SCIENTIFICA

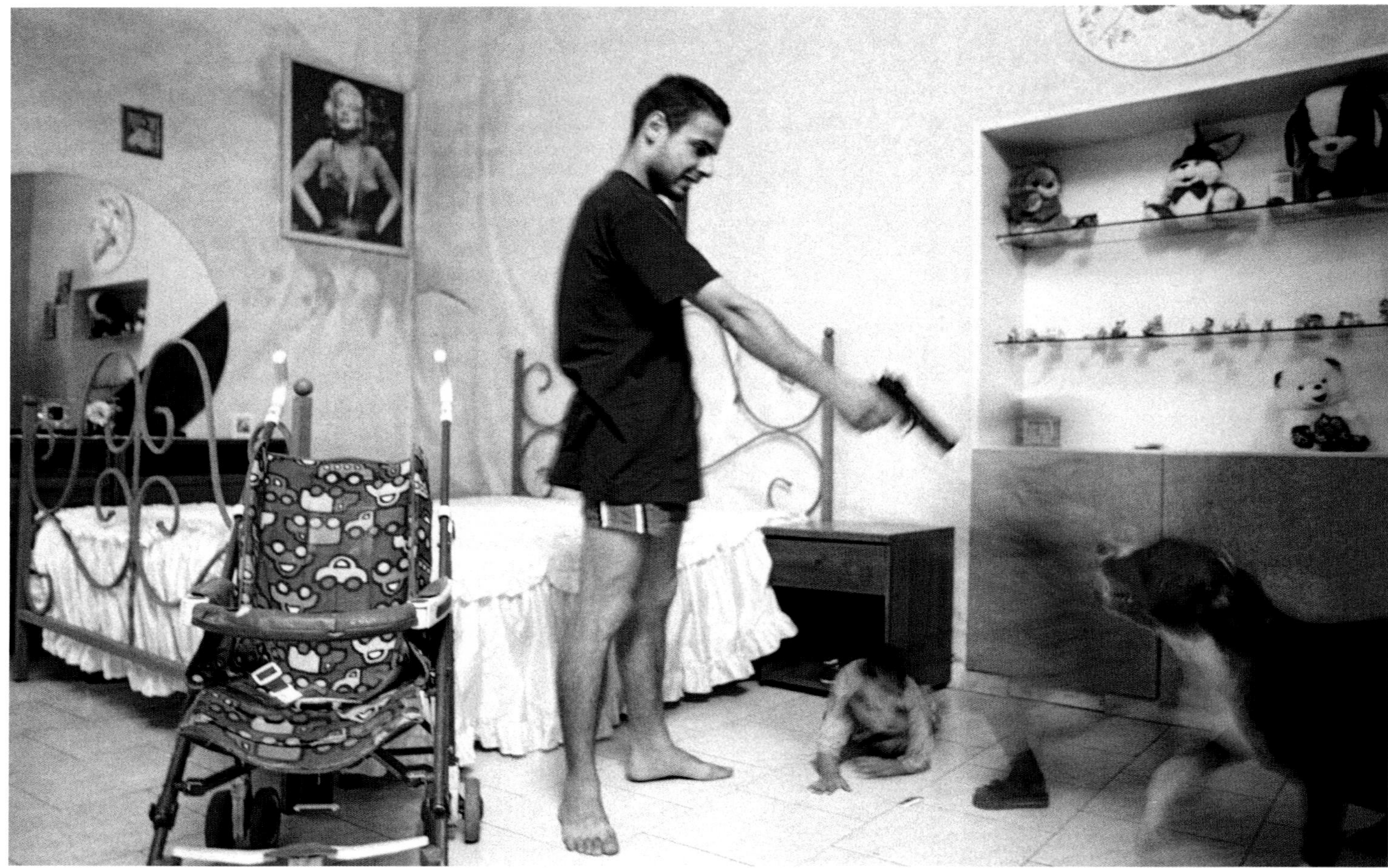

Napoli, January 2002 (MS)

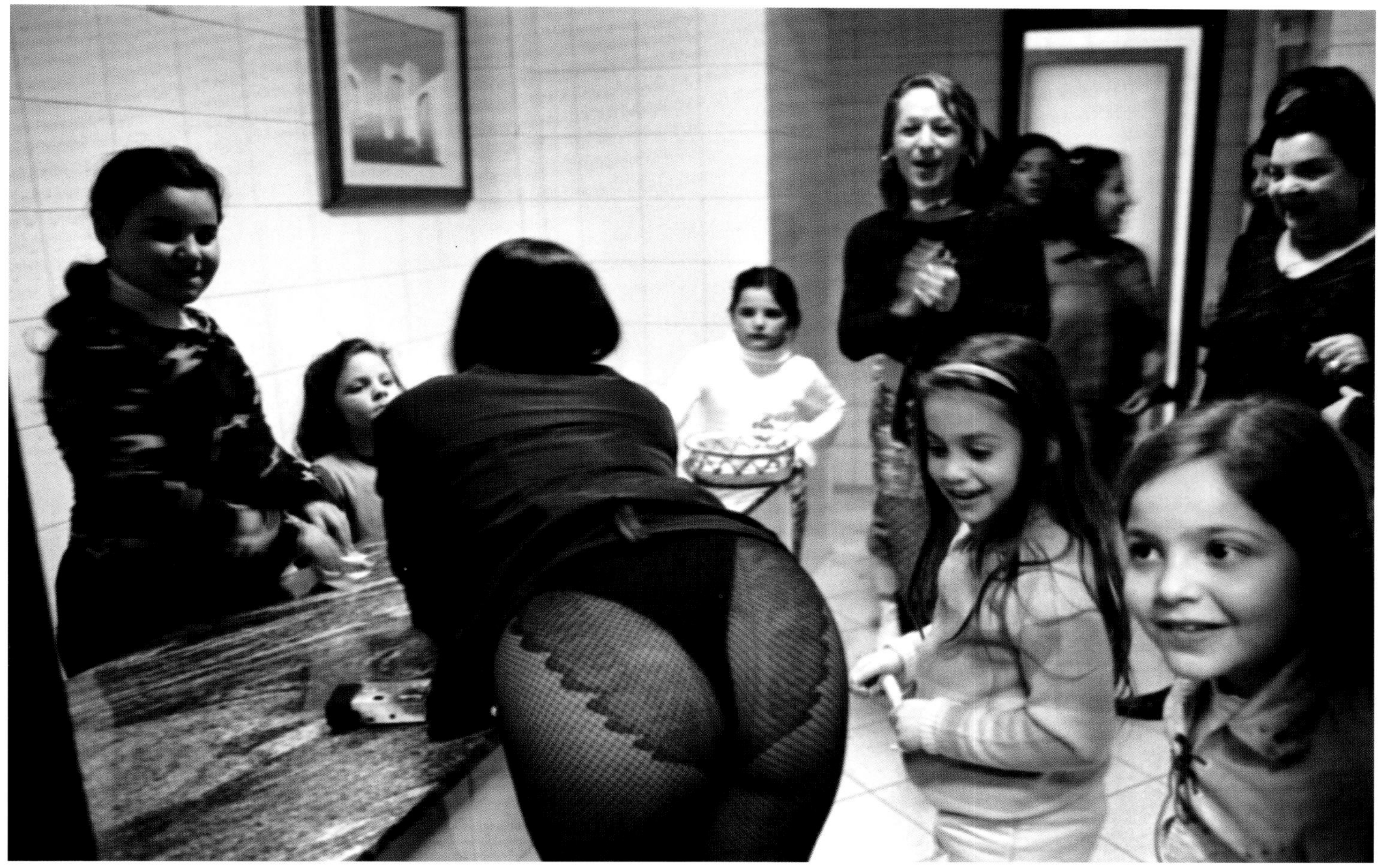

Napoli, September 2002 (MS)

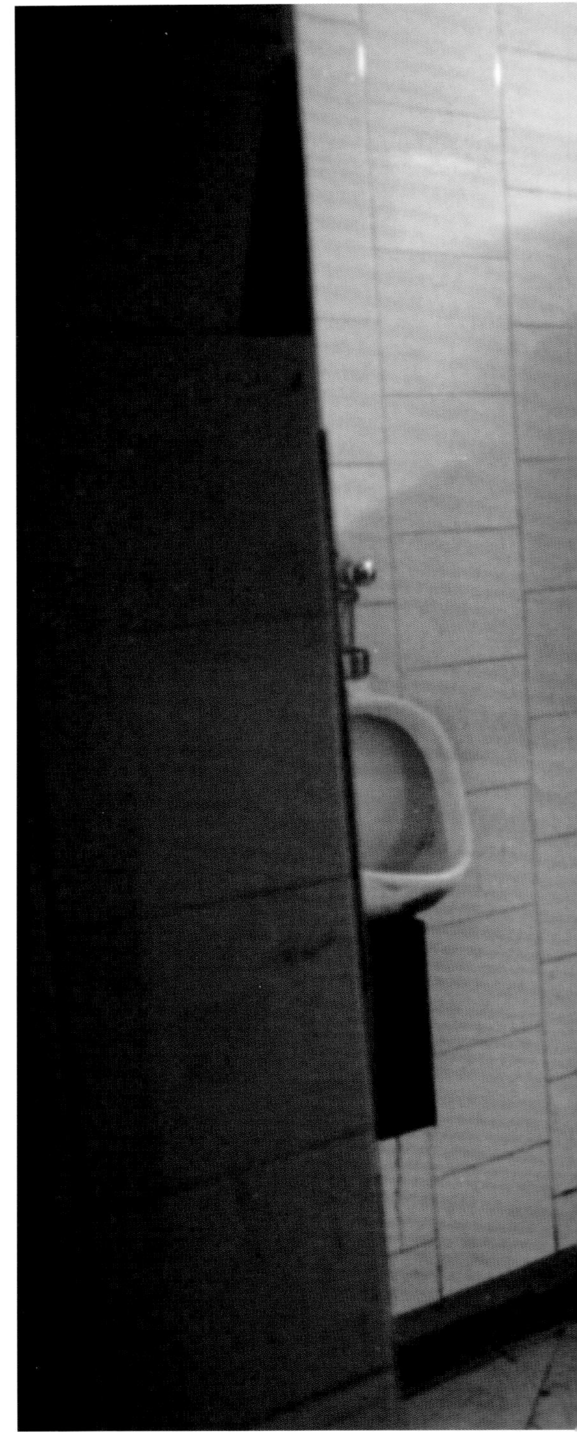

Napoli, September 2002 (MS)

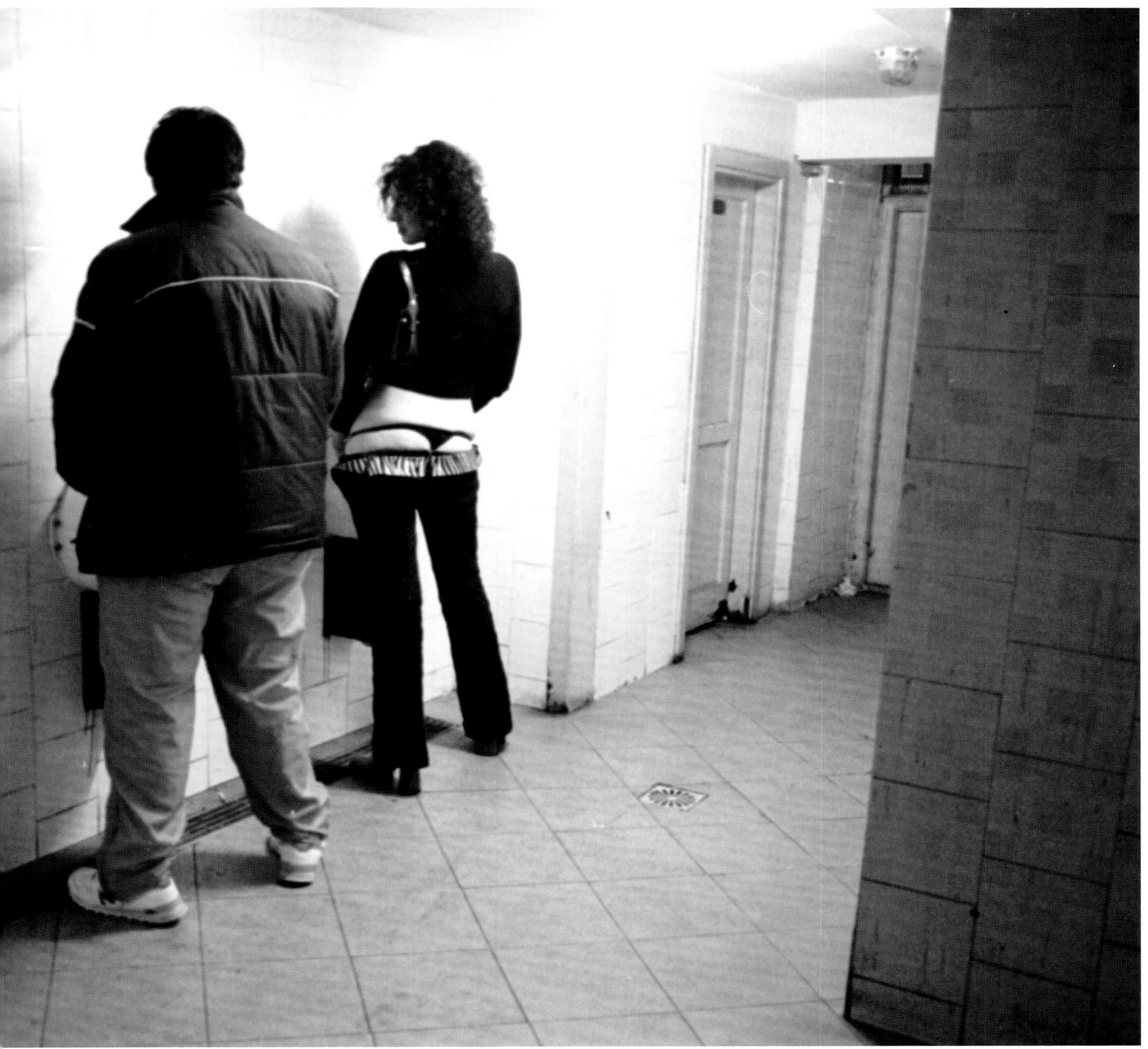

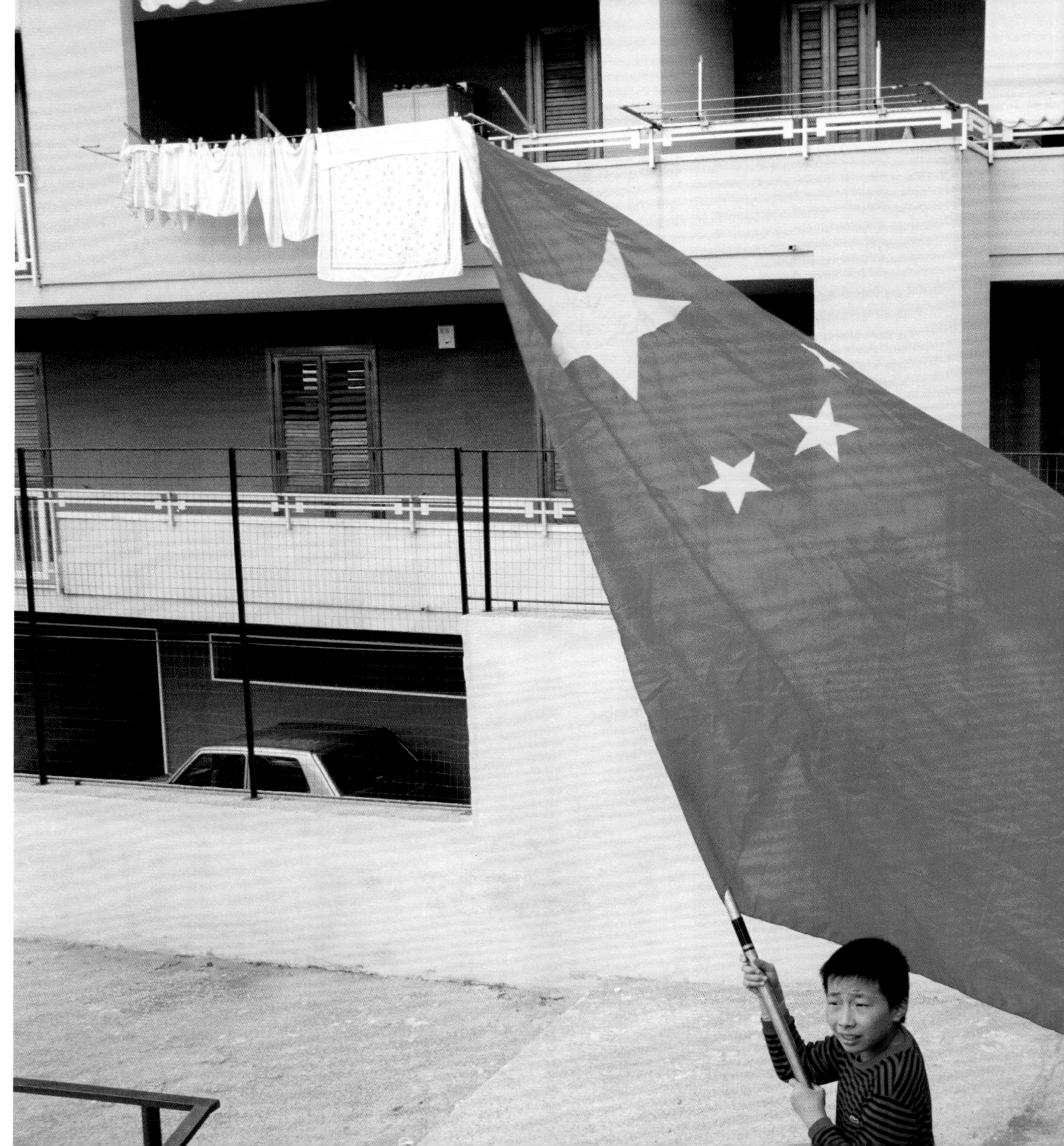

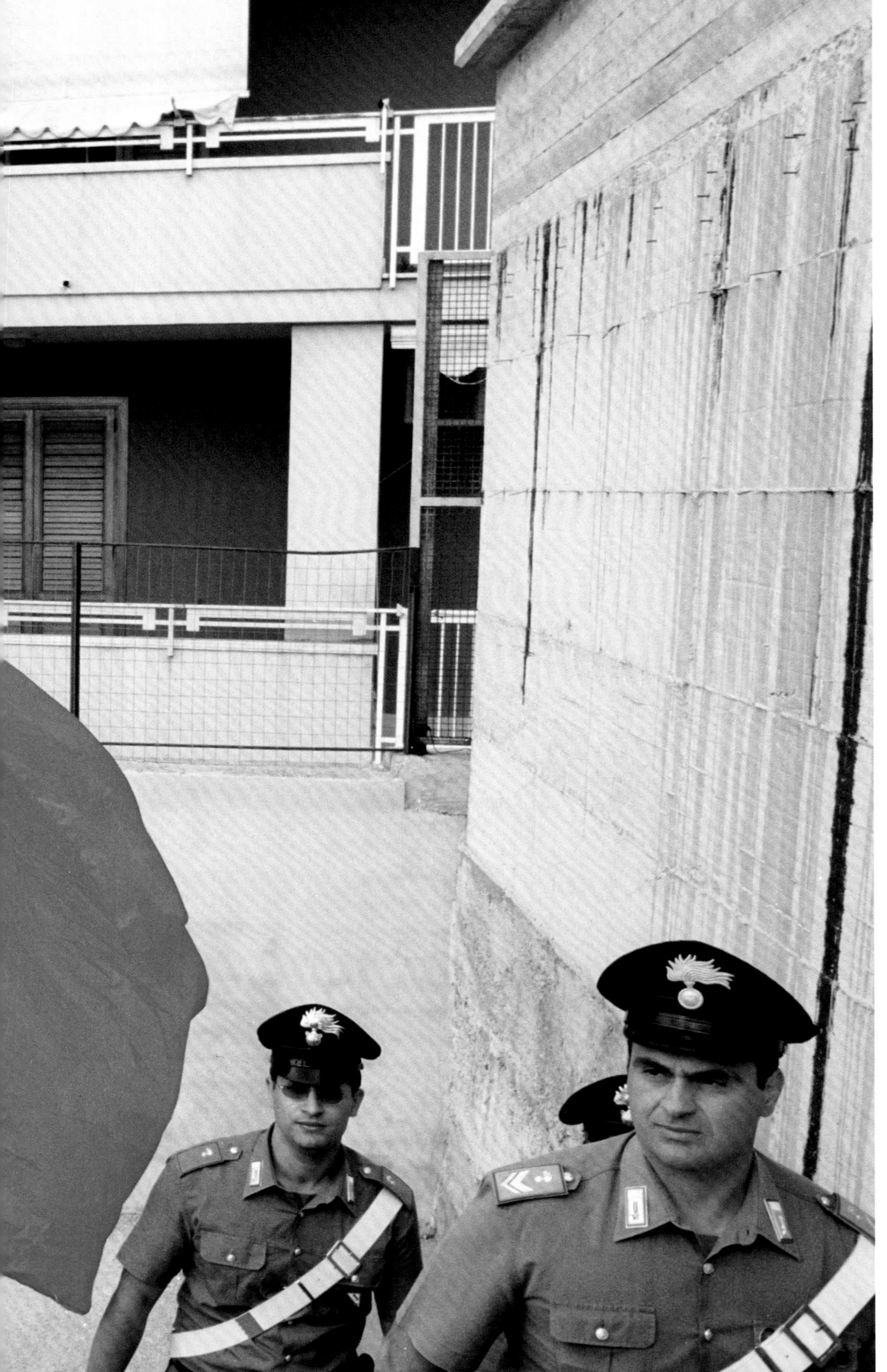

Chinese immigrant village Palma Campania,
Napoli, September 2004 (EM)

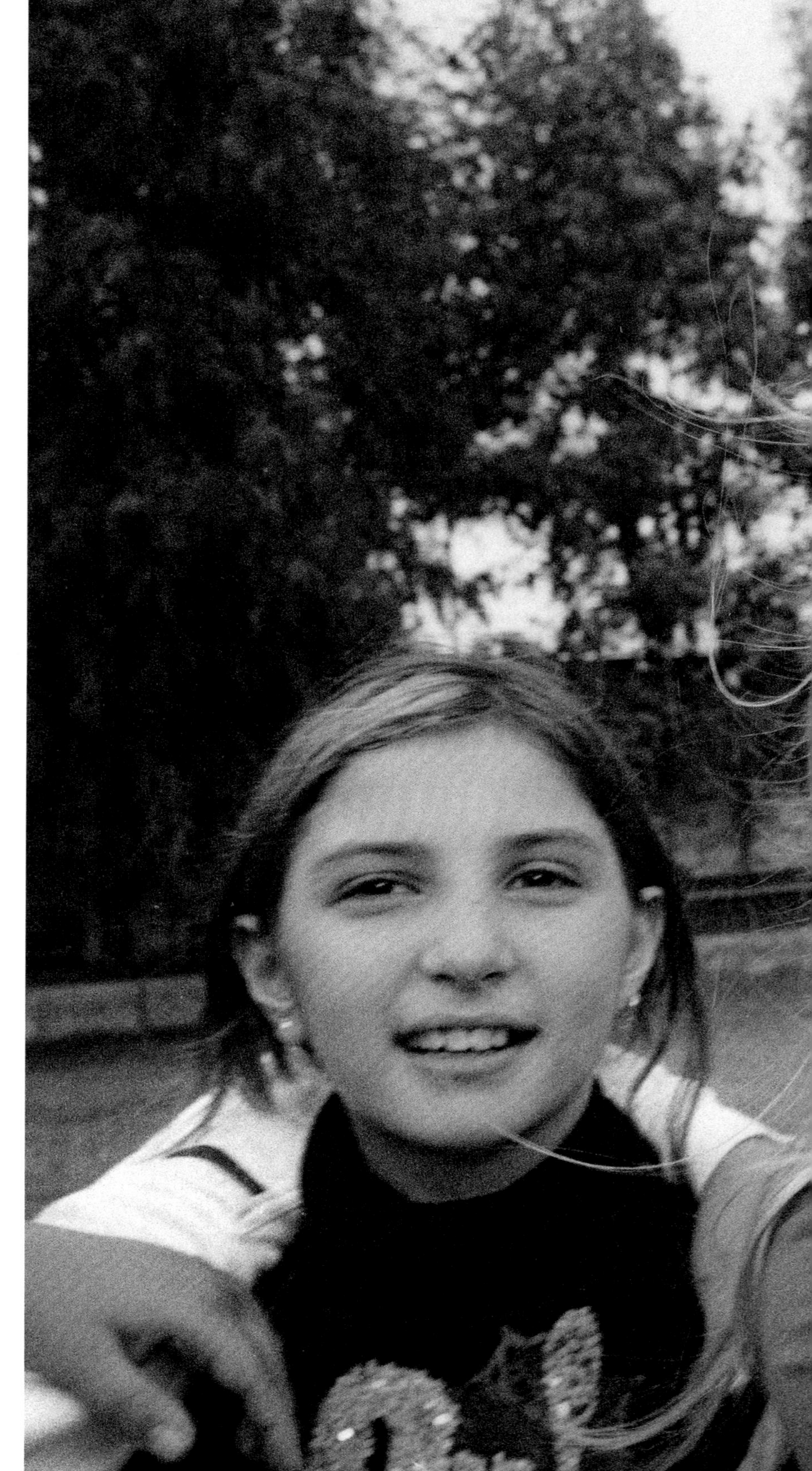

Secondigliano during the Camorra war, Napoli, January 2005 (MS)

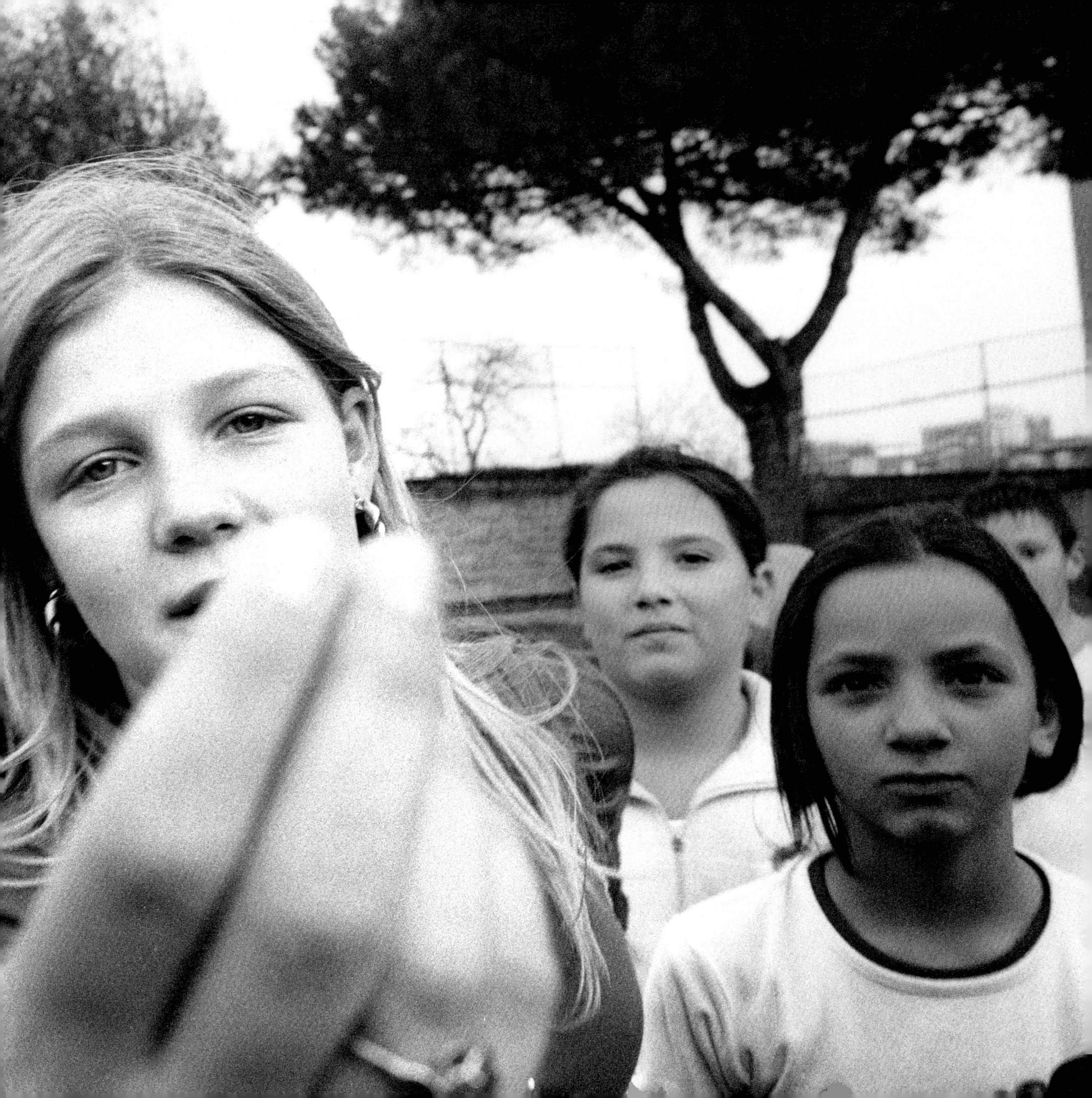

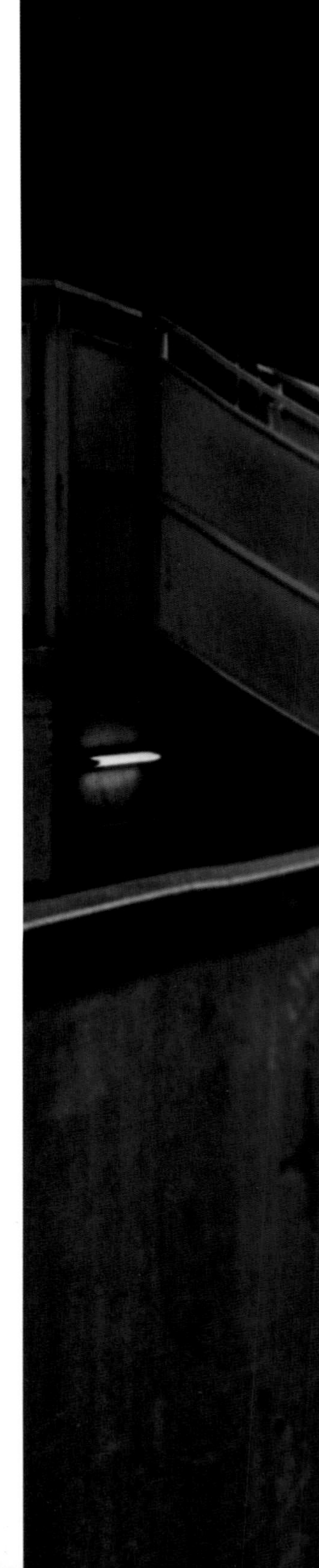

Secondigliano during the Camorra war, Napoli, January 2005 (MS)

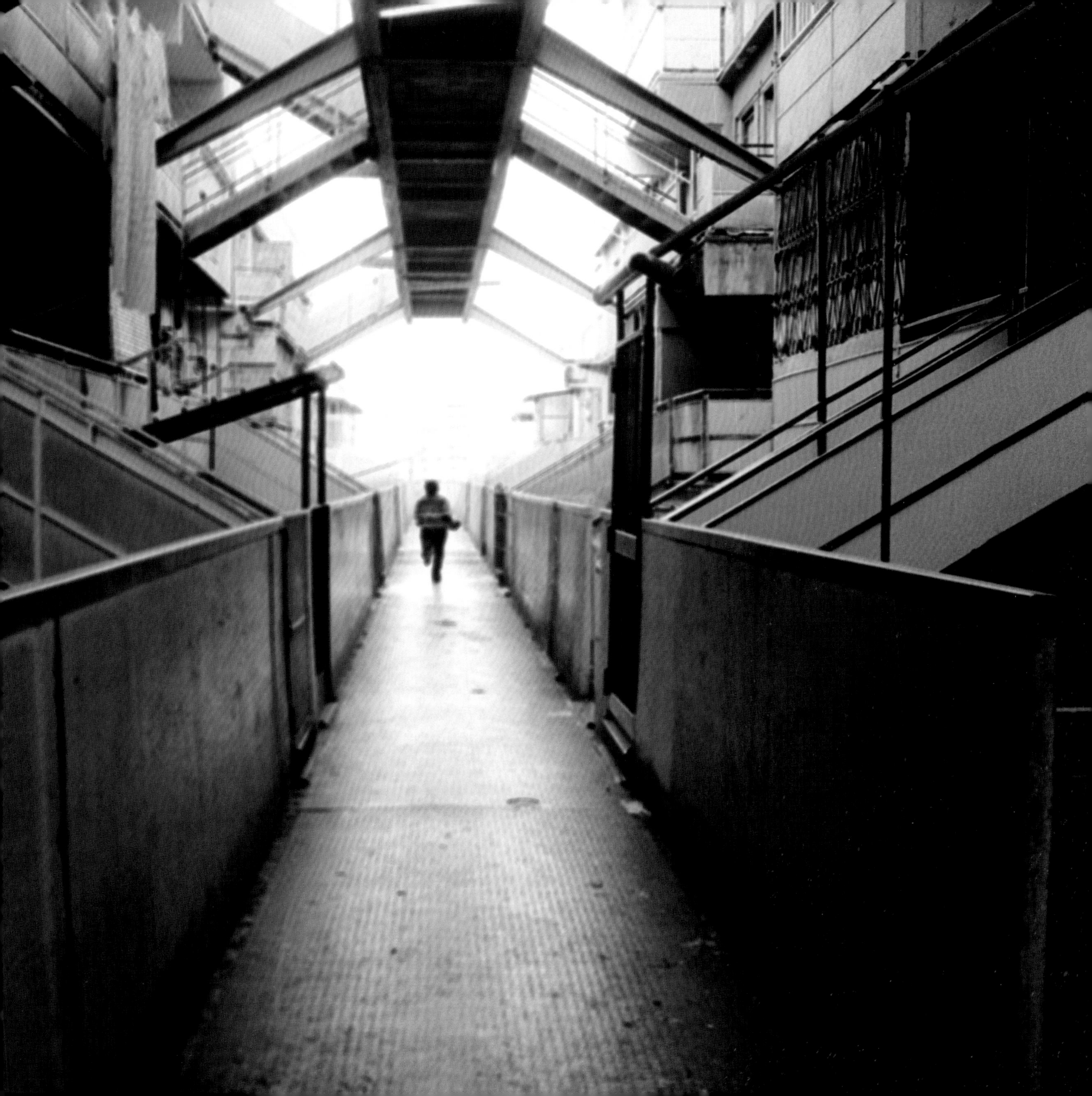

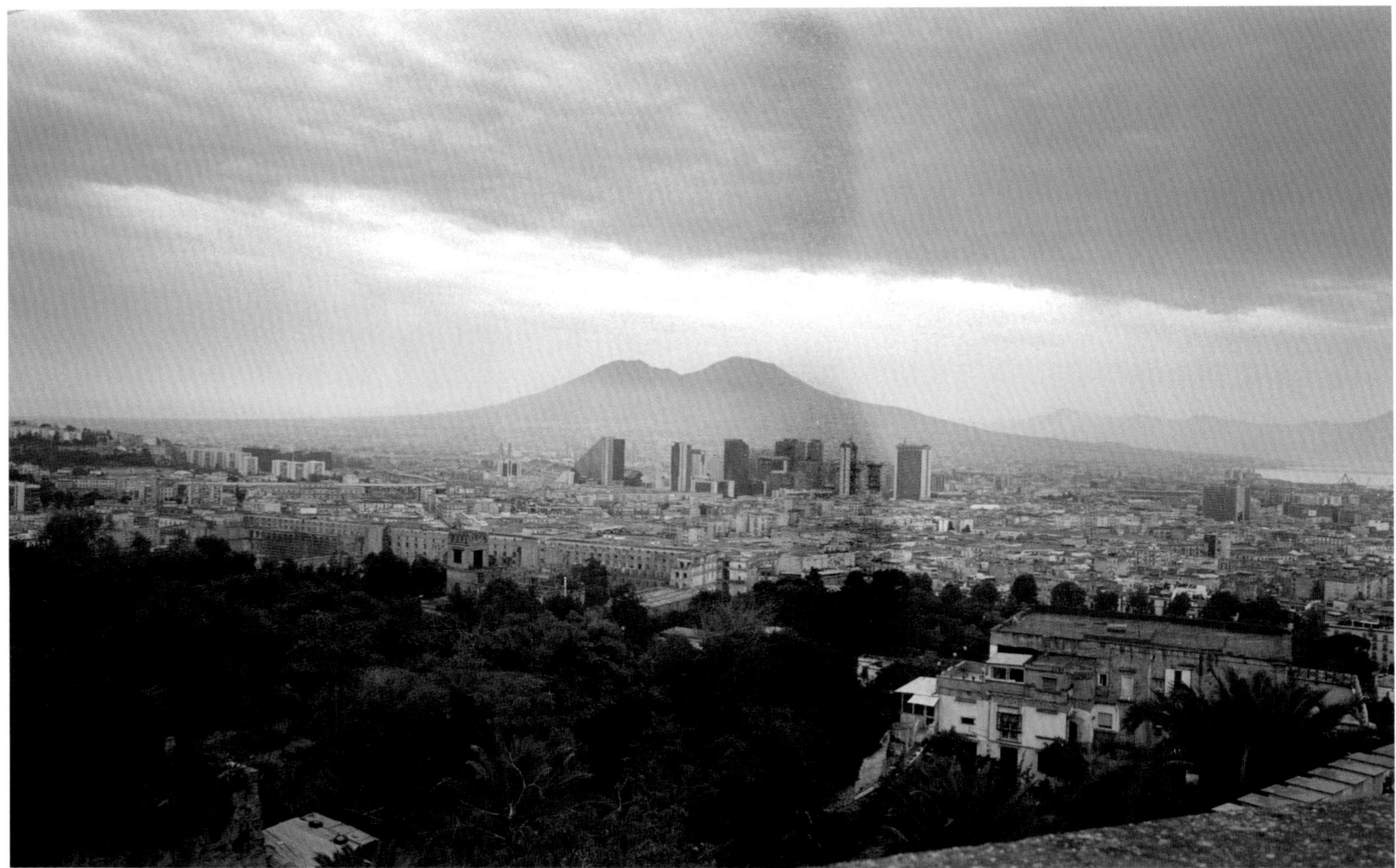

Napoli, April 2002 (MS)

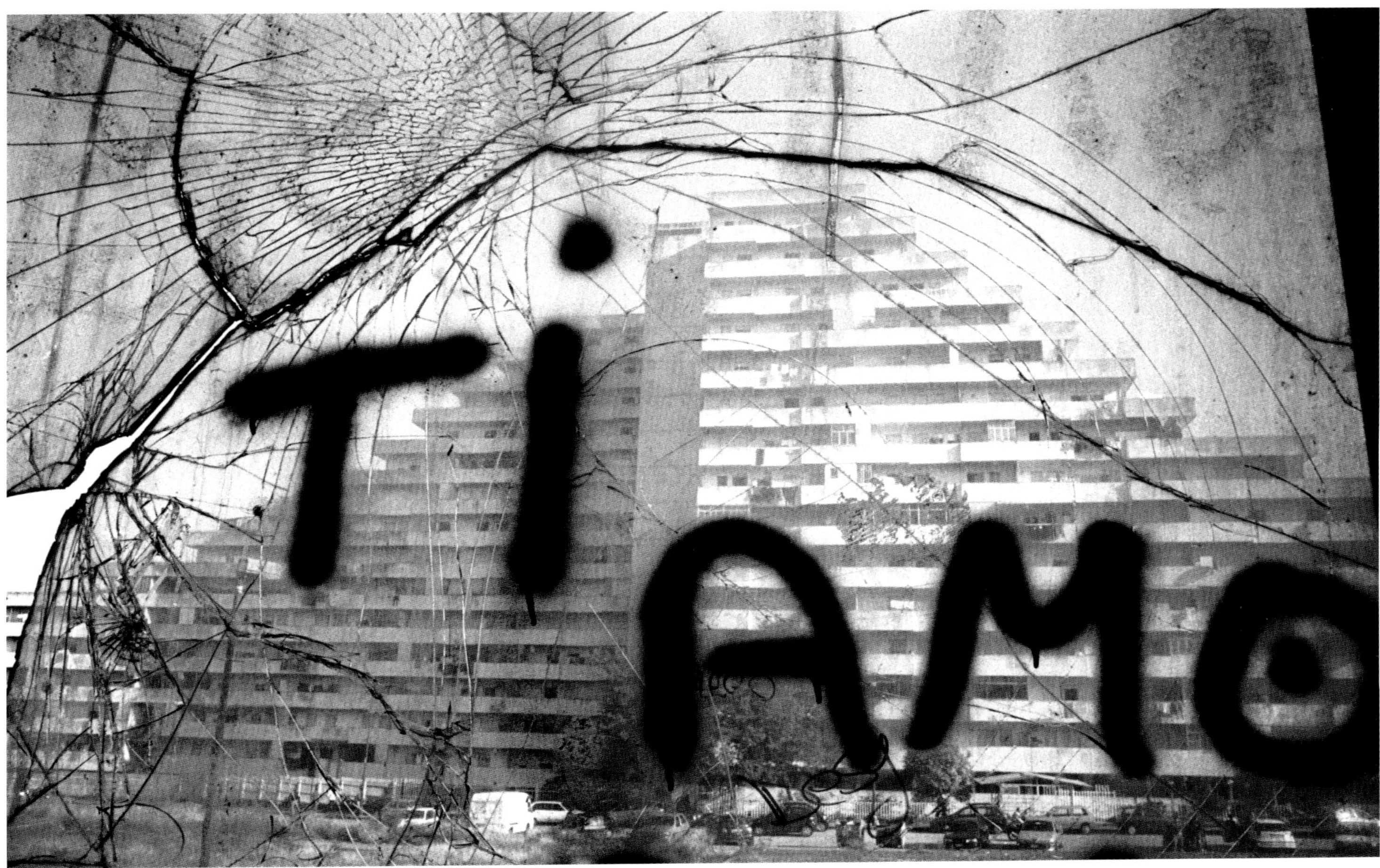


Vele di Scampia during the Camorra war, Napoli, January 2005 (MS)

# ACKNOWLEDGEMENTS

Giorgio Accardo, Diana Adu, Martin Bell, Valentino Berruti and Laura Durante, Maurizio Bono, Antonio Cadeddu, Manila Camarini, Angelo Carnielo, Stefania Celletti, Ciro the photographer from Scampia, Claudia and Giampietro, Andrea Codemo, Daniele Coralli, Alessandro Cosmelli, Alice Crose, Fabio Cuttica, don Vitaliano Della Sala, Gianluca Di Gioia, Enzo and Gina, Emanuela Evangelista, Marisa Faraoni, Andrea Frazzetta, Donatello Fumarola, Michele Gazzola, Commander Renato Giannantonio, Gigi Giannuzzi, Alessandra Grillo, Biagio Ippolito, Martina Lentini, Silvia Litardi, Luca and Consuelo, Francesco Mancuso, Paola Marchetti, Claudia Marelli, Maria Antonia, Mimmi and Fabio, Davide Monteleone, Paolo and Margherita, Nicola Parente, Mauro Parrini, Anna Paulinyi, Raffaele and Liliana Petrilli, Carmelo Porcu, Livio Quagliata, Massimo de Romanis, Ferdinando Scianna, Aurelio and Daniele Scibetta, Alessandro Scotti, Massimo Sestini, Hannah Watson

# ASSOCIATION FOR THE CENTENARY OF CGIL

All friends of Anna, Emiliano, Giancarlo, Mario, Massimo, Riccardo and Tiziana

All the Union and blue collar workers that solidly helped us to produce this project

Contrasto Agenzia
Grazia Neri Agenzia
Il Billionaire
Associazione Agrorinasce
Gli A67
Gruppo Gridas di Napoli

Thank you to everyone who contributed to the realization and distribution of this book.

Published in Great Britain in 2006
by Trolley Ltd
www.trolleybooks.com



Project Aut Photo
Project co-ordinator Anna Petrilli
Editing Tiziana Faraoni, Gigi Giannuzzi
Text editing Thomas Rees
Production assistant Hannah Watson
Design Martin Bell@fruitmachinedesign.com


A catalogue record for this book is available from the British Library.



ISBN 1-904563-49-X

Repro Centrofotolitografico

Printed in Italy

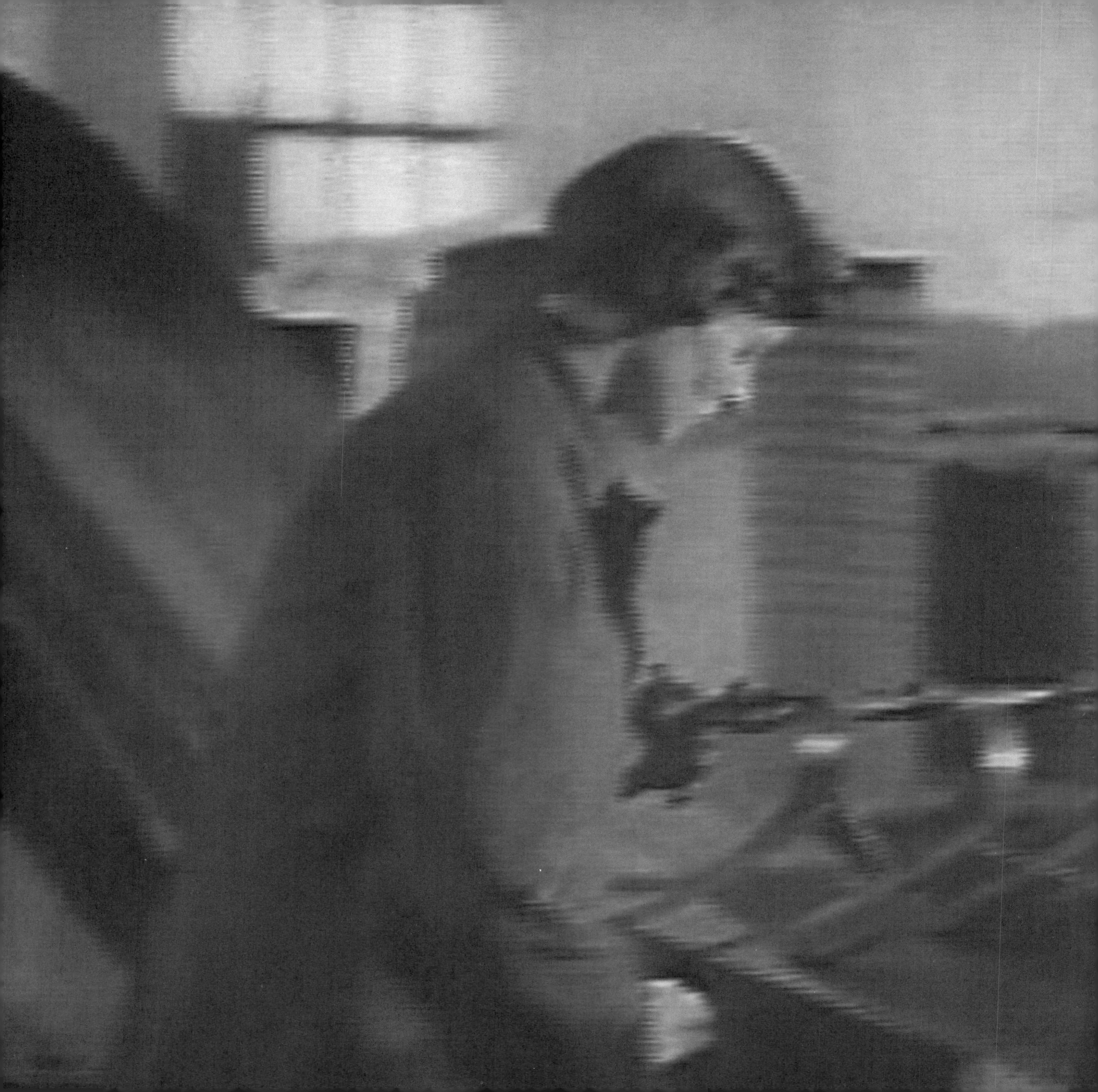